AF477853

Ink Dreams

Ink Dreams

Selections from the Fondation INK Collection

Edited by Susanna Ferrell

With additional contributions by
Einor K. Cervone
Britta Erickson
Wan Kong
Stephen Little
Celia Yang

Los Angeles County Museum of Art

DelMonico Books · D.A.P.

7 **Foreword**
Michael Govan

10 **The Fondation INK Collection at LACMA**
Stephen Little

16 **The Beauty of the Ineffable: The Fondation INK Collection**
Britta Erickson

20 **A Conversation with Gérard and Dora Cognié**
Susanna Ferrell

32 **The Spirit of Ink: Meditations, Apparitions, Dreamscapes**
Susanna Ferrell

184 **Artists in the Exhibition**

243 **Index**

250 **Acknowledgments**

253 **Board of Trustees**

255 **Image Credits**

Foreword

The Los Angeles County Museum of Art is deeply grateful to the Fondation INK and its founders, Gérard and Dora Cognié, for their generous promised gift to the museum of 400 works of contemporary Chinese and global ink art. With its focus on China, this promised gift will provide an extraordinary foundation for LACMA's rapidly expanding collection of contemporary Chinese art, and will make it possible to share this exceptional collection with our audiences here and abroad. The Fondation INK collection is additionally remarkable because while focused on leading masters of contemporary ink art in China, it also includes works of contemporary ink art by artists based in South Korea, Japan, Taiwan, Hong Kong, Singapore, Vietnam, Europe, and the United States. The collection further provides a magnificent counterpoint to LACMA's superb collection of traditional Chinese art, revealing the deep continuities between ancient and contemporary Chinese culture. While contemporary Chinese ink art has now attained global significance and reach, its links to the past demonstrate the continuing resonance and significance of Chinese culture over thousands of years.

Located in the center of Los Angeles, LACMA is a global museum in a city deeply rooted in the culture and history of China. The greater Los Angeles area is home to more than 1.5 million Asian Americans, making it one of the largest populations outside of Asia. Furthermore, in its new David Geffen Galleries, designed by Swiss architect Peter Zumthor, LACMA will tell the story of art history differently from other museums, emphasizing the heritage and cultural influence of Asia and the Pacific Rim as a starting point and reference for world history, rather than employing the European point of view often used by traditional institutions. This has proved to be a global perspective with local resonance.

In the last decade, LACMA has placed tremendous emphasis on increasing its Asian art exhibitions, acquisitions, publications, and educational programming. LACMA's combined artistic and intellectual resources have uniquely positioned the museum to mount an ambitious program that engages audiences with Chinese art and culture on a local and global scale, and our special exhibitions regularly travel throughout Asia, Europe, Latin America, and the Middle East.

We are deeply grateful to Gérard and Dora Cognié for their vision and trust in making this promised gift to LACMA, and for their support for this beautiful catalogue of our inaugural exhibition of the Fondation INK Collection.

Michael Govan
CEO and Wallis Annenberg Director
Los Angeles County Museum of Art

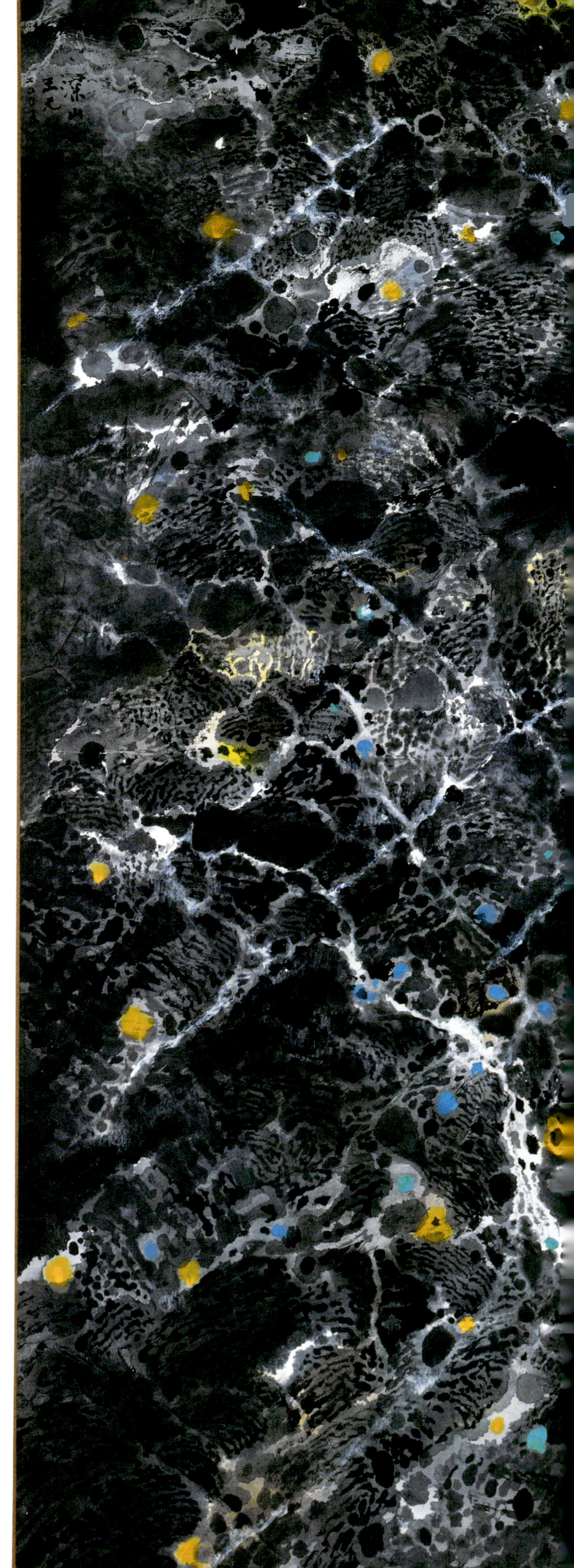

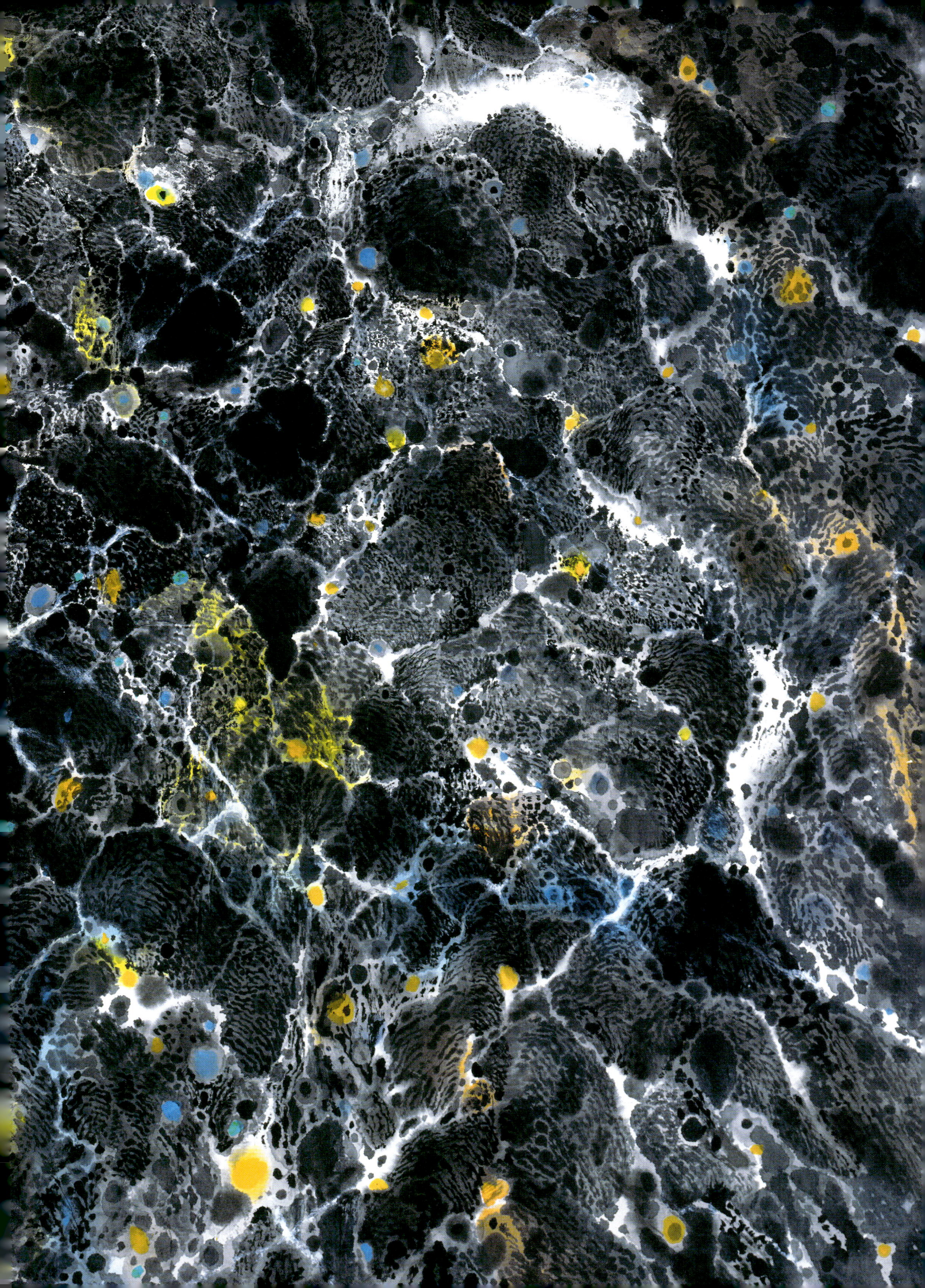

Stephen Little

The Fondation INK Collection at LACMA

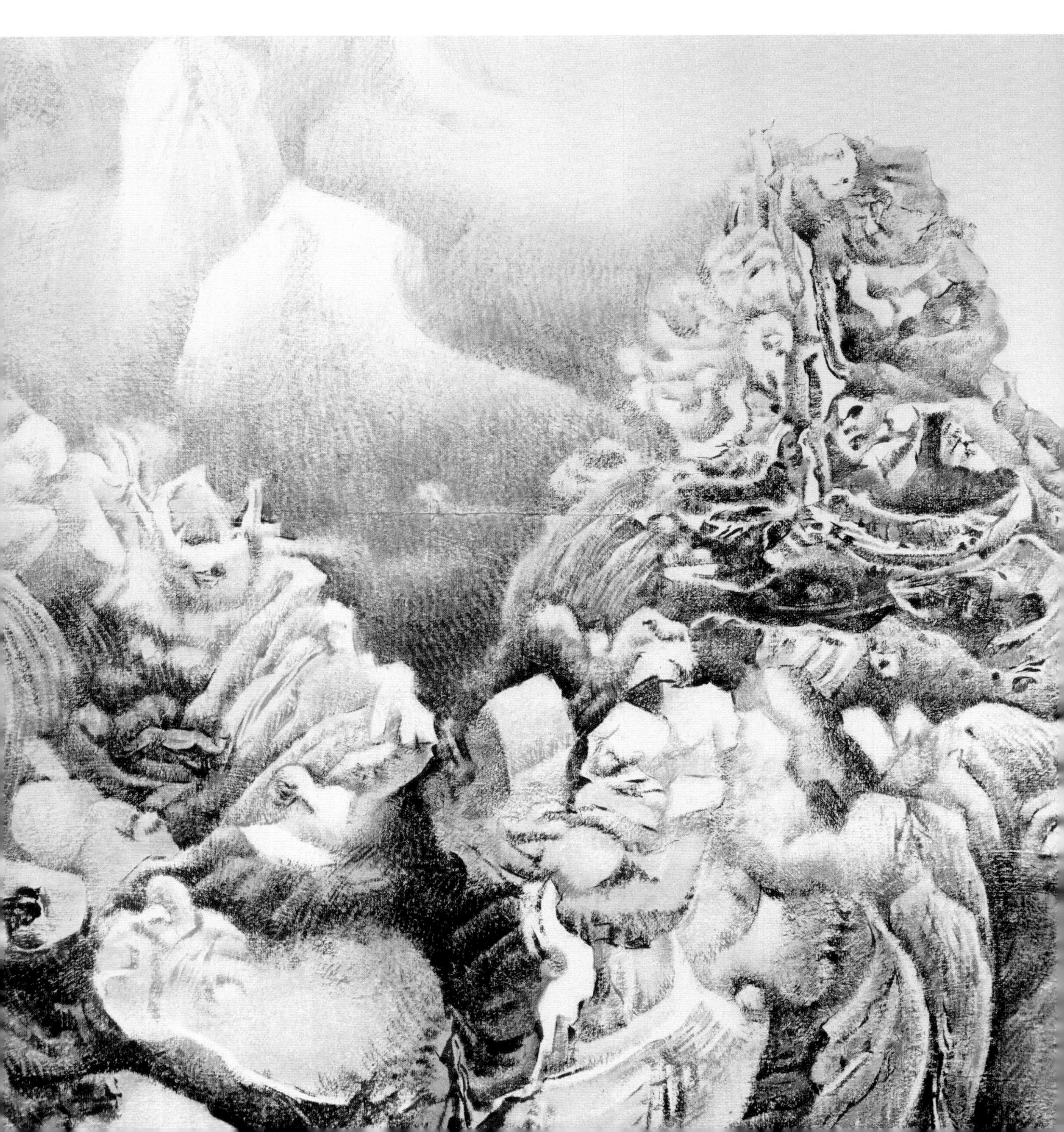

The promised gift of the Fondation INK collection of contemporary ink painting represents the largest assemblage of contemporary Chinese and global ink-related art ever donated to the Los Angeles County Museum of Art (LACMA). Created over the past 20 years by French collectors Gérard and Dora Cognié, who reside in Geneva, the Fondation INK gift comprises 400 works, the majority being Chinese ink paintings. Gérard Cognié is a retired industry executive in the field of imaging technology, and Dora Cognié is a medical doctor specializing in dermatology. Besides their interest in visual arts, they are both active philanthropists, and are the founders of Fondation Dora, an organization dedicated to helping children with special needs, and the Fondation INK. This inaugural exhibition of the Fondation INK Collection at LACMA is a tribute to the Cogniés' extraordinary taste, curiosity, discernment, and generosity.

The Fondation INK Collection will dramatically transform LACMA's contemporary Chinese art holdings. Over 100 contemporary artists are represented in the collection, which includes works by Chinese artists Bingyi, gu wenda, Li Huasheng, Li Huayi, Li Jin, Lin Tianmiao, Liu Dan, Liu Guosong, Lui Shou-kwan, Chen Haiyan, Qiu Shihua, Wang Dongling, Wang Tiande, Wucius Wong, Xu Bing, Yang Jiechang, Zhang Yu, Zheng Chongbin, and many others. In addition to Chinese artists from mainland China, Taiwan, Hong Kong, and Singapore, this promised gift includes works by leading artists from South Korea, Japan, Vietnam, Europe, and the United States; among these are Park Seo-Bo, Lee Ufan, Kitamura Junko, Suzuki Osamu, Shirazeh Houshiary, Jorma Puranen, Matti Kujasalo, Ophélie Asch, Irma Blank, and Michael Cherney. The majority of these artists work in a visual idiom deeply informed by the aesthetic and time-honored history of Chinese ink painting. The collection comprises primarily ink paintings and calligraphy, along with a significant selection of photography; among the photographers represented are Shi Guorui, Hai Bo, Hiroshi Sugimoto, and Min Byung Hun. Among the many highlights are Li Huasheng's *104* (2001; p. 52), Li Huayi's *Landscape* (2009; p. 142), Li Jin's *Party in the Garden* (2008), Lin Tianmiao's *Seeing Shadows No. 35* (2007; p. 98), Liu Dan's *Untitled* (2012; p. 170), Qiu Zhijie's *Monuments: Revolutionary Slogans of Successive Dynasties* (2007), Shi Guorui's *New Beijing CCTV* (2007; p. 112), Wang Dongling's *The Heart Sutra*

Liu Dan, *Untitled*, 2012 (detail)

(2016), Liu Guosong's *Jiuzhaigou Series #48: Sea of Floating Ice* (2004; p. 109), Hiroshi Sugimoto's *Lightning Fields 143* (2009; p. 115), and Idris Khan's *Numbers* (2015). This introductory exhibition is the first of many to explore the full depth and breadth of the Fondation INK Collection.

In addition to enabling LACMA to present Asian contemporary art in greater depth to our international audience, the promised gift of the Fondation INK Collection will make it possible for the museum to utilize the collection as a key research and teaching tool for undergraduate and graduate students, fellows, interns, and scholars studying Asian art history in the greater Los Angeles area and beyond. LACMA's Chinese Art Department will work with other curatorial departments to study and exhibit works from our collection, in relation to works from other parts of the world, other historical periods, and other mediums. The Fondation INK Collection represents a major transformative gift that will propel LACMA into the forefront of American art museums that collect, exhibit, publish, and promote contemporary Asian art and culture in a global context. As Gérard and Dora Cognié observed when announcing their promised gift in 2018, the collection will also spearhead an important new understanding of global ink art and ink aesthetics, as well as provide a model for other such initiatives throughout the world. Thanks to the Cogniés' generosity, LACMA has already shown important works from the collection in the exhibitions *Wu Bin: Ten Views of a Lingbi Stone* (2017–18) and *Sam Francis and Japan* (2021). Over the next several years, the museum will publish a series of systematic catalogues of the entire Fondation INK Collection promised gift.

Among the reasons that this promised gift is of special relevance is the fact that it demonstrates the astonishing degree to which the ancient art of Chinese ink painting has evolved over time and is still relevant in the present world. The contemporary renaissance of ink painting in East Asia and around the globe comprises myriad forms, many of which are represented in the Fondation INK Collection. The multiplicity of forms and styles is such that it is impossible to make sweeping generalizations regarding the phenomenon of contemporary ink art. Nonetheless, it is noteworthy that knowledge of the origins and history of this tradition is shared among many contemporary practitioners. The tradition's antiquity is significant: evidence of brushes used to paint extends to roughly 5000 BCE, in the Chinese Neolithic period. The earliest evidence of writing Chinese characters dates to the 13th century BCE, during the Shang dynasty in the early Bronze Age. The earliest surviving Chinese texts are divinatory inscriptions incised into the scapulae (shoulder blades) of cattle and the plastrons (lower shells) of turtles, and individuals' and clan names cast into the walls of ritual bronze vessels.

From the time of the earliest texts on Chinese painting, in the Six Dynasties Period (420–589), painting was described as a means of expression and of achieving a deeper understanding of nature and of the universe (just as early texts on calligraphy, dating to roughly the same period, refer to writing as a means of communication, of personal expression, and of mirroring the forces and shapes of nature).[1] Key to opening these windows of understanding was the artist's ability to see, embody, and express the resonant *qi* (energy) embodied in the subject, be it an insect, a human being, or a mountain. It is not surprising that the first of Xie He's *Six Laws of Painting* (compiled ca. 500 CE) states, "[Engender a sense of] life movement through spirit resonance [*qiyun shendong*]."

1 For informative essays on the development of the Six Dynasties Period aesthetic matrix connecting calligraphy, painting, music, and literature, see Zong-qi Cai, ed., *Chinese Aesthetics: The Ordering of Literature, the Arts, and the Universe in the Six Dynasties* (Honolulu: University of Hawai'i Press, 2004).

That working with brush and ink, and exploring the expressive potentials of brushwork, could become an artistic obsession is already alluded to in a late Han-dynasty polemical text attacking excessive attachment to the newly ascendant forms of calligraphic cursive script. This text, "A Pox on the Draft (Cursive) Script" (*Fei caoshu*), written around 200 CE by the critic Zhao Yi, mocks contemporaneous calligraphers who burned the midnight oil perfecting their cursive script:

> At night they are diligent without resting; by day they do not stop to eat. They will wear out a brush in ten days, and in one month use several cakes of ink. Their collars and sleeves are as though dyed dark; their lips and teeth are perpetually black [from sucking the ink-laden brush tips to a fine point].[2]

2 William Acker, trans., *Some T'ang and Pre-T'ang Texts on Chinese Painting* (Leiden: P. Brill, 1954), vol. 1, lvi–lvii.

There is a subtlety to the movements of the brush, and the manipulations of the monochromatic hues and textures of ink, that few other forms of visual expression can match. As early as the Tang dynasty, the writer and critic Zhang Yanyuan (active ca. 815–ca. 875) referred to the "five colors of ink" in celebrating the medium's subtle expressive powers of allusion, as opposed to mere description—in other words, the ability of ink to perceive hidden inner realities as opposed to mere outer forms:

> If by using ink a painter can allude to the five colors, we say that he has grasped the mind. But if an artist's mind is fixed on true colors, the essence of things will escape him.[3]

3 In this vein, see Wu Hung, *Variations of Ink: A Dialogue with Zhang Yanyuan* (New York: Chambers Fine Art, 2002).

Numerous early Chinese texts on painting discuss the challenges inherent in balancing the outer and inner realities of a landscape through the vehicle of painting. *A Note on the Art of the Brush* (*Bifa ji*) by Jing Hao (ca. 870–ca. 930) contains the following passage, part of a longer conversation between a young artist and a rustic old man he encounters in a grotto in the Taihang Mountains, located on the border of Hebei and Shanxi provinces. At one point, the old man says,

> Painting [*hua*] is equivalent to measuring [*hua*]. One examines the objects and grasps their reality [*zhen*]. One must grasp the outward appearance from the outward reality of the object, and the inner reality [*shi*] from the inner reality of the object. One must not take the outward appearance and call it the inner reality. If you do not know this method [of understanding truth], you may even get lifelikeness but never achieve reality in painting.[4]

4 Susan Bush and Hsio-yen Shih, trans., *Early Chinese Texts on Painting* (Cambridge, Mass.: Harvard University Press, 1985), 146 (with slight changes).

It is important to recognize that one cannot separate the history of East Asian ink painting from the history of calligraphy, for both forms of expression rest on the same theoretical and practical foundations, and often utilize the same tools and materials. It is significant, for these reasons, that there are many superb calligraphic works in the Fondation INK Collection, as seen in examples by such contemporary artists as Wang Dongling and Fung Ming Chip.

In East Asia, both painting and calligraphy had early on established fundamental rules and guidelines, the mastery of which has always been seen as necessary for any degree of advancement. The greatest talents, however, not only found it necessary to break the rules, but did so with such creativity that both disciplines advanced in new and unexpected directions. What is notable about the current renaissance of ink painting is that boundaries are once again being broken in many astonishing ways.

Chinese, Korean, and Japanese ink painting has now achieved a global status, but this global recognition did not happen overnight. Awareness of ink painting in the West began to manifest well over a century ago (indeed, in the 19th century), with the creation of the first European and American collections of East Asian paintings. During most of the intervening decades, however, knowledge of the traditions of ink painting and the closely related art of calligraphy was largely the domain of a small group of specialists—primarily professors, curators, artists, and art dealers—as well as collectors and other aficionados. Today, the transformation of the ancient traditions of ink painting is an international phenomenon, with increasing awareness among practitioners around the globe, and with growing collections being formed by private collectors and museums, within and beyond East Asia.

The promised gift of the Fondation INK Collection to LACMA is significant on several levels. First, it will transform LACMA into the largest and most important American museum collection of contemporary ink art. Second, it will vastly increase the ability of the museum to research and exhibit contemporary ink art, and to utilize the Fondation INK Collection for teaching the history of ink art, as practiced in Asia and globally, to university students in Los Angeles and beyond—specifically, the Fondation INK Collection will play a major role in LACMA becoming a key resource for teaching the history of East Asian art and culture at universities in Southern California, as well as part of LACMA's recently established joint master's degree partnership with Arizona State University in Tempe, and in our ongoing Mellon Undergraduate Fellowship program in art history and museology. Third, since its announcement two years ago, the promised gift of the Fondation INK Collection has been the catalyst for many other major gifts of contemporary Chinese art to LACMA, from artists, collectors, and gallerists around the world. Fourth, the promised gift of the Fondation INK Collection coincides with LACMA's partnership with the Yuz Museum in Shanghai, founded by Indonesian-Chinese collector Budi Tek in 2014, with the forthcoming major gift to LACMA from the Yuz Foundation's enormous collection of contemporary Chinese art, as well as the creation of LACMA's new display space in Macau. All of these activities will facilitate connecting the past to the present (and vice versa), and in particular making the extraordinary achievements of the Old Masters of Asian ink painting relevant for the present in ways that are unambiguously contemporary.

Britta Erickson

The Beauty of the Ineffable

The Fondation INK Collection

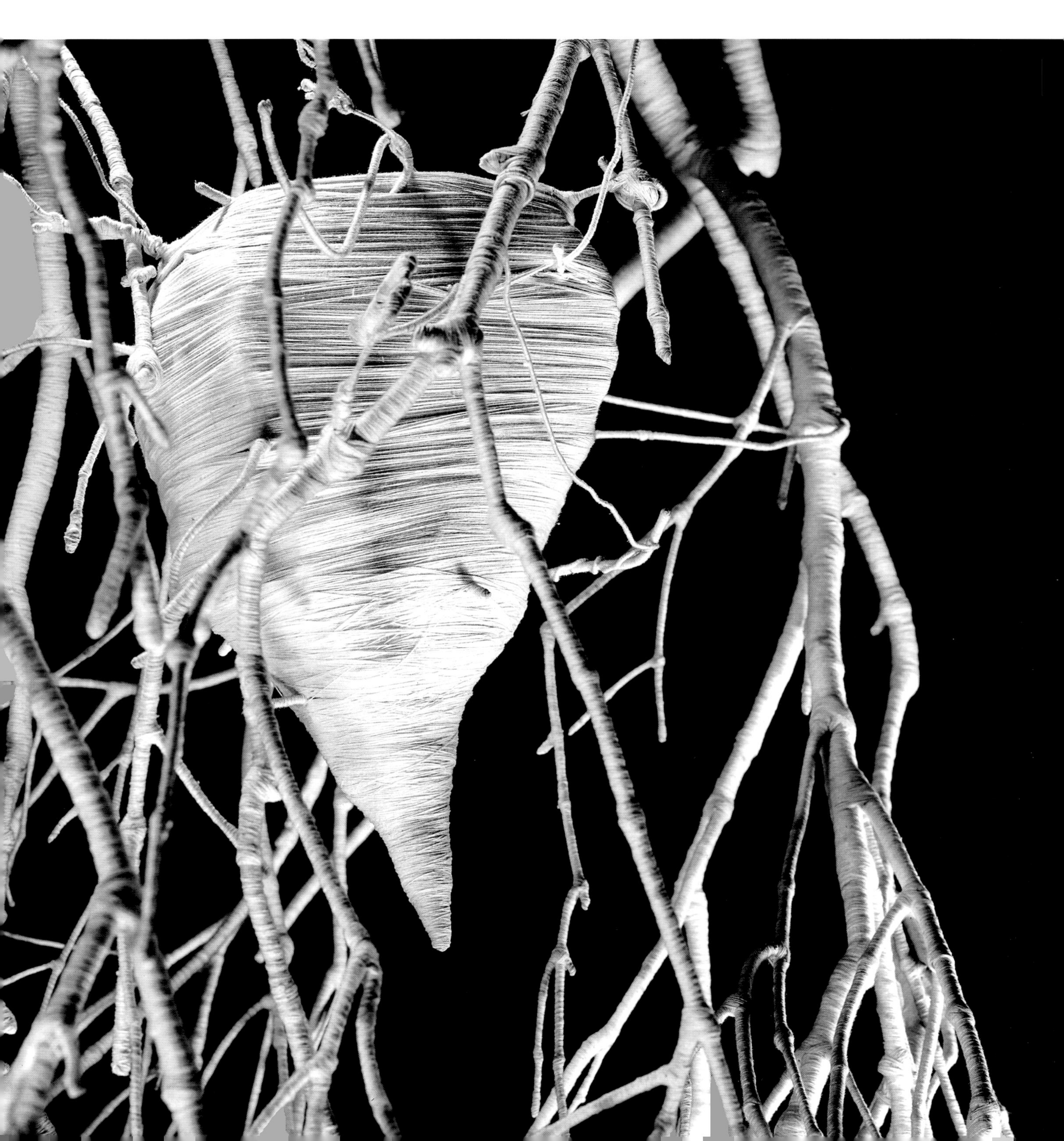

Formed over the course of almost two decades, Gérard and Dora Cognié's Fondation INK Collection expresses a personal and open-minded aesthetic. Historically grounded in the Chinese ink painting tradition through works by such mid- and later 20th-century masters as Lui Shou-kwan and Liu Guosong—great innovators whose painting is rooted in a firm understanding of the past—the collection reaches outward from there temporally as well as geographically and in terms of medium. The delight of a private art collection such as the Cogniés' is that it is formed with absolute freedom to follow an instinctive sense of what belongs. There are no institutional overseers tasked with upholding mysterious imperatives, and acquisitions do not require layers of approval. With a private collection, the parameters shaping it need not even be explicit: they can remain as an undefined aesthetic instinct that brings coherence to the assembled works of art.

The Fondation INK Collection makes a welcome statement for our time. In identifying an ink aesthetic, it locates a distinctive quality that spans continents and cultures. This may turn on the desire to explore the ineffable. How better to lay bare the shared essence of humanity than by revealing a commonality expressed through art? This quality is an antidote to the overwhelming torrent of information that is the uncomfortable hallmark of our era, when to define precisely is a goal, often leaving little room for subtlety. In such a time, we should cherish the rare opportunity presented by the Fondation INK Collection to consider that which is undefinable: after all, such is the crux of our existence.

Mr. Cognié was an experienced collector of European art when, on a business trip to Shanghai in 2002, he set aside a few days to visit galleries showing Chinese contemporary art, a field largely new to him. He found himself interested and impressed. His first purchase in China, of two ink paintings by Wang Tiande, marked the start of his interest in creating an ink collection. "I had never seen anything like that before," he explained, "and I started thinking about building a collection around this kind of art work and aesthetics."[1] From that point onward, Mr. Cognié, with the support of his wife Dora, began actively seeking out works of art whose aesthetics connected with those of ink painting, regardless of medium or geographical/cultural origin.

1 Gérard Cognié quotes are from an email sent in response to the author's questions.

Lin Tianmiao, *The Tree*, 2010 (detail)

While Chinese ink painting forms the core of the collection, the Fondation embraces ink painting from other parts of East and Southeast Asia, as well as photography, sculpture, oil painting, woodcut, installation, video, and ceramic art. The cultural and national diversity of artists outside of Asia is notable, including Finland, the United States, the United Kingdom, France, Germany, and so on. The idea of the collection in all its diversity coalesced as Mr. Cognié observed the intersection, in terms of aesthetics and/or mediums, of his newly acquired Chinese ink paintings with areas of art where he already had no small expertise.

In recent decades, art historians and critics have grappled with questions central to a definition of ink painting and its significance, including the degree to which it is desirable to adhere to traditional materials, techniques, and philosophies. If it veers from those latter elements, how far can it go before no longer being construed as ink painting? To what extent can—or should—it respond to and become integrated with the international contemporary art realm? To venture one step further—and into territory that I would argue is entirely specious and simplistic—is it even possible for ink painting to *be* contemporary? Of course, not everyone is perplexed or even engaged or entertained by such issues. For artists and collectors, there is no need for such dogmatism. The artist chooses the mediums that are most effective for the purpose, wielding them according to an instinctive aesthetic, and the collector selects the works of art that resonate with him or her. There is a deep communication between artist and collector via the work of art. Critics and art historians strive to parse this communication using words, a tool outside the essential communication that is at play: that is why they may find themselves drawn into the debate over the definitions of ink painting.

An essential aspect of much Chinese ink painting is the extent to which it is intended to propel a profound connection between the artist's state of mind and the viewer via the work of art. In the language of traditional Chinese painting philosophy, this is known as resonance. There is a latent resonance in the work of art imparted by the artist and reactivated by the viewer's open and knowing mind. The kernel is not easy to pin down: perhaps it is not even desirable to do so. As Mr. Cognié relates, "It is difficult for me to describe what I call ink painting aesthetics; the best way would be to use some words which come to my mind like 'balance, meditation, empty space, controlled energy.' I do realize that this is personal and other people may have different criteria." The sense that the understanding of such art is personal is a corollary to the fact that artists working within this nebulous aesthetic often infuse their art with deeply felt and highly nuanced emotional and philosophical sensibilities. For the viewer to be entirely open to a work of art is to create a space of communion, a respite from our fraught times, and also an opportunity for self-cultivation. In Chinese philosophy, the latter opportunity is considered of key importance in both the creation and appreciation of art.

How do we experience the works of art in the Fondation INK Collection? The mind's sometimes frustrated natural attempts to bring the many seemingly out-of-focus images, such as those by Jorma Puranen and Qiu Shihua, into crisp resolution catalyzes a space of mental respite. Other works, for example Bingyi's and Zheng Chongbin's paintings, and Hiroshi Sugimoto's lightning photographs, beguile the viewer into considering the relationship between humans and natural forces. And there are many pieces created via repetition, often in a meditative state, by artists Irma Blank, Max Cole, Shirazeh Houshiary, Li Huasheng, and others: following their path invites a parallel contemplative state. Through various mechanisms, the works of art in the collection call forth a deeply felt response, but the ability to define those responses remains elusive: it is the expression of the ineffable that hums through the collection.

Creatively and thoughtfully composed, the Fondation INK Collection generates a shared space for the various works of art to animate, enhance, or otherwise enrich one another. The viewer is invited into this precious space, to experience a resonance with the works of art. The collection thus sparks new considerations of the nature and meaning of an ink aesthetic.

One day in 2008, I was in Shanghai and received an invitation from Mr. Cognié, to meet over breakfast and talk about his interest in ink painting. I was intrigued and accepted the invitation, not knowing that this would be the beginning of something special. It is my great good fortune and privilege to have been able to contribute as an advisor to the formation of the Fondation INK Collection, not only sharing my knowledge, but also learning from the Cogniés' point of view and experience.

Susanna Ferrell

A Conversation with Gérard and Dora Cognié

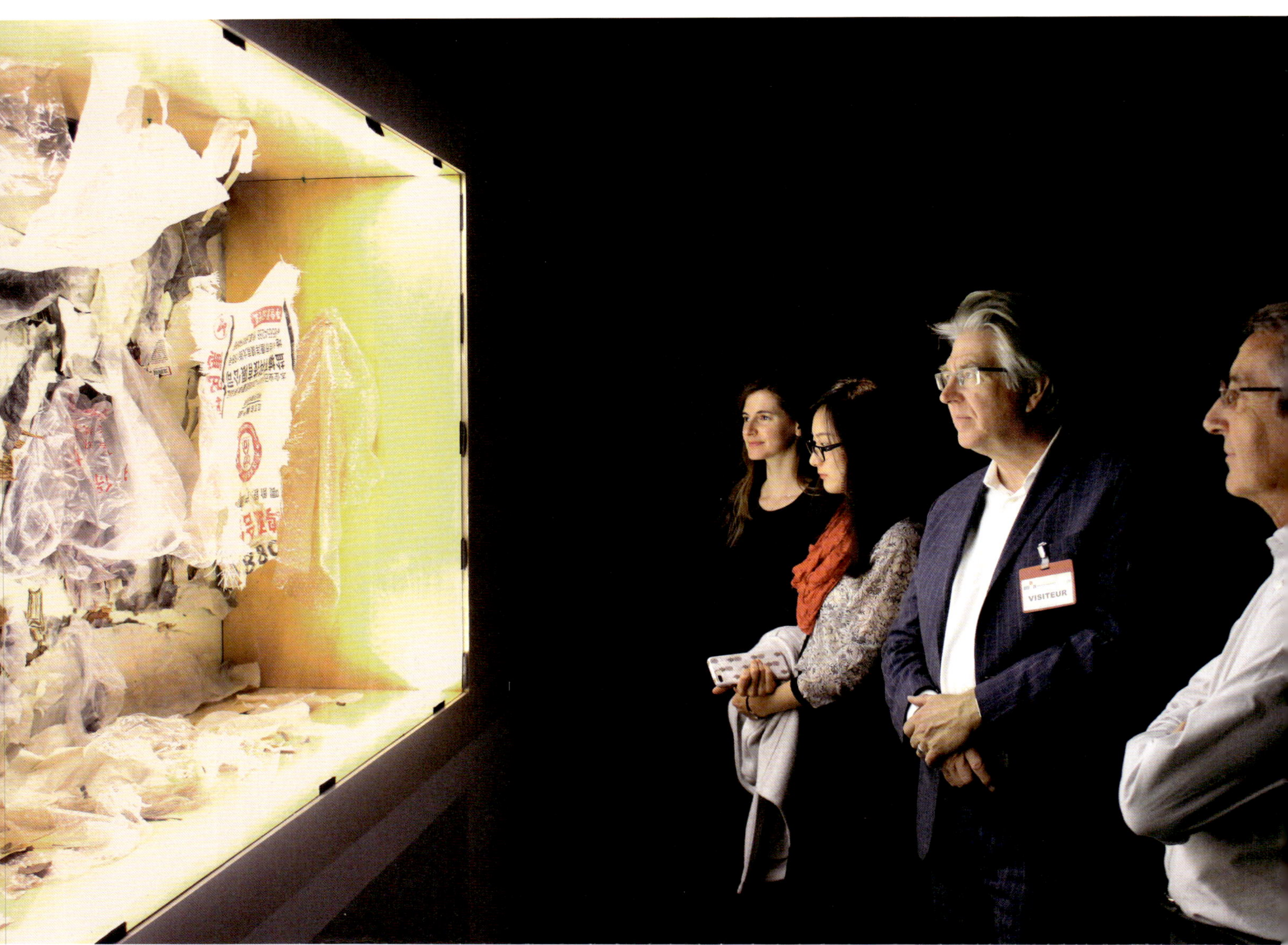

Mr. Cognié and curators Stephen Little, Wan Kong, and Einor Cervone look at a work by Xu Bing in Geneva, 2018. Photo by Susanna Ferrell

After years of planning, phone calls, and in-person discussion, I joined Gérard and Dora Cognié in digital space for a conversation about their experiences building the Fondation INK Collection. Amidst the COVID-19 pandemic, we connected via video call, bridging the nearly 6,000-mile/10,000-kilometer gap between myself in Los Angeles and the Cogniés in Geneva. The following interview is compiled from excerpts of this video call, which took place on the California morning/Geneva evening of August 26, 2020.

SUSANNA FERRELL
Many of the first works you collected were not by Chinese contemporary ink painters but School of Paris artists, which could seem to be a more likely fit for two French collectors. How did you first become interested in Asian art?

GÉRARD COGNIÉ
We started buying artworks in the '90s, but at that time we had no intention to build a collection—we were just buying works to decorate our home. There was no particular focus on any given style, but as we were living in Paris, we were exposed to a number of artists from the Nouvelle École de Paris, especially those related to the "Lyrical Abstraction" movement. We liked this style, and we bought a few pieces by artists like Elvire Jan, Henri Michaux, and Chu Teh-Chun. Looking back, it is interesting to note that artists of Chinese origin active in France like Chu Teh-Chun and Zao Wou-Ki were part of that movement.

It was only in 2002 that we became interested in Chinese contemporary art by visiting an exhibition called *Paris-Pekin*. This exhibition of young Chinese artists was based on the collection of Myriam and Guy Ullens, Belgian collectors. It was curated by Johnson Chang of Hanart TZ Gallery, and the artworks were primarily oil paintings, but there were also a few ink paintings. The show was a sensation in Paris. We had not heard of Ullens or Chang before, but I can say that we were very impressed by the exhibition—it was new, energetic, a real eye-opener. As I had the opportunity to go to Shanghai a few weeks later for my business, I decided to find out more about this subject.

SF *Was ink already at the forefront of your interests during that trip, or did this become the focus of the collection later?*

GC During my trip to Shanghai in late 2002, I was introduced to the artist Wang Tiande. I visited his studio and that's where I saw the *Chinese Clothes* series. I was very impressed, and bought two pieces from that series. During this trip, I also bought a few oil paintings (by Yin Zhaoyang) and also some photographs (by Hong Lei and Han Lei) from different galleries.

In 2003, the family moved from Paris to Geneva. There, we met a gallery owner, Leda Fletcher, who was promoting Chinese contemporary artists. We became good friends, and thanks to her, I learned a lot about Chinese contemporary art, and especially about Chinese artists living in Taiwan, like Liu Guosong and Chu Ko.

As our interest was growing and we were considering starting a collection, we realized that we had to be more selective. Ink art was what we appreciated the most. We like the visual effect of ink on paper—it is fresh, sharp, spontaneous, and there is a lot of energy coming from ink on paper. Chinese contemporary oil painting in the '90s was also interesting and energetic but, in our opinion, ink art was more refined and more original.

Later, we got a lot of help from a well-known scholar, Britta Erickson, who introduced us to some of the best ink artists in the world and helped us to identify the different trends of the ink art scene.

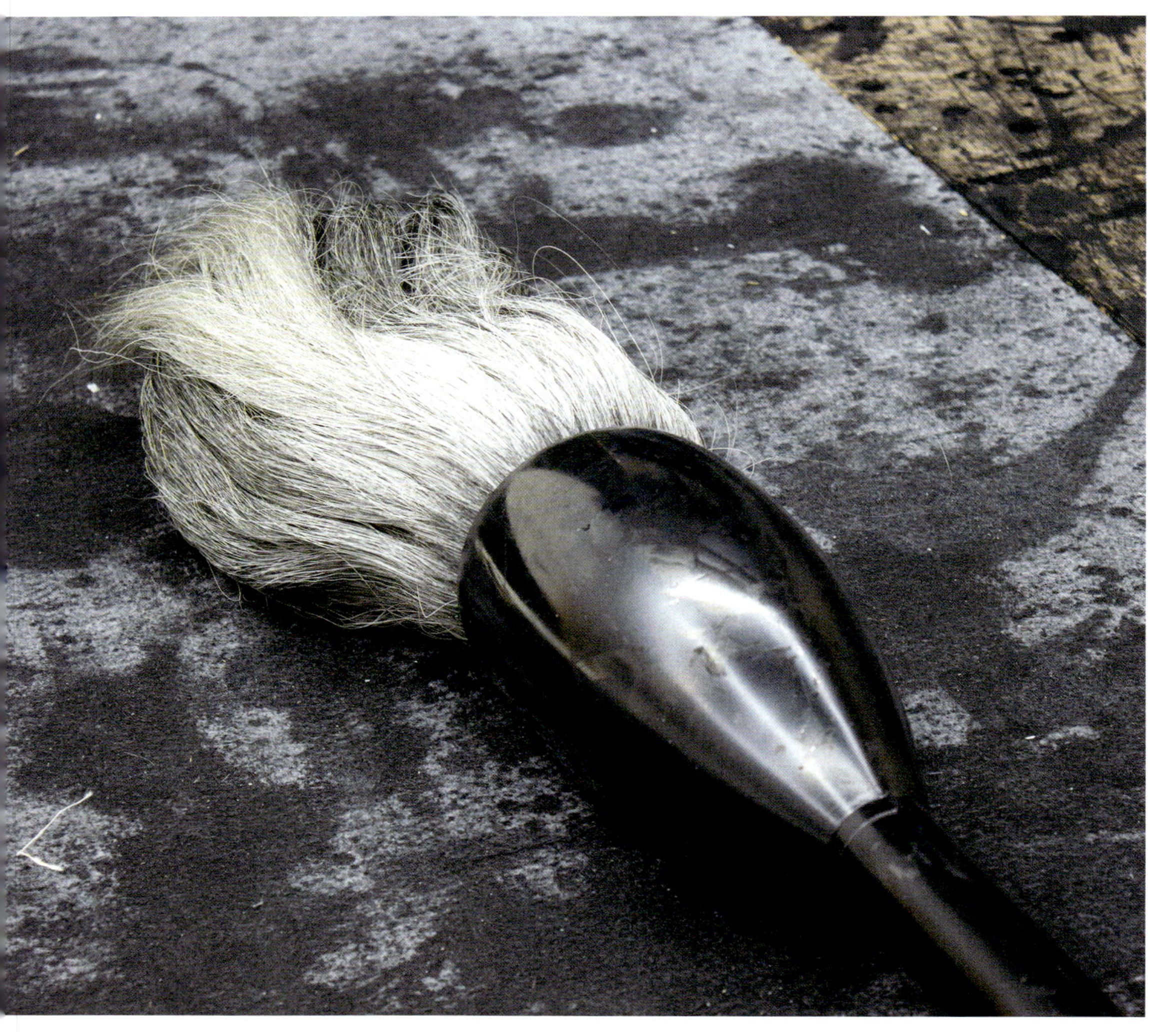

A large brush resting on the floor of Kim Ho-deuk's studio, Yeoju City, Gyeonggi Province, South Korea, November 2018

SF *What, to you, is "ink art"? Who qualifies as a Chinese contemporary ink artist?*

GC We would prefer to use the term "contemporary ink artist." Not to discount the term *Chinese*, as the majority of our collection is formed with artworks by Chinese artists, but there are artists from other countries who, in our opinion, qualify as well, so we do not want to restrict "ink art" to a country or even a region. Yes, ink art is rooted in Asia, but we believe that it can be a global artistic expression.

To give a definition of ink art is quite difficult, and each person may have a different opinion; actually, there is no right or wrong opinion as this is highly personal. In our view, contemporary ink art is rooted in the traditional Chinese technique of using ink on paper to create subjects like calligraphy, landscape, flower, etc., but, it goes beyond in terms of subjects (notably to abstraction) and also in the types of mediums (photography, sculptures, videos, etc.). In our opinion, those additional subjects and mediums do qualify as long as they produce an emotional result consistent with what we would expect from a more traditional ink painting.

SF *What does it mean to you to be a collector? Was there anything that surprised you about the collecting process?*

GC We did not get any formal training about collecting so we learned along the way; as the collection was growing, we found the administrative and logistical aspects more complicated than anticipated, but eventually we did adjust to it. Overall, it has been a very valuable experience. We have been exposed to incredible artworks that we would not have seen otherwise, and we have also met and developed relationships with very interesting people: first the artists, but also the curators, museum executives, gallery owners. We discovered that to be a collector of ink art, you have to travel a lot as we always want to see an artwork in person before making a decision to purchase it.

SF *You also collected Vietnamese art early on. What sparked your interest there?*

GC Dora and I went to Vietnam 27 years ago to adopt two children, and in 2006 I started working for a French NGO active there. I was in charge of an education program, so I was going twice a year and—I don't remember exactly when, maybe in 2007—I met an American lady, Suzanne Lecht, who had started an art gallery in Hanoi in the '90s. She knew a lot about contemporary art in Vietnam, and she introduced me to several young ink artists, and that's how I started to collect ink art by Vietnamese artists.

SF *Mr. Cognié, you took the first steps into collecting contemporary ink art, whereas Mrs. Cognié, you became more involved later on in the process. Mrs. Cognié, what were your first impressions of ink art?*

DORA COGNIÉ
In the beginning, I didn't know much about ink art and I saw only the artworks Gérard bought, which were hanging in our apartment. I liked them very much. At that time, I was staying at home and taking care of the children, so I did not travel with Gérard, but I was very supportive. When I had more flexibility to travel, I first went to Vietnam. It is a special country for us, and I met some of the Vietnamese artists Gérard is talking about. My first trip to China was in 2012, and there I met several artists and became much more involved in choosing the artworks and collecting. That's how I really came to understand the technique of ink art, the artists, and also the Chinese country.

SF *Mr. Cognié, has the collecting process changed since Mrs. Cognié became more involved?*

GC It did not change from the direction point of view, but I became a little bit more...demanding. Before making a purchasing decision, I always wanted to see the artwork, and if possible meet the artist. I had always been quite selective, but I became even more particular as there were now two of us to decide. When you know that you are going to show an artwork to another person and ask their opinion to make a decision, you want to be sure that you show him or her the best option [laughs].

DC When I was visiting the artists' studios with Gérard, I discovered that he had a very good connection with the artists. I often noticed that the artist was very happy when he or she realized that Gérard has a good eye—that's often what the artists said. When we have to choose between two pieces, Gérard always chooses the better one, and the artists often say, "You're right, that's my preferred one, too." So I had the feeling that the artists were impressed by Gérard's taste, and that was nice. I felt that there was some special relationship, good respect, between Gérard and the artists. Sometimes, as we had picked the best one, the artist said, "Oh, this one is not for sale" [laughs].

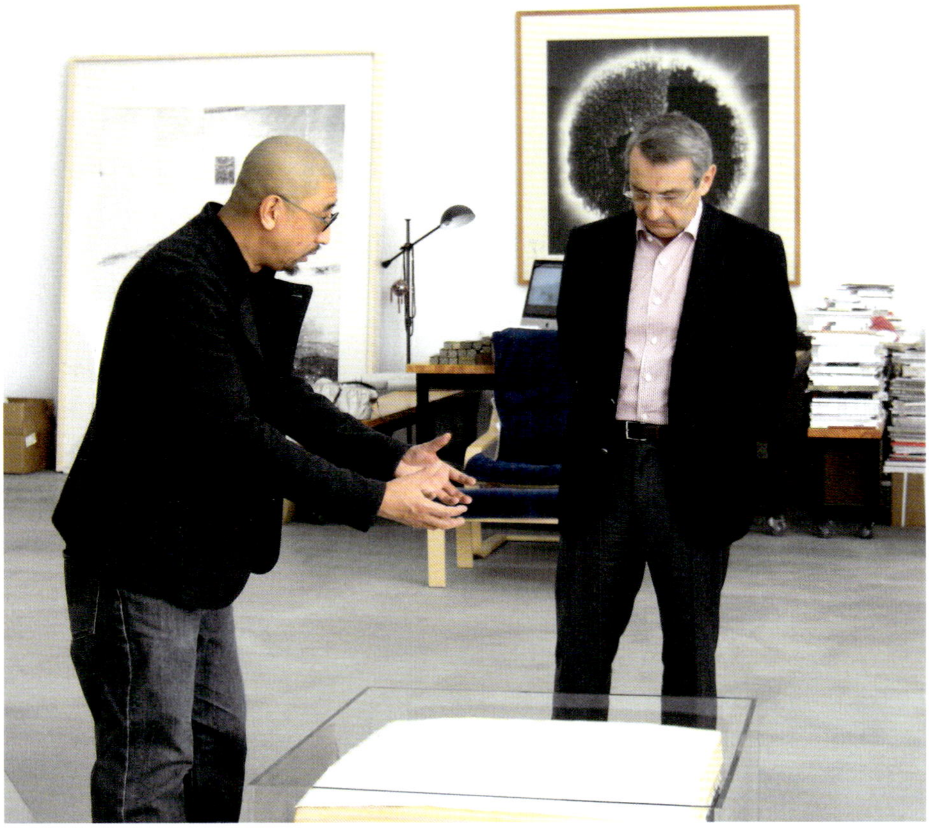

Mr. Cognié with Zhang Yu, in the artist's Beijing studio, 2015

SF *Did your impression change when you saw the works in the artists' studios, versus seeing them for the first time in your home?*

DC Yes, because I understood much better how they were doing their work. I saw the different kinds of paper, the ink. I saw all the various techniques going into the work that I couldn't imagine before. Also, I was very interested by the scholar's rocks I saw in different gardens in China—I'd never seen anything like that before, and I was impressed to see how this subject was used by several artists.

SF *What qualities do you look for when you are searching for a work to add to your collection? Is it important or necessary for a work to have a concept or philosophy behind it?*

GC When buying a new artwork, the most important factor is the emotional impact I may or may not feel when looking at it; however, this criterion is necessary but not sufficient to decide to collect a piece. The artwork should also fit other criteria: artworks that explore the idea of meditation or the action of writing are at the heart of our collection. We do not always make a conscious decision to collect an artwork that fits one of those two concepts, but as we look back, we can say that most do.

Abstract compositions, landscapes, especially mountains landscapes, and calligraphy are our preferred subjects. From a visual point of view, we look for the right balance or tension between the energy and the harmony of the composition. We are also quite strict about the quality of the execution. We are also careful in buying into a new artist—I mean new for the collection—because each time we do that, we are making a conscious decision to continue to follow that artist's work. Whenever possible, we try to meet the artist and understand his or her philosophy and how he or she is evolving.

SF *How do you see Western artists fitting into an ink art collection?*

GC As mentioned earlier, we do not evaluate artists by their nationality but by who they are and what they are doing, so it does not make a difference to us what country they come from. Are Chu Teh-Chun and Zao Wou-Ki Western or Chinese artists? In China, they are probably viewed as Chinese artists, although French curators would include them in the Nouvelle École de Paris. Some of the Lyrical Abstraction artists I mentioned earlier (Jan, Michaux) created ink works on paper so they fit very well with our collection. More recently, we acquired works by Irma Blank, a German artist who explores the act of writing. She is working on canvas and on paper, and her pieces also fit very well in our collection.

SF *How do you see the artists in your collection who work in mediums outside of ink, for example, photography, video, or ceramics, as fitting into the category of ink art?*

GC On the photographic side, many artists in the collection fit very well. Take Idris Khan's work on writing, or Min Byung Hun's foggy landscapes, or Hiroshi Sugimoto. Other photographers are situated more at the fringe of our ink art definition—I am thinking of Isabel Muñoz or Jonas Dahlberg, for example—but they are extremely good and not too far from the spirit of ink art, so we could not resist adding them to the collection!

SF *Many of the Chinese artists in your collection are from the generation that grew up during the Cultural Revolution [1966–76]; however, you have acquired pieces by much younger artists as well. Do you see a difference between the artistic interests of these different generations of artists?*

GC We are always looking for young promising artists—it is quite exciting to start supporting a young artist and see his or her development.

If we look at ink art, I do not see a significant difference between the generations born in the 1930s–40s and the one born in the 1960s–70s. If you take Li Huasheng, for example, he was born in the '40s, and initially his style was somewhat traditional, at least until the '90s. He then moved completely to abstraction, and not only to abstraction—his artworks became like a kind of performance.

Now, if you look at another artist I like, Wang Tiande, who was born later in the '60s, he has a different style, more figurative and uses techniques like cigarettes burns. But I don't find Wang Tiande more or less modern than Li Huasheng, they are just different. To sum up, I see significant differences between ink artists born in the second half of the 20th century, but those differences are specific to the individual artists and not to the period in which they were born.

SF *Of the many artists you have met, is there anyone whose philosophies have particularly resonated with you?*

GC If there is one artist for whom I have a great esteem, it's Li Huasheng. I like his earlier work, which is somewhat traditional, figurative work—simple and very elegant. But I also admire him because of the abstract work he did later, he changed his style completely and went into this linear process based on meditation. He was really free to do whatever he liked to do. He did not care about commercial things. So he was really a free artist. It was not just a question of the way he worked or what he did, but also the way he behaved relative to his art. I really admired him.

Li Huasheng shows Mr. and Mrs. Cognié a series of landscape paintings from the 1990s (later compiled as *Album 2* [see p. 212]) in Li's Chengdu studio, 2012

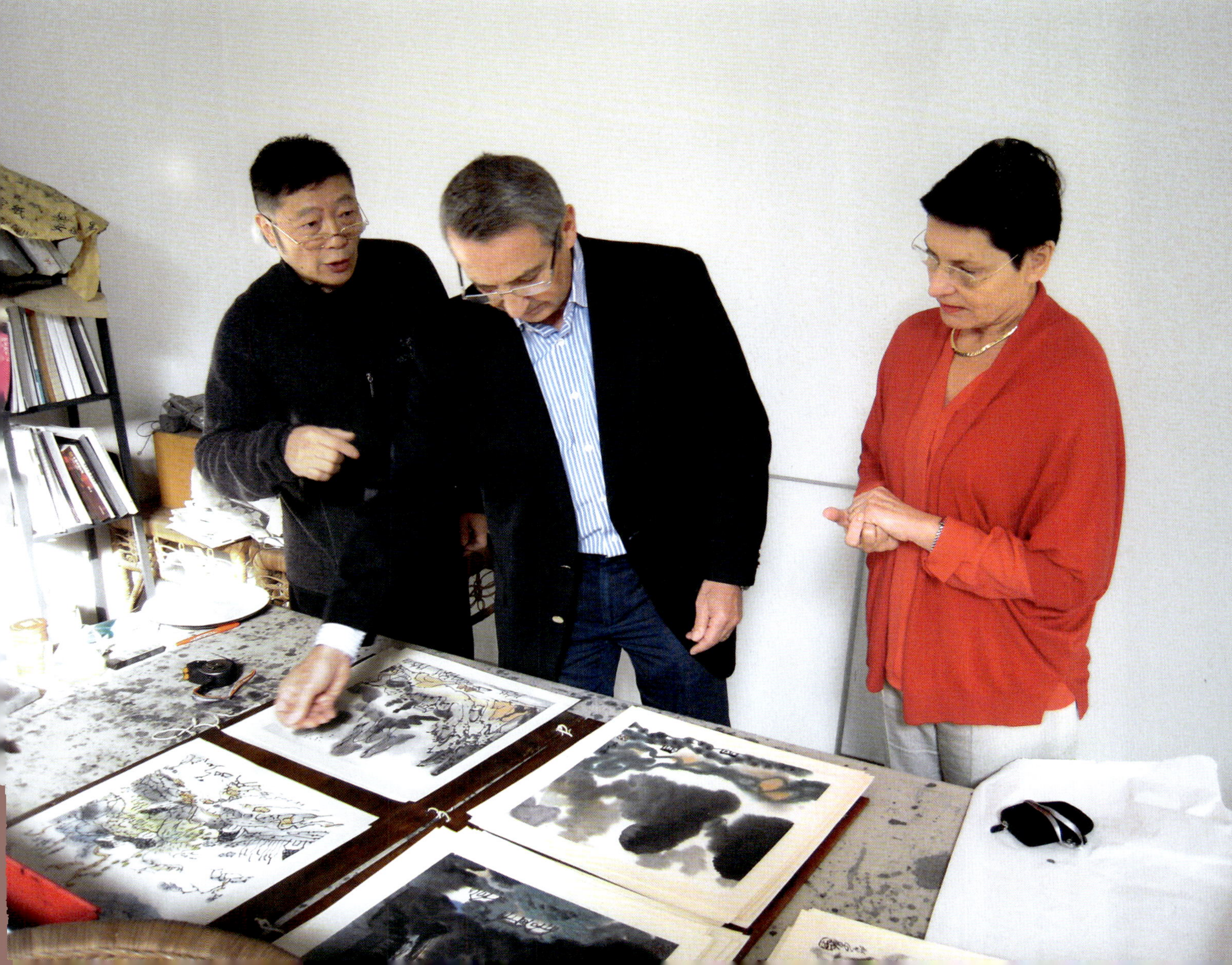

SF *Li Huasheng definitely had a unique personality. I feel that when you went to his studio, it was so clear that he was creating this work as an expression of himself, as opposed to creating art for the market. Did you meet him on that trip to China in 2012?*

GC I met him before 2012 and later on several occasions with Dora. Each visit would last a full day—he was a big talker and, as I do not speak Mandarin, Britta was translating and she did it very well. During each visit, it took a long time before we could actually go into the studio and see his latest works—normally he would show us the best pieces only in the last hour! But each visit was a great experience. Actually, we discussed the possibility of going to Tibet together, as he had been there and was planning another trip. As I'm very interested in hiking, I was thinking of joining him but, unfortunately, he recently passed away.

SF *To me, these studio visits are at the heart of your collecting process—you have developed a unique and intentional way of consistently expanding your collection to include artworks from new locations. Could you speak about this process of your collecting trips?*

GC Initially, we did not have a specific plan. I mentioned Vietnam before—I did not go to Vietnam for collecting, it just happened that I met some people there who introduced me to the local art scene. It was a bit similar for South Korea; when I was in Shanghai in the early 2000s, I went to an event where young Korean artists were presenting their works: ink on paper, videos, installation. I was really impressed by what I saw. At that time, I was also going to South Korea for my business. So I decided to spend some time looking at the art scene in this country, and this is how I started acquiring works by Korean artists.

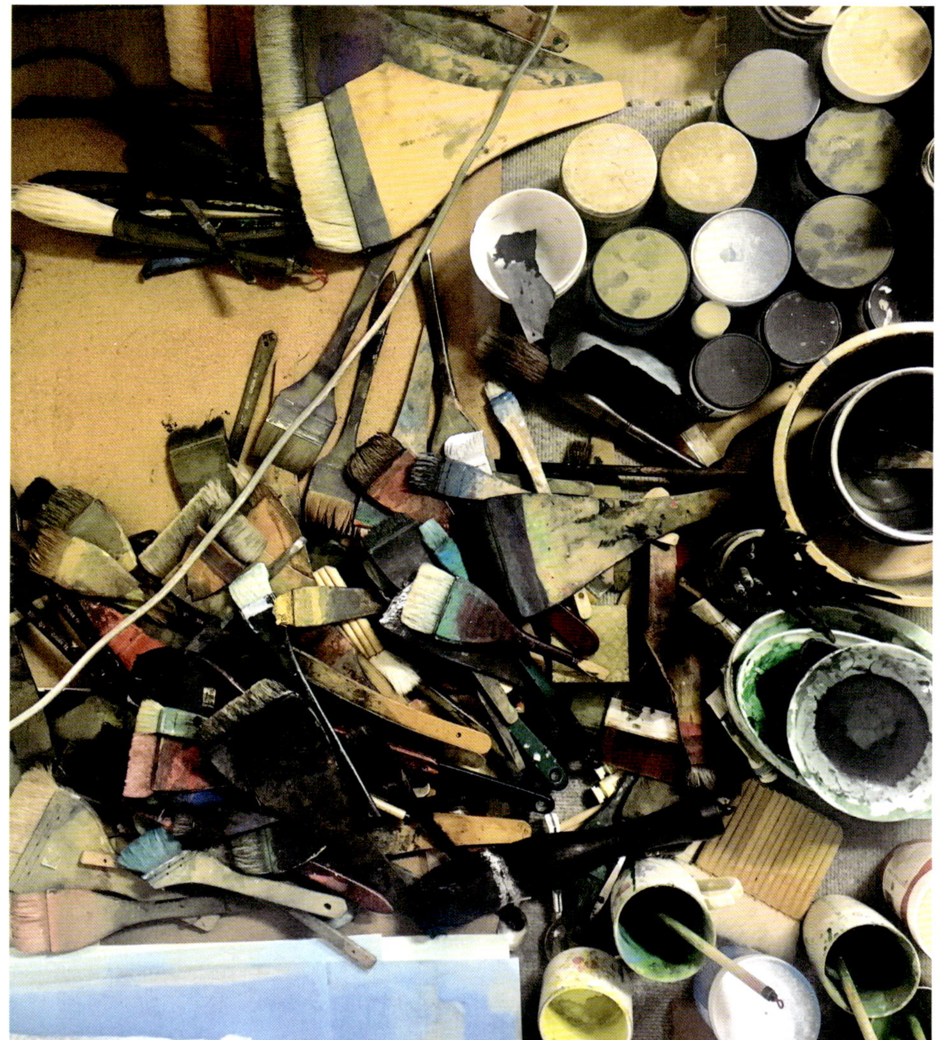

Brushes in Liu Guosong's studio, Taoyuan, Taiwan, November 2019

Because of the promised gift to LACMA, we had to make a decision: What do we do now? Do we stop or continue collecting? And if we continue collecting, how do we do it? So we decided to continue collecting, but also searching for new artists in a more systematic way—we decided that we would go to one country and really explore what's going on there, and then look at another country, and so on. We made such a trip to South Korea in 2018, and last year [2019] one in Taiwan. Now we would like to do a similar trip to Japan, but we don't know when [laughs].

SF *Could you each share some of your memories of these experiences from your travels?*

DC In Hong Kong, we met Fung Ming Chip and his wife, and now each time we go to Hong Kong we try to see them. They're very nice people and we've become good friends. So I think it's important to see an artist many times and develop a relationship.

The second example happened in Shanghai, when I met for the first time Wang Tiande. I remember Gérard showing him examples of his collection and what he had bought from him, and saying, "You're my first artist," and Tiande was so proud and so happy—it was a very nice moment.

GC A funny thing happened one day in New York. Dora and I went to see an exhibition at the Metropolitan Museum about ink art [*Ink Art: Past as Present in Contemporary China*, 2013], and as we were roaming the show, we spotted a couple. The woman was French, and the man was Chinese. We did not know them, but they asked us, in front of a piece of art, "Can you take a picture of us?" And then we started to talk about the specific work behind them and the man said he was a friend of the artist and was an artist as well, and I said, "Oh, you're an artist! What's your name?" And he said "My name is Wei Ligang." Actually, a few months before, I had bought a work by him, so I showed him the picture of his piece on my phone! Later on, I visited his studio, and we developed a good relationship, but you see, you can also meet Chinese artists in a New York museum [laughs].

SF *Clearly, you are very international in your travels, and I know that you considered many museums all over the world before deciding upon LACMA as the new home of your collection. Why did you decide to place your collection here?*

GC As the collection was growing, we had to make a decision on what to do with it—our long-term objective was to share this collection as much as possible with the public. We reviewed various alternatives, including setting up our own museum, but concluded that an existing museum that would have a good use of the collection would be the best option.

We discussed the possibility with several institutions; most were specialized in Asian art and were looking at our collection mainly from that perspective. This was too narrow in our opinion. LACMA had a much more global approach, and this was a decisive factor. We had a good relationship from the start with LACMA management, especially Stephen Little, and that was a big help.

SF *Your collection is still growing. What's on the horizon? What do you hope for your collection to become?*

GC Yes, we continue to collect. Our focus at the moment is to expand to places where ink art is active but not so known on the global scene. We recently organized trips to South Korea and Taiwan, where we found very good ink artists, some little known outside their countries. We plan to do the same in Japan for ink art and also for contemporary ceramics, which could be a good fit for our collection.

We also plan to have Fondation INK becoming more active in promoting ink art to the public in places where this art form is little known. This is certainly the case in Europe, and this will give us plenty of things to do.

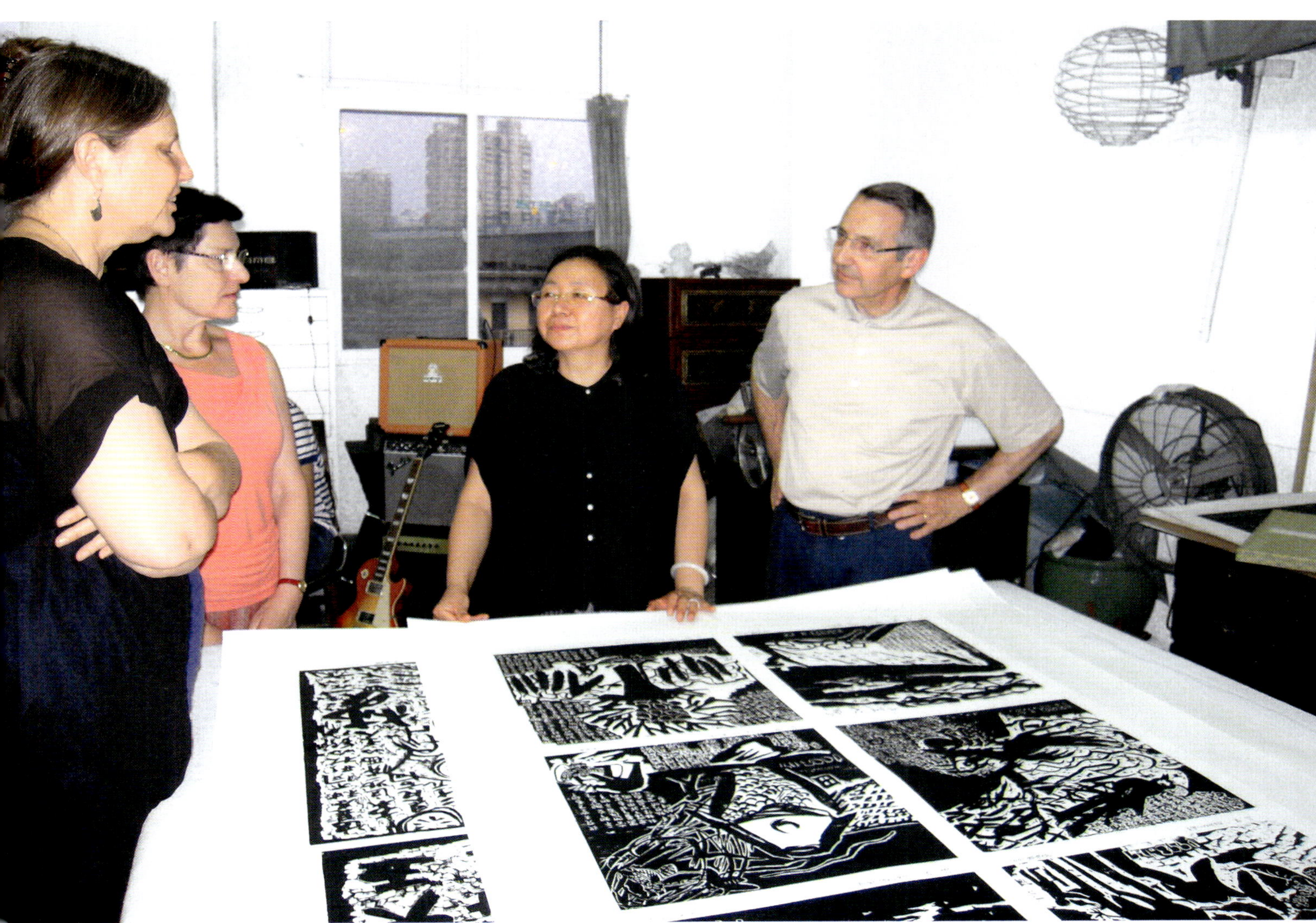

Britta Erickson, Dora Cognié, Chen Haiyan, and Gérard Cognié look at woodblock prints at Chen's Hangzhou studio, 2012

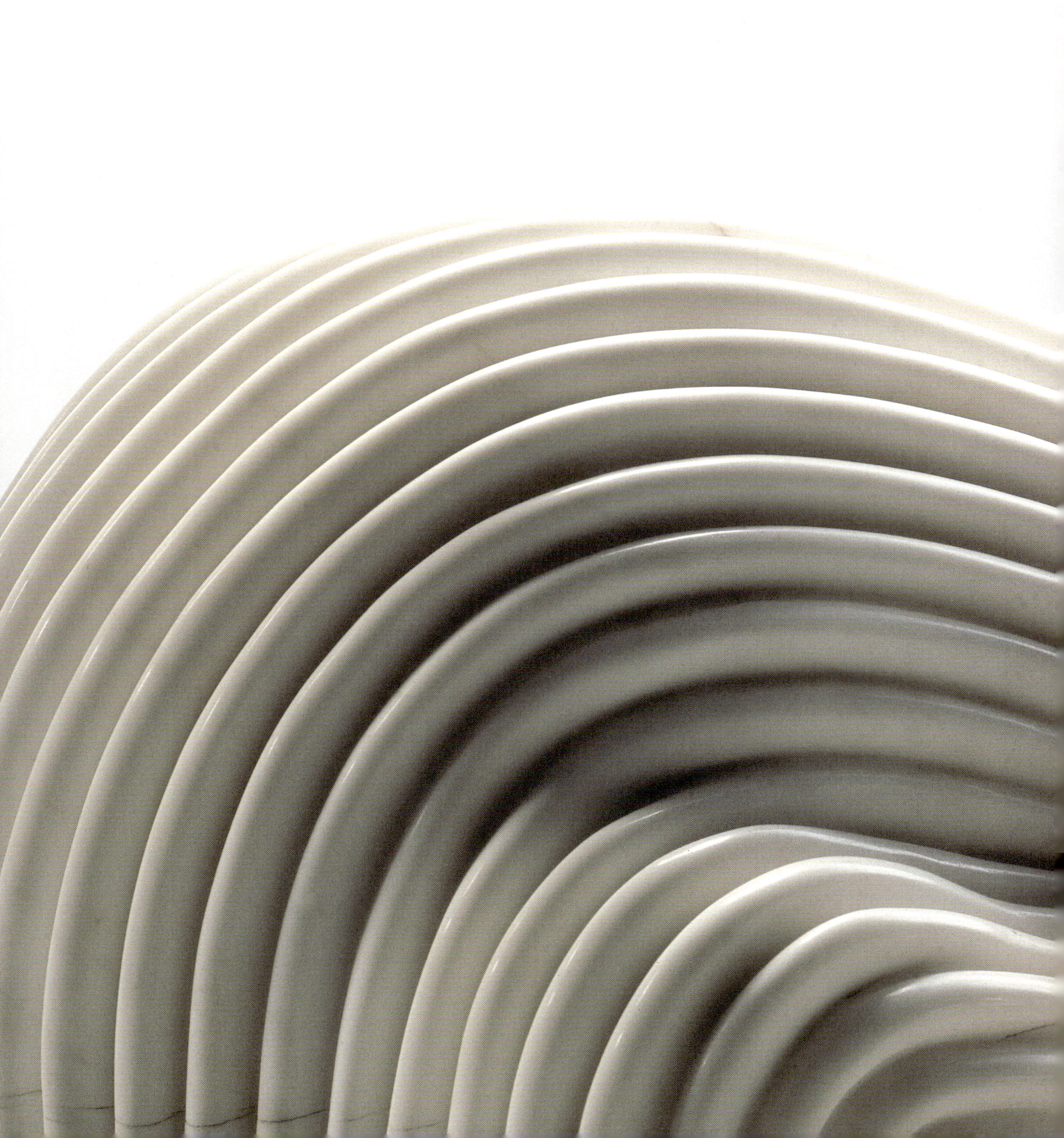

The Spirit of Ink

Meditations, Apparitions, Dreamscapes

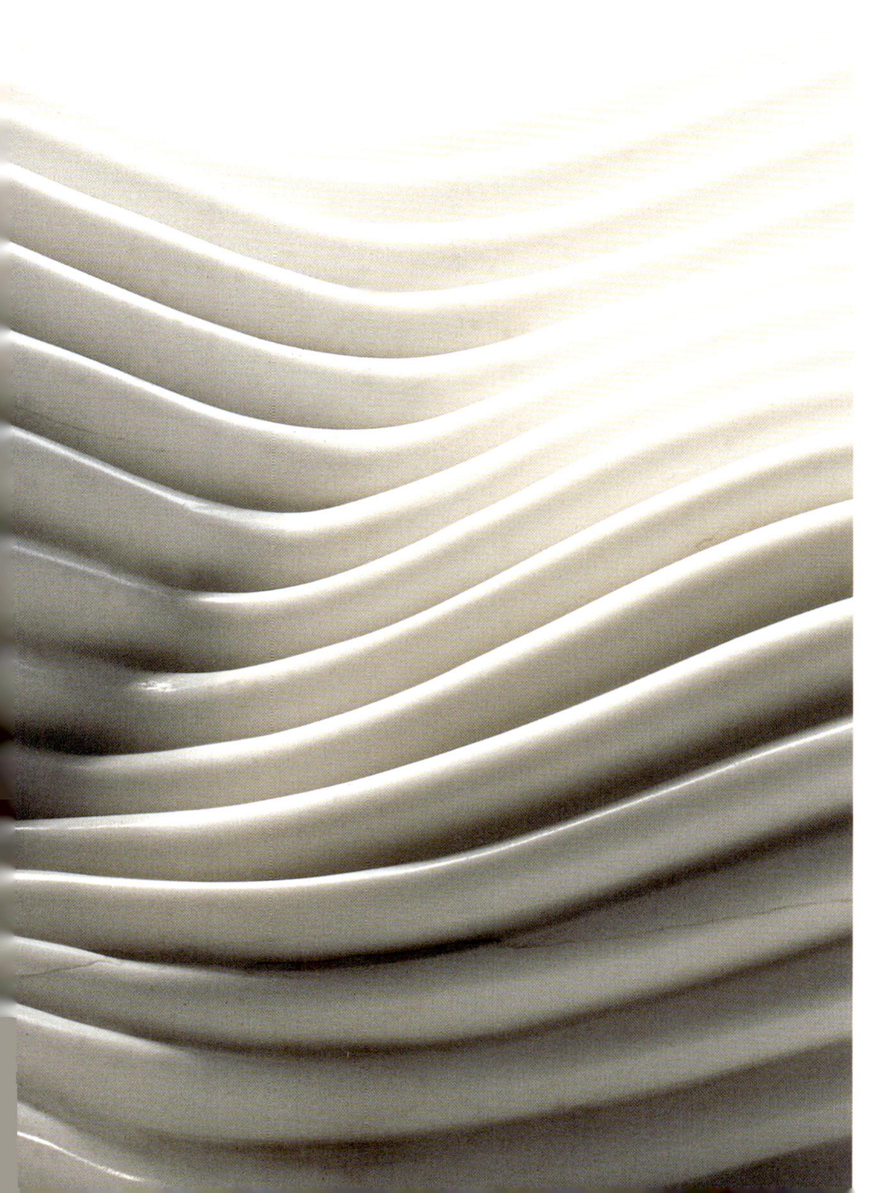

Susanna Ferrell

Ink Dreams: Selections from the Fondation INK Collection offers a fresh view on the global role of one of the great artistic heritages, East Asian ink painting. In China, ink painting materials and philosophy can be traced back over millennia, expanding over the centuries into an entity with global reach, through its aesthetics, philosophy, materials, and practice. Collectors Dora and Gérard Cognié have recognized a *spirit* of ink painting that transcends medium or place of origin. *Ink Dreams* seeks to elucidate the soft qualities of ink in the context of a contemporary, globalizing[1] art world, by recognizing three themes deeply embedded in ink art history: meditations, apparitions, and dreamscapes.

1 Although the term "global contemporary art world" can sometimes have the connotation of a homogenized setting, conforming to historically Western European artistic traditions, I use it throughout this essay to describe the expanded accessibility of and connection between distinctive global art practices and practitioners.

While the interpretation that contemporary ink art is not defined by physical materials or place of origin claims some novelty, there is in fact a *tradition* of ink artists traversing the understood bounds of this mode of painting—that is to say, there is a precedent, set by ink artists past, for making exceptions. For example, although historically most ink painting was produced by East Asian artists, no history of Chinese court painting would be complete without mention of Giuseppe Castiglione (fig. 1), an Italian Jesuit missionary who spent half a century painting in the courts of Emperors Kangxi, Yongzheng, and Qianlong. His style fused Chinese and Italian traditions, adopting the Chinese mediums of ink and mineral pigments as well as compositional elements, while relying on the style and techniques of his training in Renaissance Italy—resulting, for example, in a composition of three-

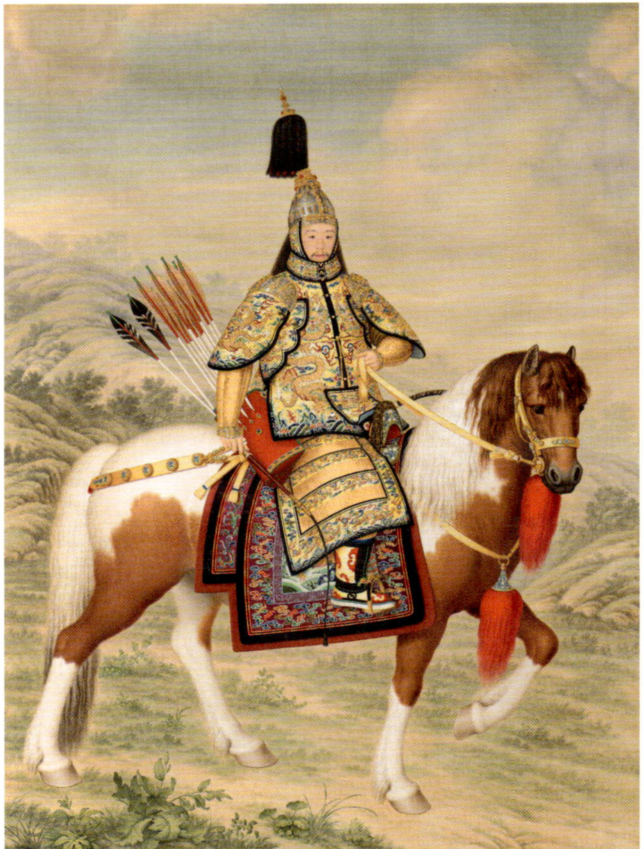

Fig. 1 Giuseppe Castiglione (1688–1766), *The Qianlong Emperor in Ceremonial Armor on Horseback*, 1739. Hanging scroll: ink and color on silk, 130⅞ × 91⅜ in. (332.5 × 232 cm). The Palace Museum, Beijing

dimensional horses sited against a relatively flattened landscape. Therefore, it was already established centuries ago that one does not have to be of East Asian descent to create ink art.

In the present day, cross-cultural exchange is significantly more commonplace than it was during Castiglione's lifetime—one simply has to hop on a plane, take a long nap, and awaken in a new country. Or, with lesser commitment, surf the ever-expanding internet, which has ushered in a new era in which resources on Asian and Western[2] art histories are readily available to anyone with a connection. Naturally, then, more artists from outside of Asia have embraced ink aesthetics or otherwise found inspiration in Asian art history.

2 I will be using "Western" throughout this essay to denote areas strongly influenced by and privileging Western European culture; it should be noted that in areas outside of Western Europe itself this is usually via imperialistic or colonial means.

The Castiglione of the 21st century may very well be Michael Cherney (p. 140), an American living in China who has been deeply committed to replicating ink aesthetics in his photography since the 1990s. Neither Cherney's heritage nor his use of photography excludes him from the ink art lineage. Chinese ink artists throughout history have forgone their traditional instruments on multiple occasions, letting fingers, fingernails, lotus pods, husks, scrunched-up paper, splashing techniques, and even their own hair take the place of the brush in an experimental fashion. The historical Chinese sources that inspire Cherney are readily apparent in his work, such that they maintain an ink art aesthetic. Furthermore, historical Chinese ink artists were confined to using the tools of their time—photography simply was not an option for artistic experimentation during, say, Castiglione's day. When photography did finally enter the canonical ink painter's domain, it became an instrument for transgressing the boundaries of the genre.

Zhang Daqian epitomizes the experimental ink artist on the cusp between ink tradition and modernity. Although he originally painted in a traditional *shuimohua* style, he began to incorporate expressive splashes of ink and wash in the 1960s. But Zhang further expanded upon the ink tradition in the late 1970s and early 1980s when he collaborated with the photographer Hu Chongxian to create photographic works in the style of traditional bird-and-flower paintings, complete

Next page Michael Cherney, *Five Peaks: Eastern, Western, Southern, Central, Northern*, 2008 (detail)

with Zhang's ink-on-photo calligraphic inscriptions (fig. 2). While it is impossible to say which artists in the Chinese ink art canon might have experimented similarly with new media, one can posit that more liberal artists of centuries past would have leaned into an opportunity to create art in such a revolutionary new medium.

When ink art originated, there was no camera, no video, no installation art, and relatively little cross-cultural exchange. However, this is not to say that the field of ink art cannot evolve with the times to include new mediums and participants. Thus far, the contemporary definition of ink art has not been adapted to fit an era in which new mediums abound and the art world is swiftly becoming more and more global. As artists encounter a never-ending stream of options and inspirations, the parameters of any given genre will change. And in fact, the physical environment, tools, and cultural milieu of ink art has transformed.

An overview of ink art from its origins to the present day reveals three persistent themes: *meditations*, or artwork related to Zen or Chan Buddhism,[3] calm repetition, or momentary phenomena or inspiration; *apparitions*, or works that center around absence, trace, or the building of layers; and *dreamscapes*, based on the tradition of expressing one's inner world through the painting of landscapes. In the contemporary era, these trends are subverted through the use of new mediums, full abstraction, and perspectives from outside of East Asia, but they nonetheless continue to inform and shape the genre of ink art.

3 "Chan" translates roughly to "meditation," as does the Japanese "Zen," "Zen" being the more commonly used romanization outside of Asia. This essay will preference the use of "Chan," as the majority of the discussed artists are Chinese, but will use "Zen" when referring specifically to a Japanese origin or source of inspiration.

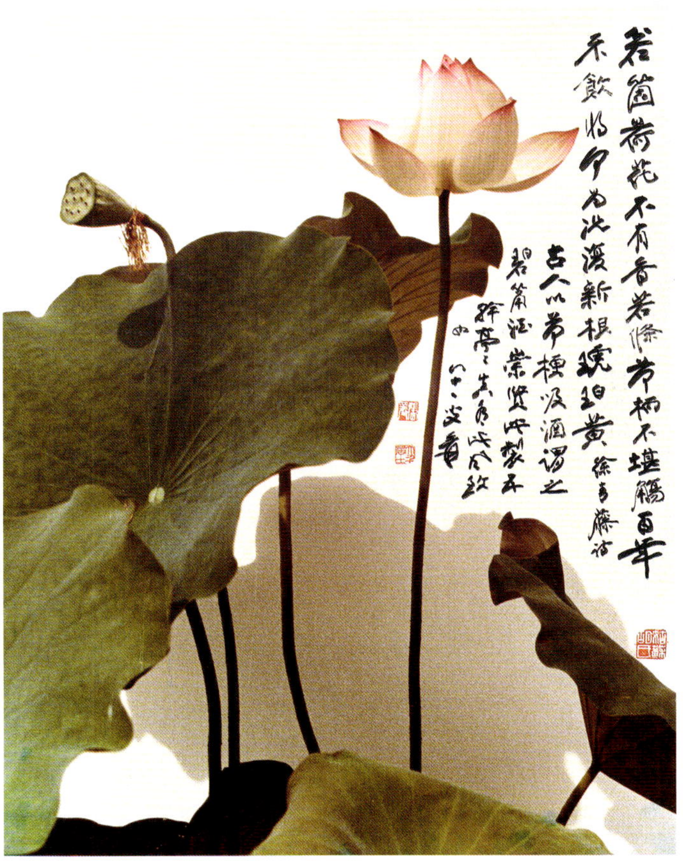

Fig. 2 Zhang Daqian and Hu Chongxian, *Jade Green Straws*, ca. 1979–82. Ink on photograph, 19½ × 14½ in. (49.5 × 36.8 cm). Yuz Museum, Shanghai

Meditations

Centuries of Prolonging

The Origins of Meditative Art More than 2,500 years ago, beneath the branches of the Bodhi Tree in Bodh Gaya, Bihar, India, Siddhartha Gautama attained enlightenment through meditation, becoming the Amitabha Buddha. This event is the first instance of Buddhist meditation, the deep contemplation of Siddhartha's surroundings itself spurring the earthly introduction of the religion. However, though Buddhism was the main vehicle by which meditation entered East Asia and was later disseminated globally, variations of the practice can be found in Christianity, Judaism, Islam, Confucianism, Daoism, and—its earliest religious context—Hinduism.

The first recorded examples of meditative art come in the form of cave paintings and sculptures, dated as early as the 2nd century BCE, located at the Ajanta Caves in Aurangabad, Maharashtra, India (fig. 3). The site was excavated by the region's ruling dynasty in order to create a 30-cave complex, made up of *viharas*, or monasteries, each with individually dug prayer halls and chambers. Artworks adorning the prayer halls depict stories from early Buddhist texts such as the *Jatakas*, and include carvings and paintings of the Amhitaba Buddha in a state of meditation.

Meditation was introduced into East Asia during the Han dynasty (206 BCE–220 CE), when Buddhist monks first brought the practice to China via the "Silk Road."[4] Later, in the 2nd century CE, missionary monks An Shigao and Lokaksema, from Iraq and Gandhara,[5] respectively, provided Chinese translations of Buddhist texts on meditation. Though Buddhism did not immediately take hold in China as a mainstream religion, it was gradually popularized over the following centuries. During the 4th century, Chinese Buddhist monks transmitted the religion to Korea, and in the 6th century it spread to Japan. From the 7th century onward, Buddhism's reach expanded into Southeast Asia and Oceania.

4 I use quotation marks around "Silk Road" here as it is somewhat of a superimposition, named by German historian Ferdinand von Richthofen in the 19th century, and does not represent a literal road but a loose assemblage of trade routes.

5 A region encompassing modern-day Pakistan and Afganistan.

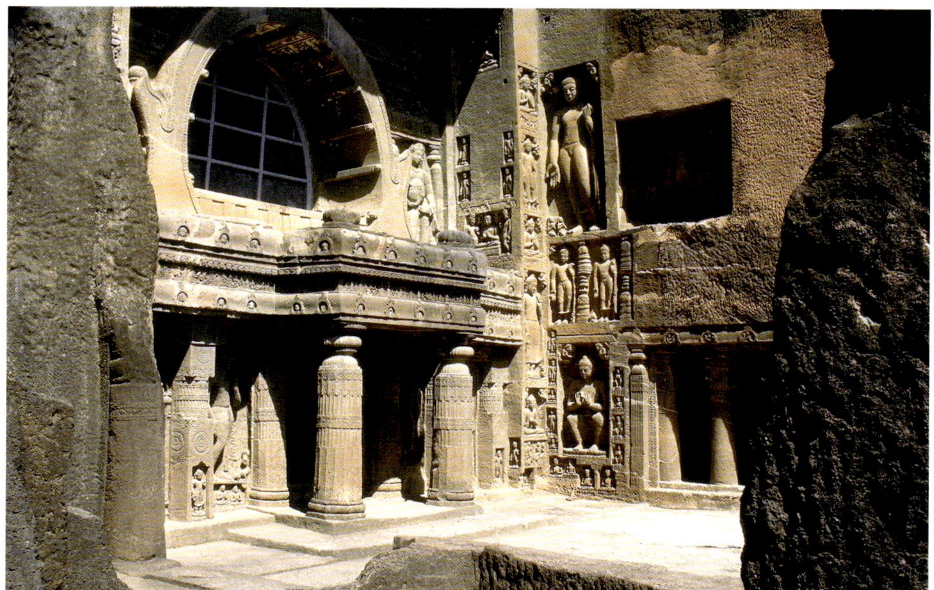

Fig. 3 The facade of the Ajanta Cave 9 *chaitya* worship hall in Aurangabad, Maharashtra, India, ca. 100 BCE–100 CE

Naturally, it was not until Buddhism had established a presence in China that Chinese Buddhist art emerged. The earliest works, dating from the 3rd to the 5th century, are murals and sculptures decorating the walls of the Kizil Caves, in what is now the Xinjiang Uyghur Autonomous Region in northwestern China (fig. 4).[6] As with the monastery paintings in the Ajanta Caves, the Kizil murals depict Buddhist stories and were likely used as inspiration for meditation and prayer in addition to didactic purposes. Iconography such as halos and mandorlas help to identify bodhisattvas, Buddhas, and the Amithaba Buddha. These early Chinese renditions of Buddhist imagery are characterized by smooth, rounded linework, rudimentary shading, and the heavy use of blue, green, red, white, and black mineral pigments.

6 Although 2nd century carvings from the Mogao Caves in Dunhuang, Gansu Province, have sparked some debate over potential Buddhist influence, these works are not conclusively Buddhist. For further information, see Minku Kim, "Claims of Buddhist Relics in the Eastern Han Tomb Murals at Horinger: Issues in the Historiography of the Introduction of Buddhism in China," *Ars Orientalis* 44 (2014); Wu Hung, "Buddhist Elements in Early Chinese Art (2nd and 3rd Centuries A.D.)," *Artibus Asiae* 47, nos. 3–4 (1986), 263–352.

But what qualities define meditation, and the artwork inspired by it? Buddhist art across cultures, commonly features richly colored illustrations of Buddhist texts as well as images of the Amitabha Buddha in a seated posture of meditation: the earliest form of meditative art. But beyond these types of direct representation, there are more abstract and phenomenological ways in which meditation can be translated to art. Techniques of meditation can be broadly categorized into two major groups: repetitive movements or utterances, usually in the form of a prayer, and prolonged contemplation. The end goal of both is to empty the self and find one's inner Buddha-nature. These techniques have been incorporated into Buddhist art, past and present, in the form of didactic paintings, landscape, and abstraction, and through the artist's approach to the creative process itself.

The Chan Buddhist sect, which stresses the importance of the independent, meditative journey, developed in the 9th century, and it was at this time that artists began to digress from illustrating Buddhist stories and wrestle with their own subjects of contemplation. The first major Chan artists were Guanxiu and Shi Ke, both practicing Chan

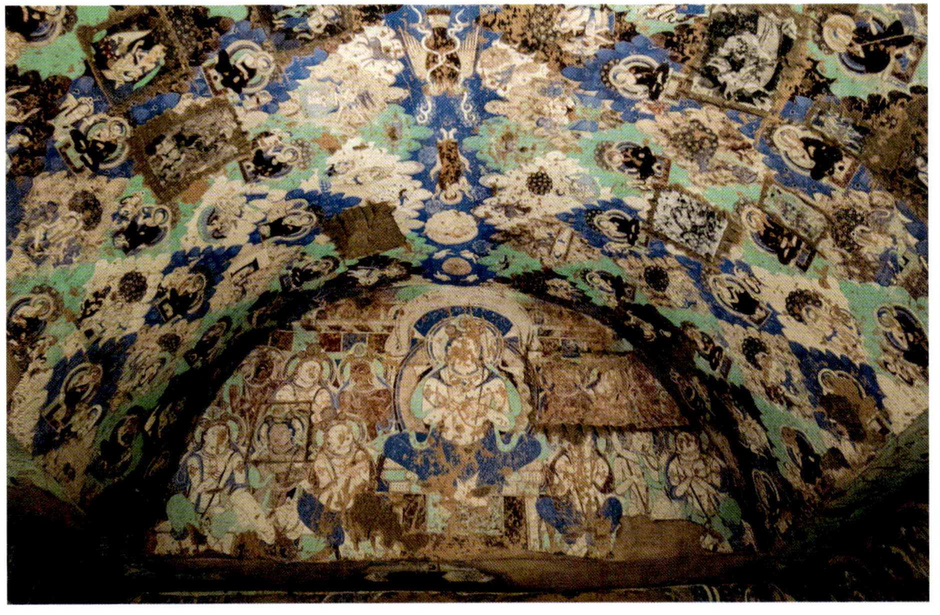

Fig. 4 Reproduction of ceiling murals from Cave 38 prominently depicting the Maitreya Buddha, along with bodhisattvas, musicians, traders, and other figures, Kizil Caves, Baicheng County, Aksu Prefecture, Xinjiang, ca. 3rd–5th century CE

Buddhists themselves (although this may seem to be a given, there were times when Buddhist art by non-Buddhists was common).

While Guanxiu's imagery centered around stories from Buddhist history, the unique style in which he painted his figures sets his work apart from typical Buddhist art of the period. He is principally known through reproductions of his long-lost paintings of the Eighteen Arhats or Luohans (fig. 5). As seen here, rather than employing the smooth linework, saturated colors, and formalization common during both the Tang dynasty (618–907) and the Five Dynasties and Ten Kingdoms Period (907–79) (fig. 6), Guanxiu's figures are nearly grotesque. Wrinkled and bony, often with agonized expressions, they reflect the reality of their ascetic lifestyle—quite the opposite of the Buddhist modes of painting popular at the time. Another distinguishing feature of Guanxiu's work is the use of monochrome black and gray ink, again atypical of prior Buddhist art. His images made space for the contemplation of the hardships specific to asceticism, returning, in a way, to the origin story of Buddhism—to Siddhartha Gautama's journey toward enlightenment.

The 10th-century artist Shi Ke established a monochrome style that would become a pillar of later Chan painting. Using monochrome ink and wash, he painted bold, expressive brushstrokes, a striking contrast to the standard practice of eliminating any trace of the artist's hand. Shi Ke, like Guanxiu, did not present his subjects as pictures of perfection but as realistically flawed beings.

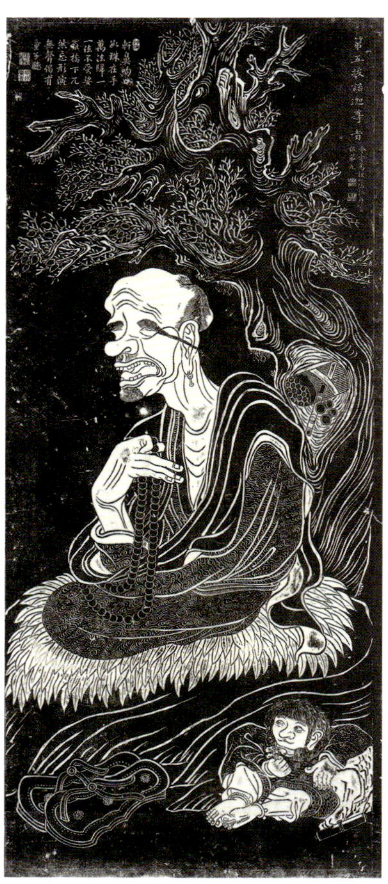

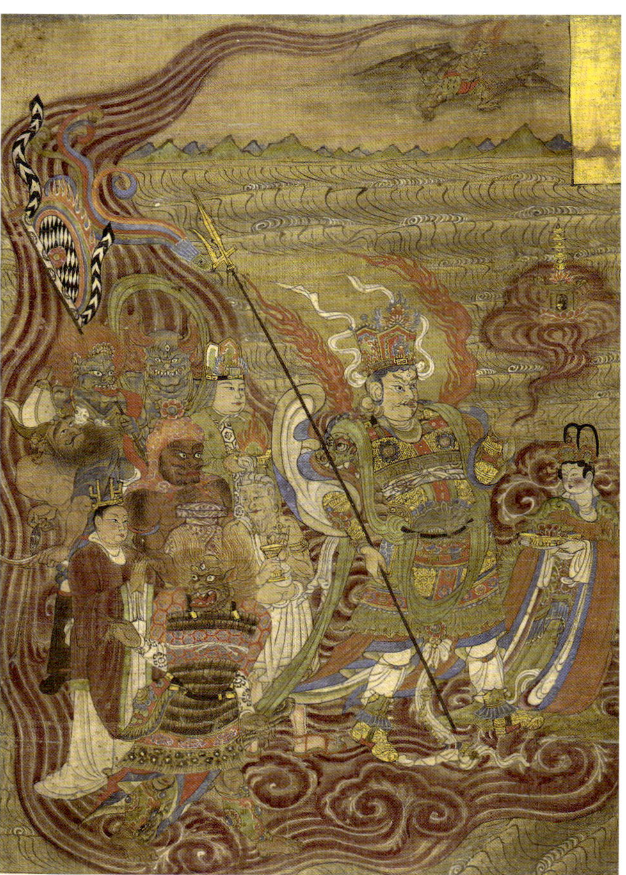

Fig. 5 Luohan, after a set attributed to Guanxiu (832–912), stone carved 1757, rubbing ca. 18th or 19th century. Ink on paper, 54⅝ × 27¾ in. (138.7 × 70.5 cm). The Metropolitan Museum of Art, New York, Gift of Miss H. C. Wagner, 1959

Fig. 6 Painting of Vaisravana, Guardian of the North, shown crossing the waters, 9th century. Hanging scroll: ink and color on silk, 14¾ × 10½ in. (37.6 × 26.6 cm). The British Museum, London

Meanwhile, according to Japanese legend, the *ensō* made its first appearance as a Zen symbol in the 9th century. The *ensō*, or circle, represents the void. When closed, it symbolizes perfection; open, it denotes the need for further cultivation or an acceptance of imperfection. Over time, the *ensō* became a recurrent subject in Japanese Buddhist painting, often paired with a short calligraphic poem. Although the form itself is elementary, it expanded the realm of Buddhist art beyond realistic or formalized images of the earthly and the spiritual worlds; and while the use of symbolic imagery was not new to Buddhist art, this is the first instance in which the image itself was completely nonrepresentational. The painting of the *ensō*, a simple, single stroke, can itself be a meditation—the act of painting the work an opportunity to empty the mind.

Among later innovators in Chan Buddhist painting are Song-dynasty artists Ma Yuan (1190–1230) and Muqi (ca. 1210–1269). Both forwent detailed, grandiose landscape paintings for scenes composed with expressive brushwork and minimal compositions, contingent in part upon negative space—"The most pertinent symbol—or rather: non-symbol—for the 'insight into one's own essential nature' in Zen painting."[7] This negative space created room to breathe, to impart one's own thoughts, and to again consider the void.

These characteristics of negative space, simple symbolism, and the artist's own contemplative experience of painting are central to the Fondation INK's collection of meditative art.

7 Helmut Brinker and Hiroshi Kanezawa, *Zen Masters of Meditation in Images and Writings* (Zurich: Artibus Asiae and Museum Rietberg Zurich, 1996).

Buddhism and Meditation Outside of Asia Buddhism was first brought to Europe after Greek colonists were exposed to Buddhism and Hinduism in India as early as the 4th century BCE. In the 1st–2nd century CE, Buddhism was further disseminated in Europe after Christian missionaries to Asia brought word of Buddhist teachings back to their homelands. However, European Christians considered the religion paganistic and its adherents in need of saving. Buddhism, and the practice of meditation along with it, began finding wider tolerance in Europe only during the Enlightenment era; later, in the early 19th century, European academics began to view Buddhism as a practice worthy of study, albeit through an exoticized and romanticized lens. The religion was not truly accepted until much later.

Buddhism surged into the United States and Europe along two major pathways during the 19th century. First, in 1844, the scholar Eugène Burnouf published texts introducing Buddhism to France, and his translation of the Lotus Sutra from Sanskrit to French was published for the first time in 1852. In the following years, scholars continued to translate Buddhist texts from Sanskrit and Pali into various European languages and published their own studies, fueling much excitement about the *exotic, new* religion—or, more accurately, the exoticized, newly recognized religion. Additionally, populations from East Asia began emigrating in larger numbers at this time, and over the next six decades established the first Buddhist temples in the Americas (1853, San Francisco; 1907, Cañete, Peru), Australia (ca. 1876–82, Thursday Island), and Europe (1909, Saint Petersburg).

Creatives from Walt Whitman to Vincent van Gogh began incorporating references to Buddhism and East Asian art into their practices. These artists set the scene for future generations, as the interest in and impact of Buddhism grew in Europe and the United States. They were followed by Impressionists, Beat poets, Abstract Expressionists, Pop, Fluxus, and Light and Space artists, and Minimalists. The influence of Buddhism in general and Zen and Chan teachings in particular on European and American art was immense.

In the mid-20th century, while Buddhism experienced a period of restriction in China, it flourished in Europe and the United States. Art practices were radically restricted in Communist China, and genres such as ink art were deemed a part of the "Old Culture" that needed to be abandoned in order for the country to advance into modernity. Equally, religion was rejected as superstitious. The accepted Socialist Realist mode was diametrically opposed to the minimalist monochrome of Buddhist art, opting for markedly colorful imagery of cheerful, industrious workers, peasants, soldiers, and officials—far from the harsh reality captured in Guanxiu's austere figures. However, in the US especially, Buddhist ideas and cultural practices became associated with a cosmopolitan sensibility in the 1960s, and its influence grew in non-Asian communities in the decades following. Artists like John Cage, Ad Reinhardt, Bill Viola, and Agnes Martin found inspiration in Buddhism during the 1950s and 1960s, and incorporated elements of Chan philosophy into their art.

During the 1990s, Buddhism experienced a second significant surge in popularity in the United States, as media attention around the religion again swelled. Today, the principles of meditation and mindfulness—adopted from Chan Buddhism—have gradually pervaded secular spaces like classrooms, gyms, spas, museums, and corporate retreats.

Meditation in Contemporary Art In two significant ways, contemporary artists have consciously or unconsciously adopted meditation in their work. The first, repetition of gesture, parallels the repeated utterance of Buddhist chants or the meditative practice of repeated sutra writing, both emptying words of their meaning. Li Huasheng (pp. 52, 73) and Zhang Yu (p. 49), for instance, echo this meditative repetition by tirelessly repeating a single action to create their paintings: for Zhang, the deliberate, rhythmical pressing of his inked or wetted fingerprint into paper; for Li, the meticulous rendering of fine-line grids over vast

Ophélie Asch, *Battle at the Craters* (*Bataille aux cratères*), 2014 (detail)

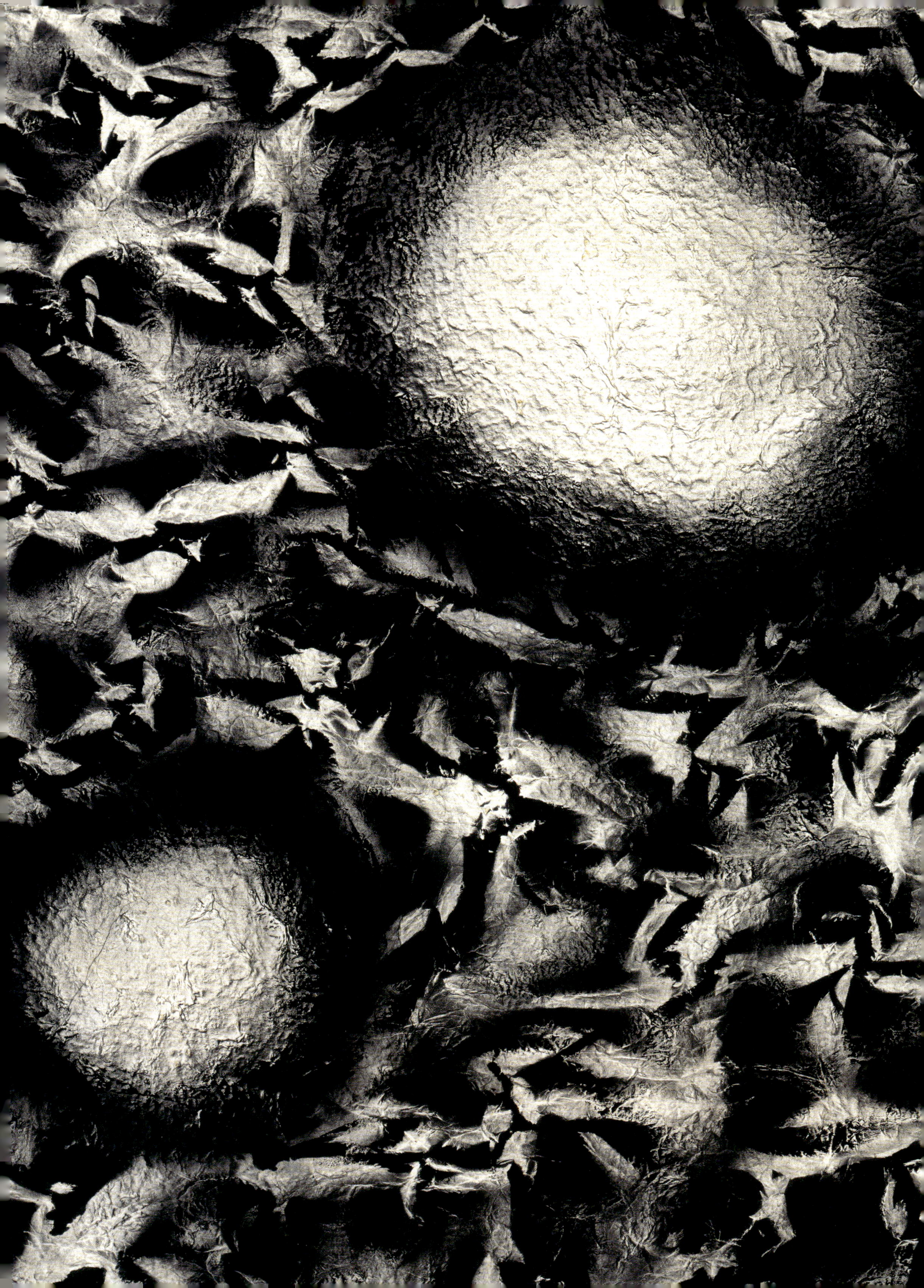

expanses of paper. The final product is not merely a painting, but a physical record of the time expended in the creation of a work: these artists embrace painting as a meditation itself, a daily practice lasting decades—a truly integral part of their lives.

Although not always acknowledged as conscious meditation, this practice of repeated mark-making constitutes a significant trend in the global contemporary art world. Irma Blank (pp. 82, 83), Matti Kujasalo (p. 71), and Max Cole (p. 80), among many others, have cultivated practices around their signature repeated marks. This approach is easily translated to sculpture, as evidenced by the work of Kitamura Junko (pp. 74, 75), who glazes her ceramics with tiny, intricate dot patterns fastidiously carved out and filled in. Further abstracting the principle of the meditative repeated mark is Sunagawa Haruhiko (p. 62), whose ruminations on line and space are often manifested through simple, repetitive geometric forms.

However, meditation is not merely repeated gesture. It also involves prolonged contemplation. Works like Qiu Shihua's *Untitled* (p. 50) require extended attention from viewers—it is only through prolonged looking that one may perceive the faint mountains of Qiu's nearly white landscape, gleaned and appreciated over time. Bingyi (p. 78) understands meditation as connection through time and space, and believes that painting is able to link *wanwu* (myriad things). Her paintings, therefore, become objects of contemplation as well. Similarly, Lui Shou-kwan affirms his meditative method through the titling of his longstanding series *Zen Paintings* (p. 79). Though Lui, Bingyi, and other artists in this section are well-informed in Chan philosophy, and others practice meditation, these are not essential prerequisites to making meditative artwork. As Lui aptly notes:

> The apprehension of Zen does not depend on a person's worshipping the Buddha, or reading the sutras, or being a Buddhist monk… the basis of Zen is man's nature—that is to say, the individual man's original nature—and it is fundamental that the apprehension of it is to be sought by cutting through the intellectual process and using means other than the reasoning faculty.[8]

8 Mei Lin Lai, "Lui Shou Kwan & Modern Ink Painting," PhD diss., University of Sydney, 2011.

These conceptual, soft qualities of meditative art allow for the subject's seamless transition into contemporary art practice, complementing abstraction, minimalism, and performance. They are not reserved solely for Buddhist artists, but available to anyone who has embraced this essential understanding of meditation.

Lui Shou-kwan, *Zen Painting A69-14*, 1969 (detail)

Plates
Meditations

Zhang Yu, *Fingerprint 2007*, 2007

Qiu Shihua, *Untitled*, 1994

Li Huasheng, *104*, 2001

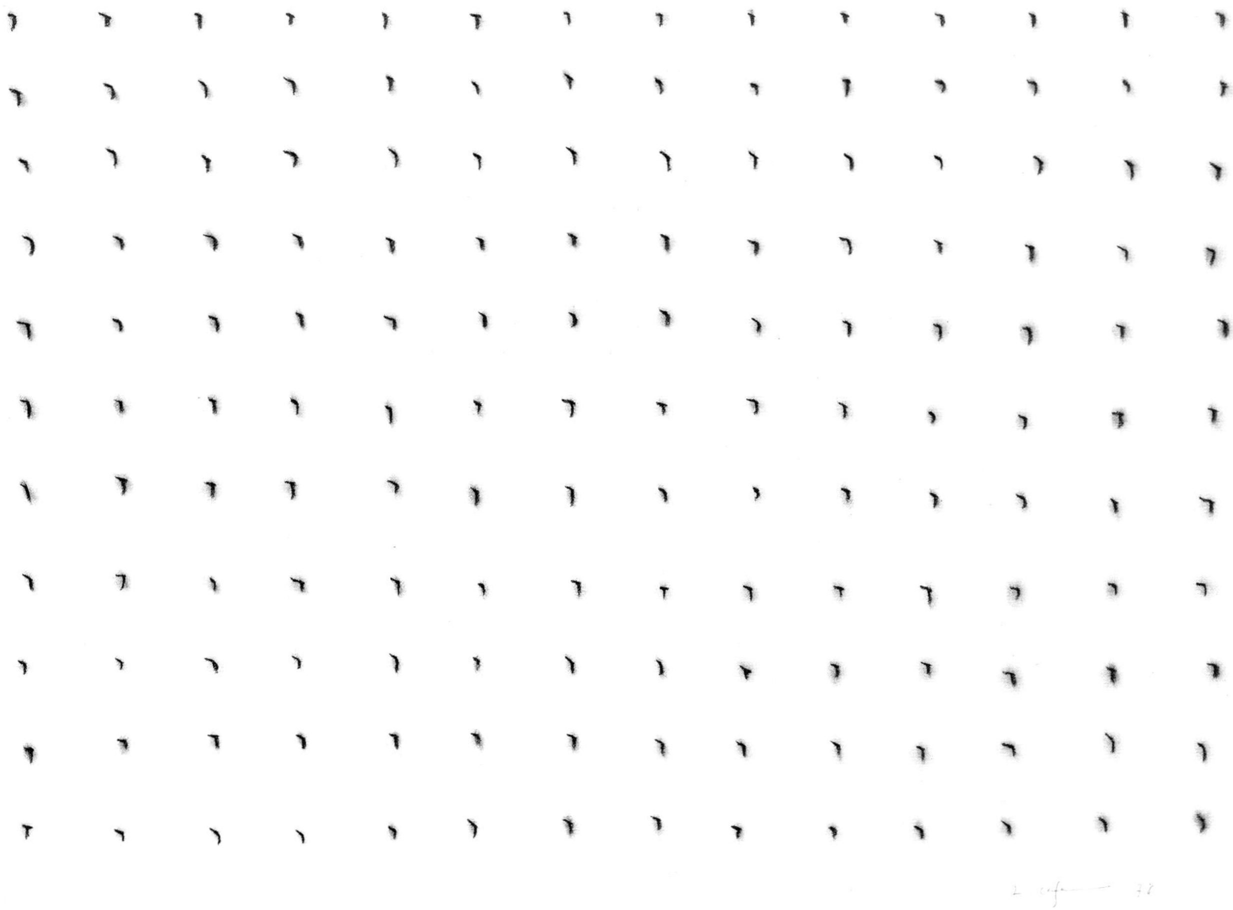

Lee Ufan, *From Point*, 1978

Chua Ek Kay, *Reflection-Breeze Passes by the Lotus Pond*, 2007

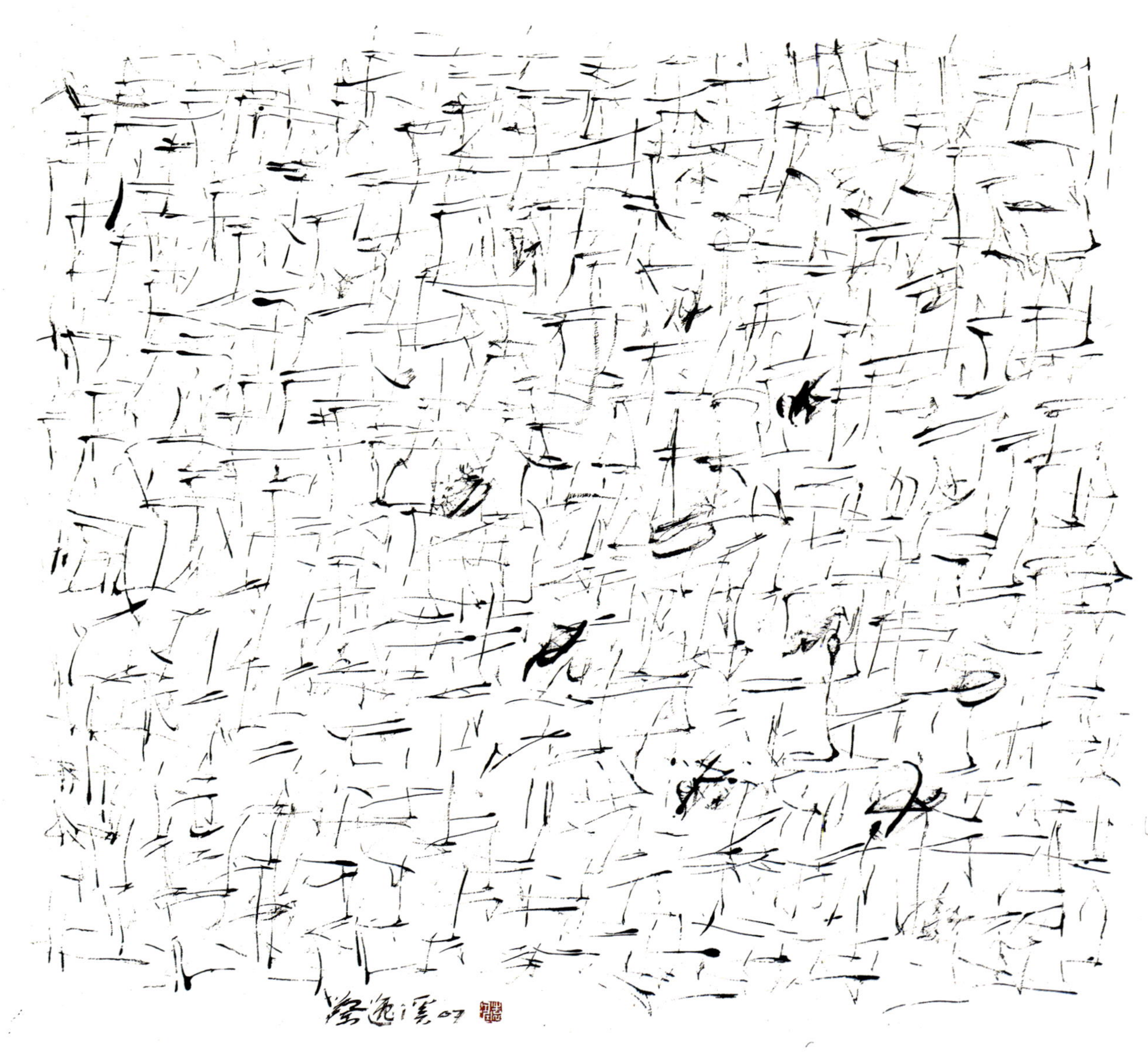

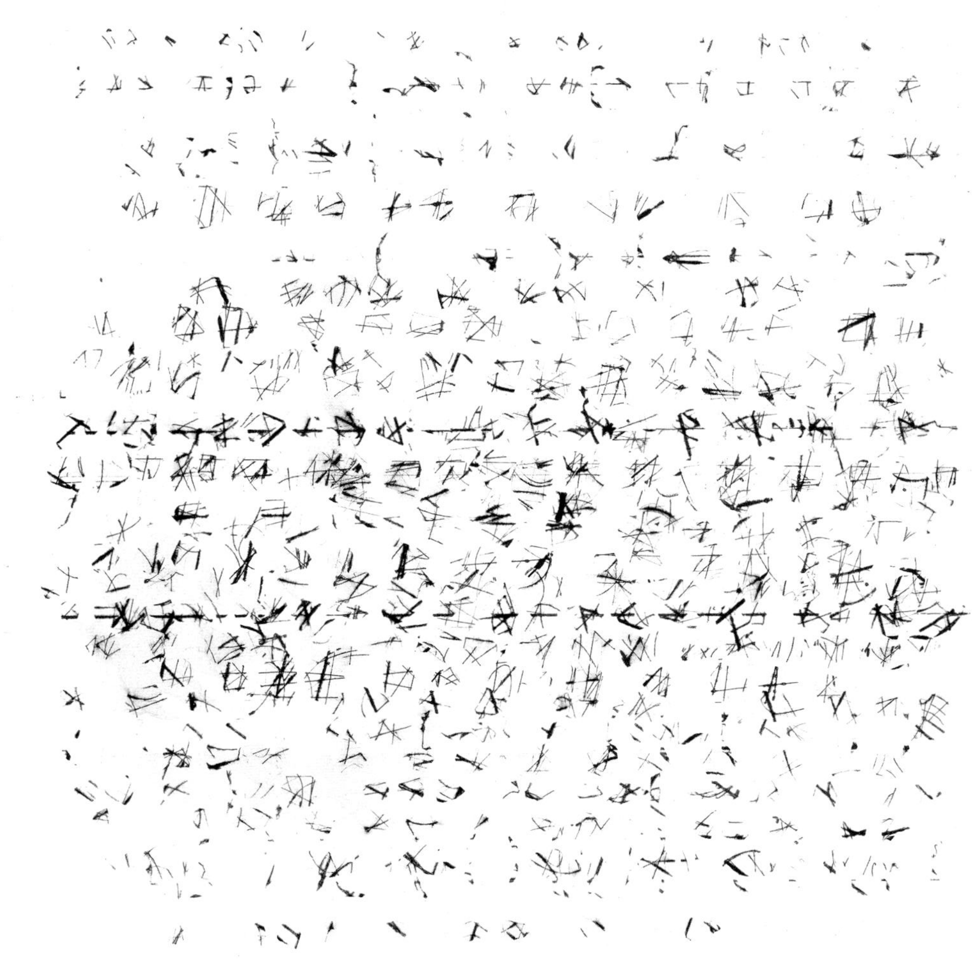

Antoine Pentsch, *Untitled XII*, 2000

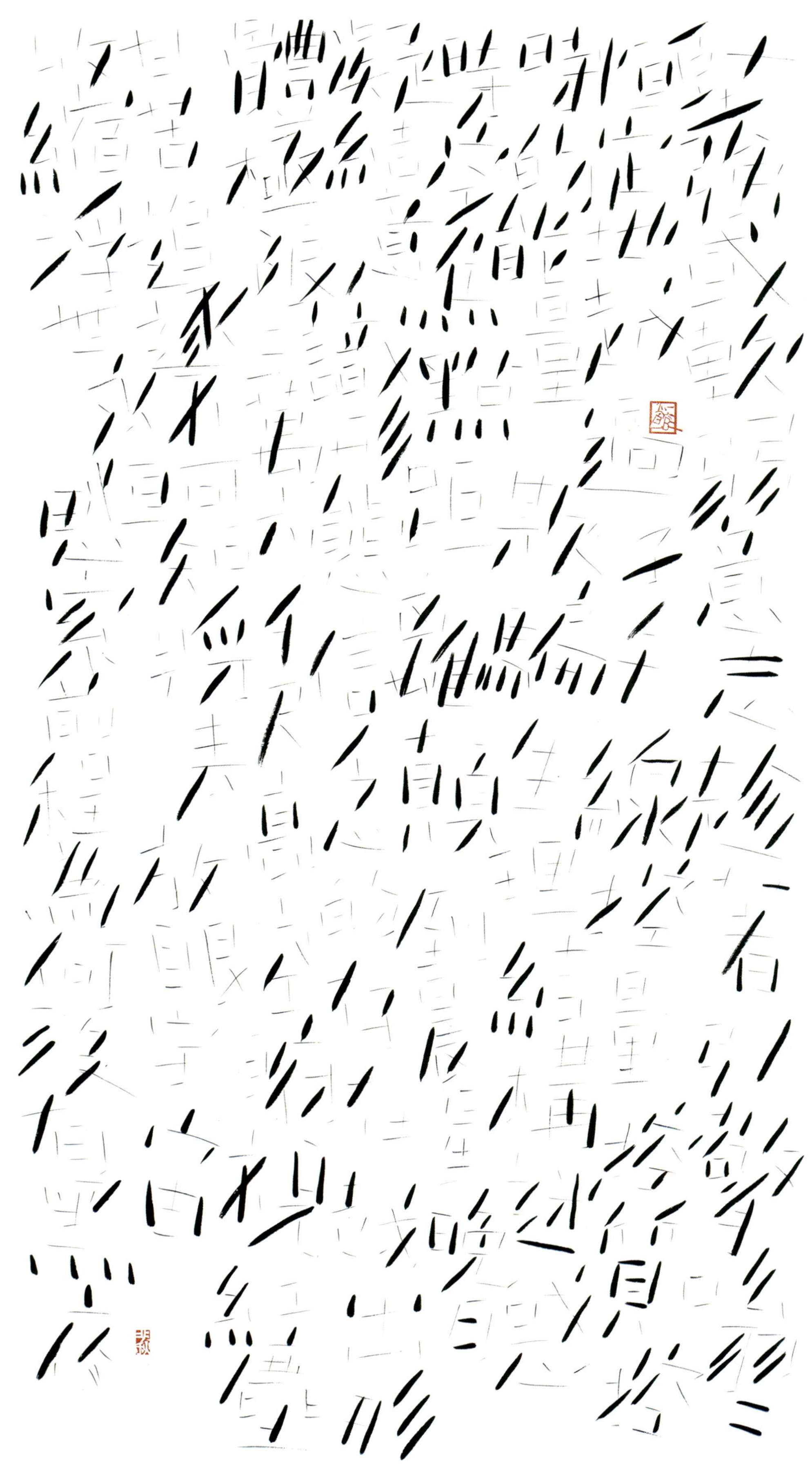

Fung Ming Chip, *Accidentally Passing, Needle Script*, 2015

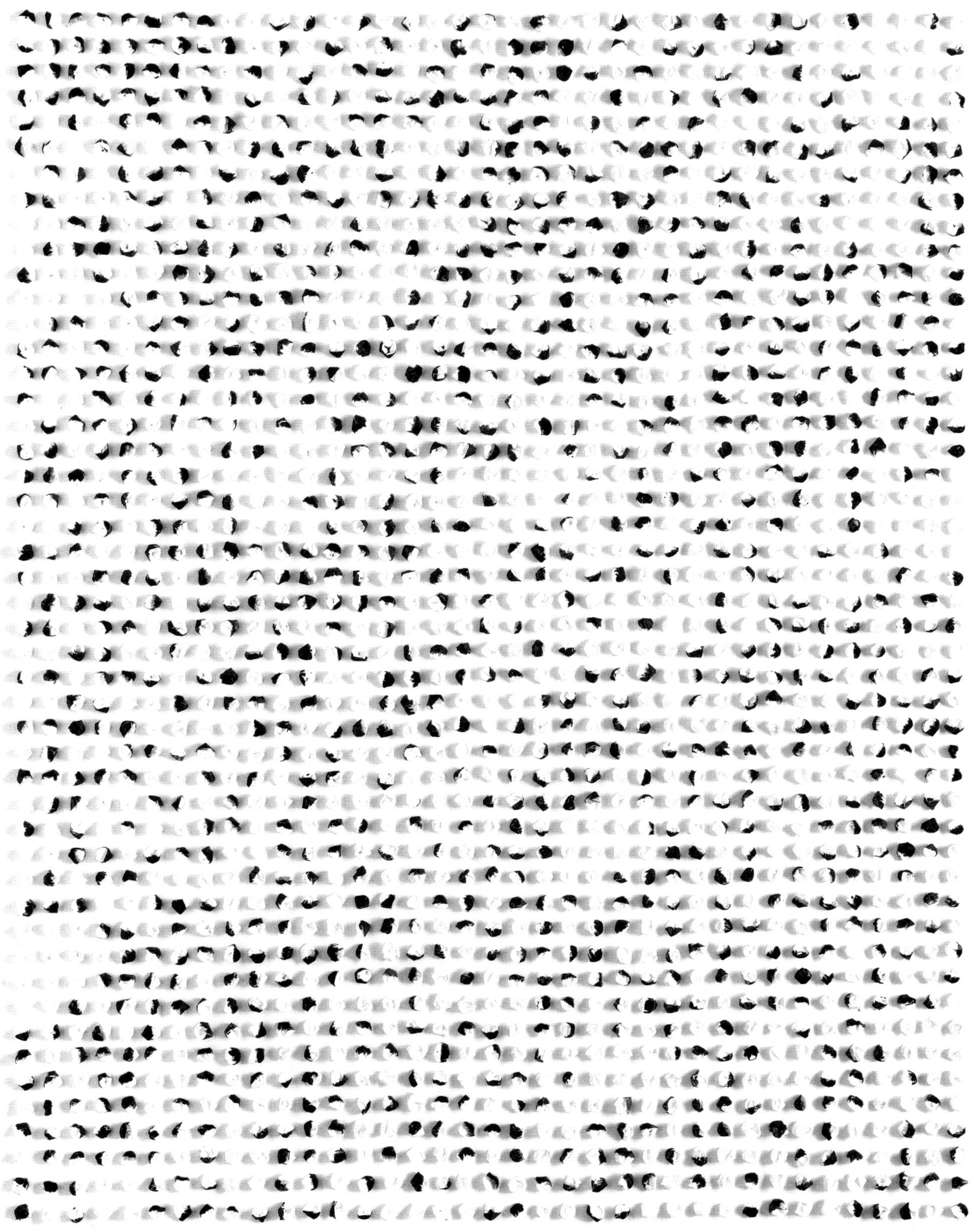

Jeong Gwang-Hee, *The Way of Reflection*, 2017

Sunagawa Haruhiko, *Convergence*, 2005–7

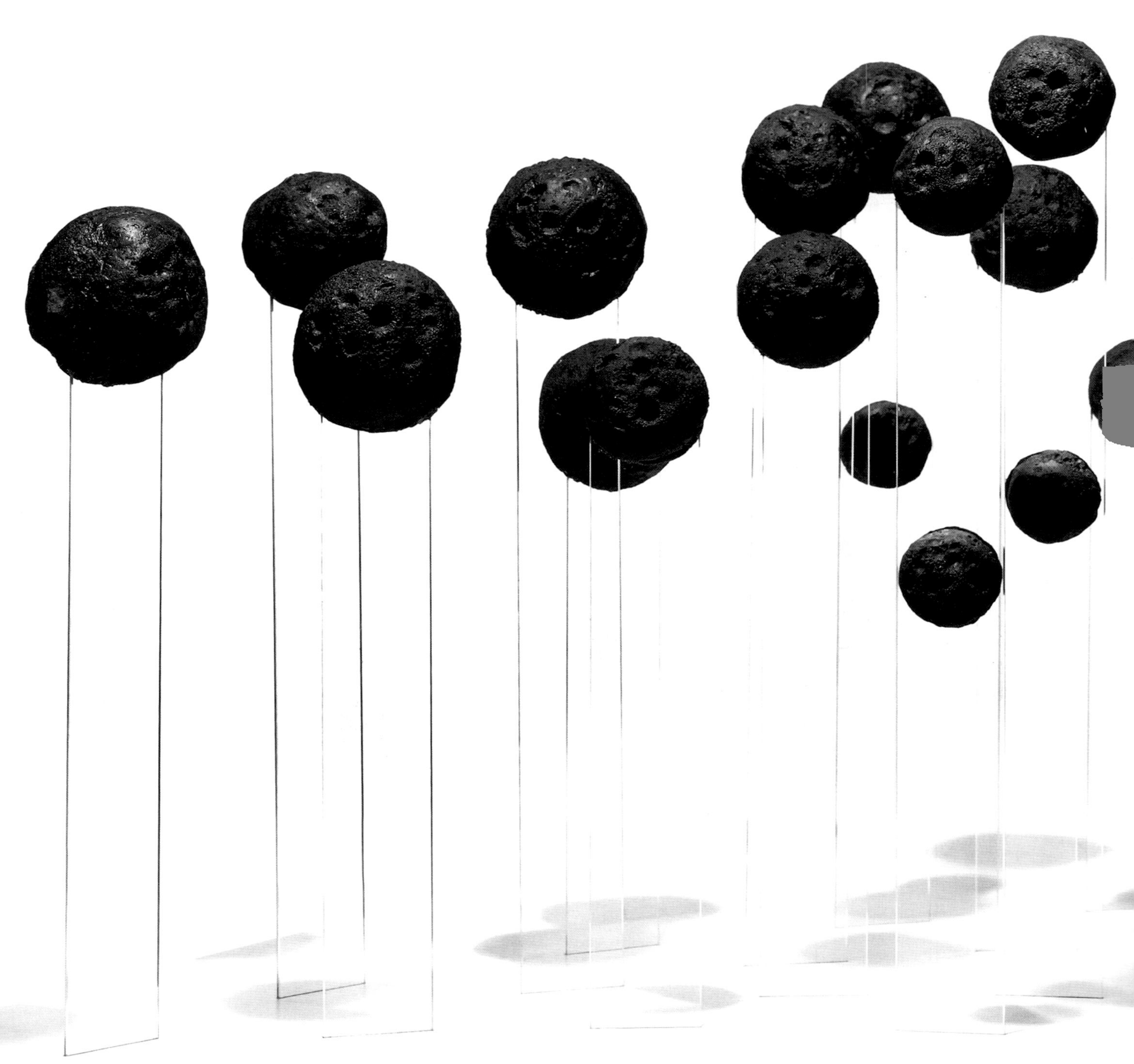

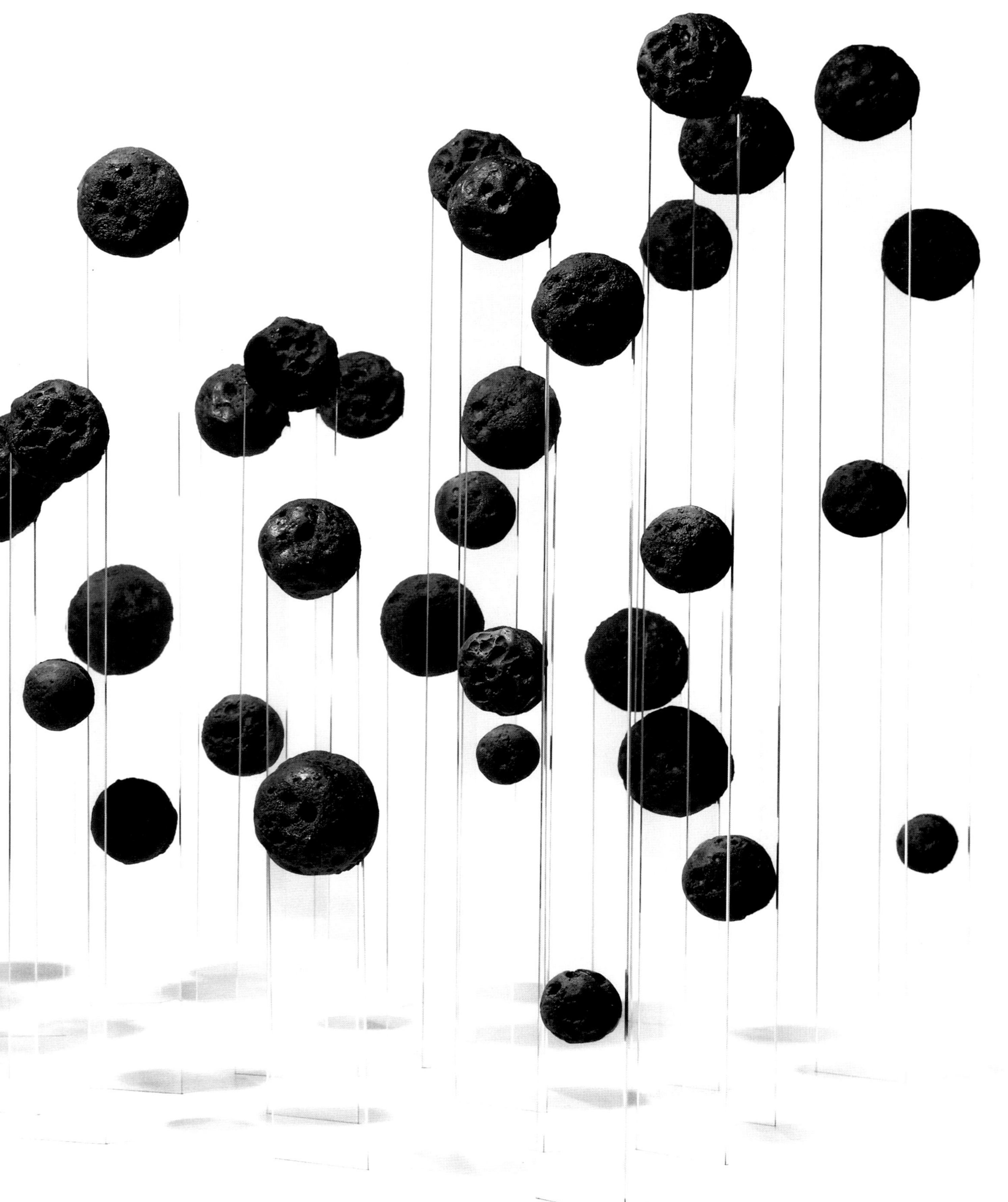

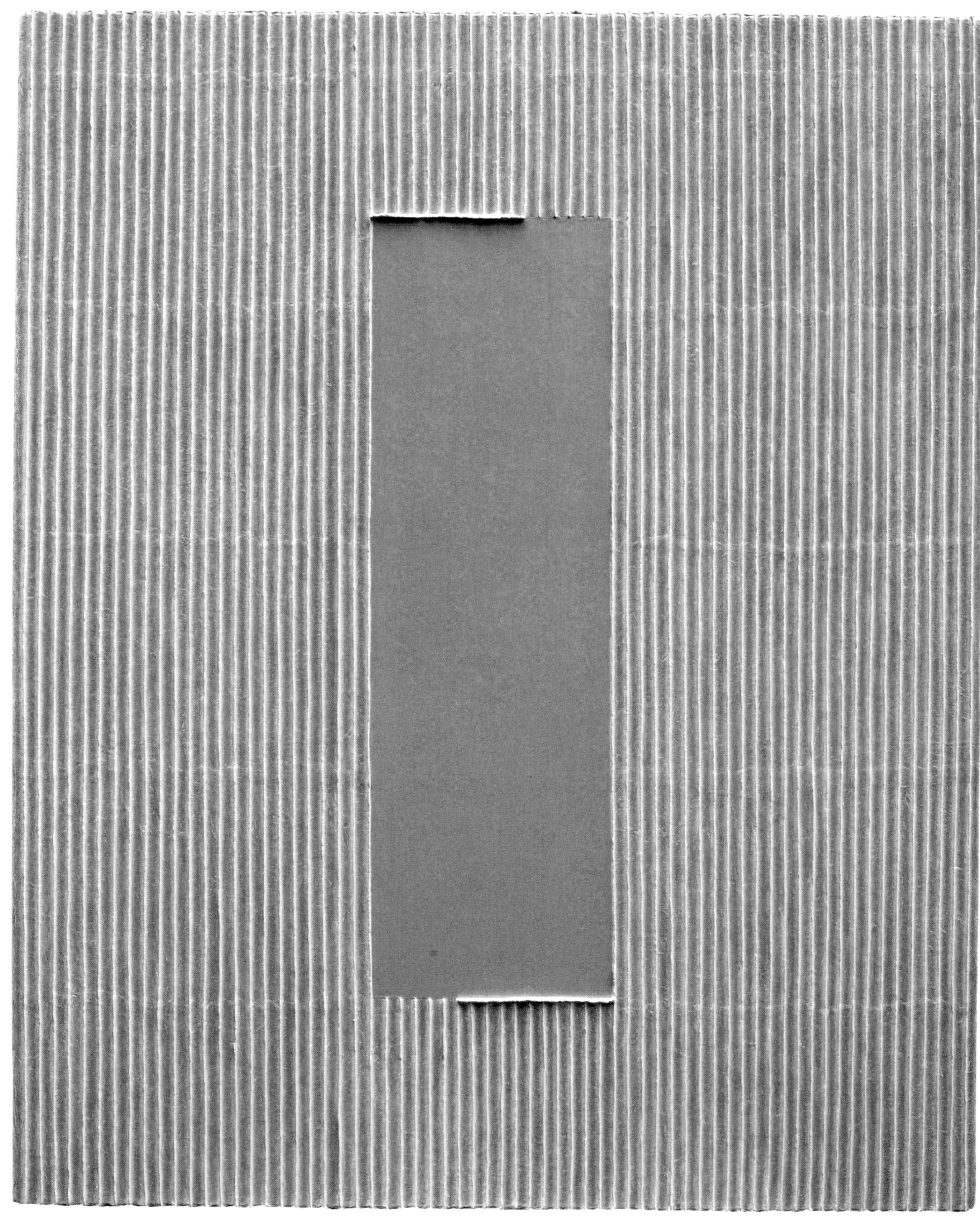

Park Seo-Bo, *Ecriture No. 080222*, 2008

Matti Braun, *Untitled*, 2009

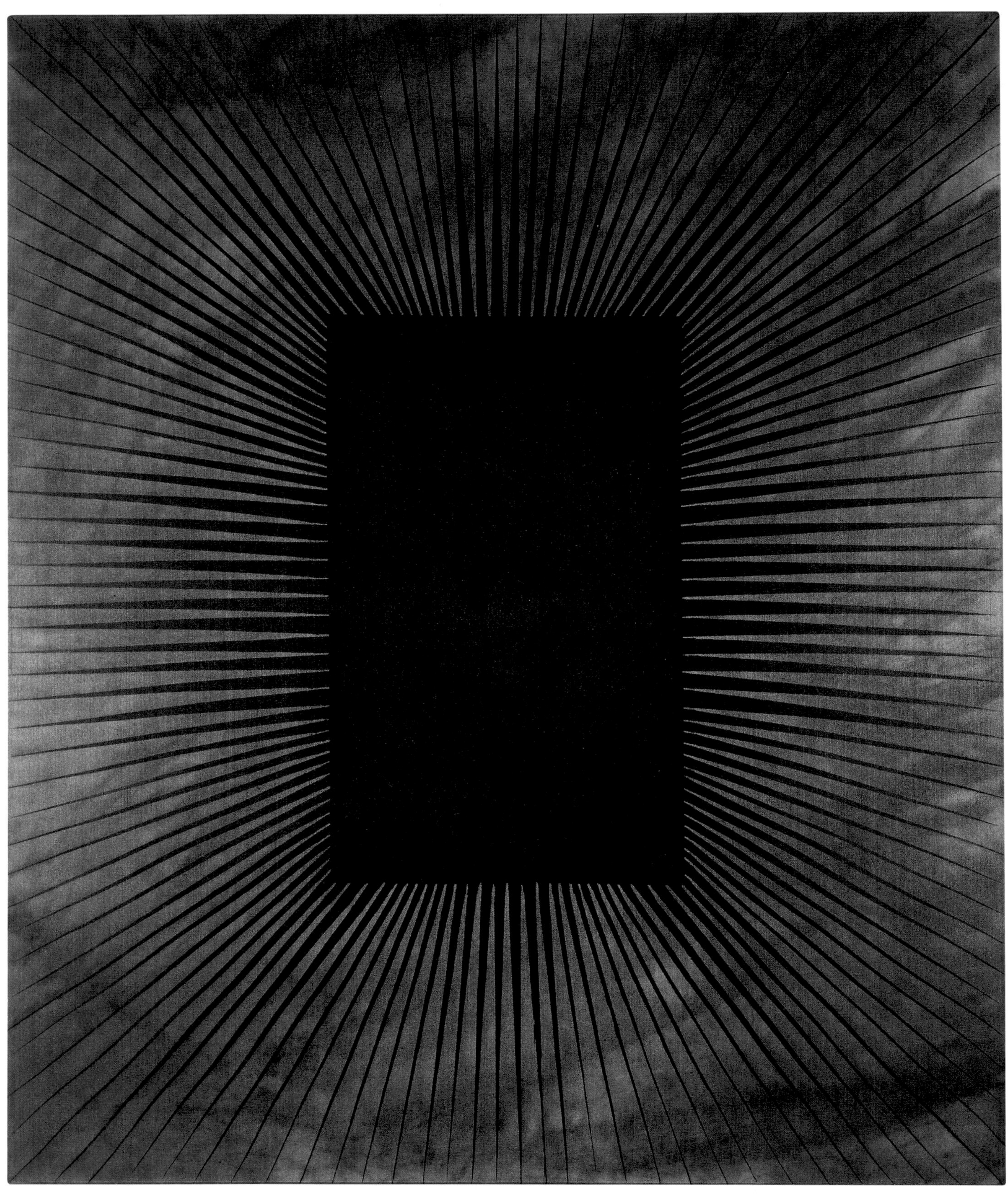

Matti Braun, *Untitled*, 2009

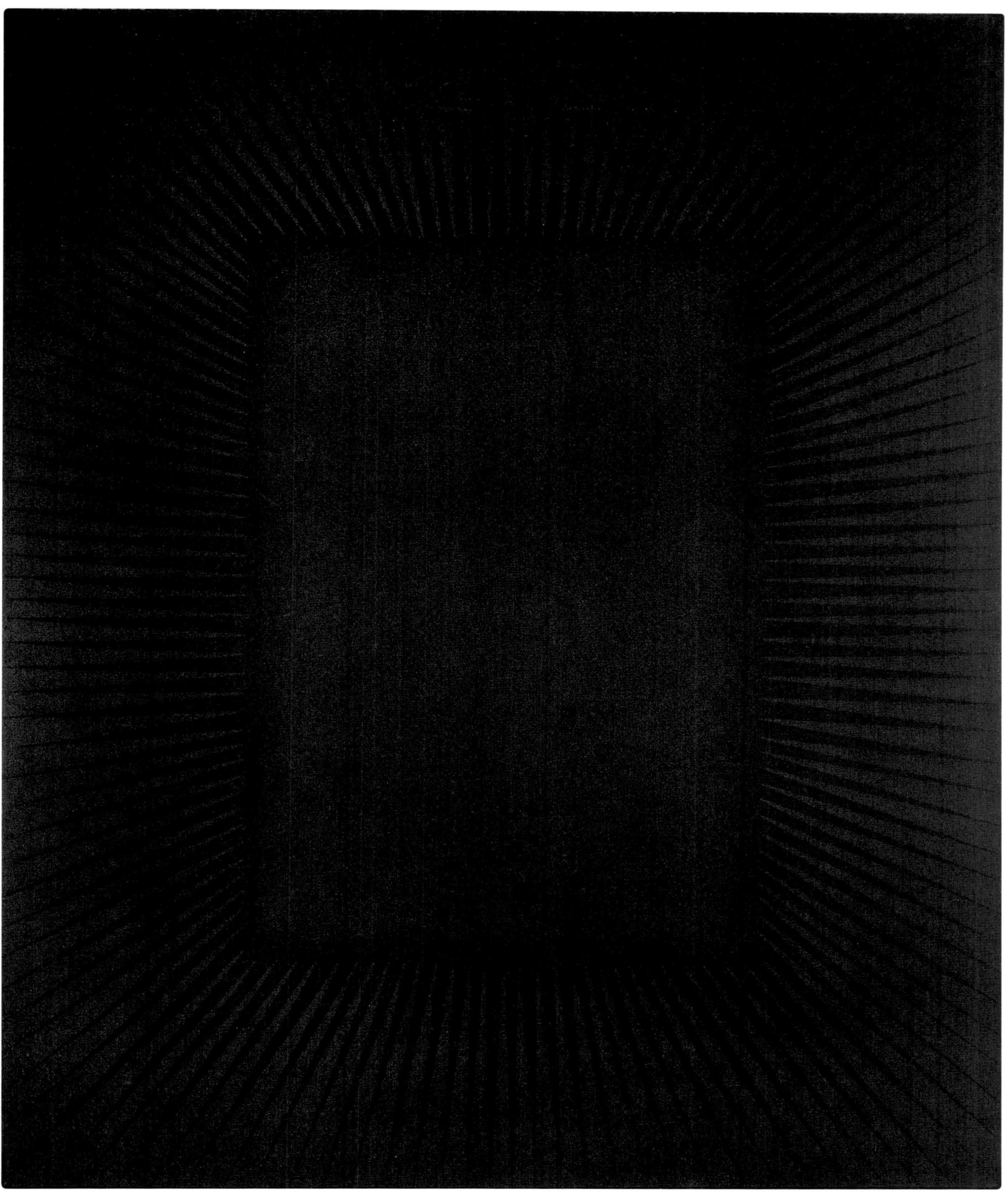

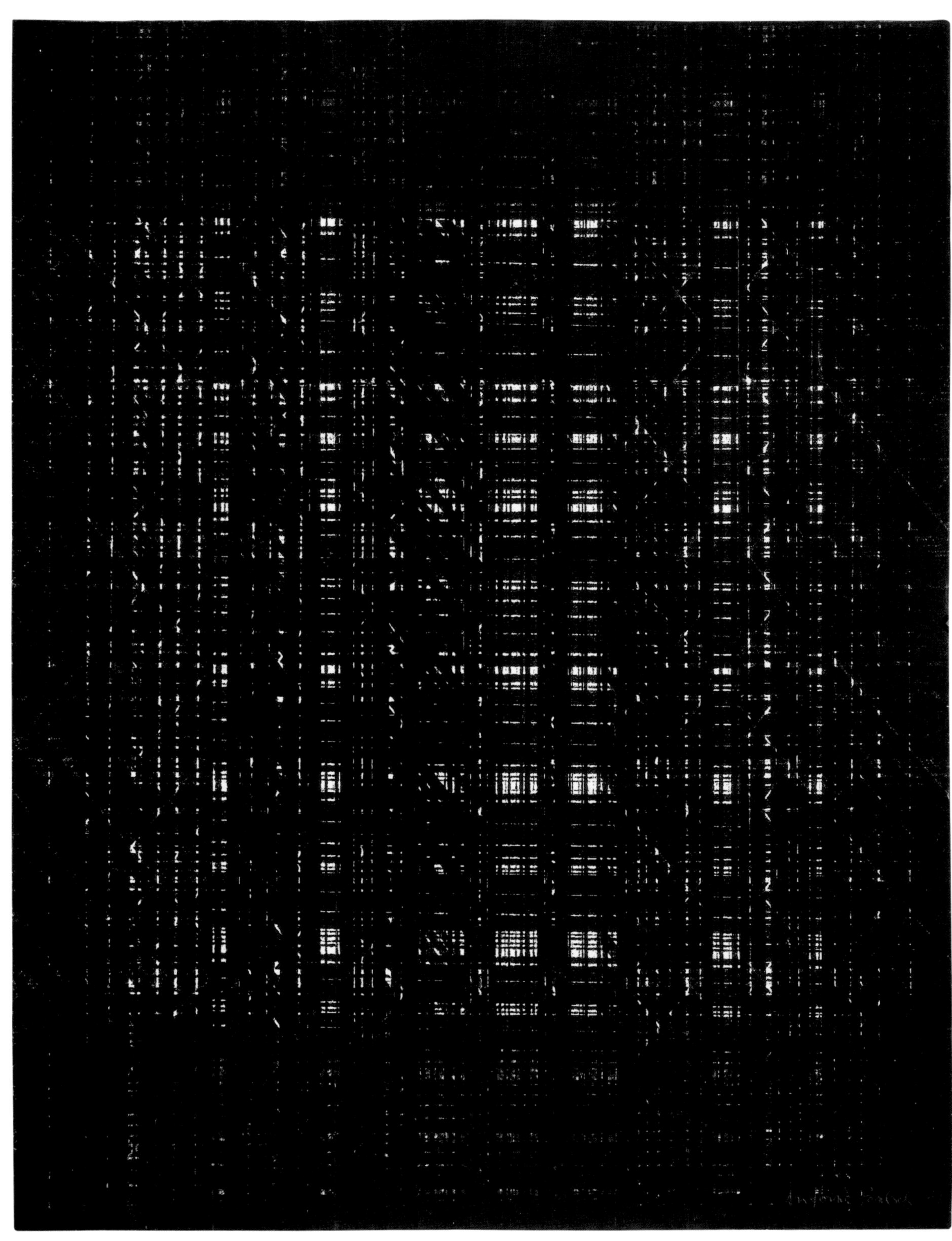

Antoine Pentsch, *Untitled*, 1989

Matti Kujasalo, *Painting*, 2011

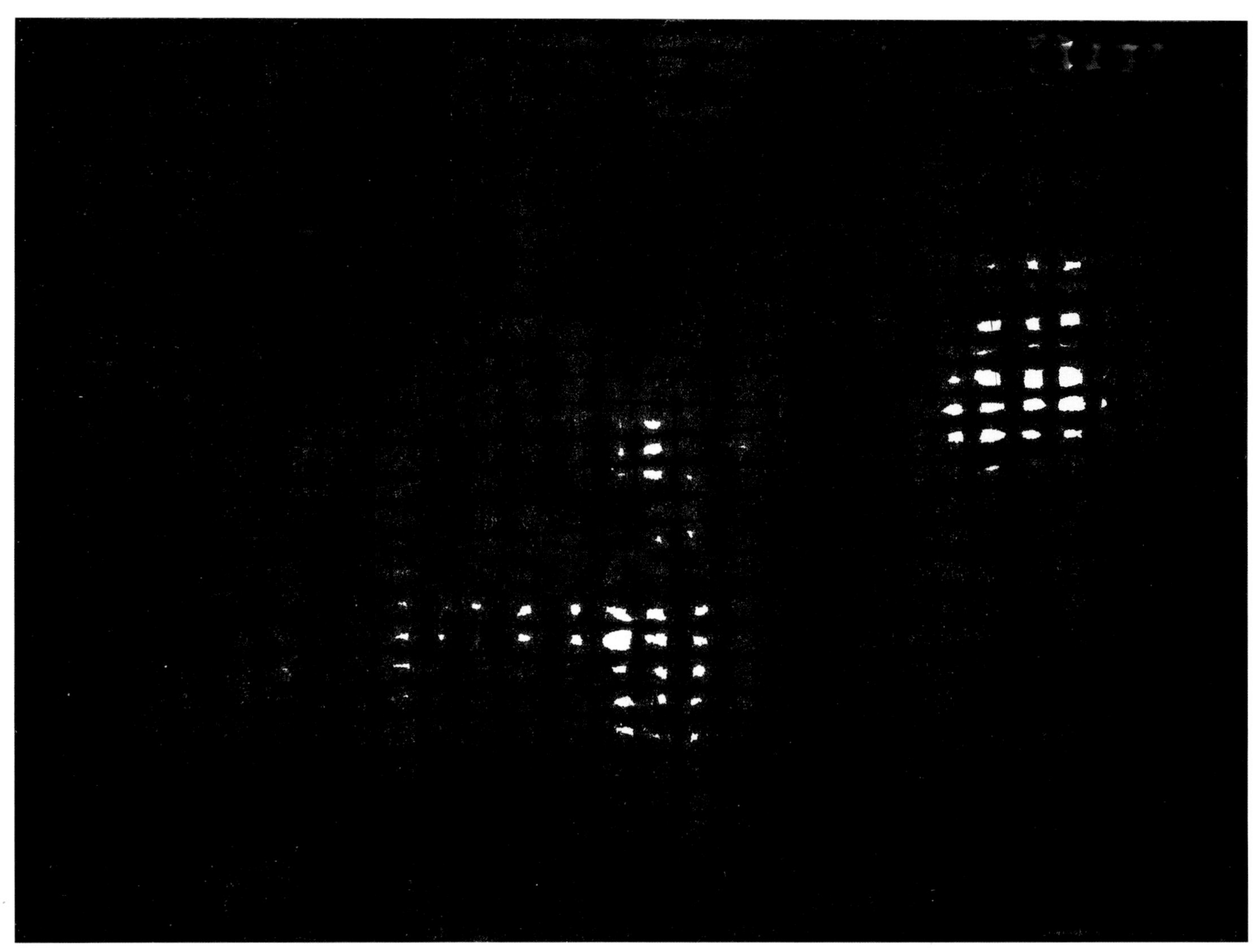

Li Huasheng, *Untitled*, 1998–2000

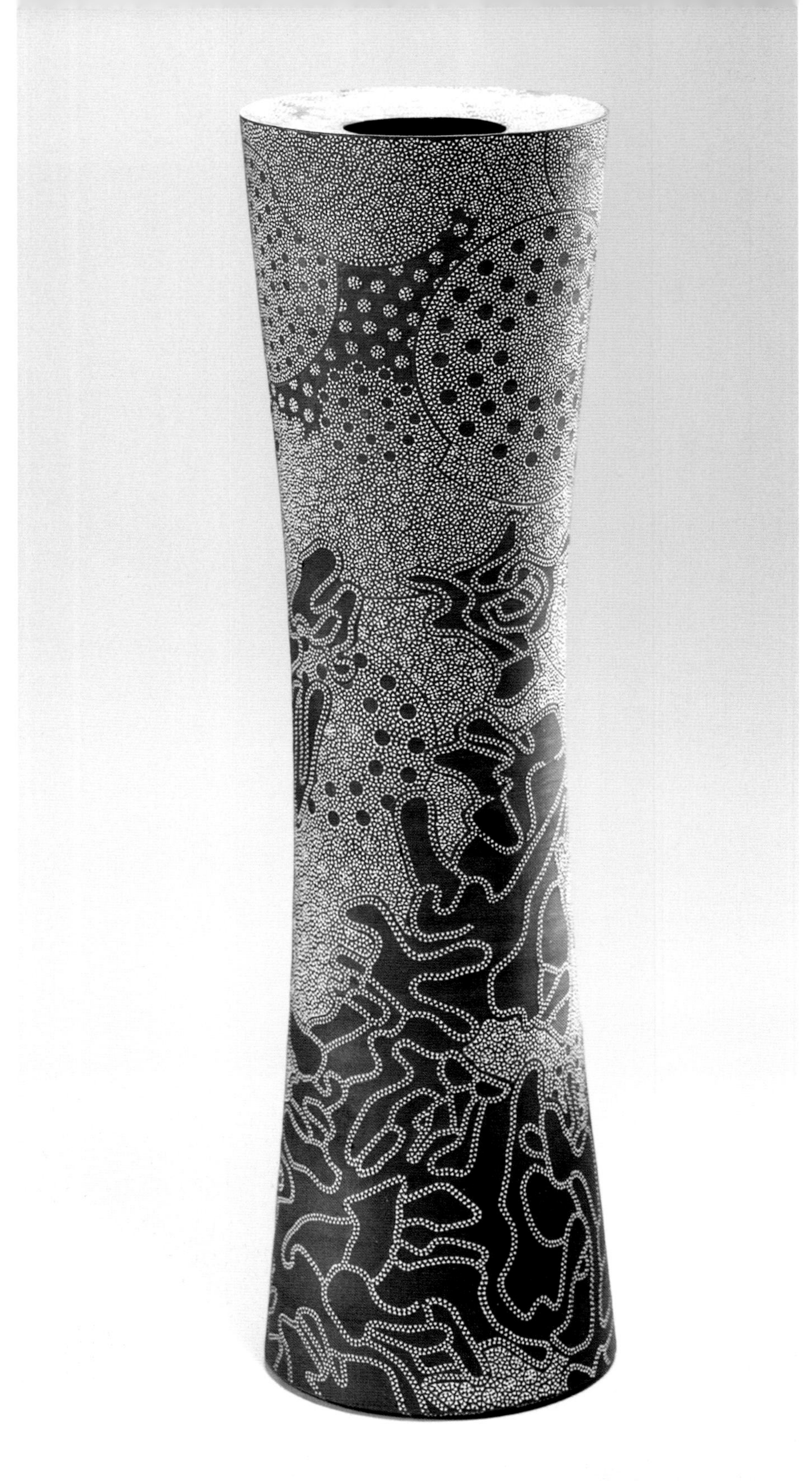

Kitamura Junko, *Vessel 08-C*, 2008

Kitamura Junko, *Vessel 08-G*, 2008

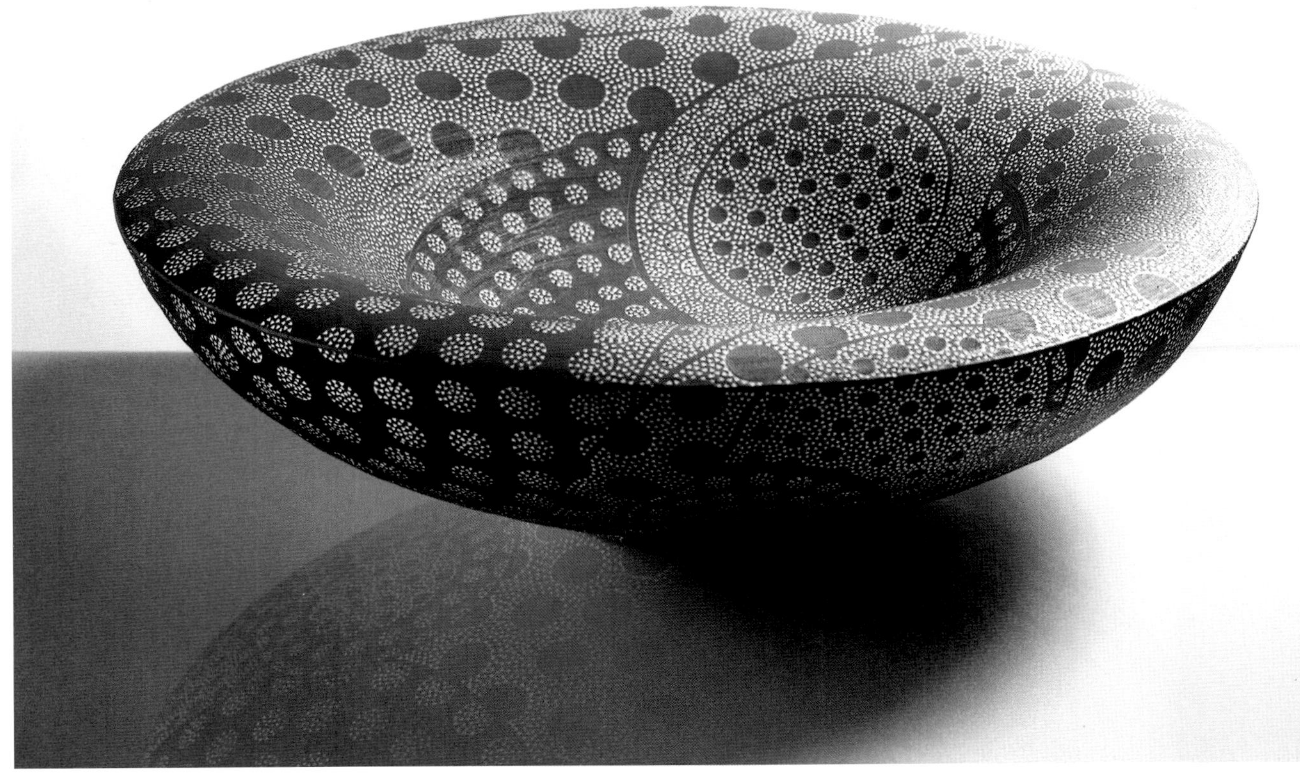

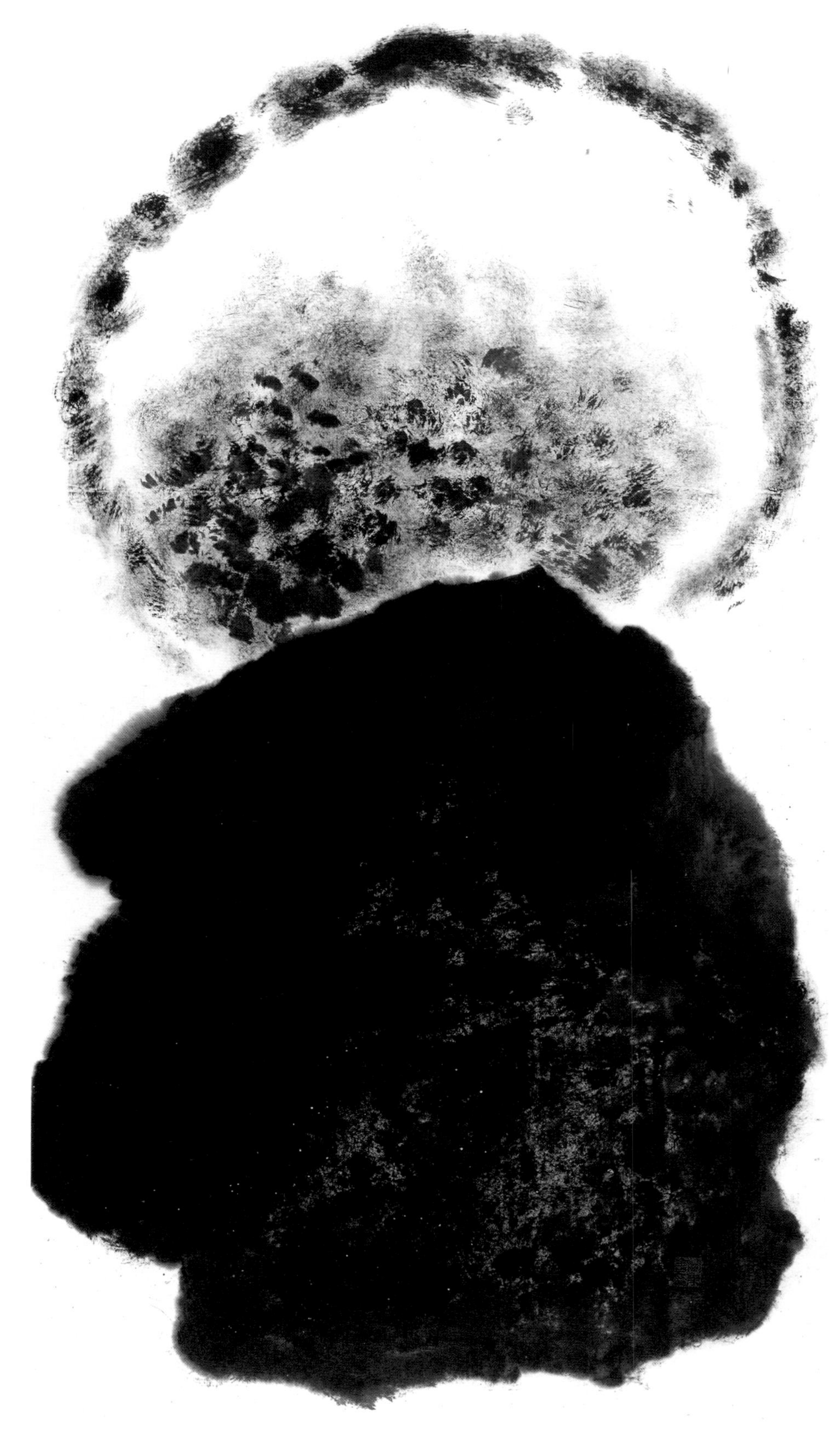

Yan Binghui, *Monument*, 1993

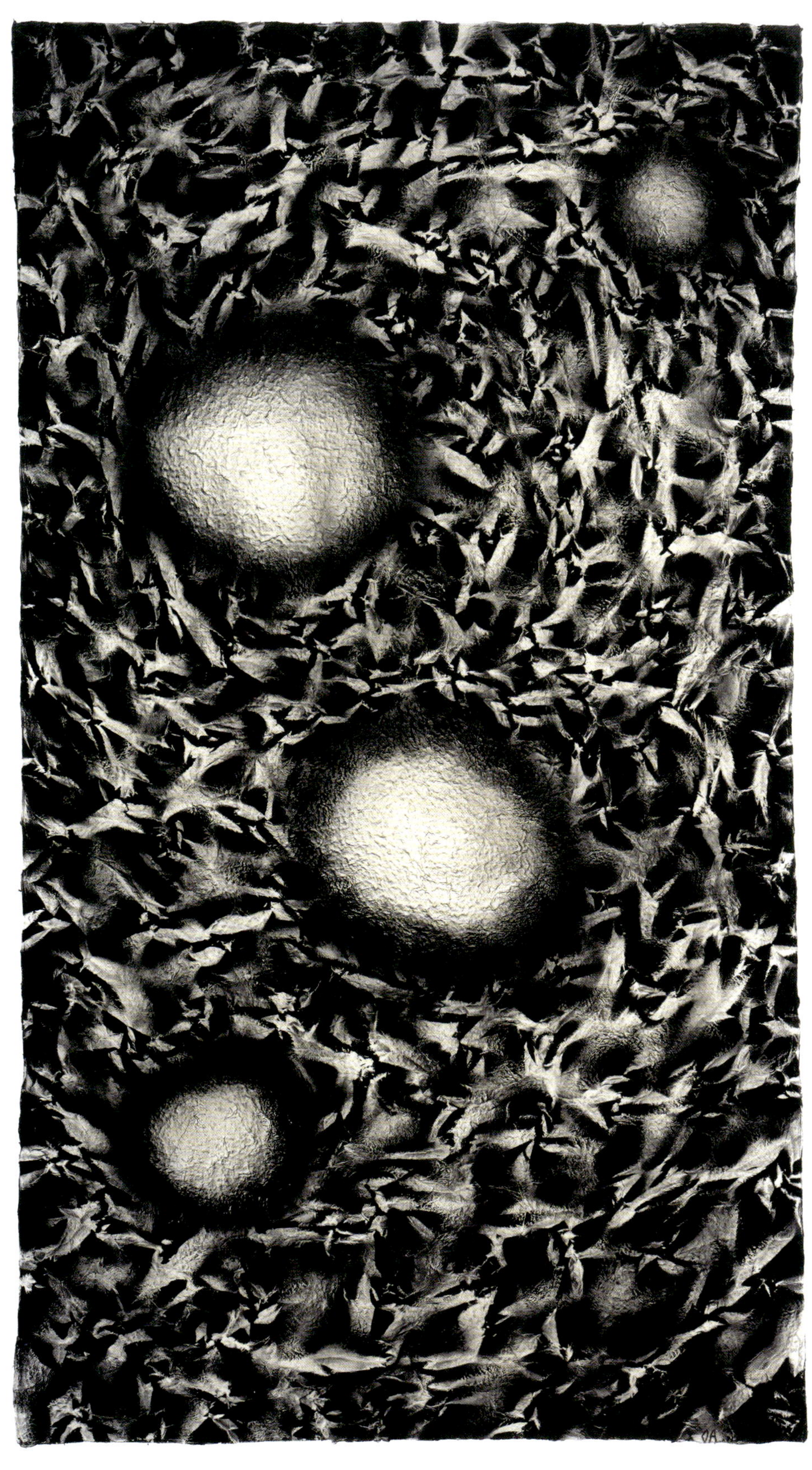

Ophélie Asch, *Battle at the Craters* (*Bataille aux cratères*), 2014

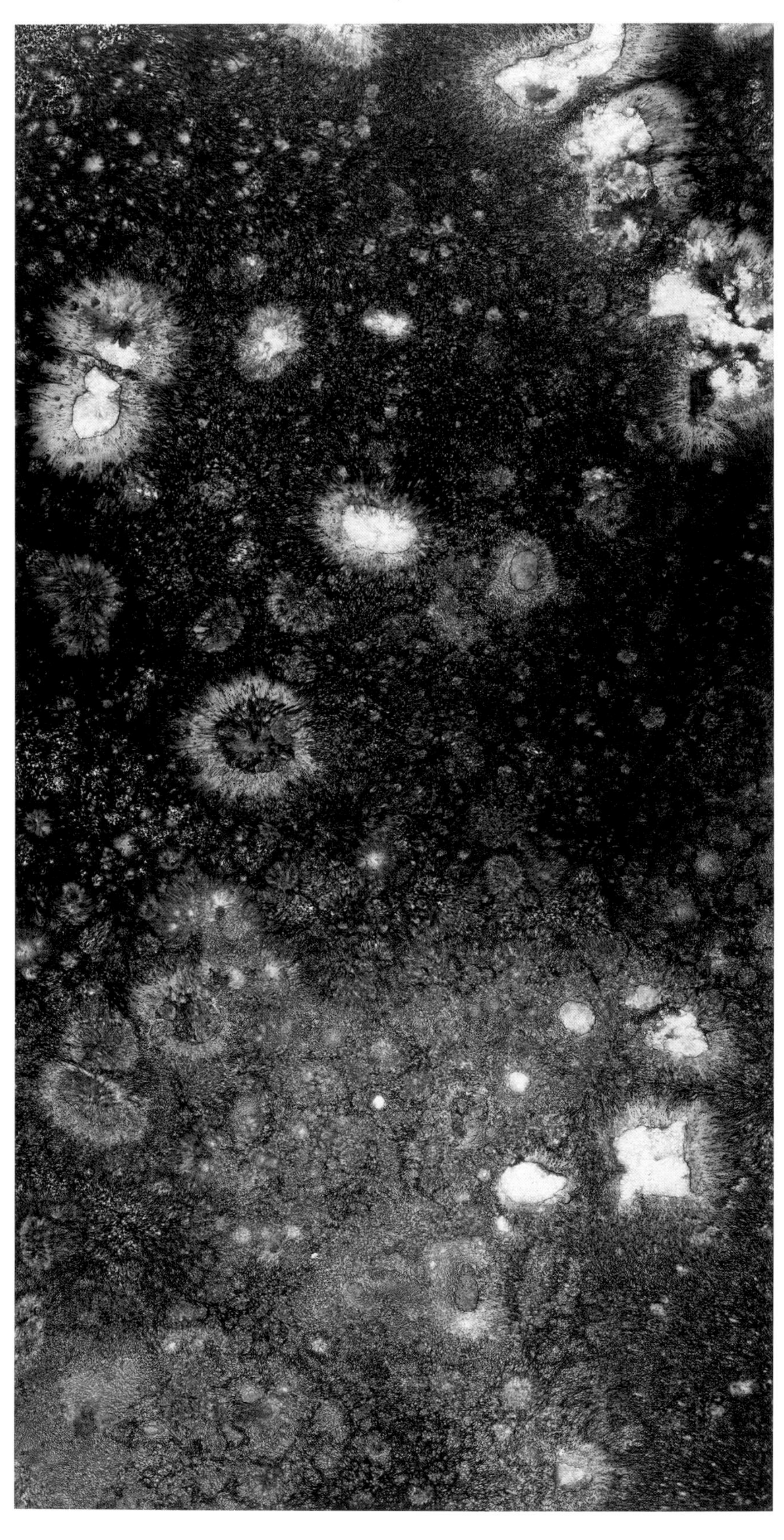

Bingyi, *Let Me Become the Universe's Plaything*, 2018

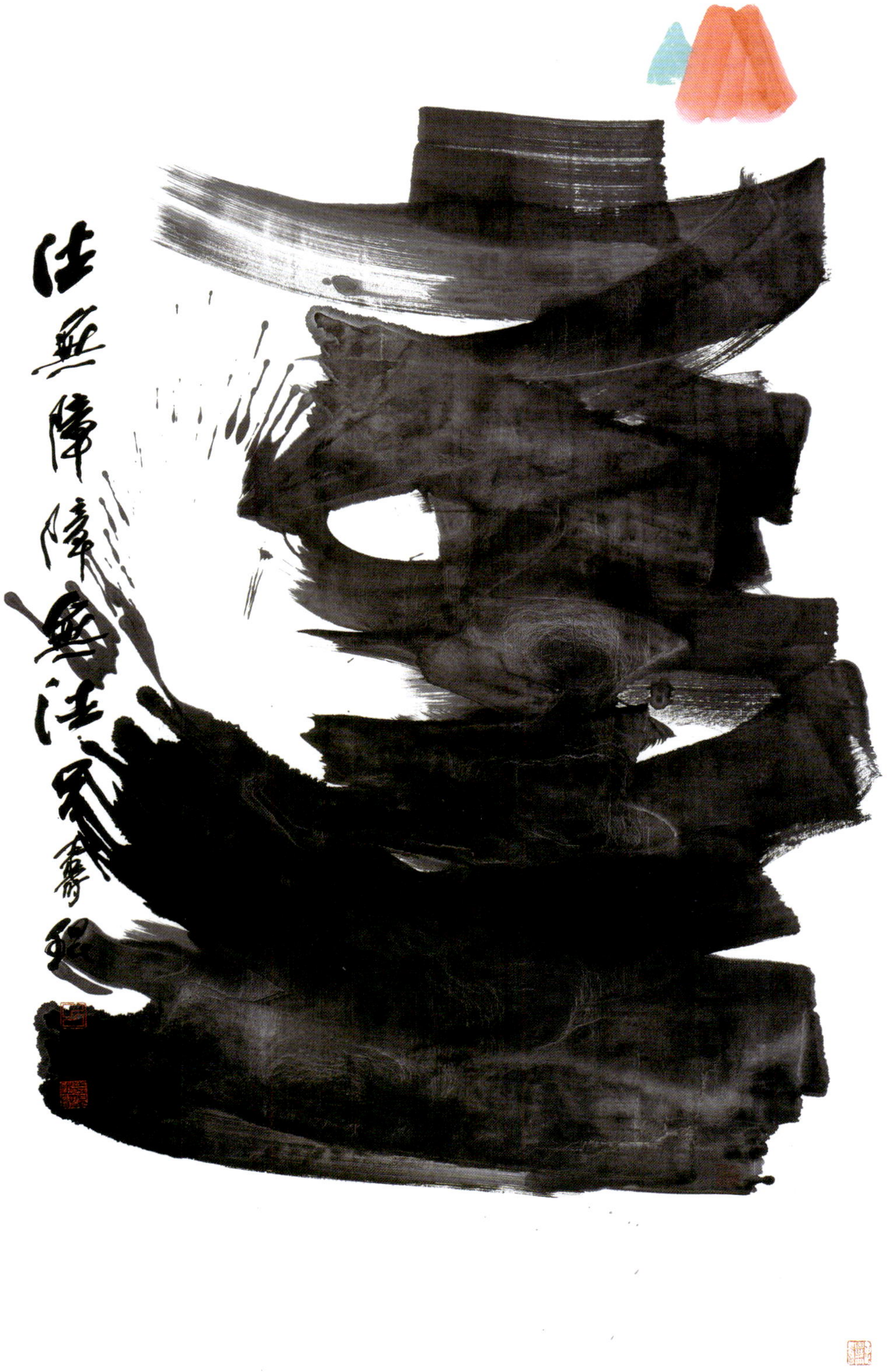

Lui Shou-kwan, *Zen Painting A69-14*, 1969

Max Cole, *Untitled*, 1999

Huang Zhiyang, *Possessing Numerous Peaks No. S-1226*, 2012

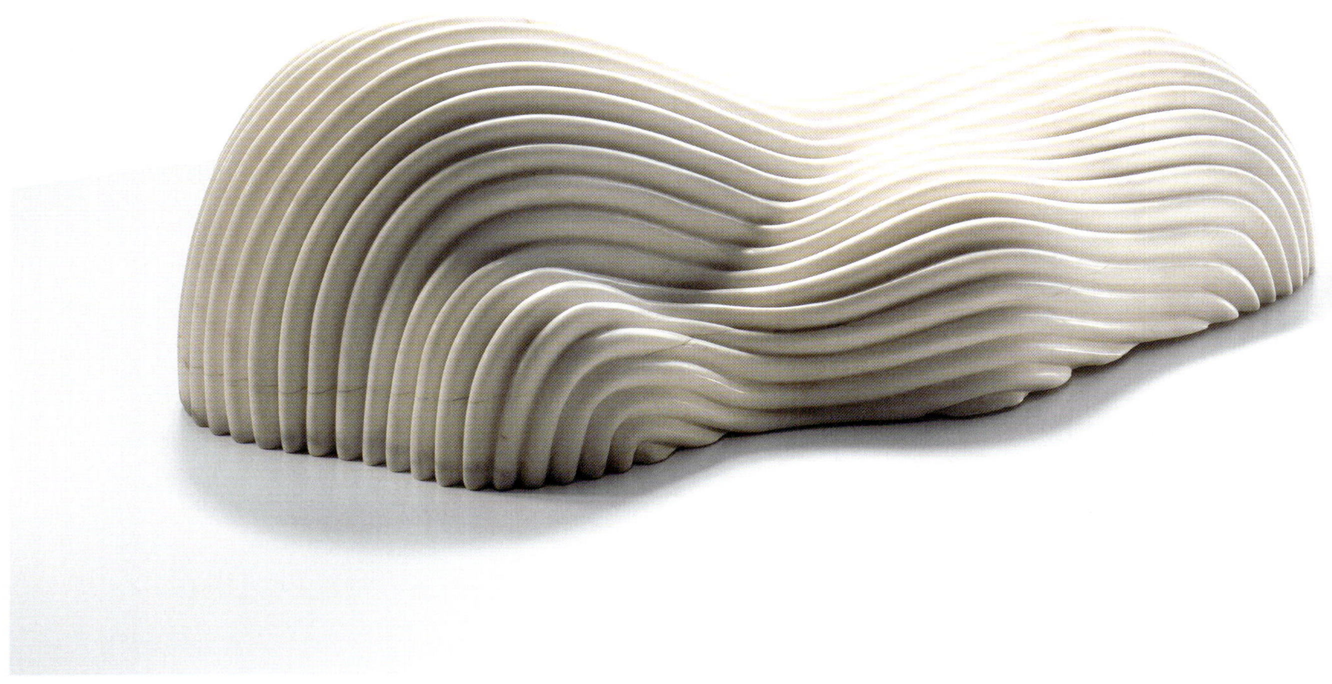

Irma Blank, *Radical Writings, Dal Libro Totale*, ca. 1984

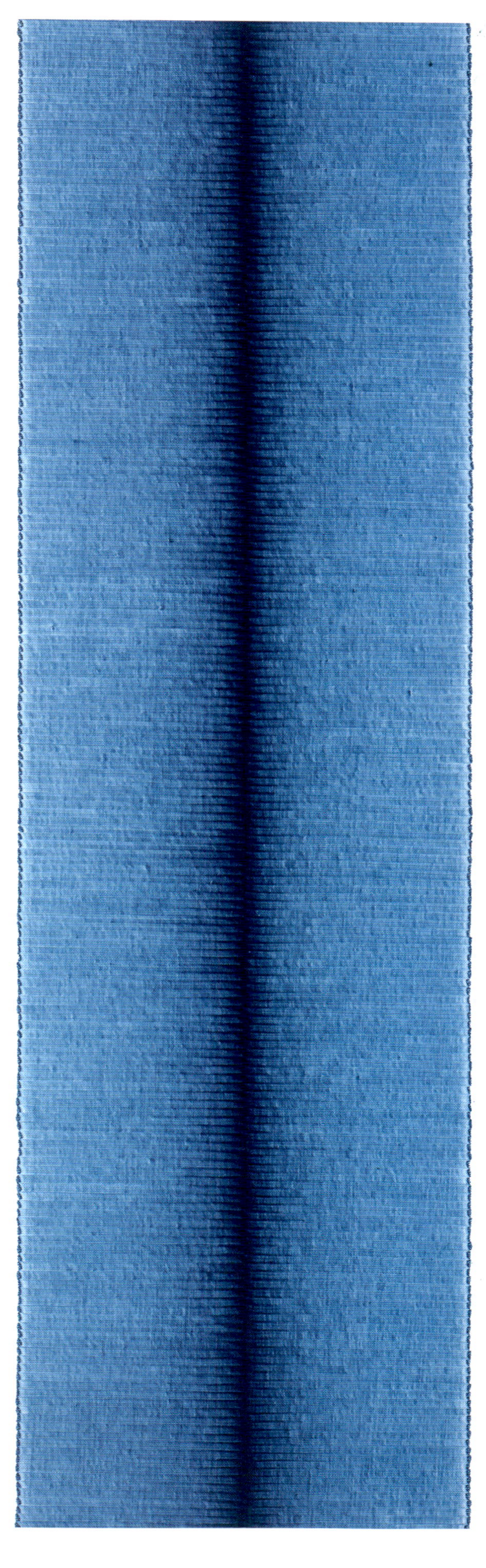

Irma Blank, *Radical Writings, Abecedarium 7-1-91*, 1991

Shirazeh Houshiary, *Torn*, 2009

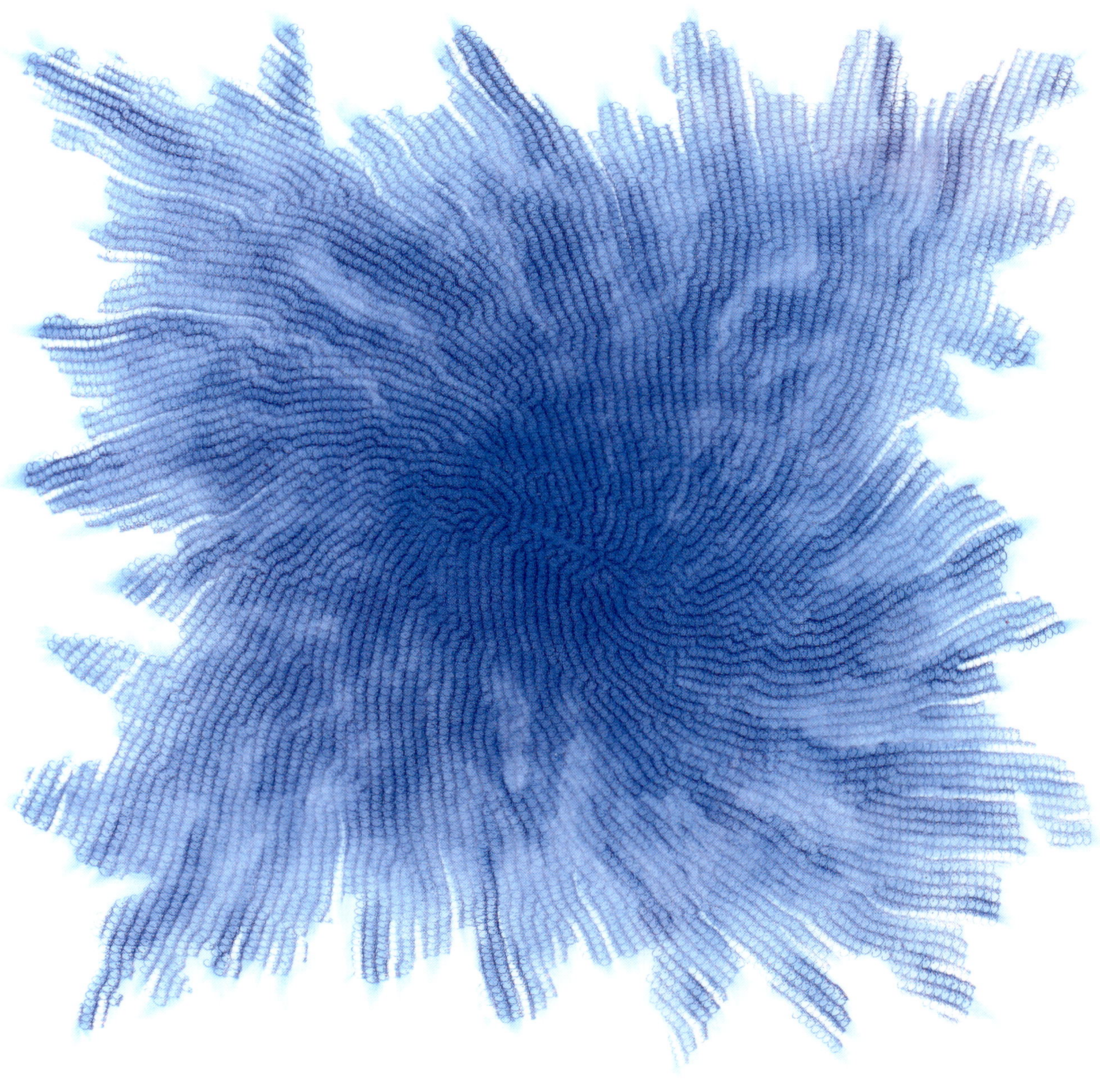

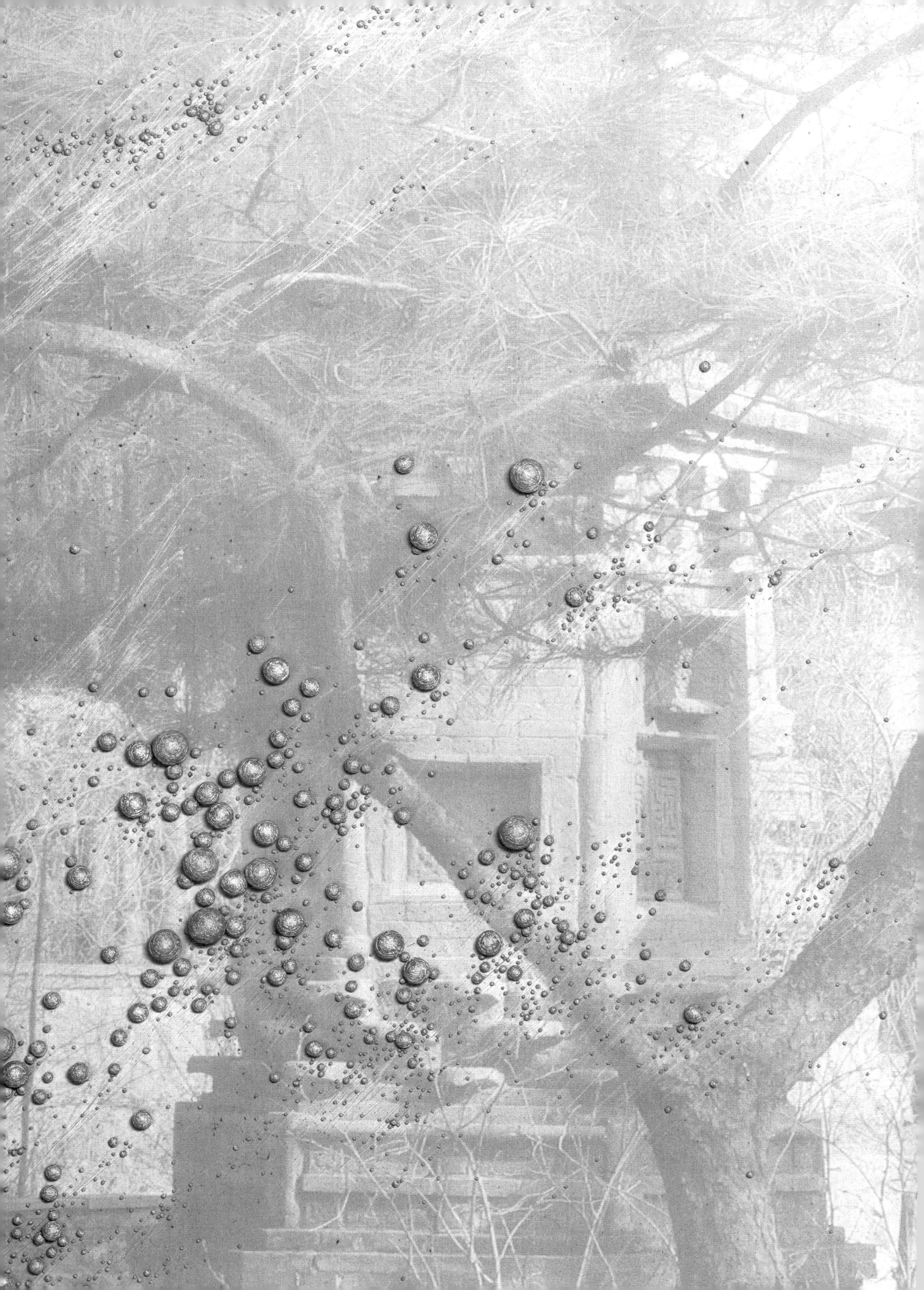

Apparitions

Presence through Absence

An apparition is, paradoxically, both present and notably absent. It is the trace of something past, no longer corporeal or even fully discernible. This section presents historical and contemporary works of ink art that use partial and total absence to aestheticize the state of both being and not being, through the layering of translucent washes, or, forgoing ink entirely, the depiction of a thick mist, a human figure, or an abstract light found in the white of the artist's blank ground.

Wanglianghua The first iteration of a designated "apparition painting" practice was *wanglianghua*,[9] which originated with the Chan monk Zhirong (1114–1193) during the Southern Song dynasty. Although none of Zhirong's work has survived, his painting style is known through descriptions by his contemporaries: astonishingly pale ink watered down to near-invisibility, his compositions existing in between a state of presence and absence, as if the intention were not to depict a figure or landscape, but to evoke the idea that one was missing. His simple brushwork gave only the roughest outline of a figure, floating amidst the nothingness of a blank background. Against the pale strokes of the figure, he detailed delicate facial features with a saturated, pitch-black ink. Following Zhirong, a small group of Southern Song painters created works in the *wanglianghua* style: namely, Liang Kai (ca. 1140–ca. 1220), Wuzhun Shifan (1178–1249), Zhiweng Ruojiang (mid-13th century), Hu Zhifu (13th century), Gong Kai (1222–1307), and others.

Although the artists featured in the Apparitions section of *Ink Dreams* were not necessarily directly inspired by the *wanglianghua* painters, their art shares characteristics with the movement, as well as a reinterpretation of what "apparition painting" could be. The muted quality that Zhirong achieved with his watered-down ink is apparent in, for example, Min Byung Hun's *Snow Land Sky Fog Gloom* (p. 102) and Lin Tianmiao's *Seeing Shadows No. 35* (p. 98)—in both cases, details are indistinct. However, these differ from the *wanglianghua* tradition in obvious ways: no sharply contrasting black ink accents, no quick, loose brushstrokes, and, in fact, no brush or ink at all—both works are photographic, *Seeing Shadows* incorporating the addition of Lin's signature white thread. These pieces take an important component of the *wanglianghua* tradition and extend it to the entirety of a work of art, evoking a blurred and uncertain vision, as it is difficult to fully discern their depicted scenes.

9 *Wanglianghua* is translated as "apparition painting." However, in order to differentiate between this specific trend and the greater concept of an apparition, I will be using *wanglianghua* to reference this specific historical practice, and "apparition" to denote a more general concept.

Min Byung Hun, *Snow Land Sky Fog Gloom*, 2005 (detail)

Phantom Mist Outside of the *wanglianghua* lineage, the motifs of mist and clouds, winding around the body of a mountain or across the surface of a lake, embody the phantasmic qualities of an apparition. They have their own significant history in Chinese ink art, often marking the break between the foreground and background of a landscape composition. These forms, as opaque as they appear, are not really *there*, however—they are depicted through an absence of ink, instead showing the solid white of the artist's paper or silk.

Although mist can be found in the works of some Chinese artists as early as the 10th century, notably those of Jing Hao (active ca. 855–930), Dong Yuan (ca. 934–962), and Juran (10th century), it was not until the 11th century, during the Northern Song dynasty, that mist or haze became a major element of landscape compositions in China, adopted by myriad artists. Guo Xi (fig. 7) and Fan Kuan (ca. 960–ca. 1030) each used an absence of ink to "paint" a cloudy separation of foreground and background, conjuring a hint of mystique in the process. The practice accelerated over succeeding generations. Li Gongnian (ca. early 12th century), Zhao Ji (Emperor Huizong, 1082–1135), Mi Fu (1051–1107), and Mi Youren (1074–1151) were all influential users of visitant mist, the latter two artists generating their own "Mi tradition" of painting. Apart from its utility in dividing spaces, mist lent a moody weight to the artist's compositions.

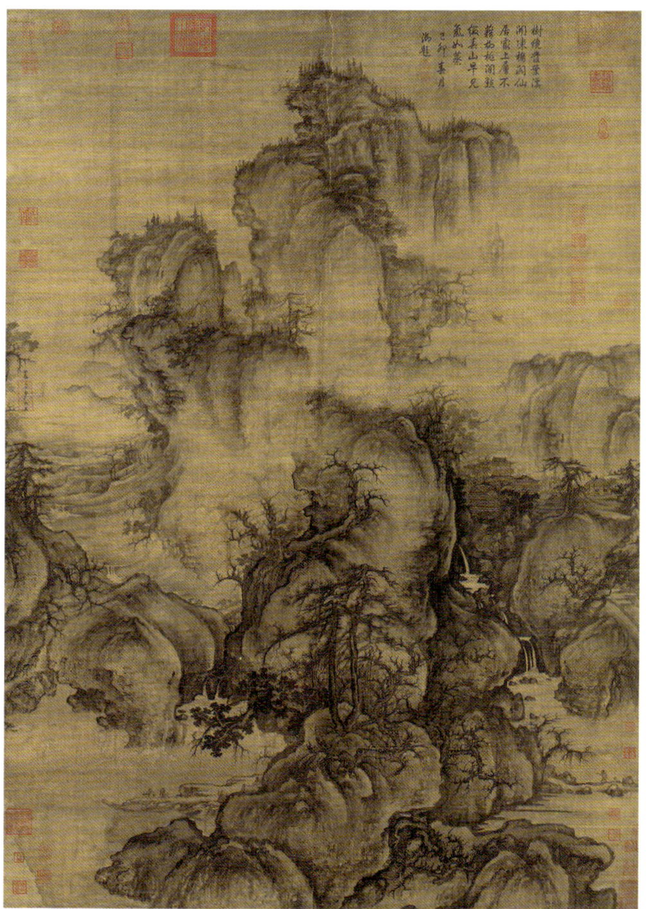

Fig. 7 Guo Xi (ca. 1020–ca. 1090), *Early Spring*, 1072. Hanging scroll: ink and color on silk, 62⅜ × 42½ in. (158.3 × 108.1 cm). The National Palace Museum, Taipei

Following these precedents, there was no period in Chinese ink art history completely devoid of the misty mountain landscape, but the subject reemerged in full force in the 17th century, continued by Mi tradition artists and others. Take, for example, Wang Hui's *Clearing after Rain over Streams and Mountains* (fig. 8). Although the influence of *wanglianghua* is likely incidental, the strokes that compose the piece are not overworked; the mountains in particular have a rough simplicity—the artist clearly did not aim for verisimilitude—and each fades into a midground of blank white paper. In painting these mountains, and more specifically, *not* painting the mist that obscures their bases, the apparition is created: the composition is orchestrated via the conspicuous absence of ink.

Like the aesthetics of *wanglianghua*, this trend has also transitioned smoothly into the contemporary art world. Absence is a defining factor in the tones and compositions of Hiroshi Sugimoto (pp. 115–17), in Liu Guosong's *Jiuzhaigou Series #48* (p. 109), Zhang Yu's *Divine Light Series No. 7: Floating Incomplete Circle* (p. 119), and Wu Chi-Tsung's *Still Life 012-Buttercup Tree* (p. 121), among other works in this and other sections of *Ink Dreams* (for example, while Park Seo-Bo's work is meditative at its very core, it is the *absence* of furrows that opens space for the viewer's own meditation [p. 65]).

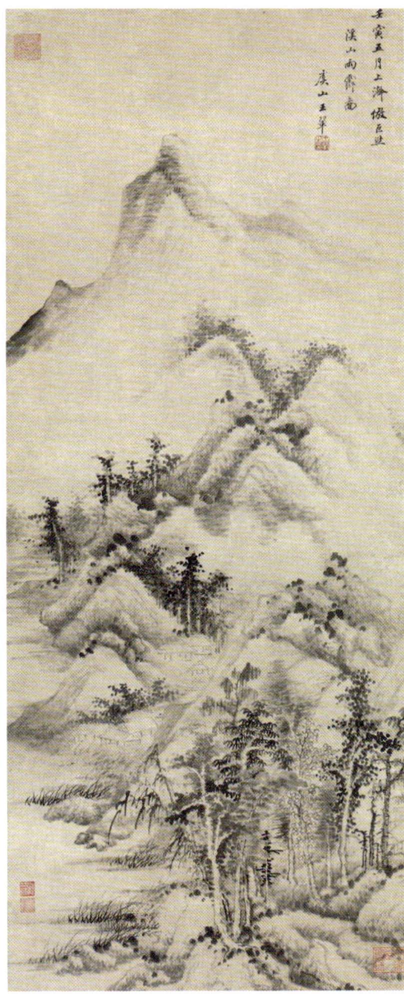

Fig. 8 Wang Hui (1632–1717), *Clearing after Rain over Streams and Mountains*, 1662. Hanging scroll: ink on paper, 44⅞ × 17⅞ in. (114 × 45.4 cm). The Metropolitan Museum of Art, New York, Bequest of John M. Crawford Jr., 1988

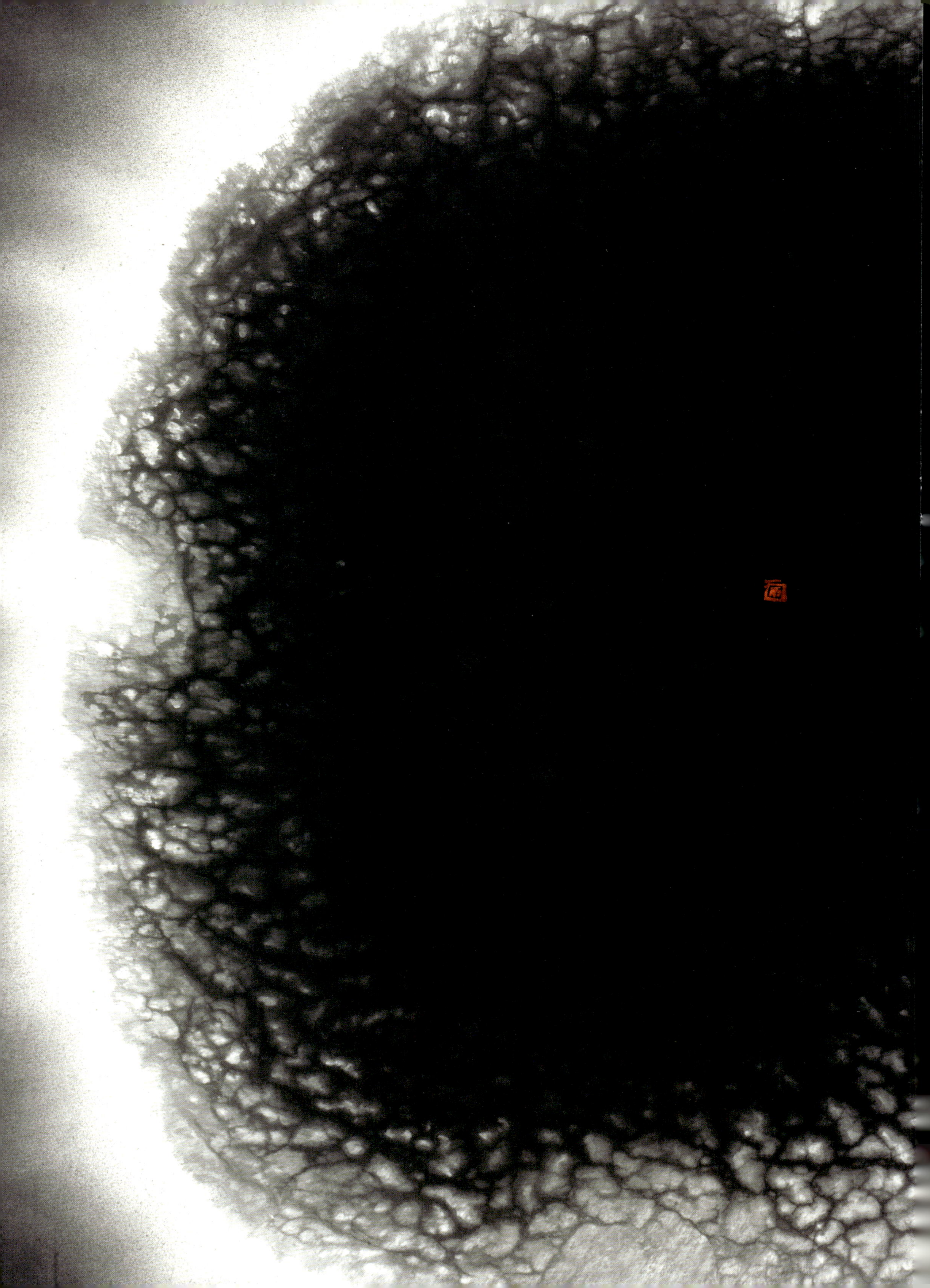

Layering A layer—something translucent; again, not quite present—can also be construed as an apparition. Layering has long been a critical component of ink painting. The styles of meticulous *gongbi* painting and loose ink-and-wash both rely upon the layering of ink. One method often used by contemporary and historical ink artists alike is to begin by painting vast washes of ink, then apply darker details (similar to the technique of *wanglianghua* artists but without the stark contrasts). Another example is the *gongbi* coloring technique of *sanfanjiuran* (literally, three layers of alum, nine layers of dye), by which the artist layers color upon color with the end result of a deep, complex shade; by inserting water-resistant alum between layers of pigment, their vibrancy is fully preserved, and the colors are not muddied as they would be if they were layered while wet.

Repeated layering is instrumental in the creation of works like Yang Jiechang's *Fingerprint: Right Ring Finger* (p. 97), Rhee Kibong's *Wet Psyche—No Wind* (p. 110), and Zheng Chongbin's *Dissolved Geometry* series (p. 95). Yang's layer upon layer of ink builds to an infinitely black work, textured with a top layer of glue to create a shining imprint of a finger. Rhee lays a thin fabric over his base painting, then further obscures the original image with a layer of Plexiglas and additional paint. Zheng applies ink and acrylic to both the front and back of xuan paper; the acrylic creates areas resistant to the watery ink, manifesting natural fractals through the combination of hydrophilic and hydrophobic paints.

Photographic works in this section embrace the use of layering in a way that was impossible throughout most of ink art history. Much of Idris Khan's art (p. 105) incorporates the digital layering of multiple images of a single scene, creating a composite image that shows glimpses of many moments but the entirety of none. Wang Gongxin's spectral *Sun Set* series (p. 111) is equally layered, white or gray streaks indicating the captured motion of the artist's subject. In Dai Guangyu's *Landscape, Ink, Ice* (pp. 106, 107), the effect of an apparition does not derive from the layering or blurring of images, the absence of ink, or the use of light values. Rather, this long-form performance-photograph shows the traces of what once existed. On the left, the viewer is presented with an image of the Chinese characters *shanshui* (landscape), painted in ink on a frozen lake. On the right, the characters have begun to disintegrate, indicating the passage of time and the natural changing of the landscape.

Although these various trends and styles in ink art history have not previously been recognized as related, they all depend upon the underlying principle of communicating presence through absence. By extrapolating these qualities of hazy landscapes, faint figures, and layered ink, and cohering them into a single soft quality, "apparitions," a continuum from historical painting to contemporary ink art becomes evident.

Zhang Yu, *Divine Light Series No. 7: Floating Incomplete Circle*, 1994 (detail)

Plates
Apparitions

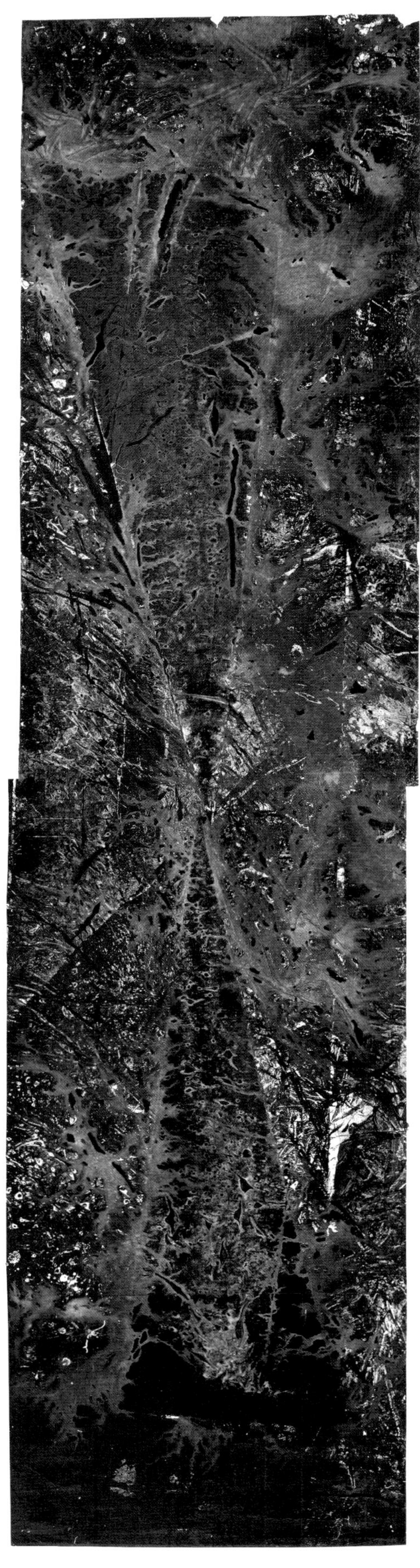

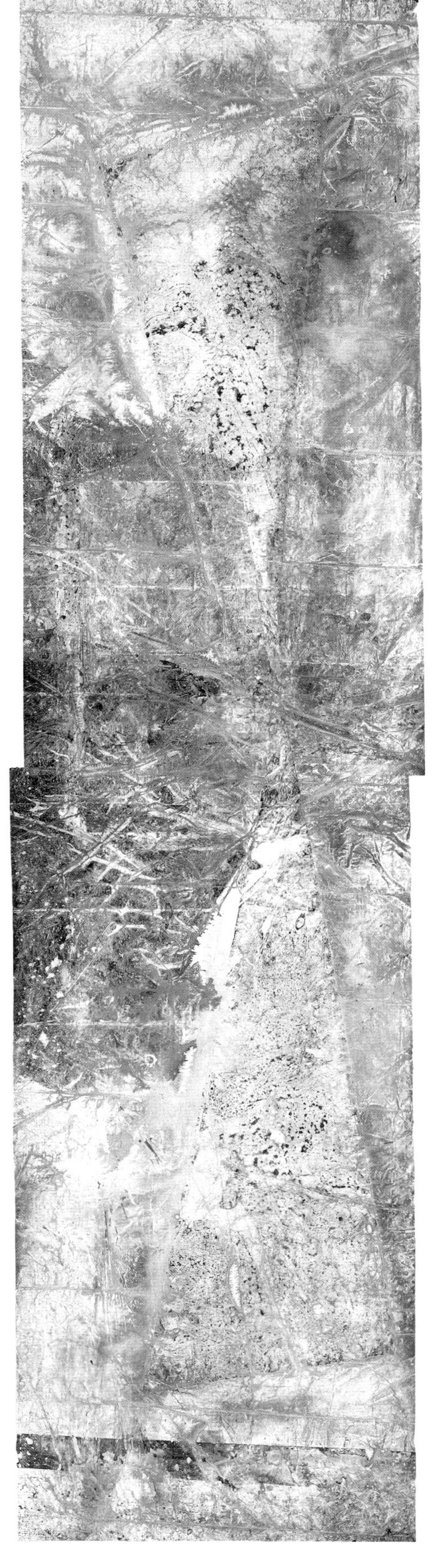

Zheng Chongbin, *Dissolved Geometry B*, 2012
Zheng Chongbin, *Dissolved Geometry C*, 2012

Yang Jiechang, *Fingerprint: Right Ring Finger*, 1992–94

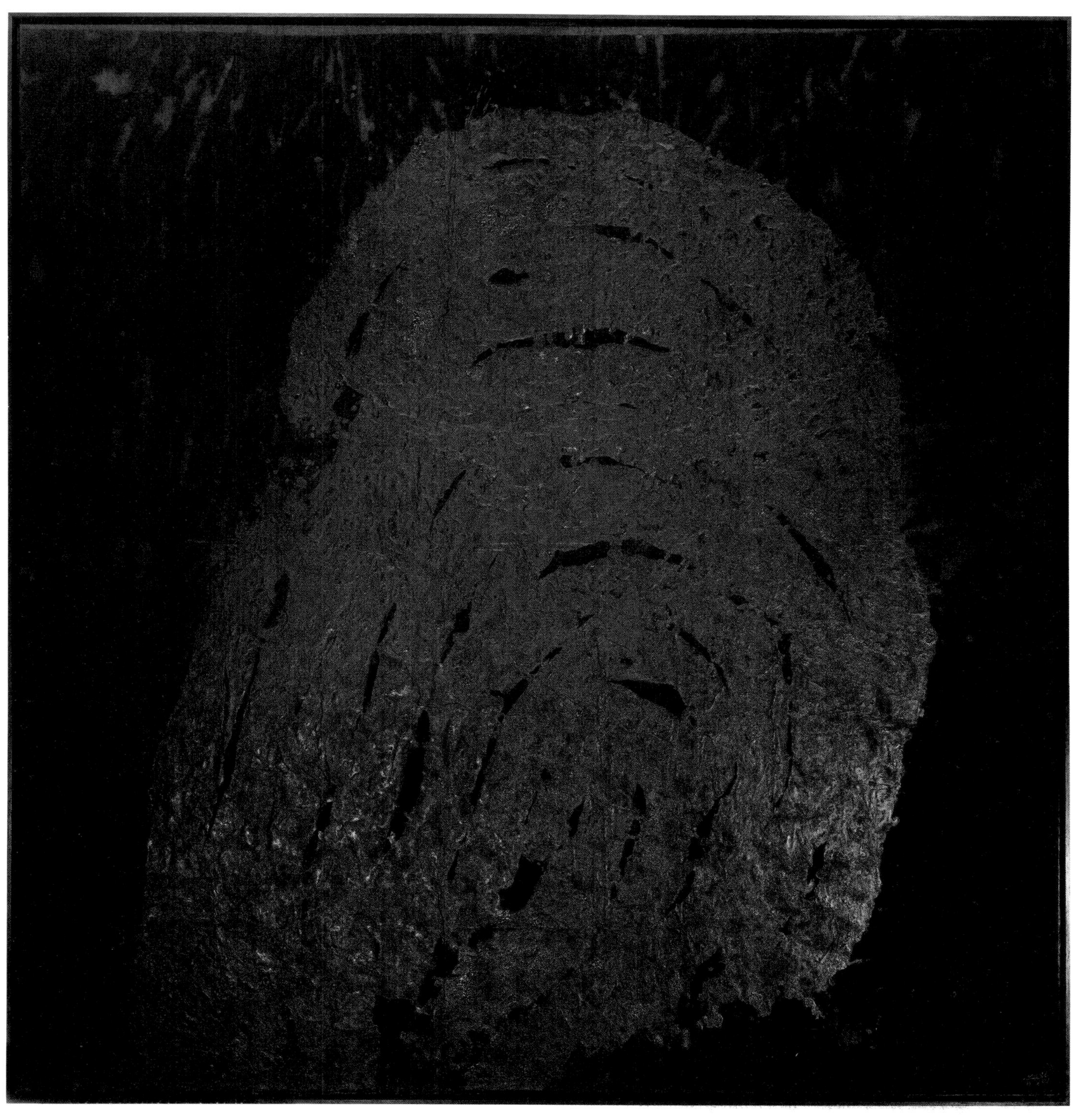

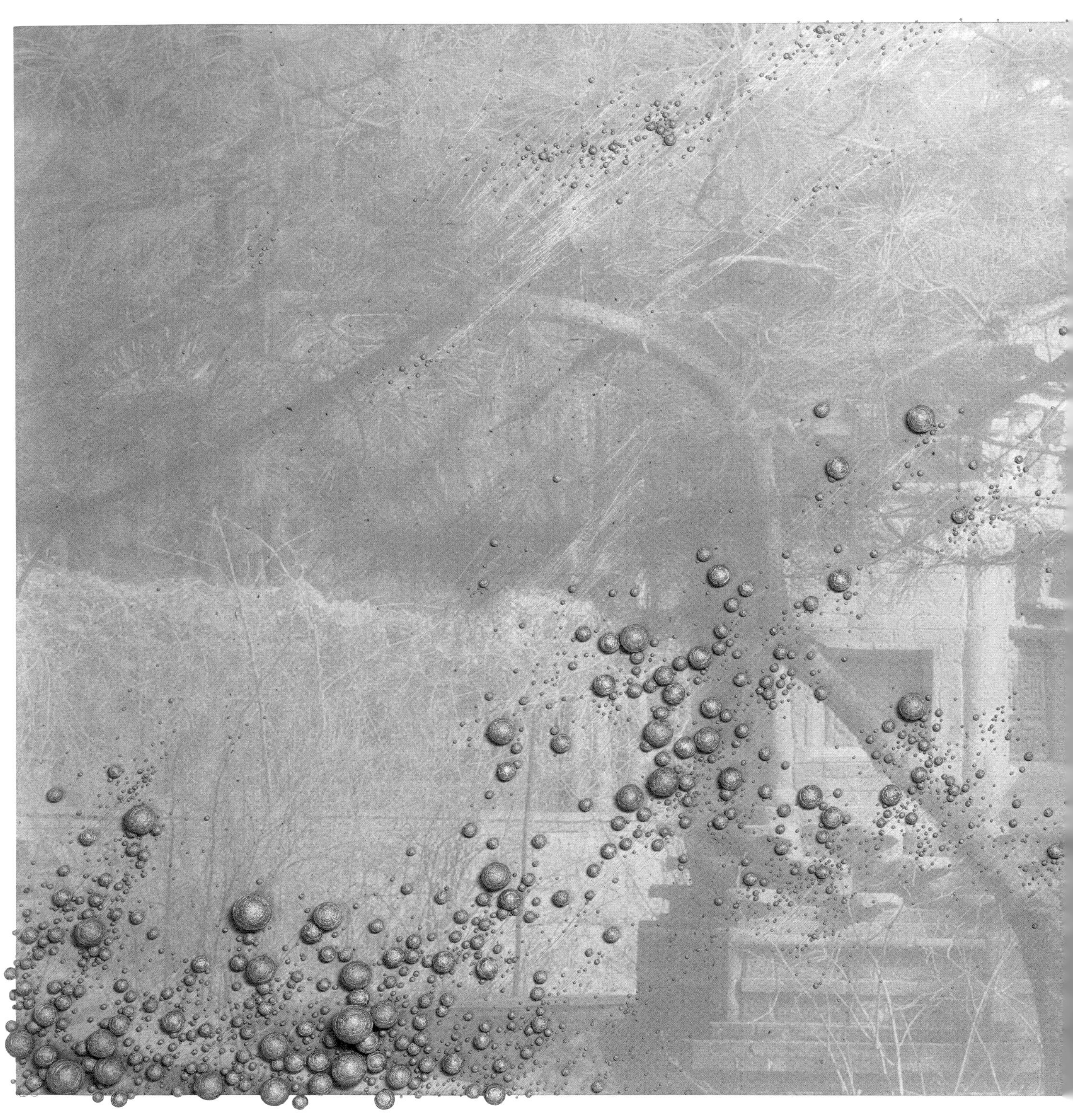

Lin Tianmiao, *Seeing Shadows No. 35*, 2007

Seeing Shadow No.35

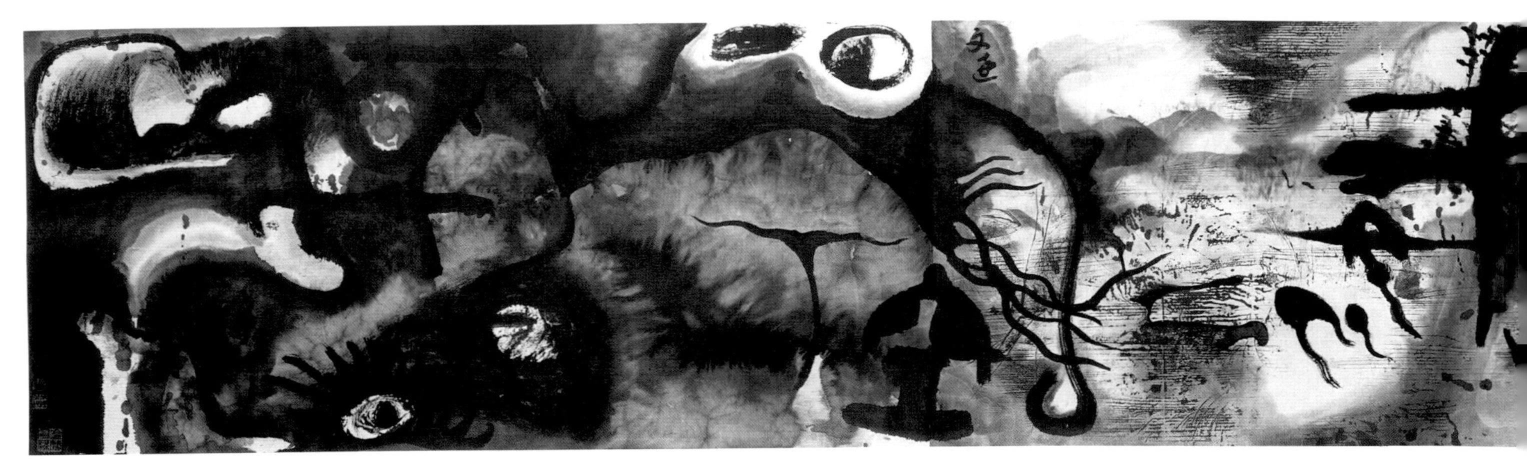

gu wenda, *surrealist landscape #3*, 1982

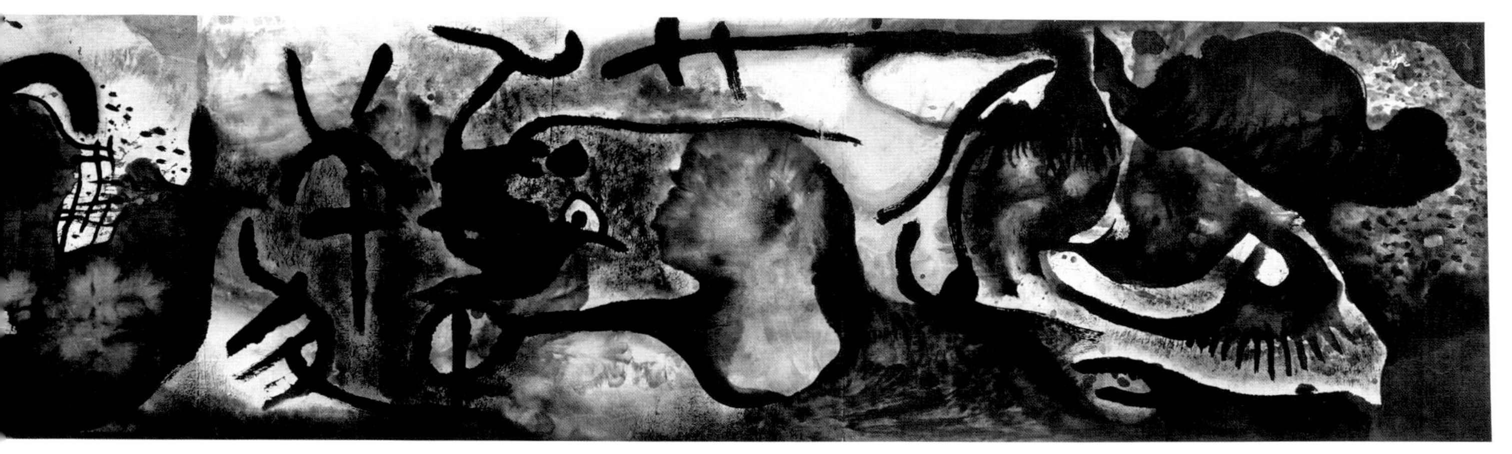

Min Byung Hun, *Snow Land Sky Fog Gloom*, 2005

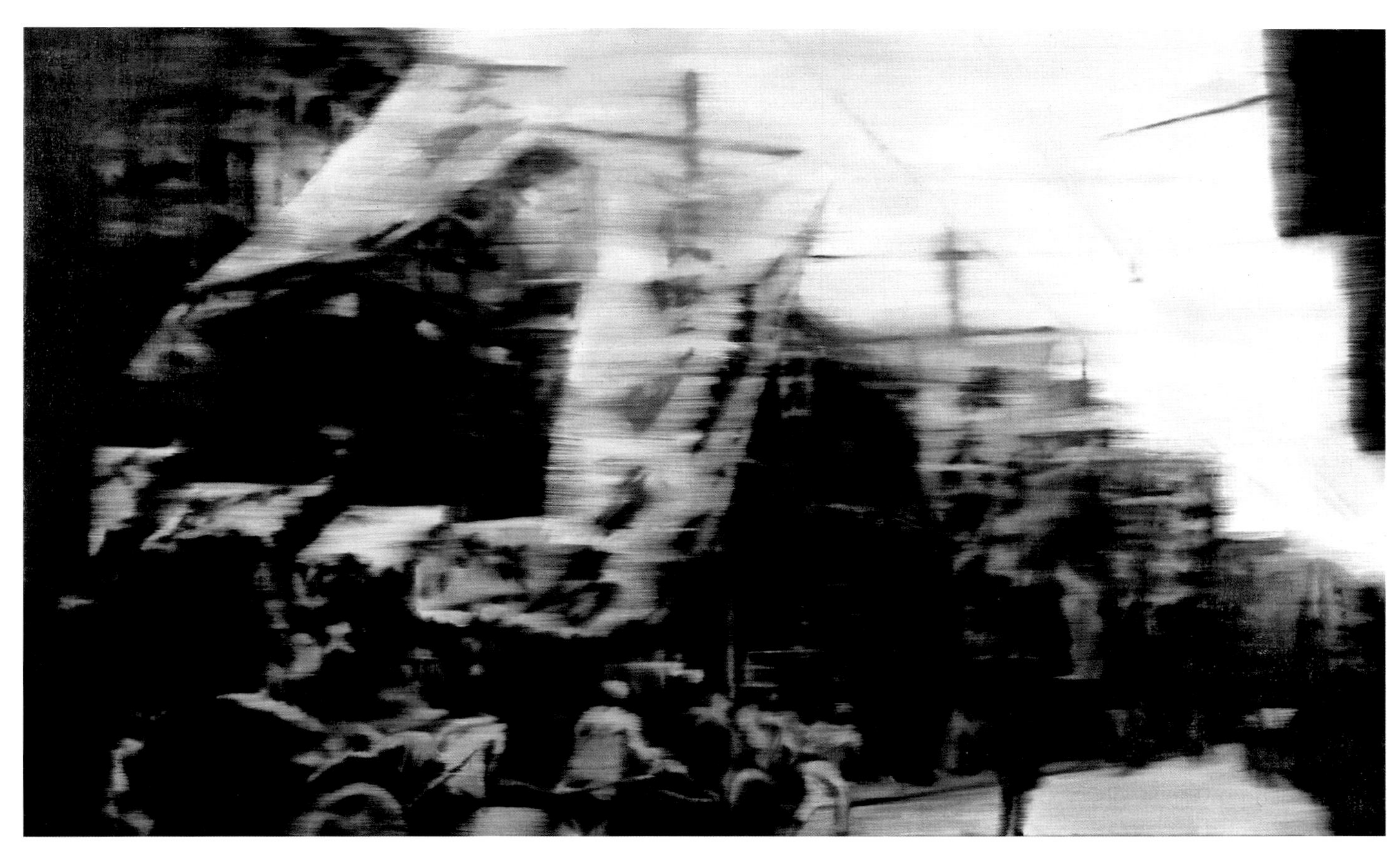

Chen Bolan, *A Street View of Shanghai*, 2007

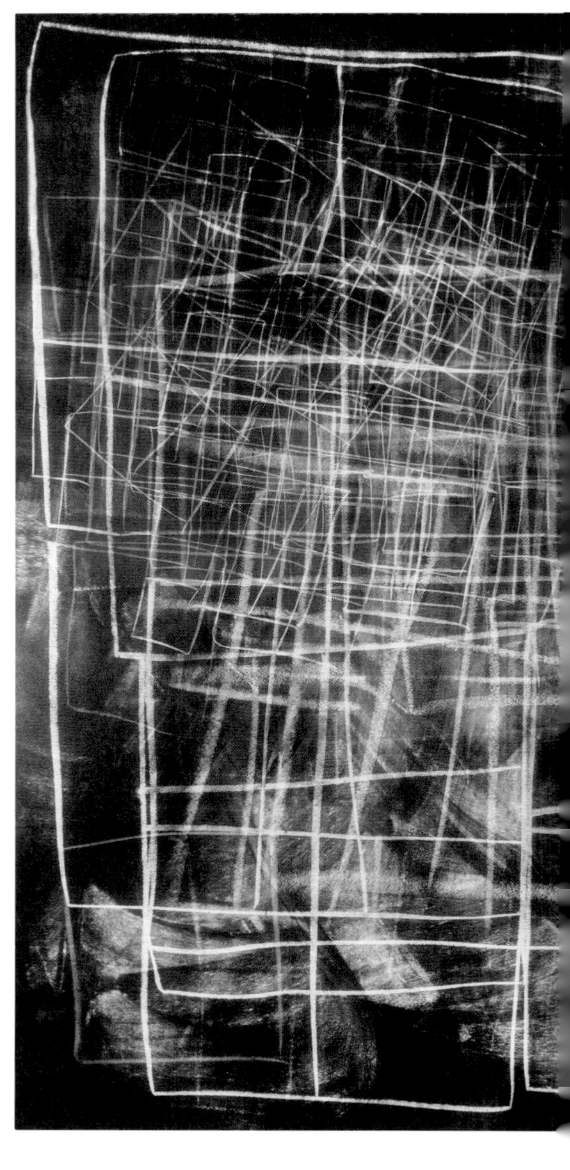

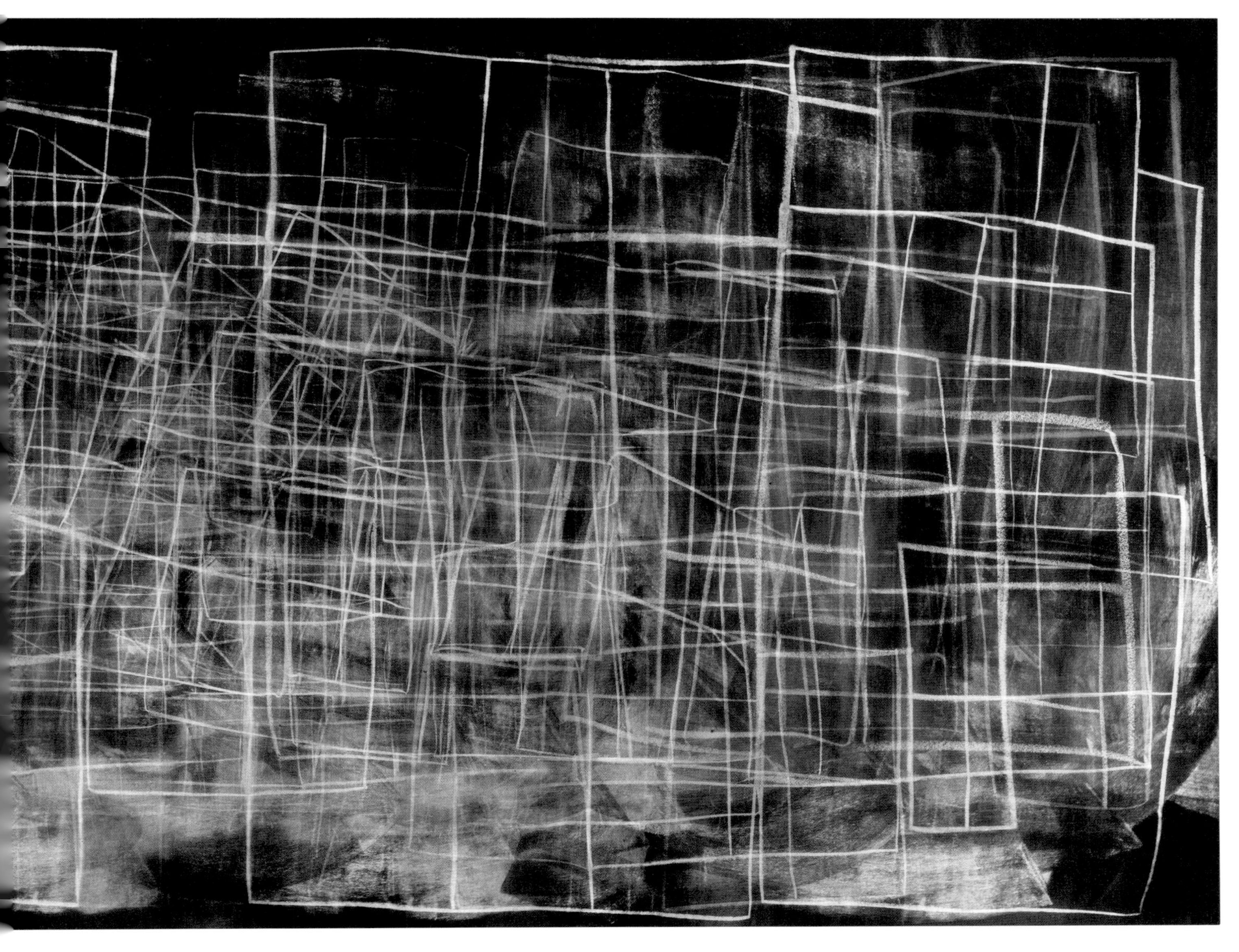

Idris Khan, *Untitled*, 2013

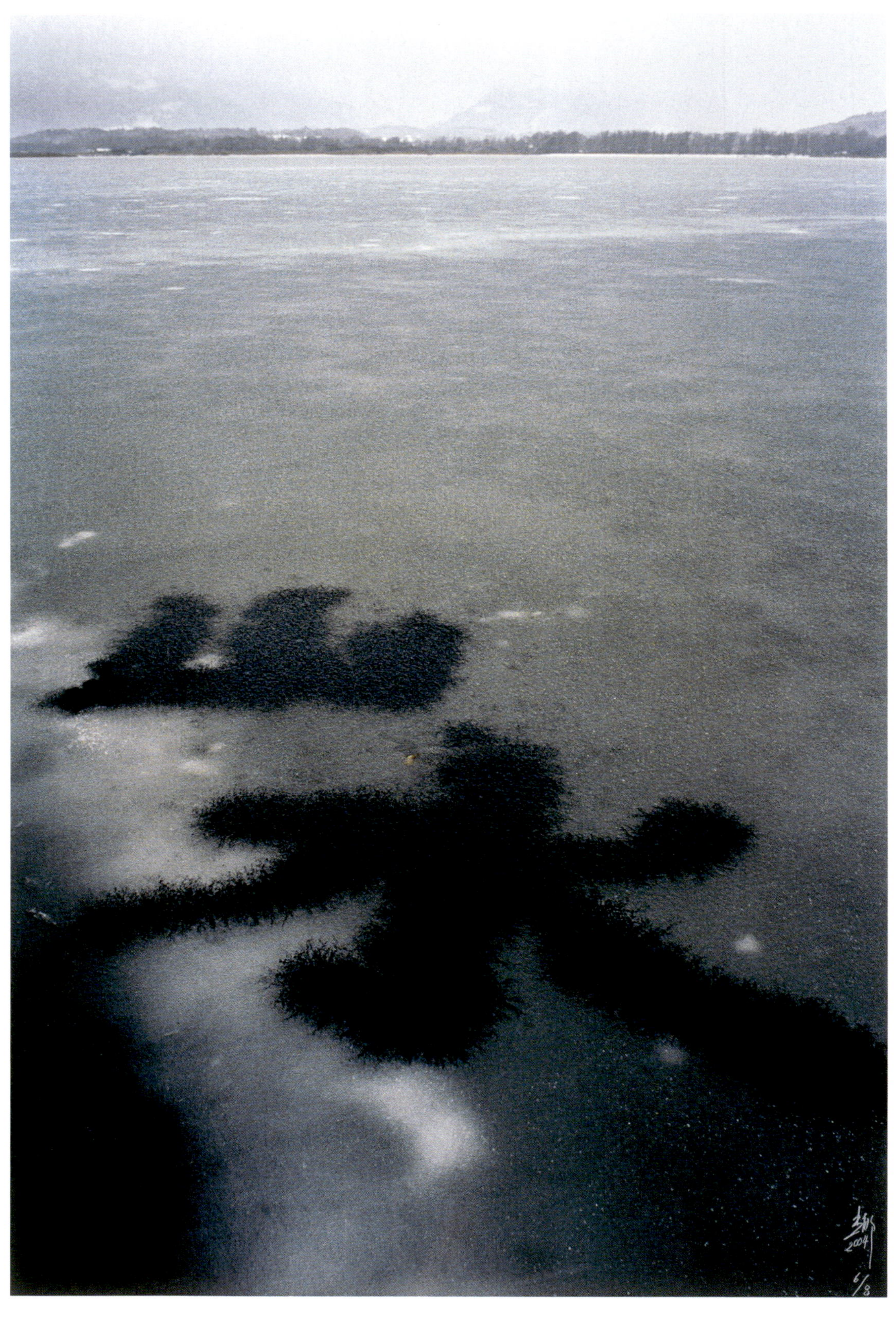

Dai Guangyu, *Landscape, Ink, Ice*, 2004

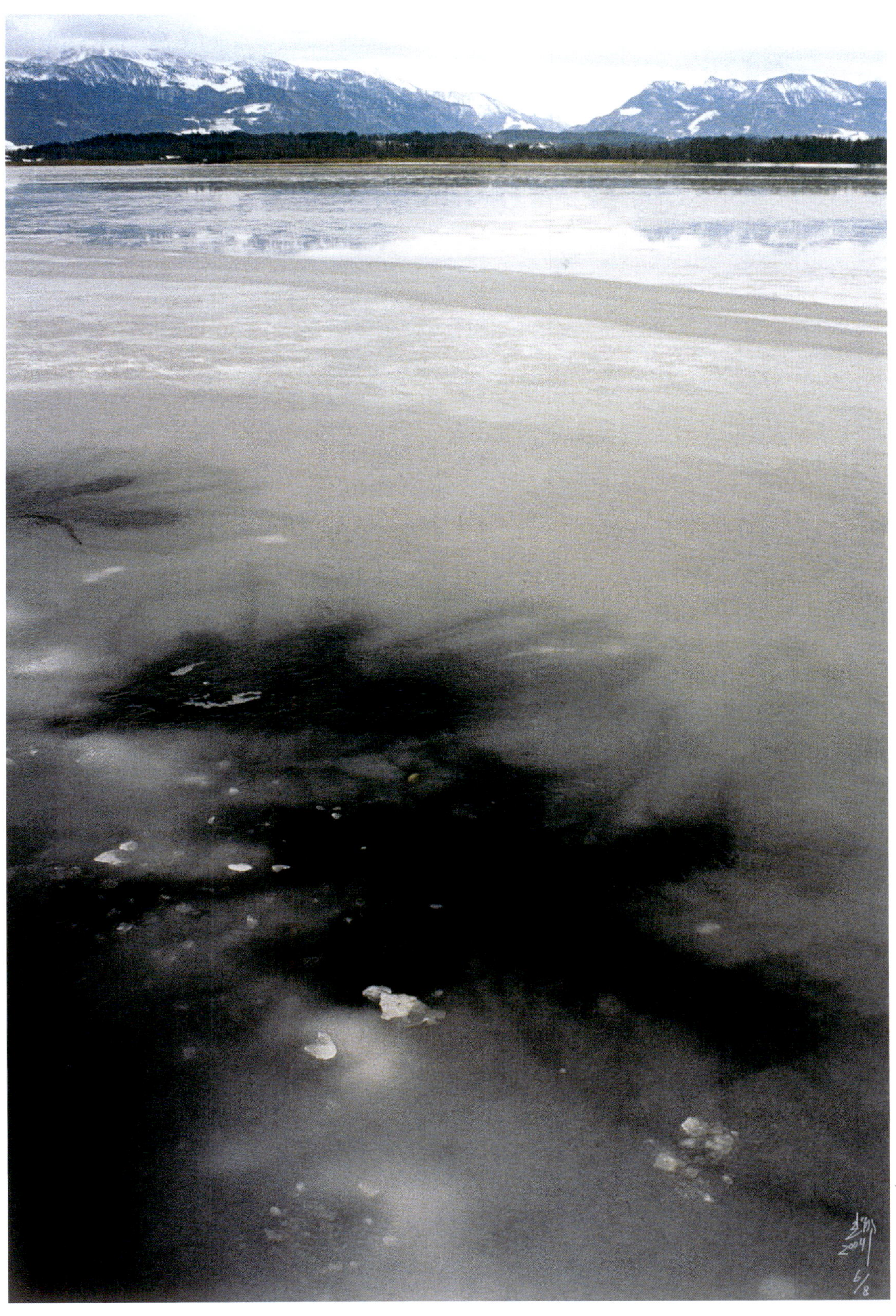

Liu Guosong, *Jiuzhaigou Series #48: Sea of Floating Ice*, 2004

Rhee Kibong, *Wet Psyche–No Wind*, 2010

Wang Gongxin, *Sun Set 5*, 2004

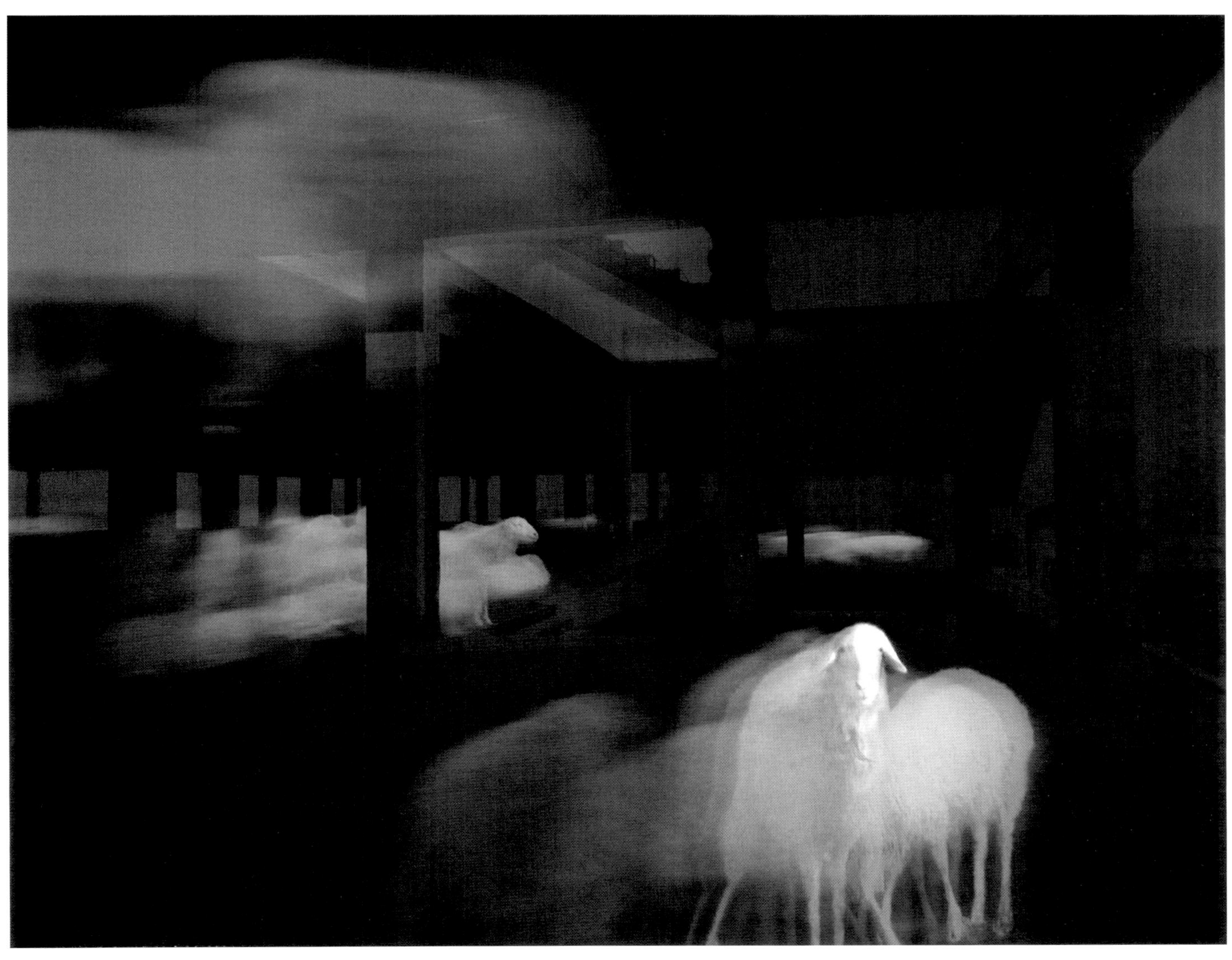

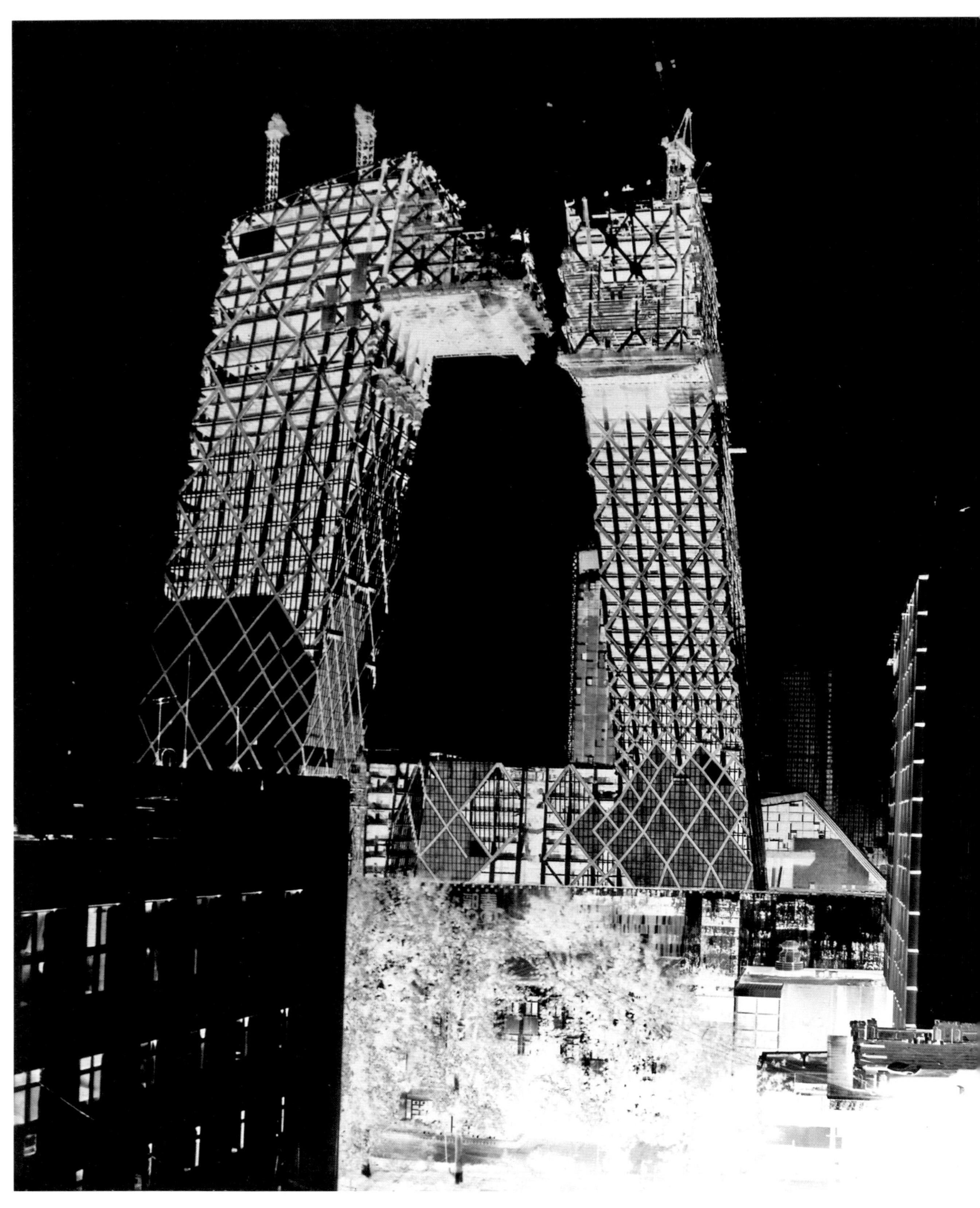

Shi Guorui, *New Beijing CCTV*, 2007

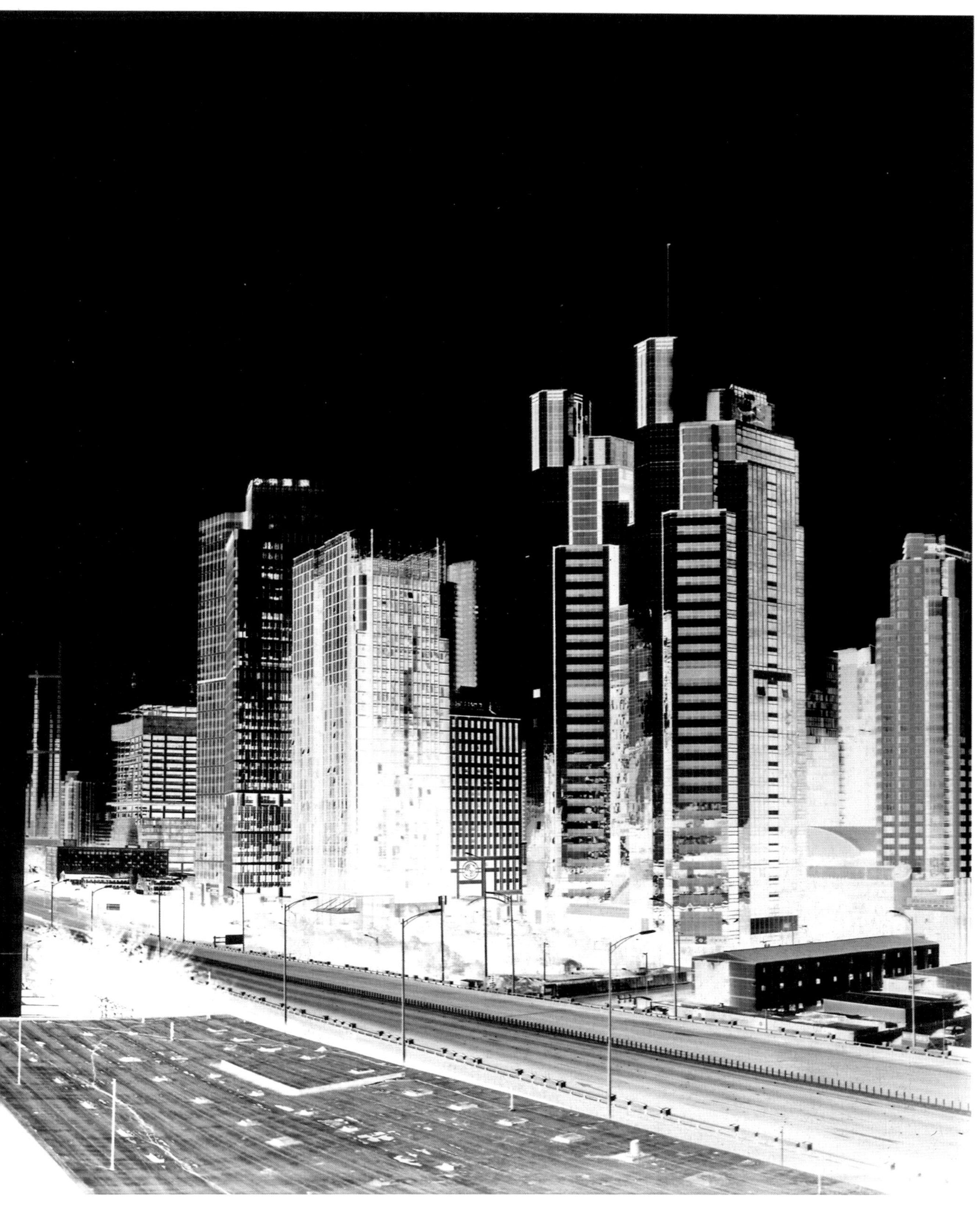

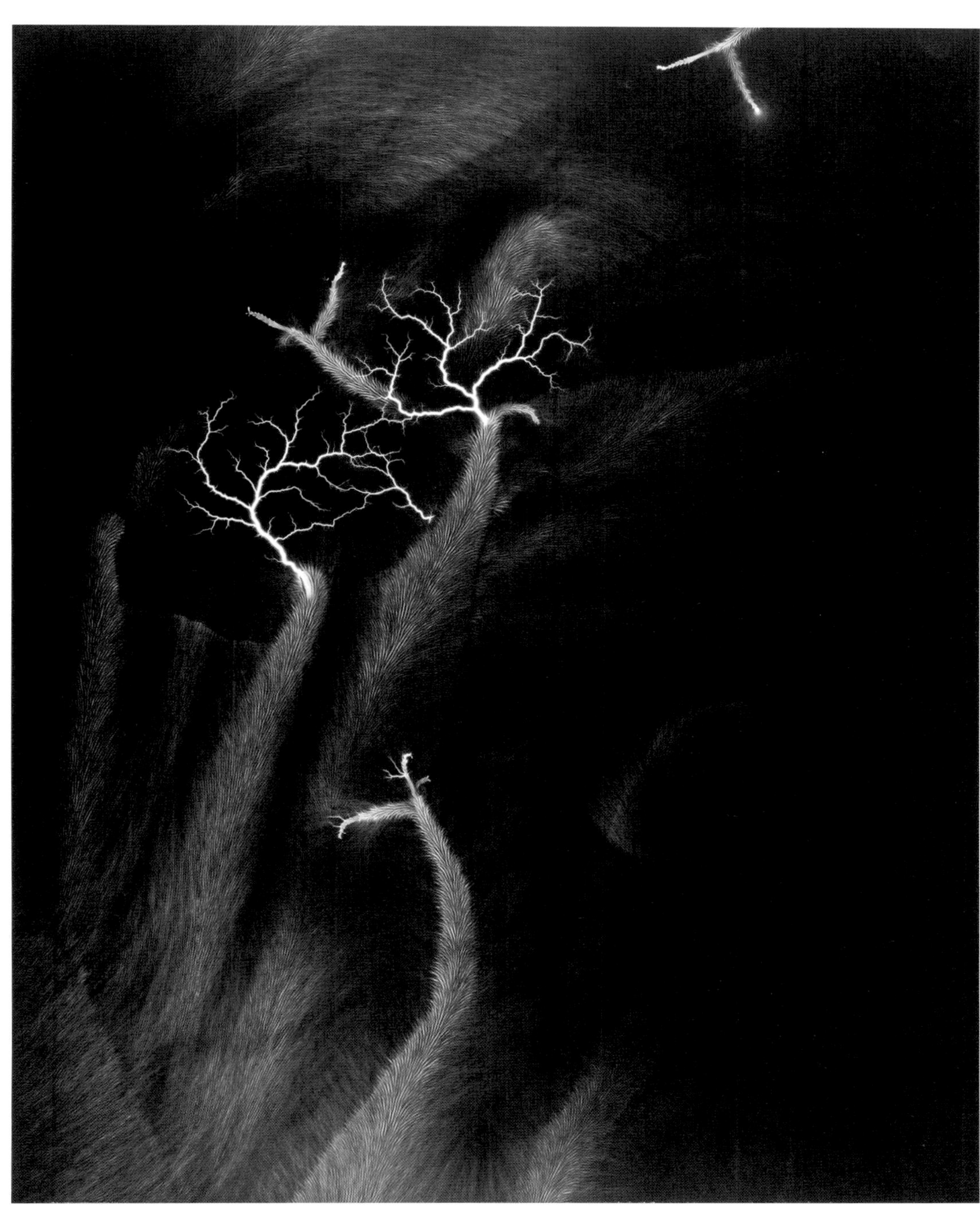

Hiroshi Sugimoto, *Lightning Field 119*, 2009

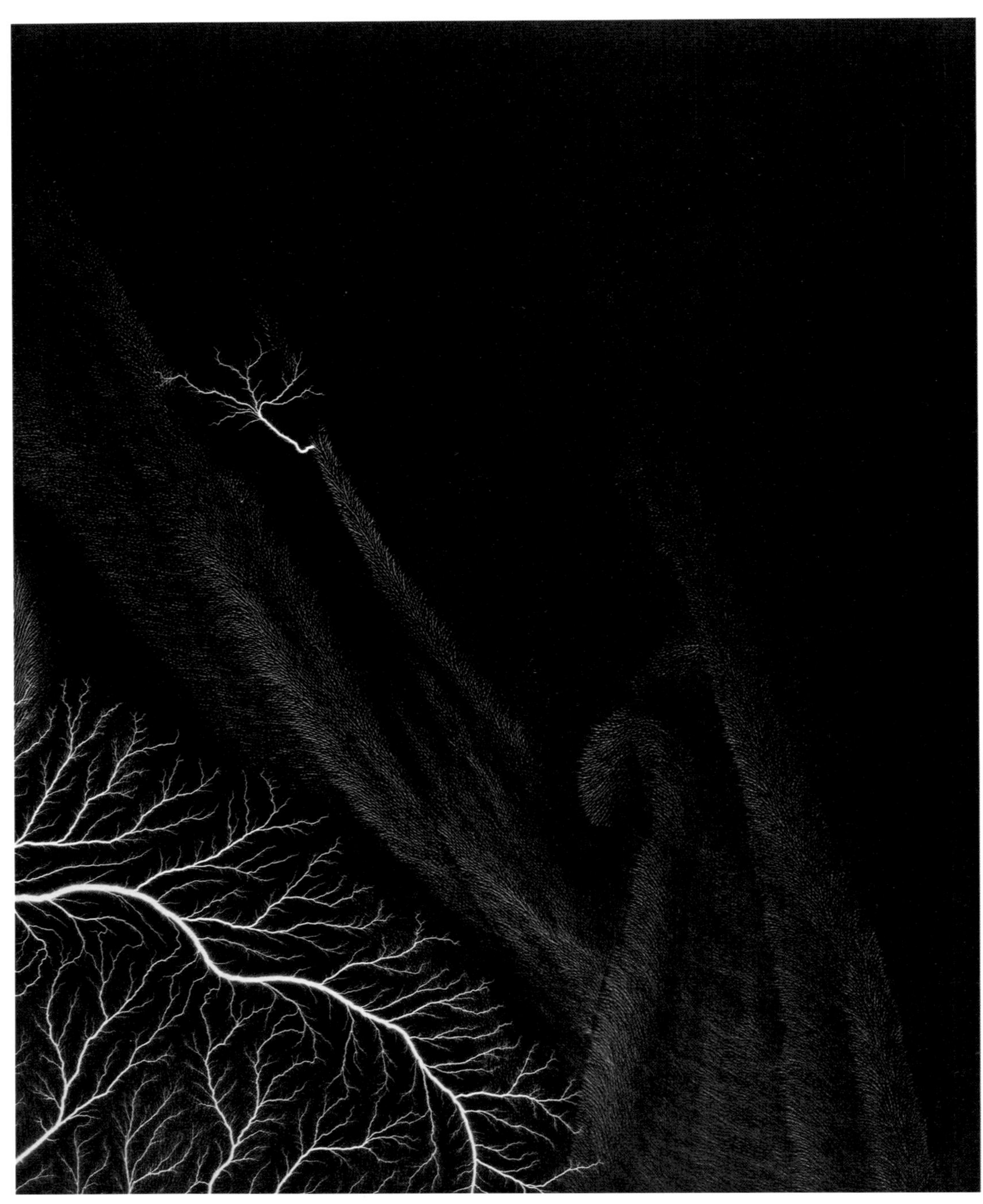

Hiroshi Sugimoto, *Lightning Field 143*, 2009

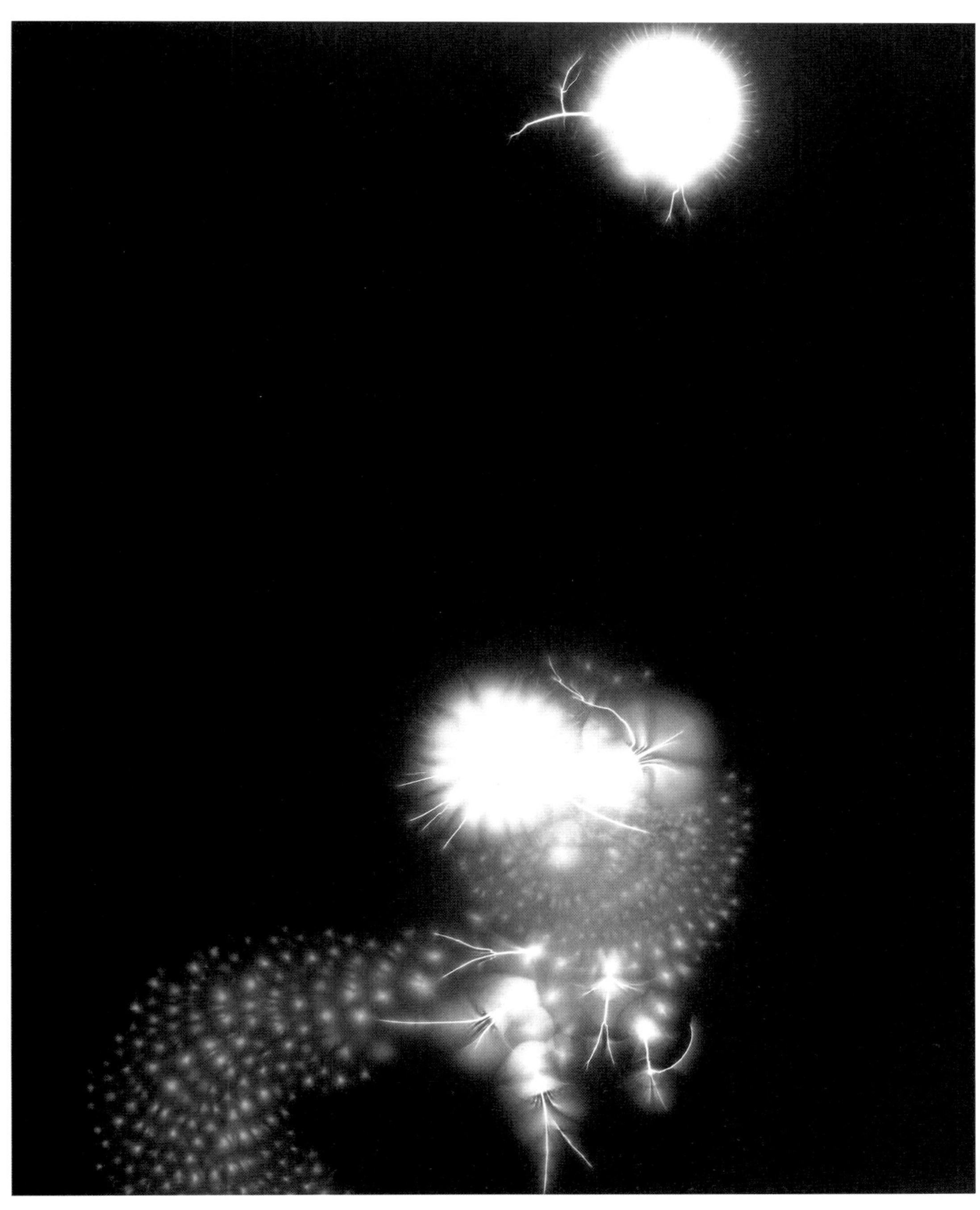

Hiroshi Sugimoto, *Lightning Field 138*, 2009

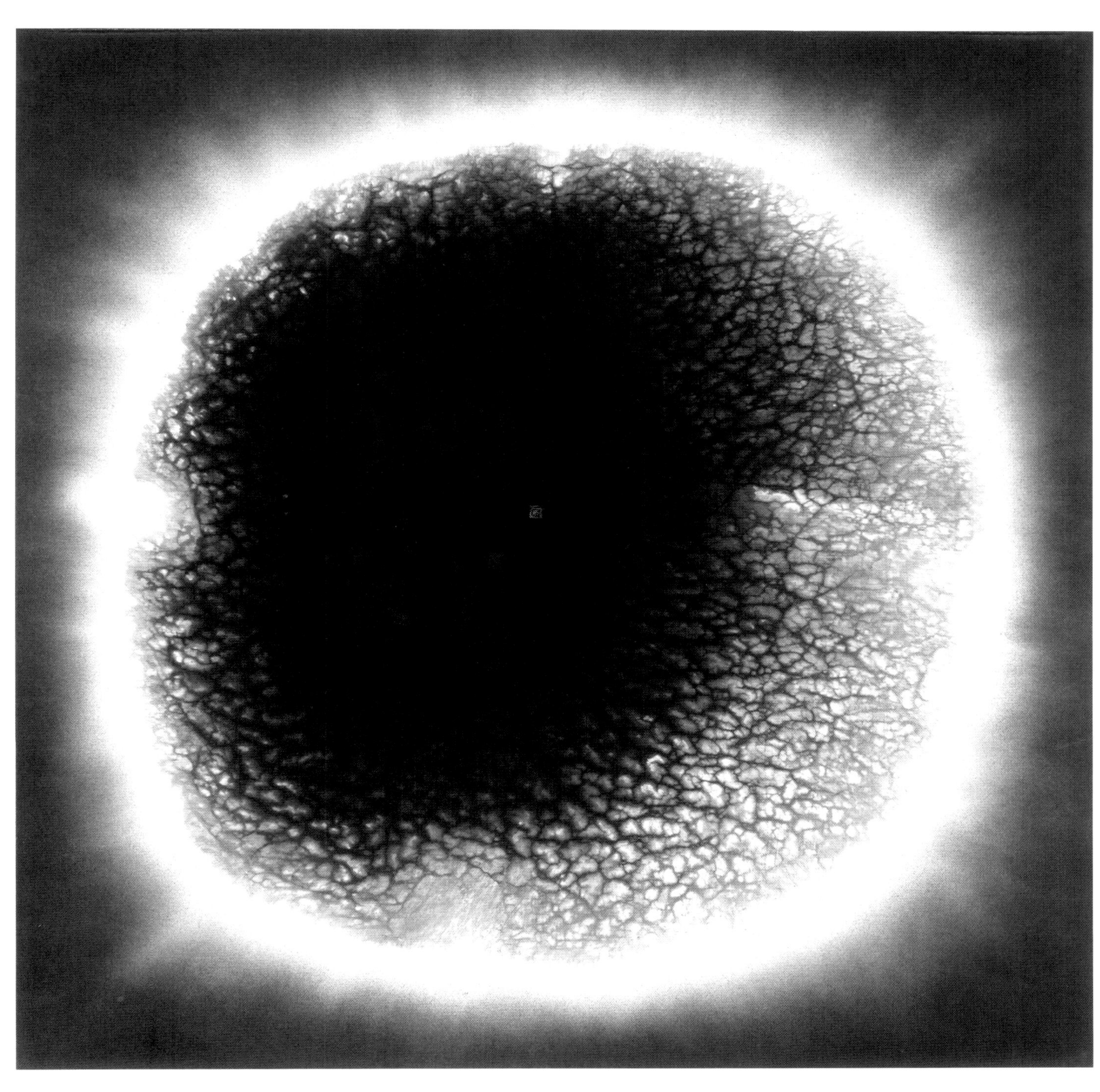

Zhang Yu, *Divine Light Series No. 7: Floating Incomplete Circle*, 1994

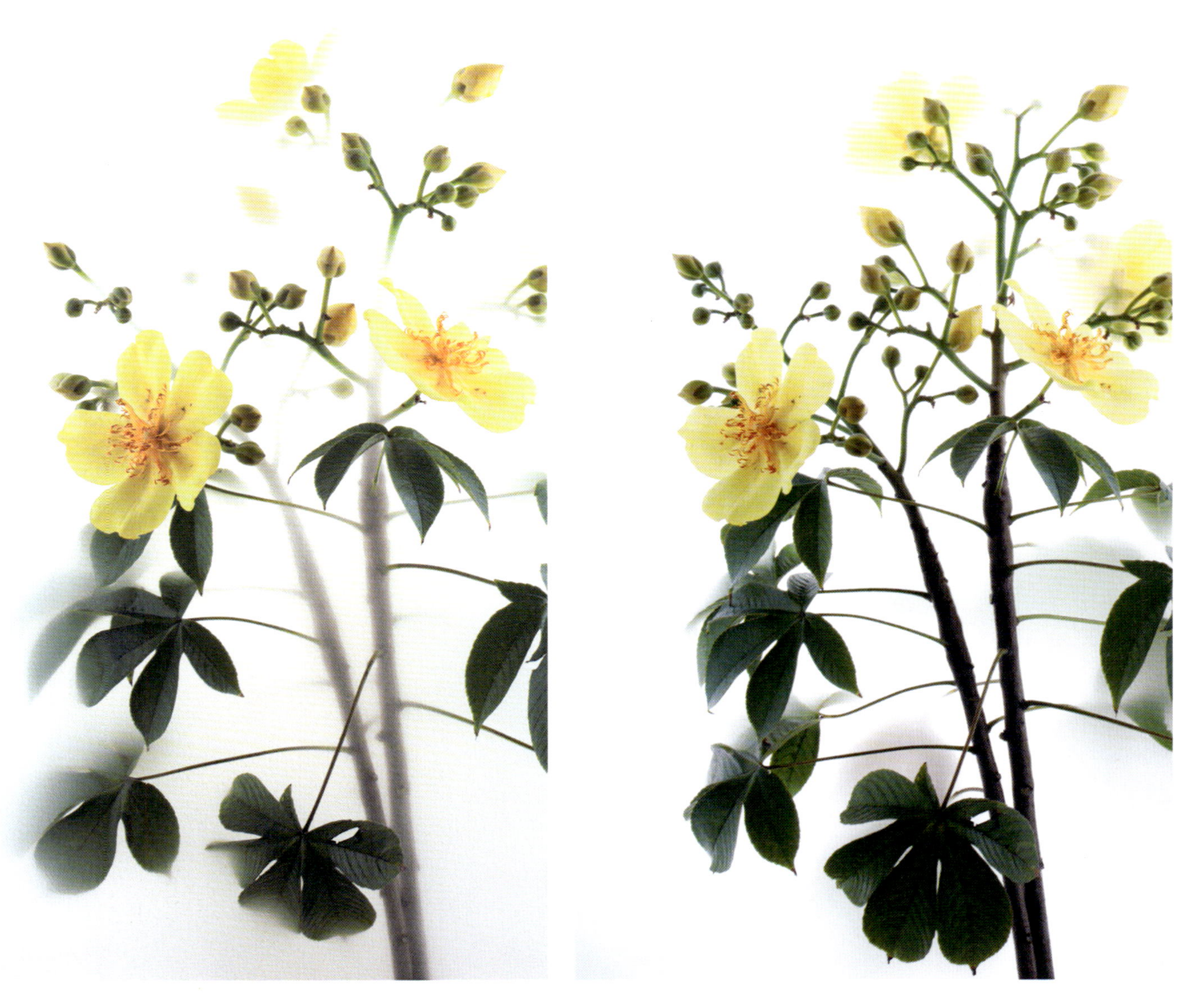

Wu Chi-Tsung, *Still Life 012-Buttercup Tree*, 2019

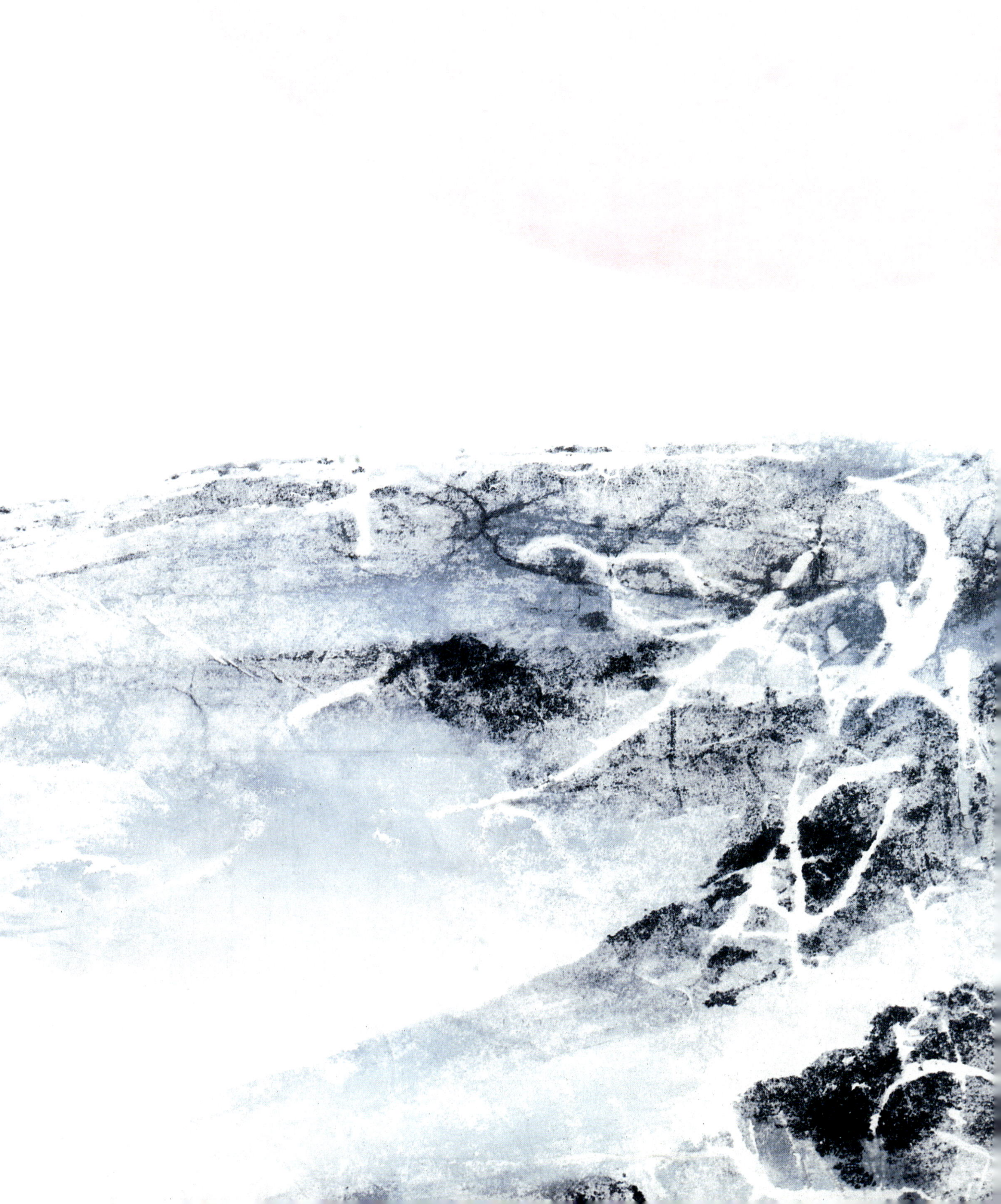

Dreamscapes

Landscapes of the Heart

Literati of the Song Dynasty Around 550 CE, the esteemed art historian Xie He outlined the six principles of Chinese painting in his *Record of the Classification of Old Painters*. Of the six, two were deemed of the utmost importance: the first principle, *qiyun* (spirit resonance), the energy communicated by an artist through a painting; and the third principle, that the painted image should relate to the formal likeness of the subject.

These tenets stood undisputed for centuries, until they were finally challenged in the Northern Song dynasty (960–1127). Beginning at this time, literati intellectuals moved from capturing the likeness of the land around them to painting works that reflected and symbolized their unique interior worlds—a principle that would prove its endurance throughout the following centuries. The eminent writer and painter Su Shi (1037–1101) begins a short poem with this bead of wisdom:

> If anyone discusses painting in terms of formal likeness,
> His understanding is close to that of a child.[10]

The inner landscape[11]—the mountains and rivers that flow through the mind—became the subject of the works of Chinese literati artists and writers who, like Su Shi, valued the process of self-expression over realistic depiction. The Northern Song literati sought not to translate what they saw into their paintings, but to spontaneously record on paper or silk the landscape that came to them intuitively. This land-

10 Susan Bush and Hsio-yen Shih, eds., *Early Chinese Texts on Painting* (Cambridge, Mass.: Harvard University Press, 1985), 224.

11 This is an interpretation of the Chinese xinjing, xin meaning heart and jing meaning view or scenery—thus, the landscape of the heart or mind.

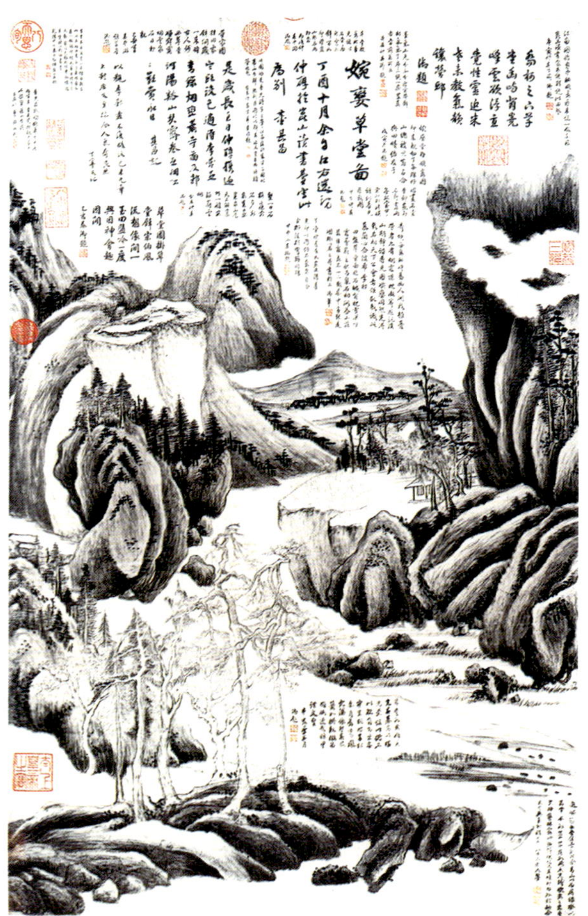

Fig. 9 Dong Qichang (1555–1636), *Wanluan Thatched Hall*, 1597. Hanging scroll: ink and colors on paper, 4½ × 14½ in. (11.3 × 36.8 cm). Private collection

Xu Bing, *Background Story: Ink Variation (from Lui Shou-kwan)*, 2016 (detail)

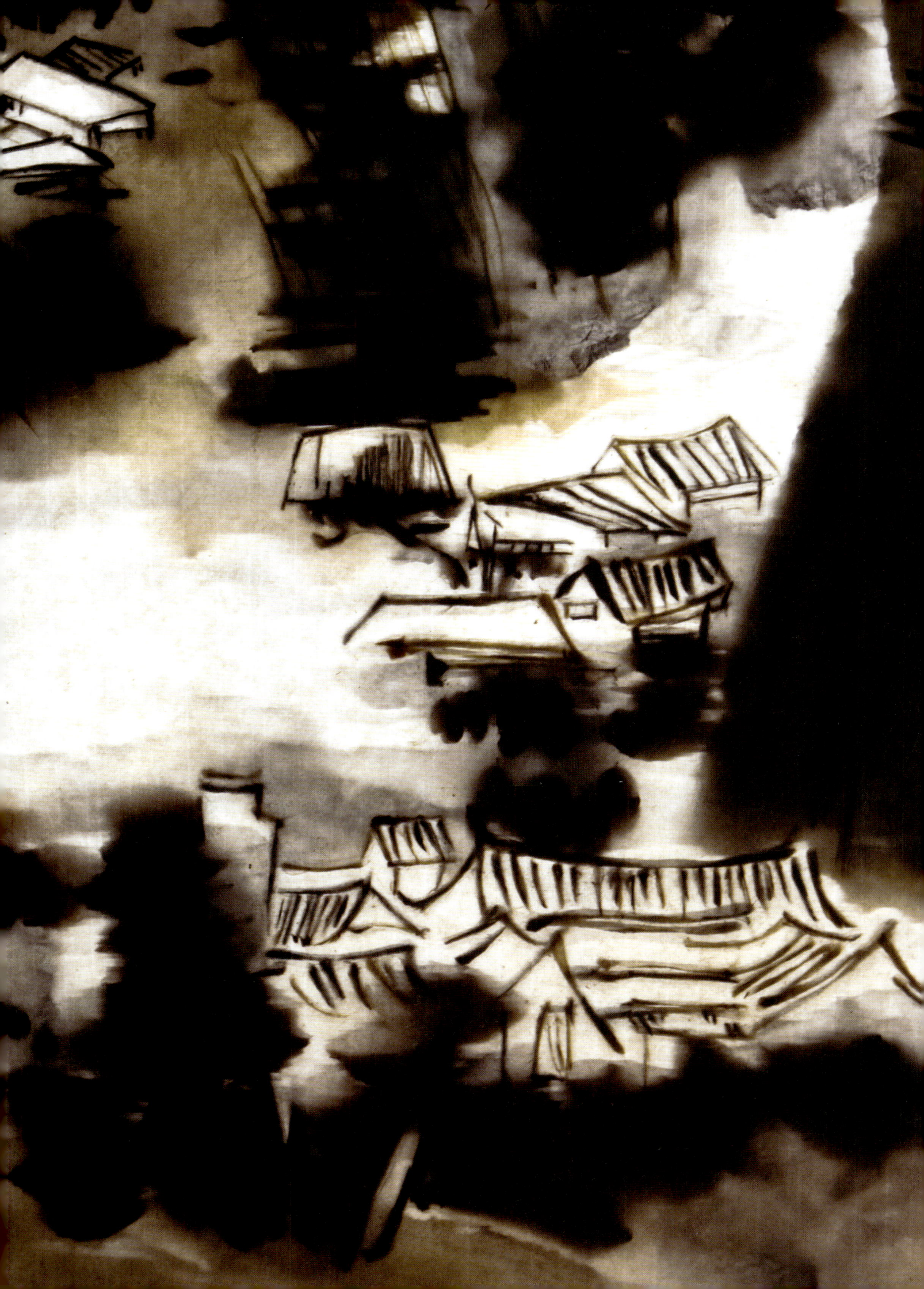

scape might have plants that would not naturally grow together, streams flowing as if from nowhere, craggy cliffs that could not physically bear their own load.

Consider Dong Qichang's *Wanluan Thatched Hall* (fig. 9). Although the rocks in the foreground appear as if they might be found in real life, this illusion quickly fades as the eye wanders toward the middle- and background. The lumpy rock formations to the right demonstrate the artist's interest in texture and shading, but reflect more the folds of the mind than of natural stone; the trees and mountains of unrealistic scales somehow mesh into the shared picture plane. Dong Qichang's expressive landscape is crowded, bold, fantastical, and deeply personal—for the only nature it reflects is that of his inner world.

The Contemporary Landscape Today, a number of ink artists declaratively identify with these lauded literati painters. They are knowledgeable about Chinese art history and seek self-expression in their landscape paintings. As with the subjects of meditations and apparitions, the world giving rise to the imaginary landscape has changed dramatically since the genre was first established. Besides the new tools and influences described above, the artists within the Dreamscapes grouping are also immersed in a physical and social environment markedly different from that of their predecessors.

This scenery continues to change at a rapid pace. While it was once common in China for reclusive artists to find themselves deep within majestic, untouched nature, their contemporary surroundings are increasingly urban. Today, many artists in China keep studios in high-rise apartment buildings, developed arts districts, or dedicated studio complexes. In the work of some, like Liu Dan (p. 170), this built-up, urban landscape is nowhere in sight—a true literatus, his works reflect the mindscape of a Northern Song painter, depicted with meticulous, detailed brushwork in a classic monochrome. Others, like Xu Bing have subverted the landscape tradition to reflect the current environment, and notably, the degradation caused by pollution. In his series *Background Story* (pp. 158–61), he re-creates specific landscape paintings from ink art history using dried grasses, leaves, and trash in the place of ink and brush. The resulting composition is flattened behind the front pane of a light box, disguising the work's component parts but affecting the appearance of an ink painting.

Yang Shih-Chih, *Modern Landscape*, 2008 (detail)

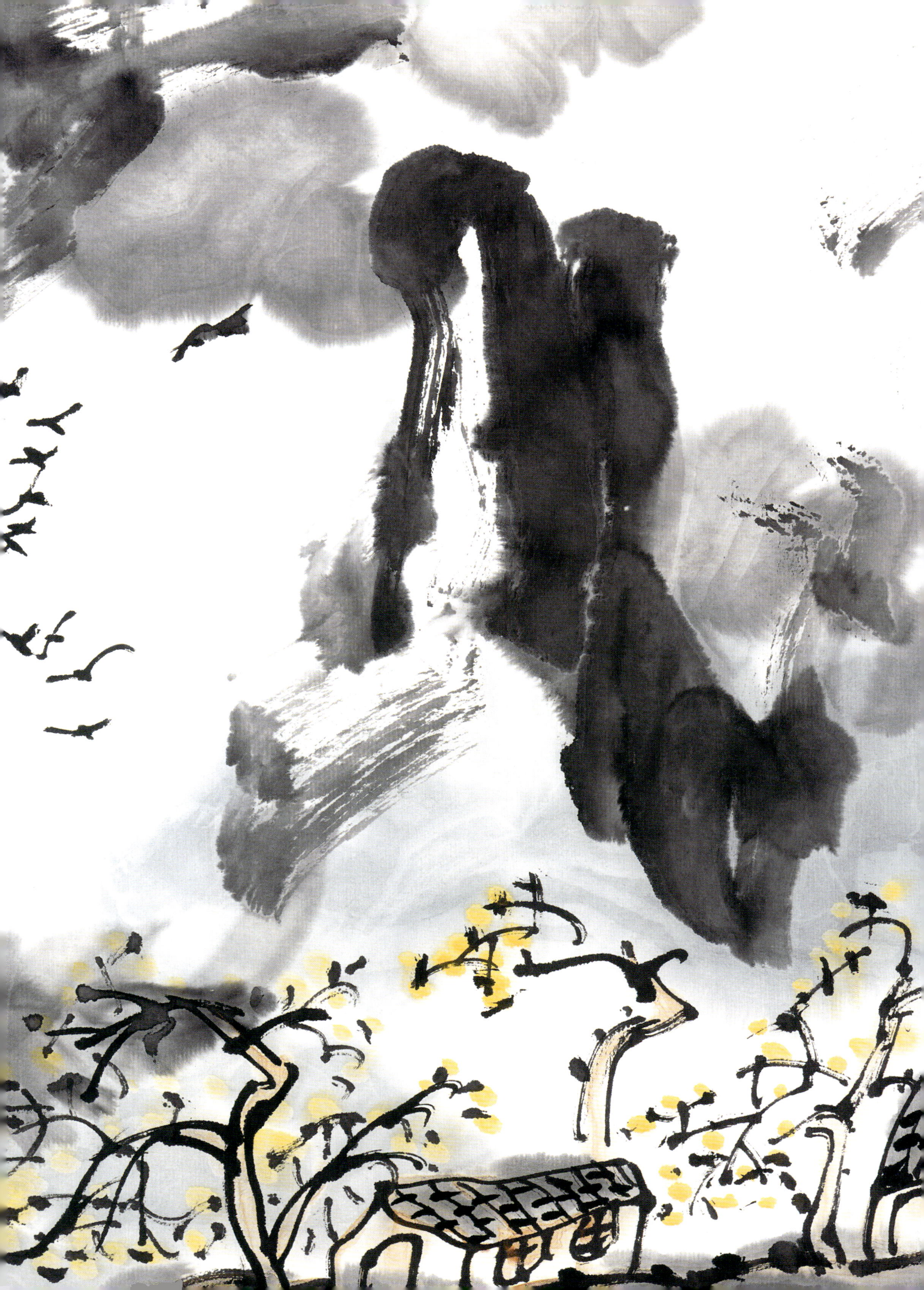

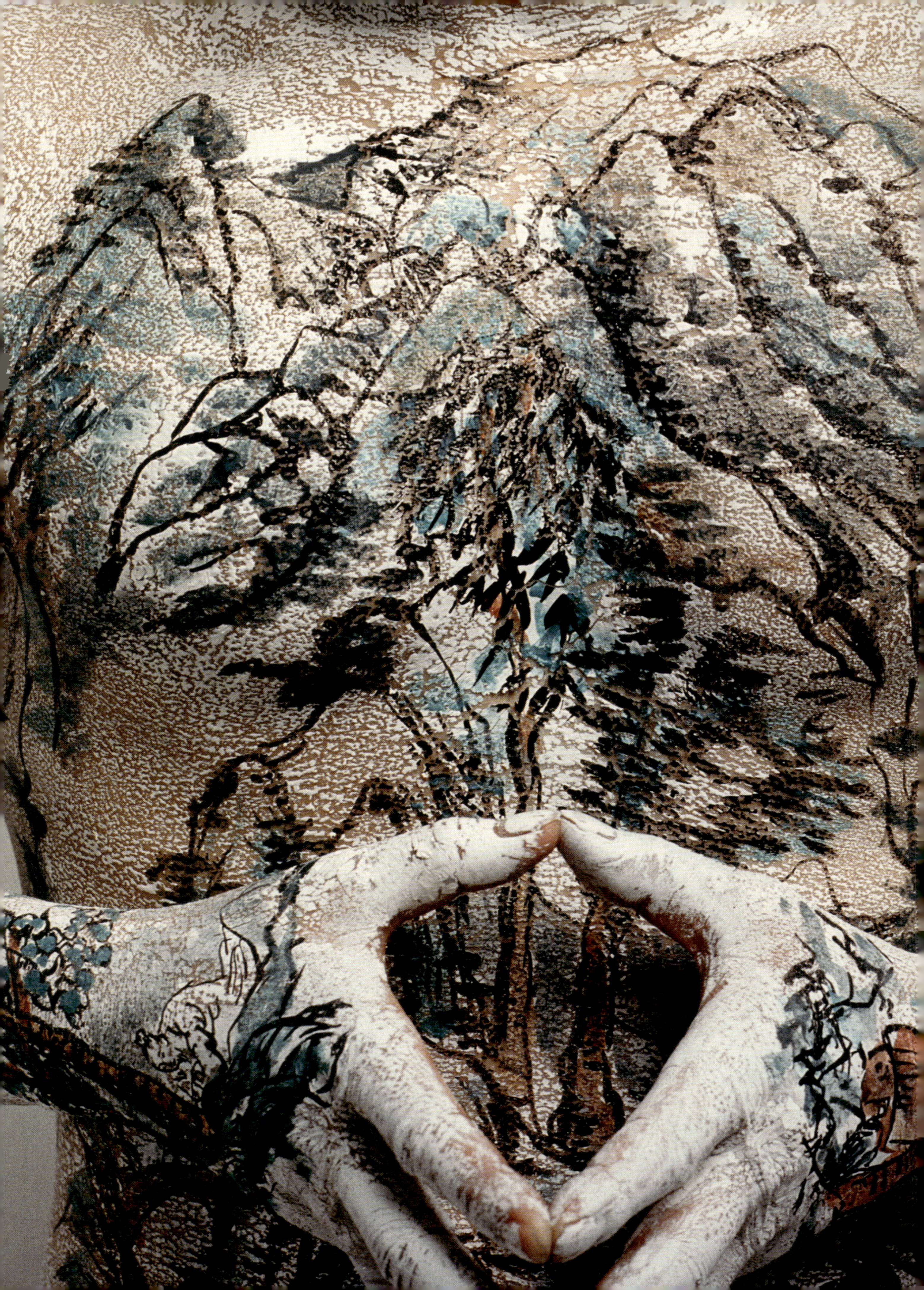

Some artists, like Li Huayi (p. 143), Leung Kui-ting (p. 175), Wucius Wong (p. 179) and Kim Ho-deuk (p. 153), show little interest in depicting a fully wrought landscape. The central focus of their work, in fact, is not the scene itself, but the pattern-like repetition of natural forms. Li uses cracks in a stone's surface or the roots of a tree; Leung repeats a mixture of plants, cliffs, and geometric shapes; Kim's work is meditative, his mountains composed with spontaneously repeated peaks. Though Wong's rivers and mountains may be misread as purely abstract, his rendering of texture with natural elements is a refined practice in contemporary ink landscape painting.

Again, as is true for meditation and apparition, the dreamscape can be communicated through photography as well. Hong Lei (pp. 154, 155), Huang Yan (p. 152), and Hai Bo (p. 147) each translate the subject to this modern medium, showing us landscapes in which elements of reality are composed in such a way as to produce a surreal effect.

Finally, the dreamscapes created by Chen Haiyan (p. 171) are, in fact, based on the artist's actual dreams. Chen goes one step beyond the original literati artists: instead of simply letting her waking subconscious flow out onto her paper, her inspiration comes entirely from the late-night processing of her unconscious mind.

Huang Yan, *Chinese Shanshui Tattoo Series No. 7*, 1999 (detail)

Plates
Dreamscapes

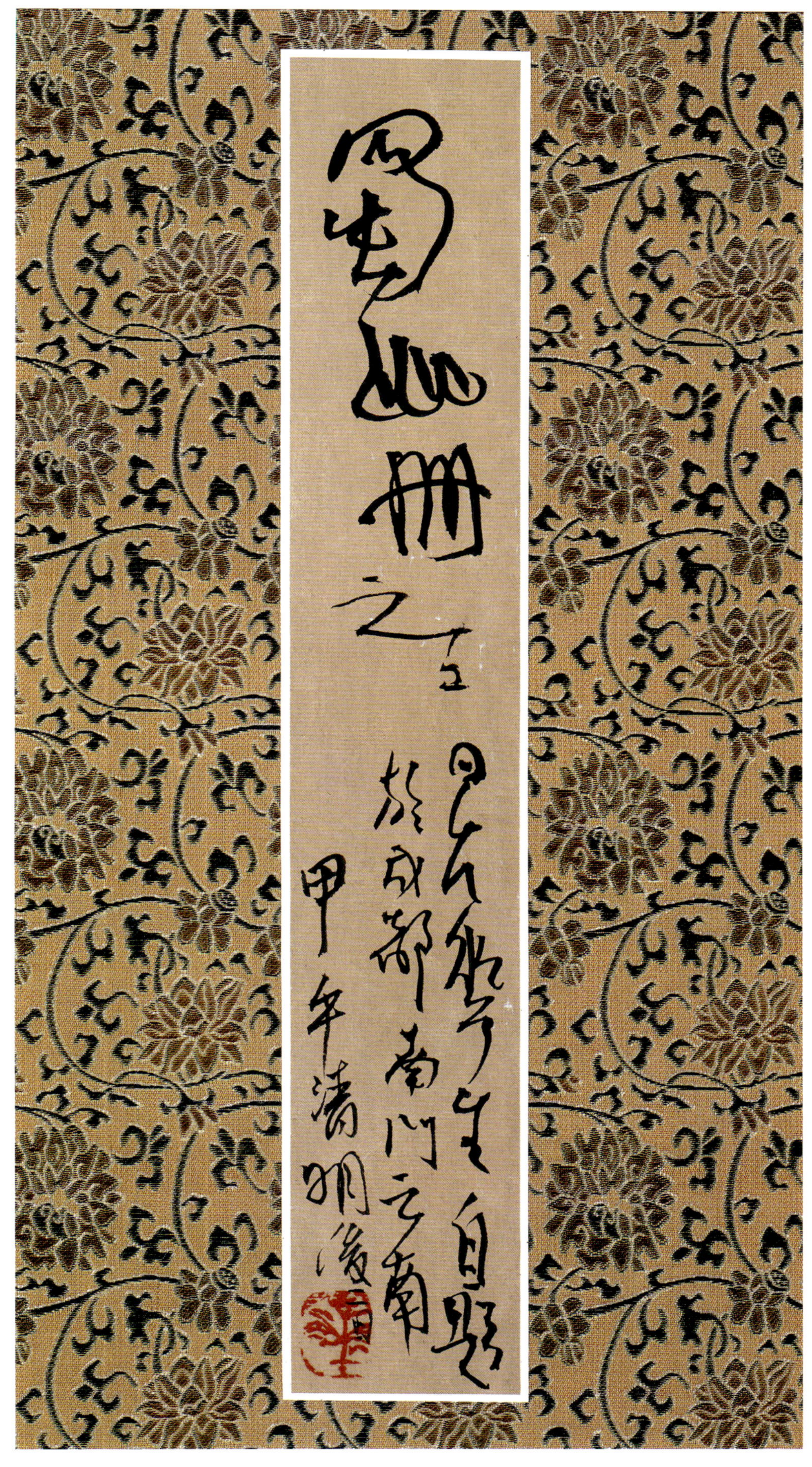

Li Huasheng, *Album 2*, 1990s

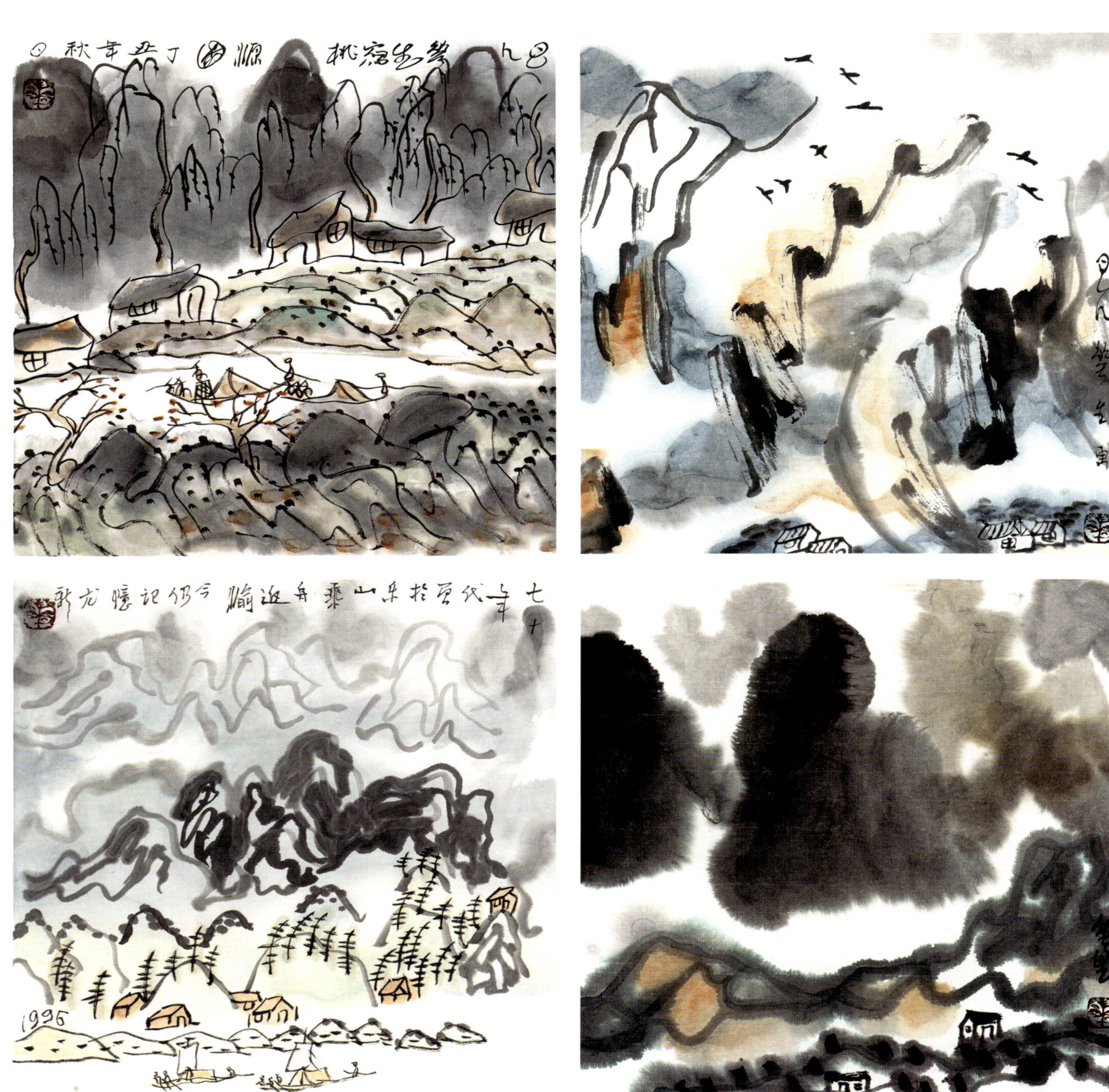

Li Huasheng, *Album 2*, 1990s

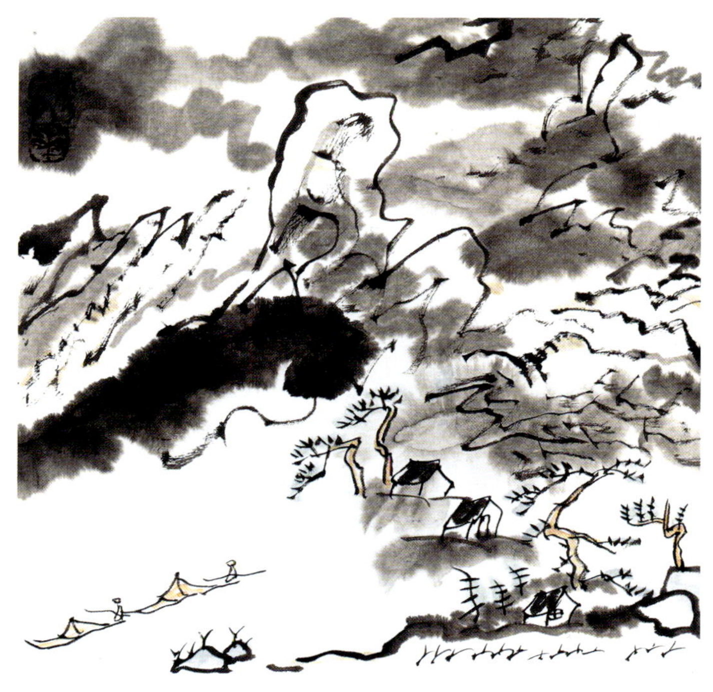

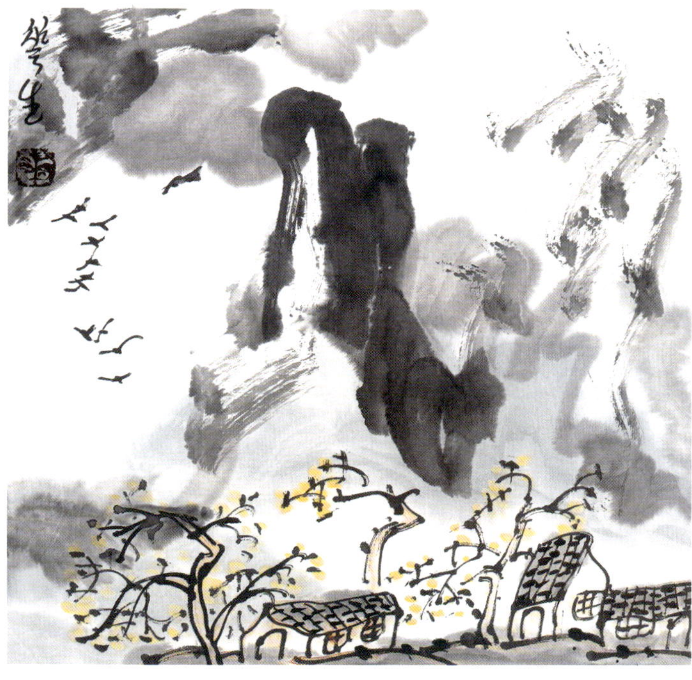

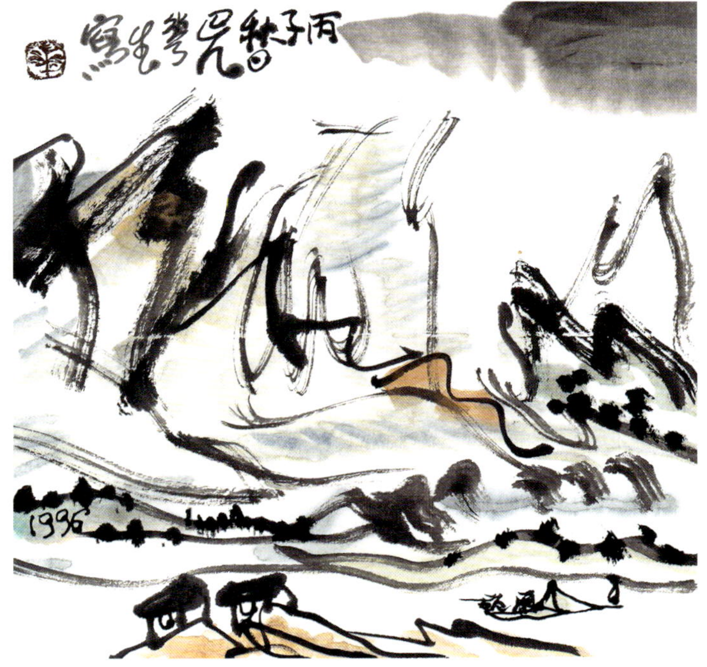

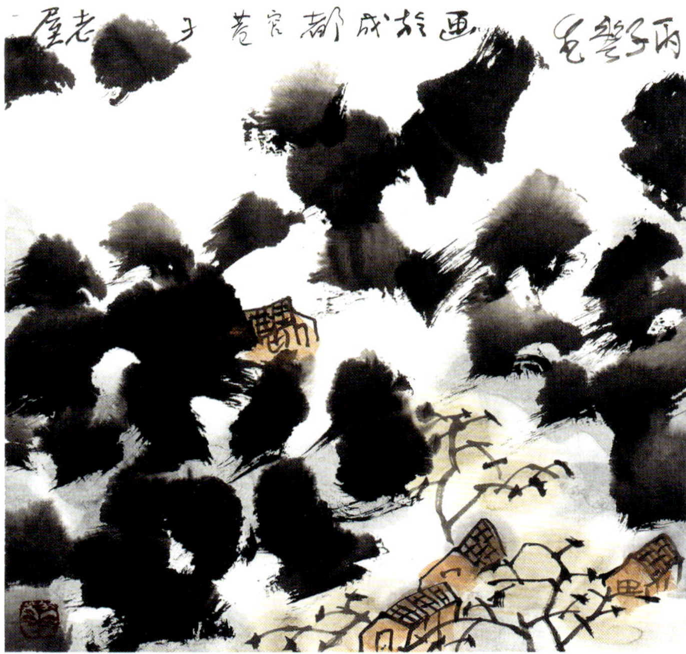

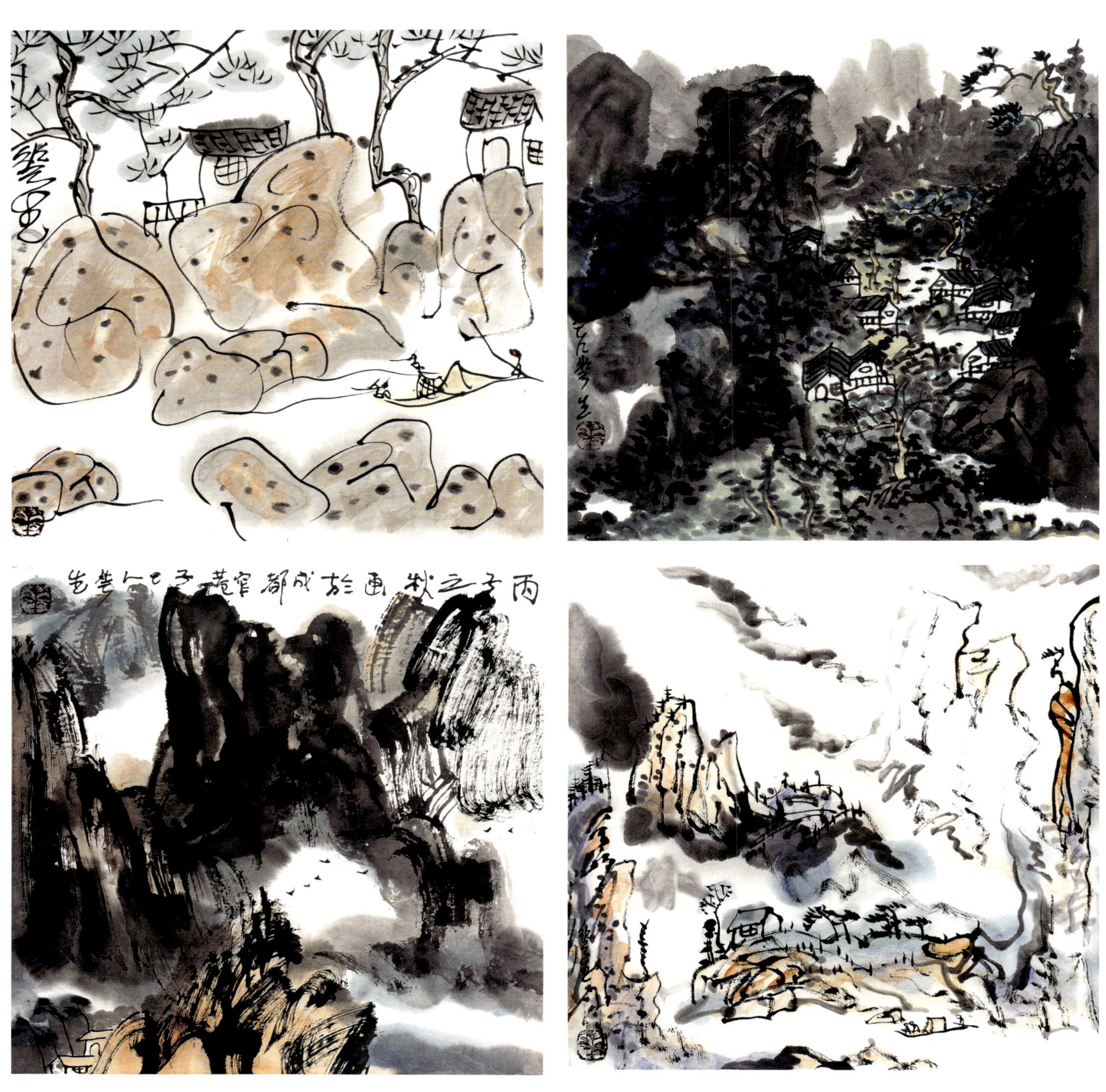

Li Huasheng, *Album 2*, 1990s

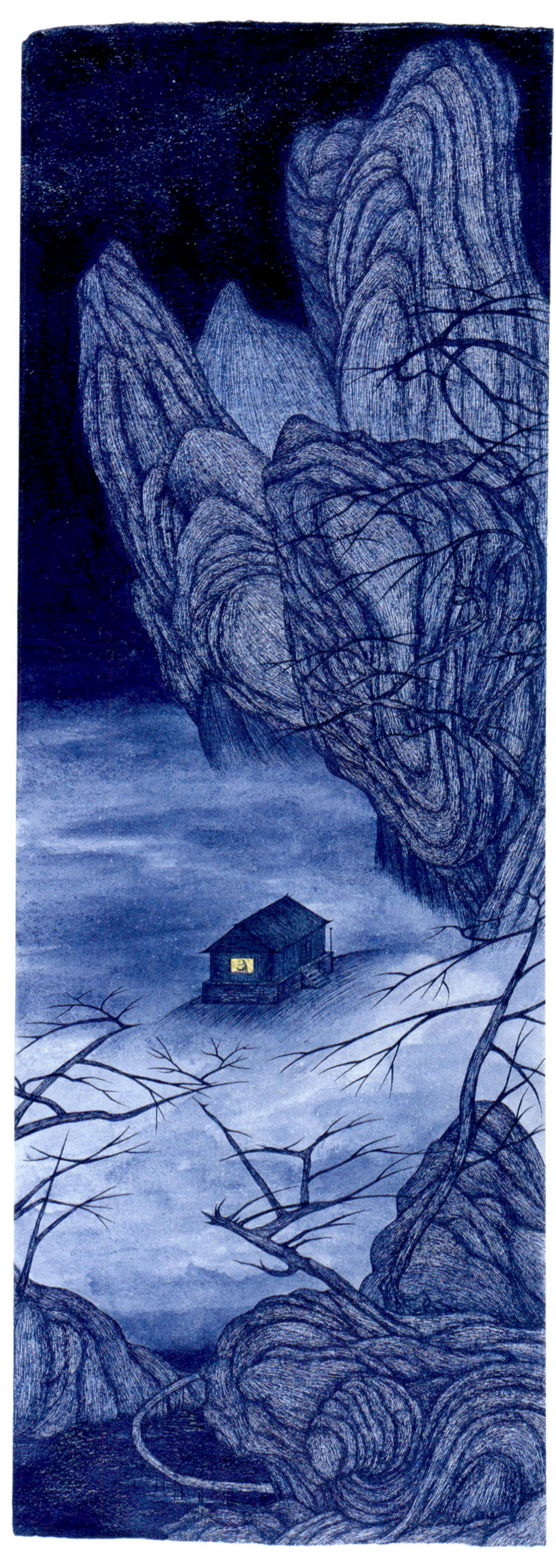

Yao Jui-Chung, *Wonderful: Secret Lover in Golden House*, 2007

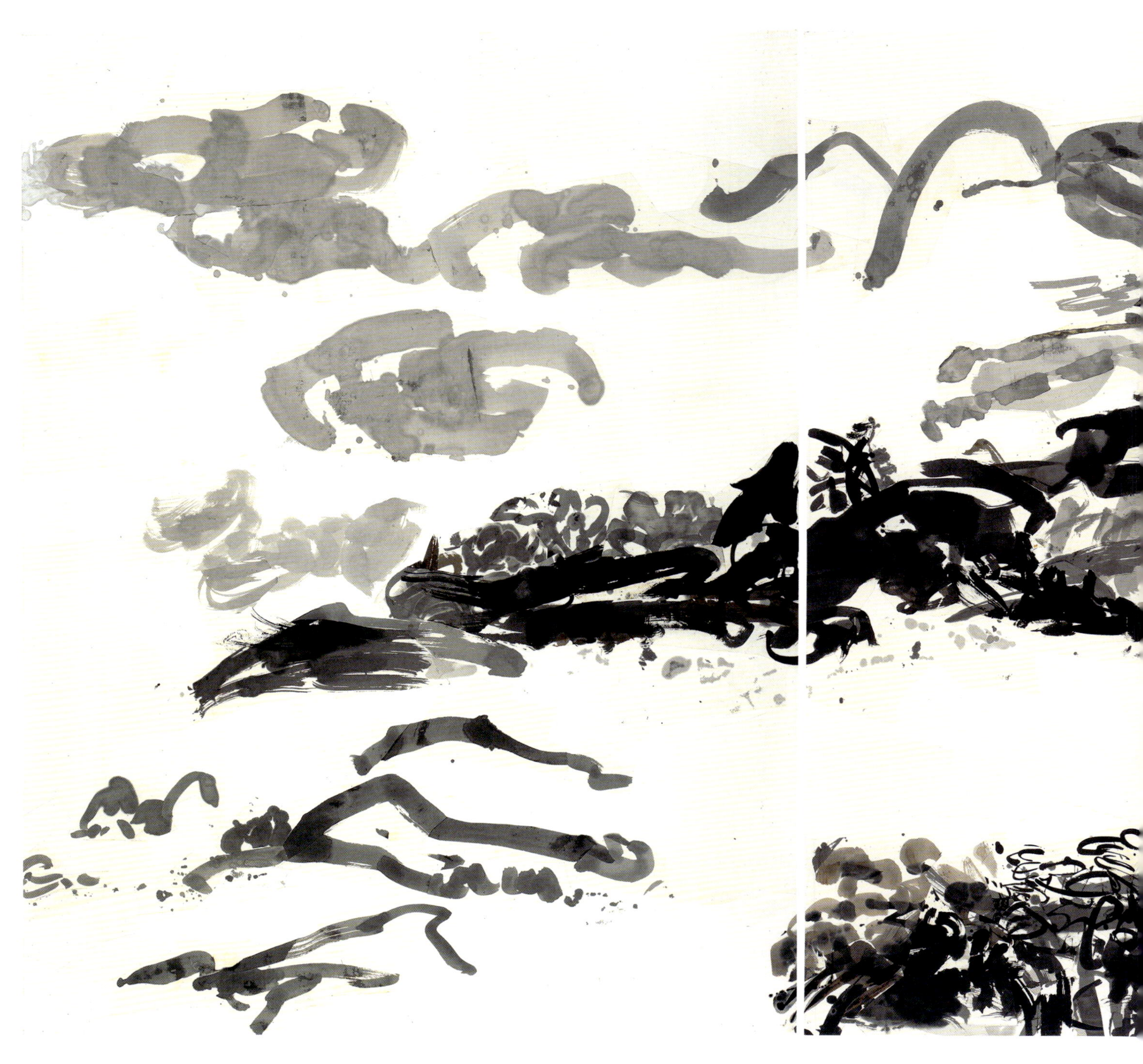

Yang Shih-Chih, *Modern Landscape*, 2008

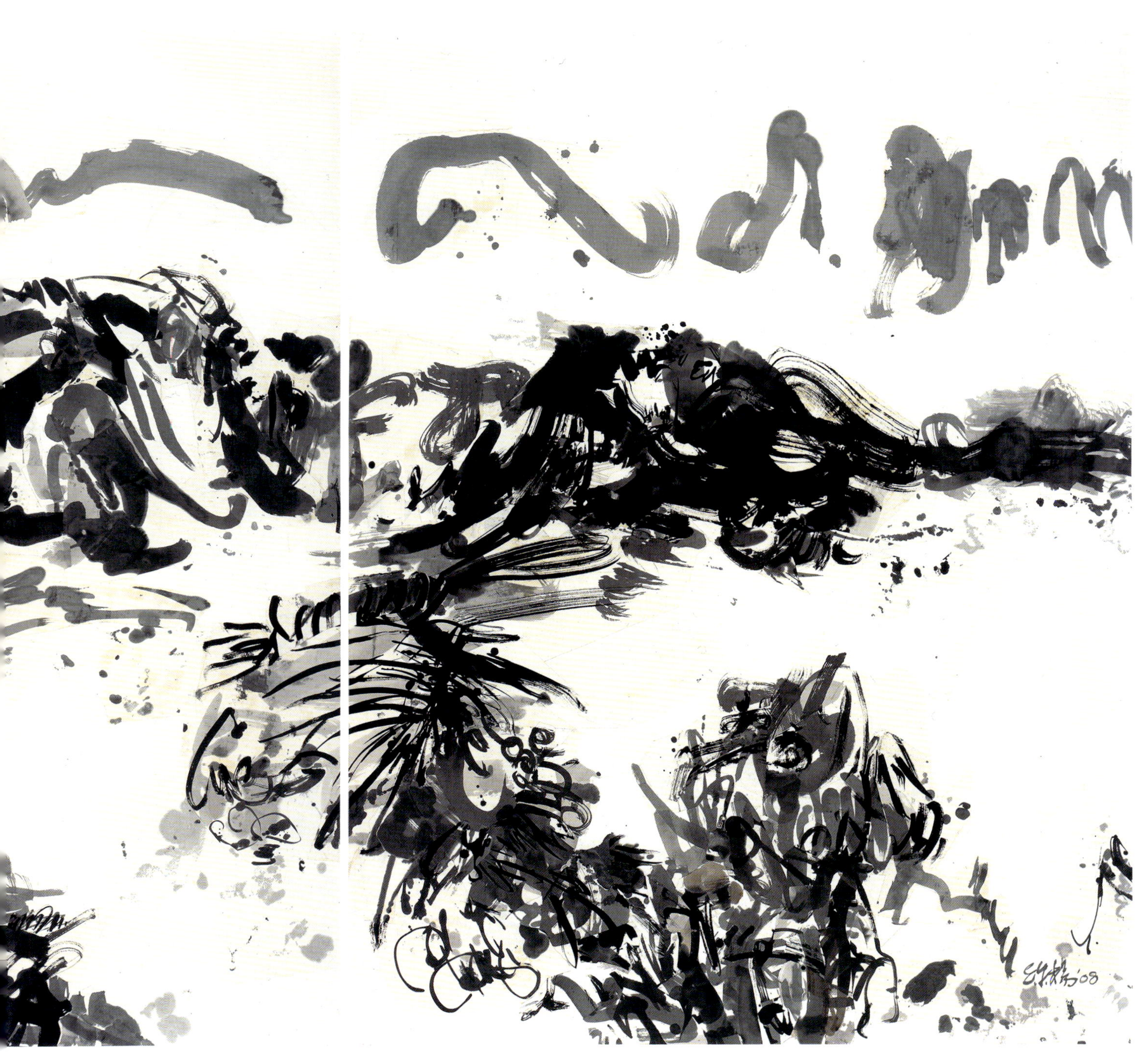

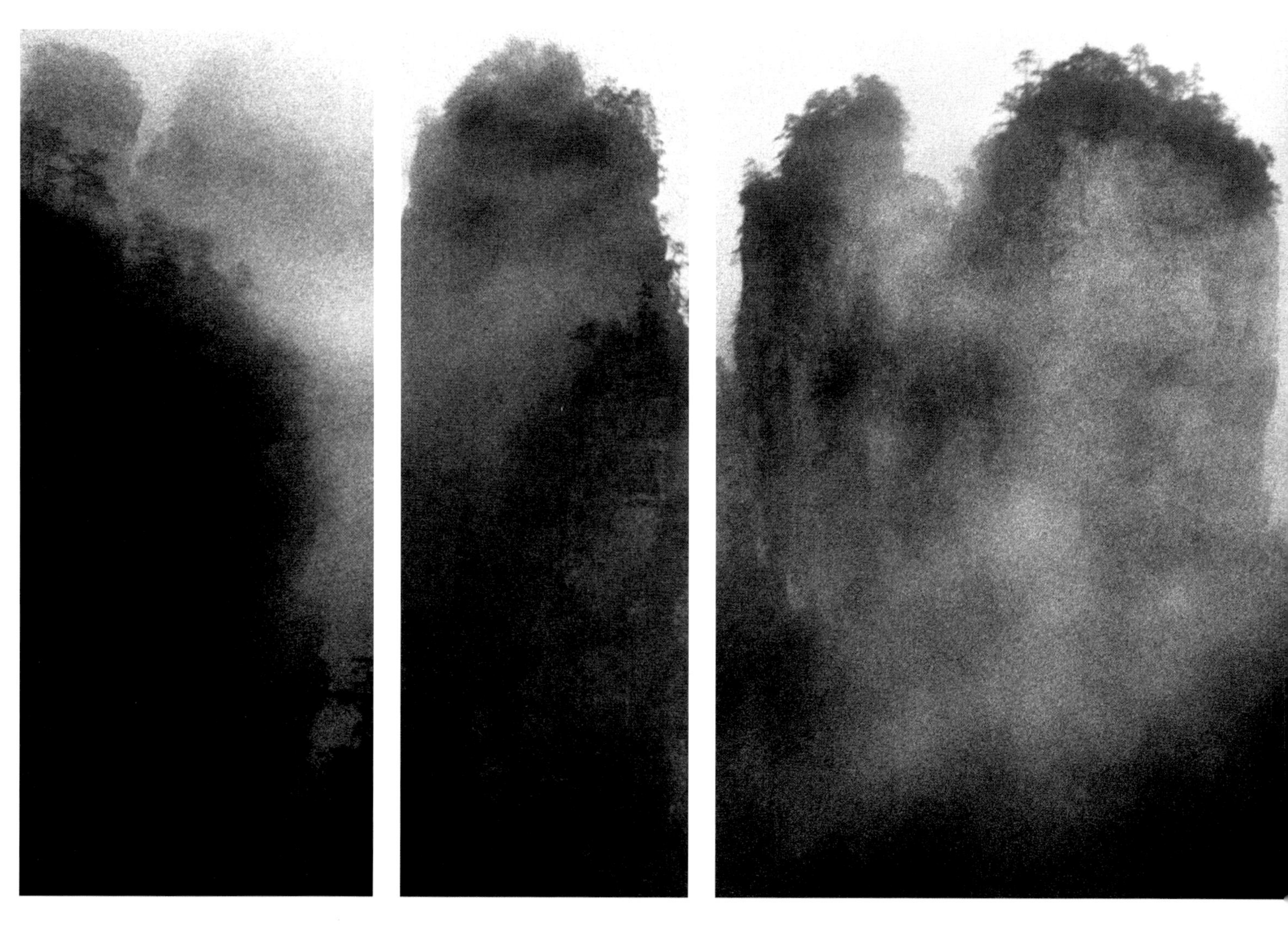

Michael Cherney, *Five Peaks: Eastern, Western, Southern, Central, Northern*, 2008

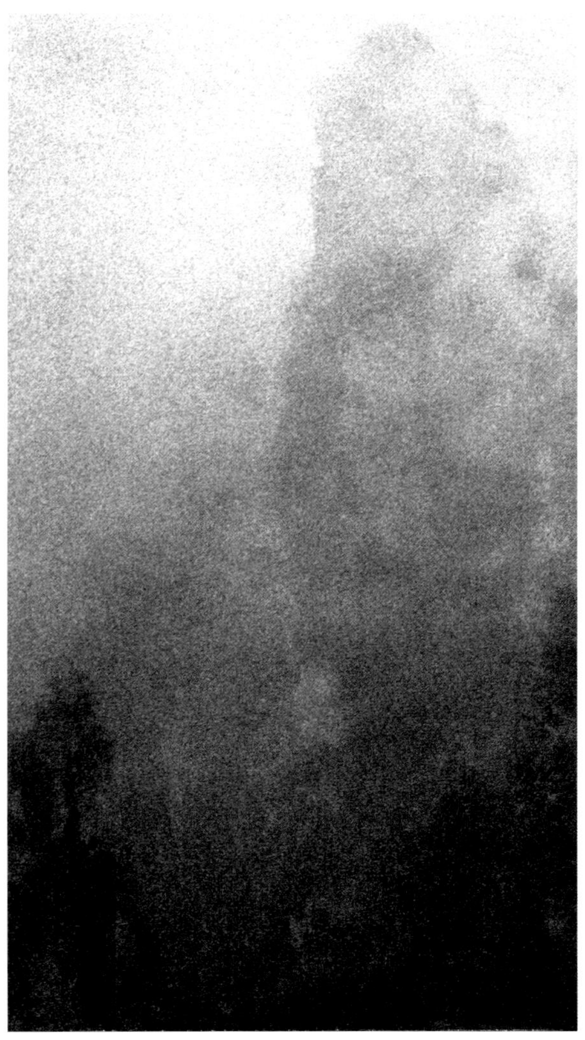

Li Huayi, *Landscape*, 2009

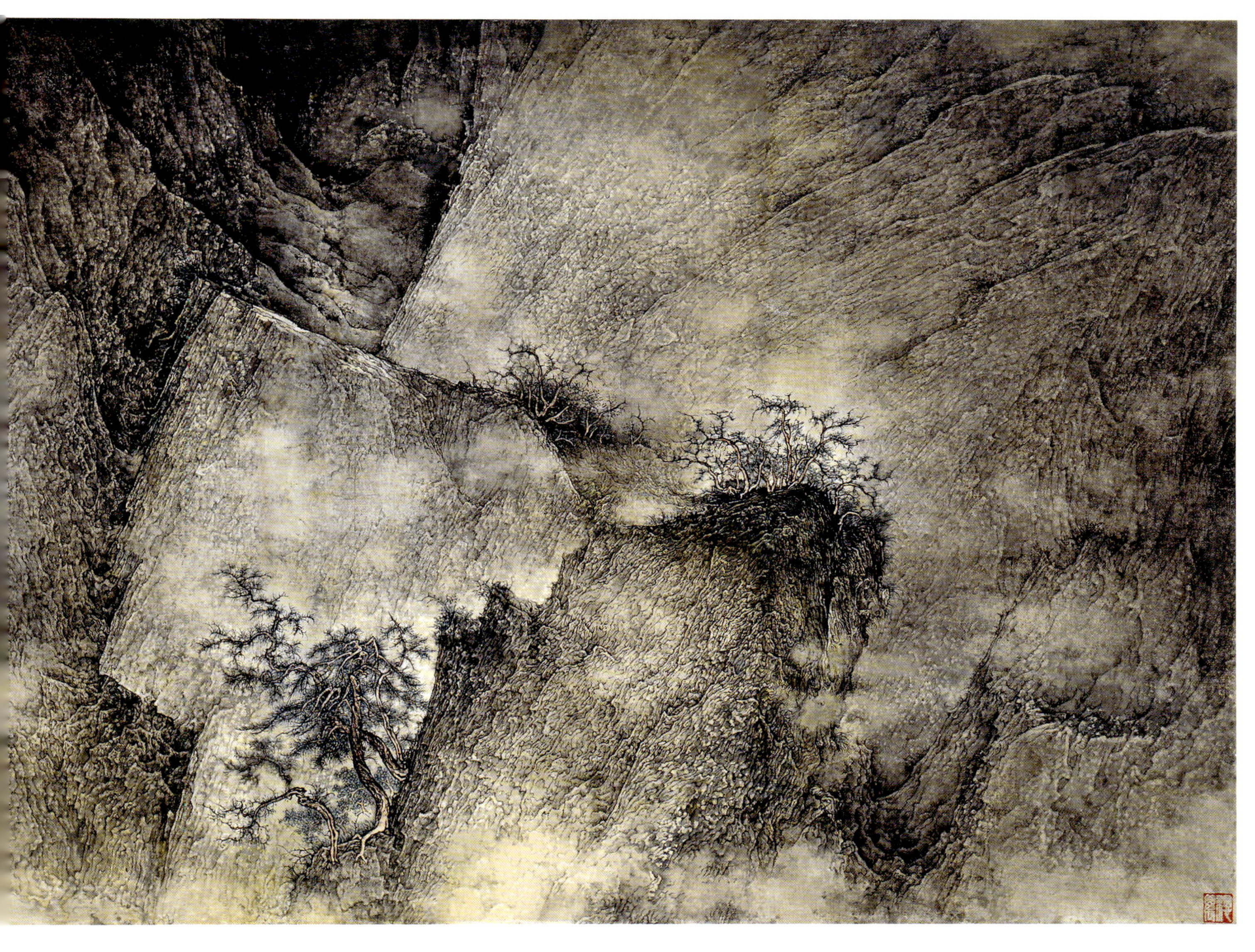

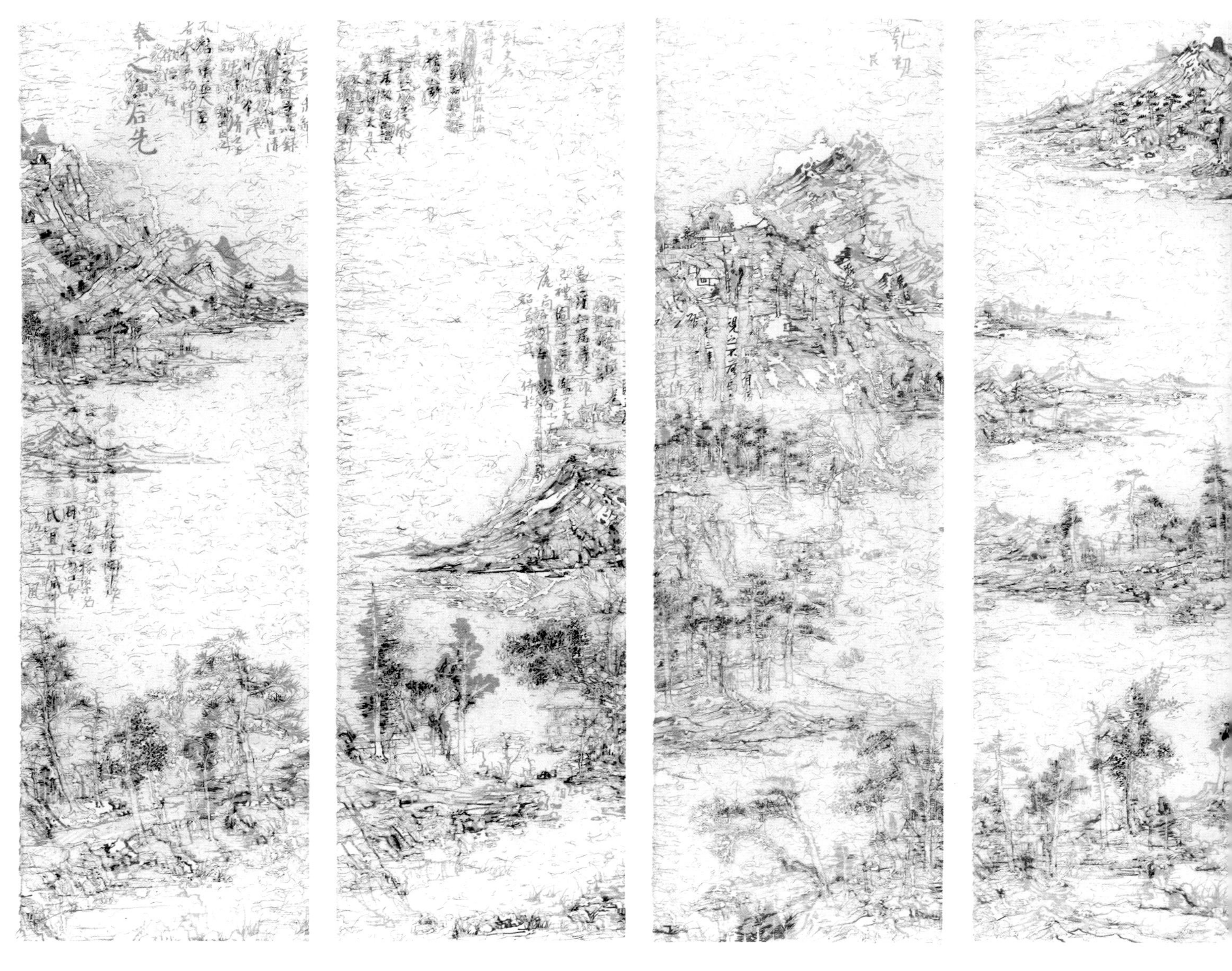

Wang Tiande, *Untitled*, 2013

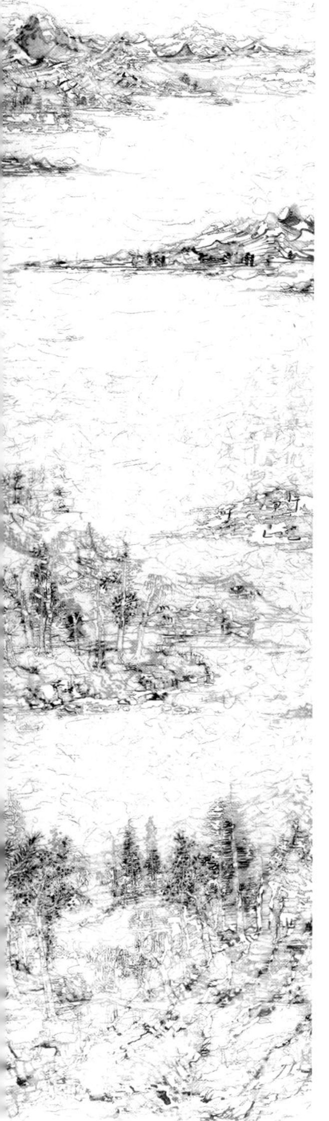

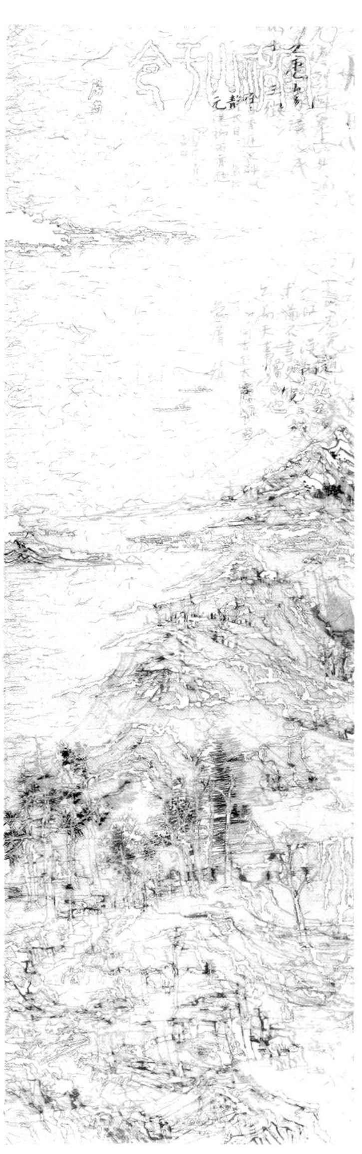

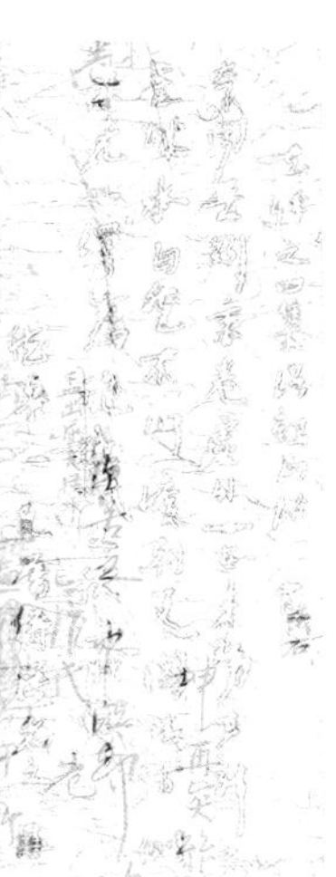

Hai Bo, *Blue Bridge*, 2004

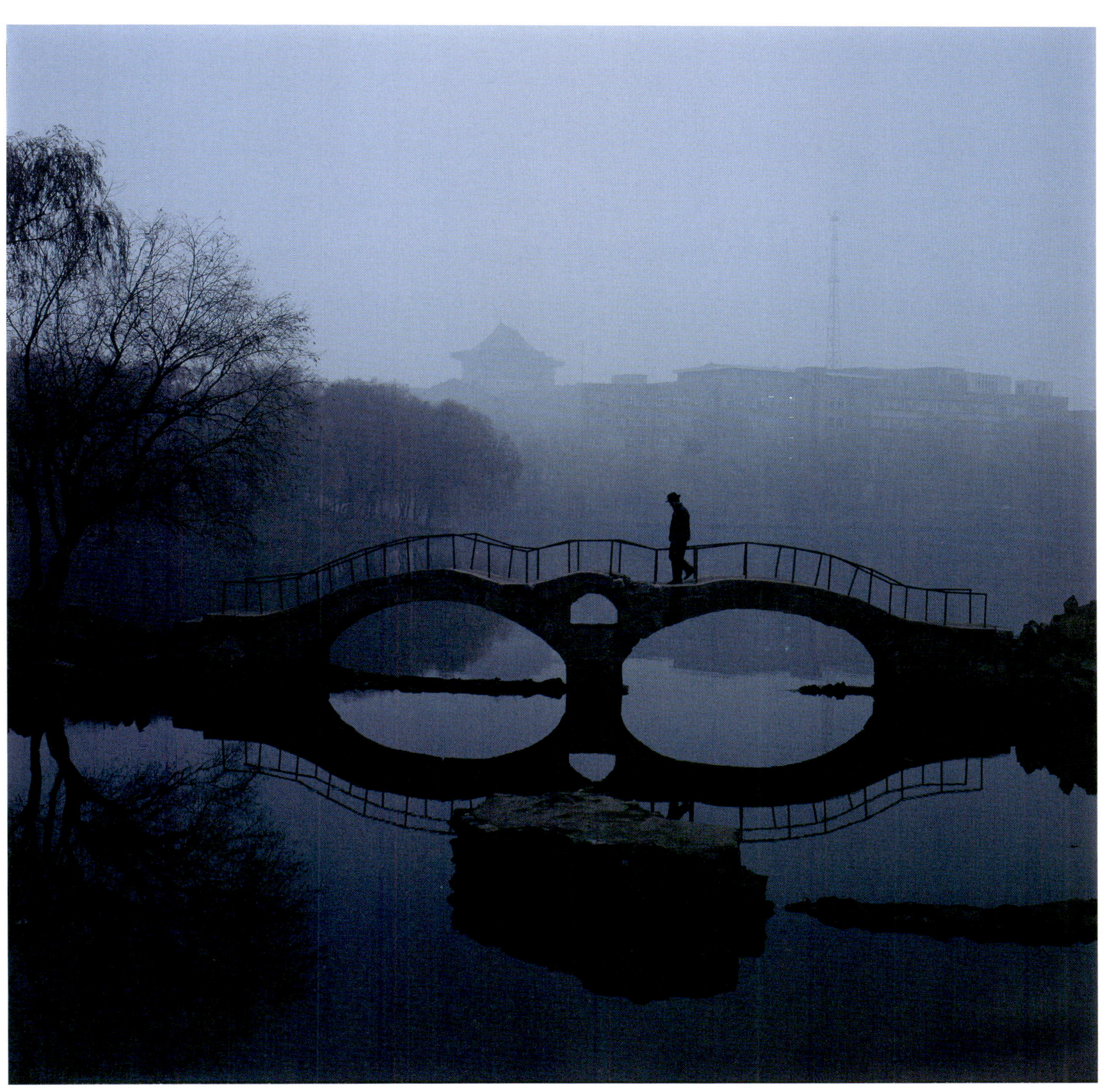

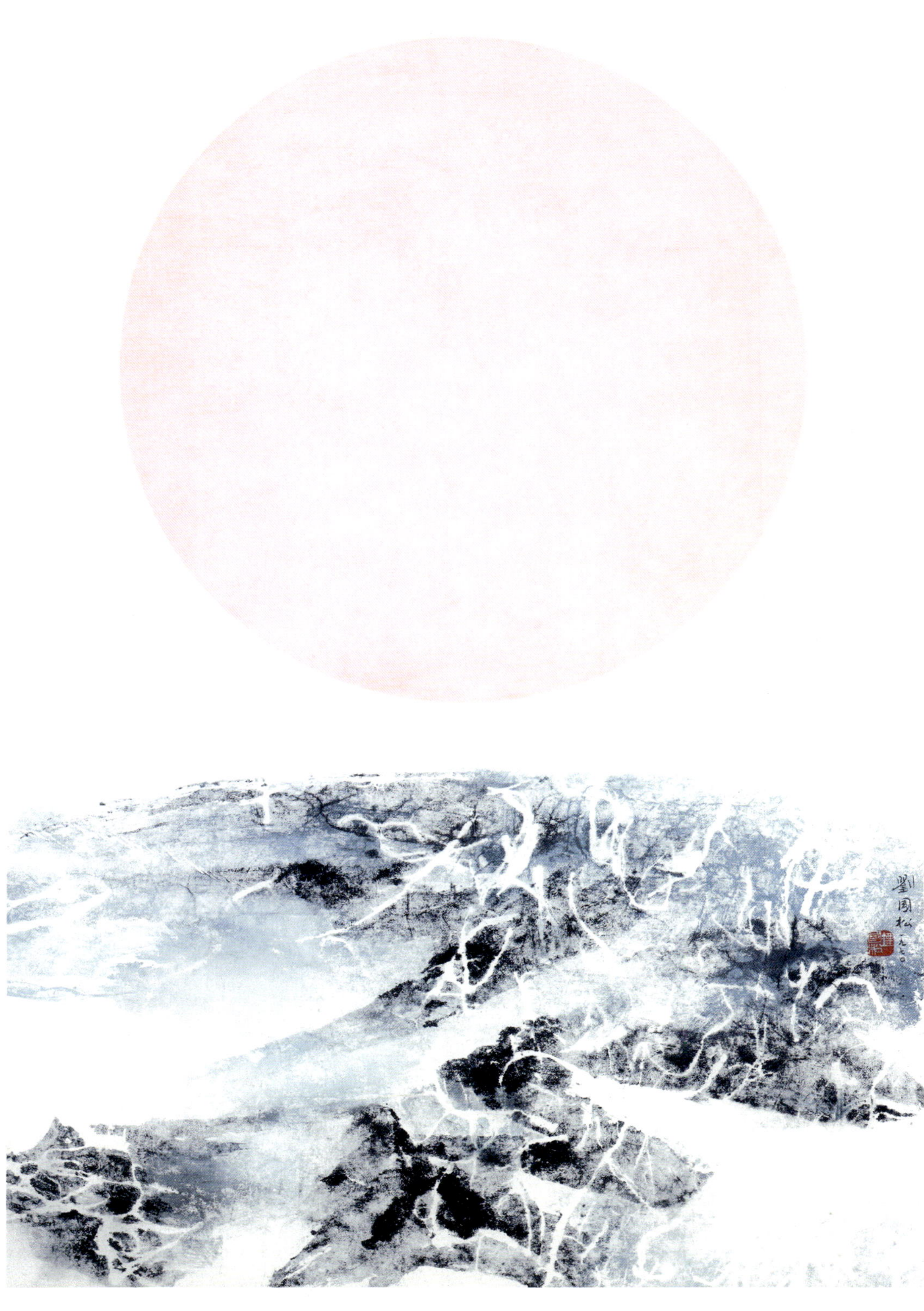

Liu Guosong, *Moon Series: It'll Soon Be White All Over*, 1970

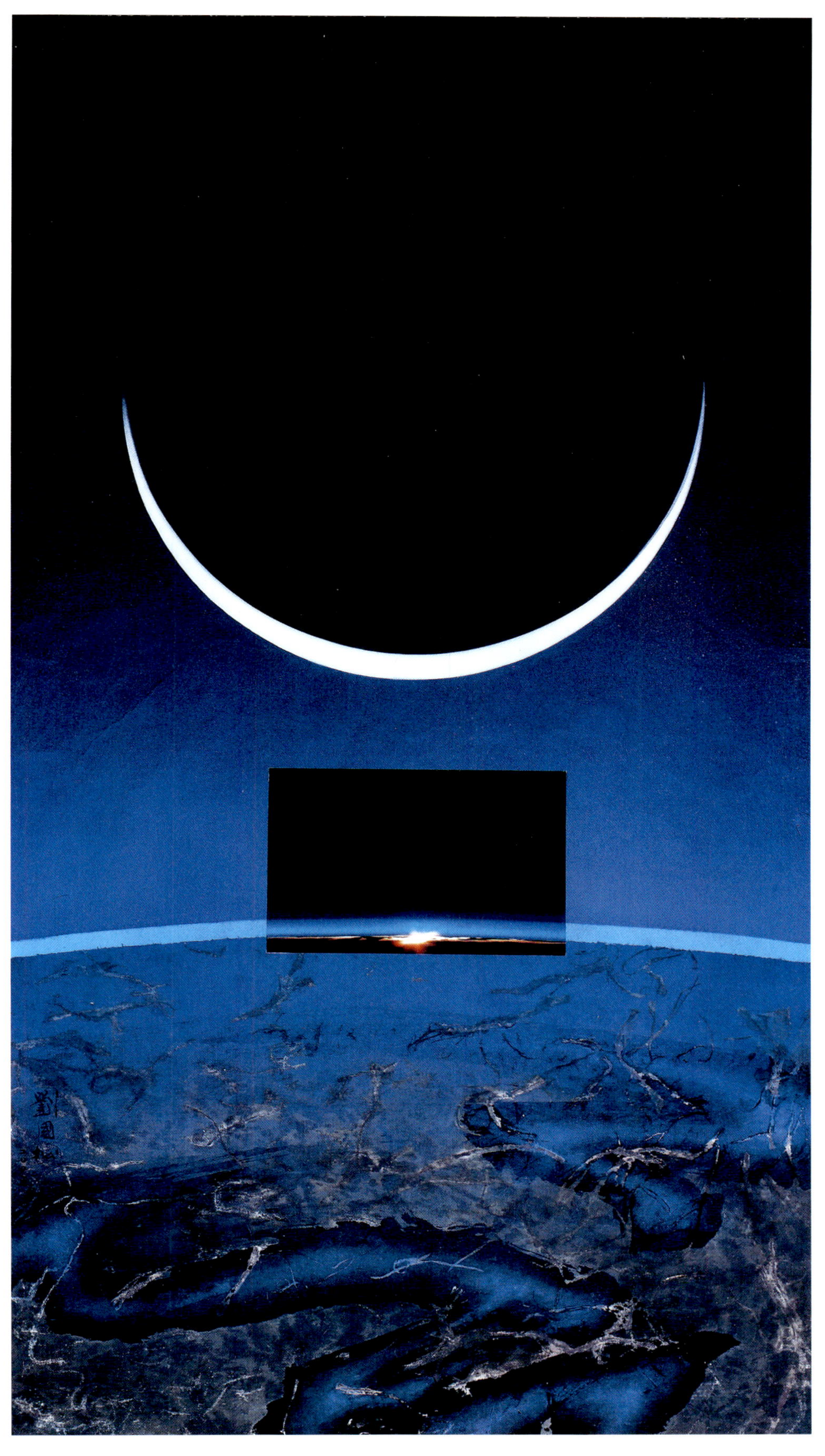

Liu Guosong, *Moon Series: Daybreak*, 2005

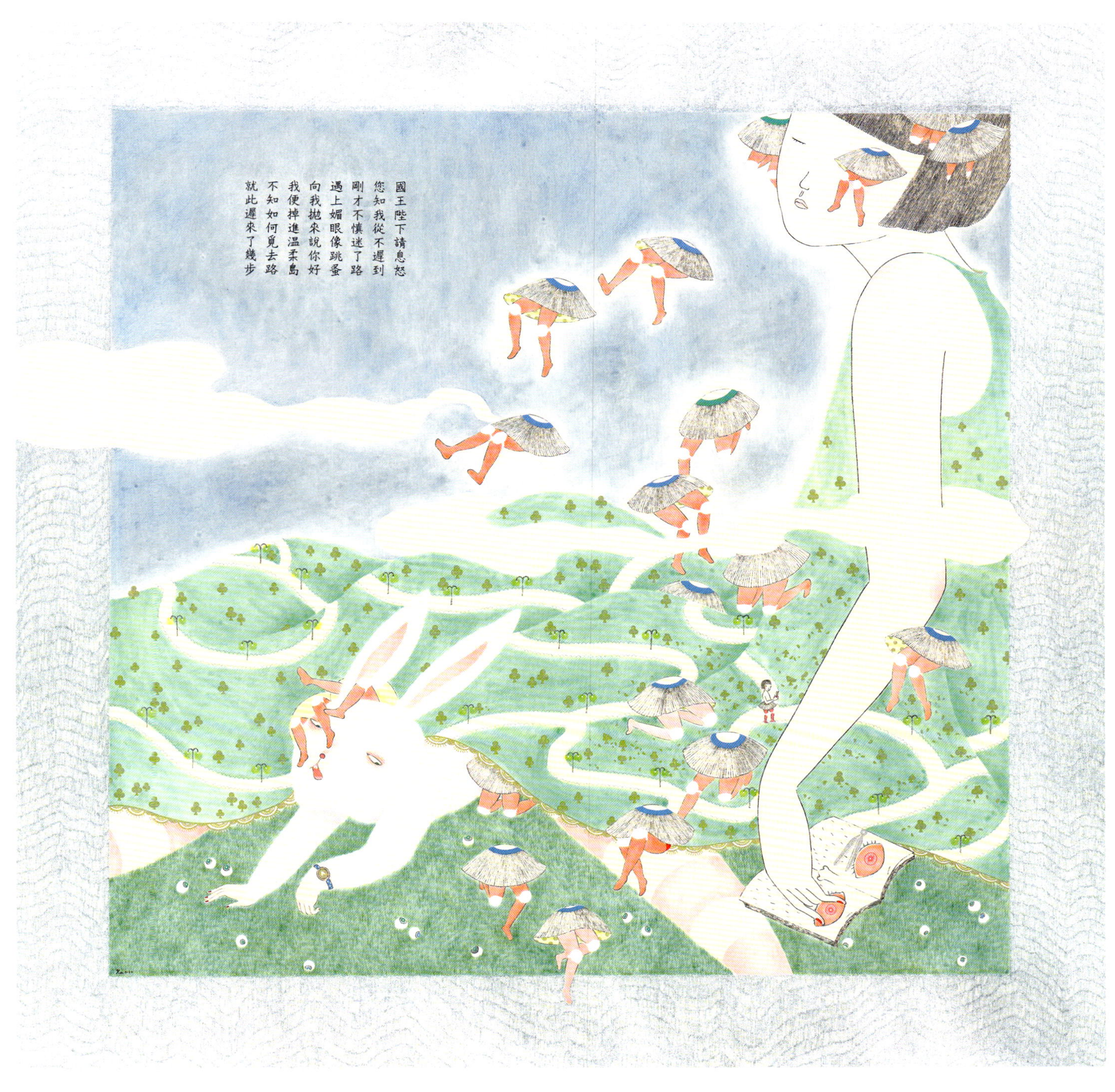

Joey Leung Ka-yin, *Late Rabbit*, 2010

Huang Yan, *Chinese Shanshui Tattoo Series No. 7*, 1999

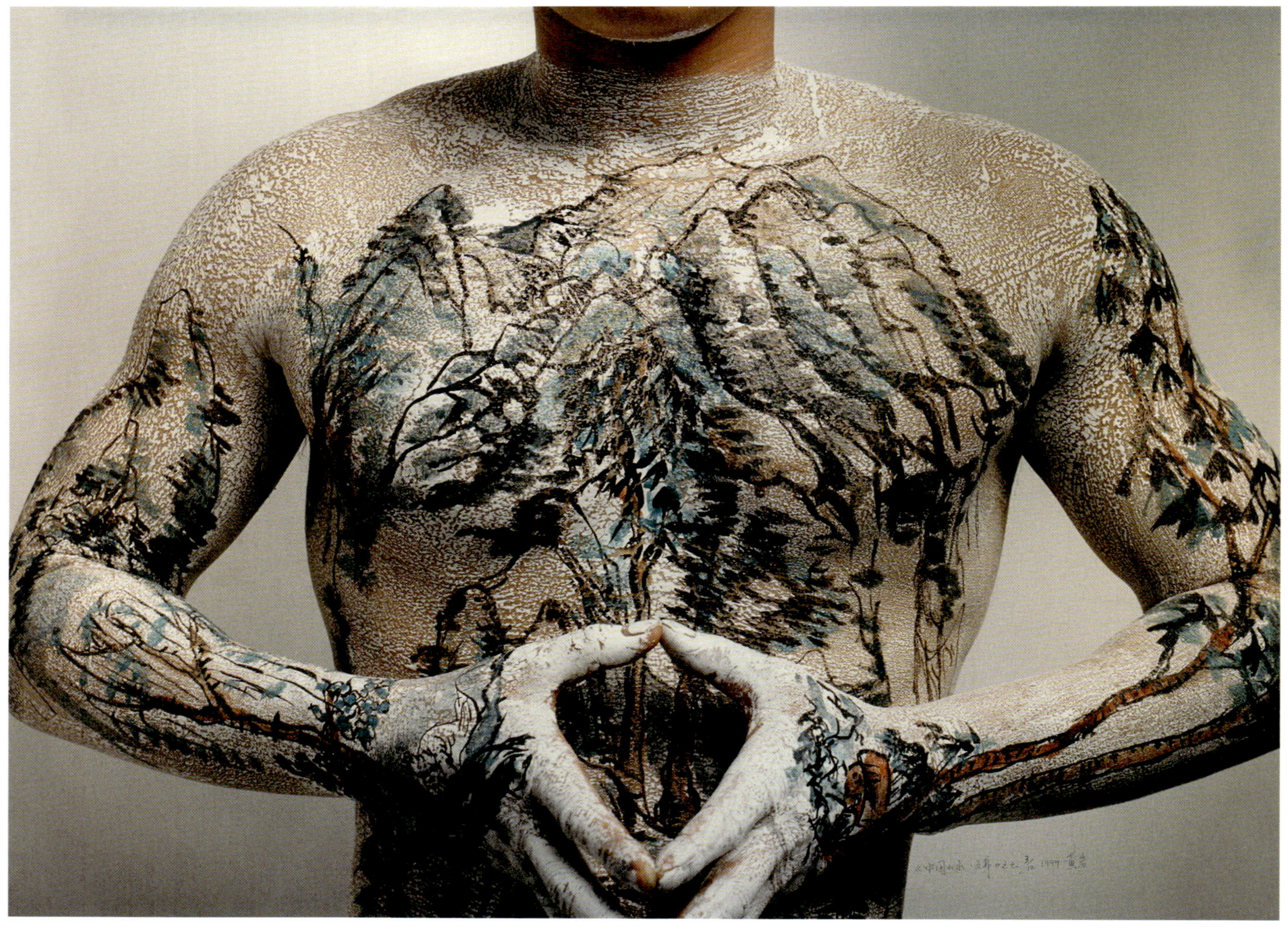

Kim Ho-deuk, *San, San* (*Mountain, Mountain*), 2018

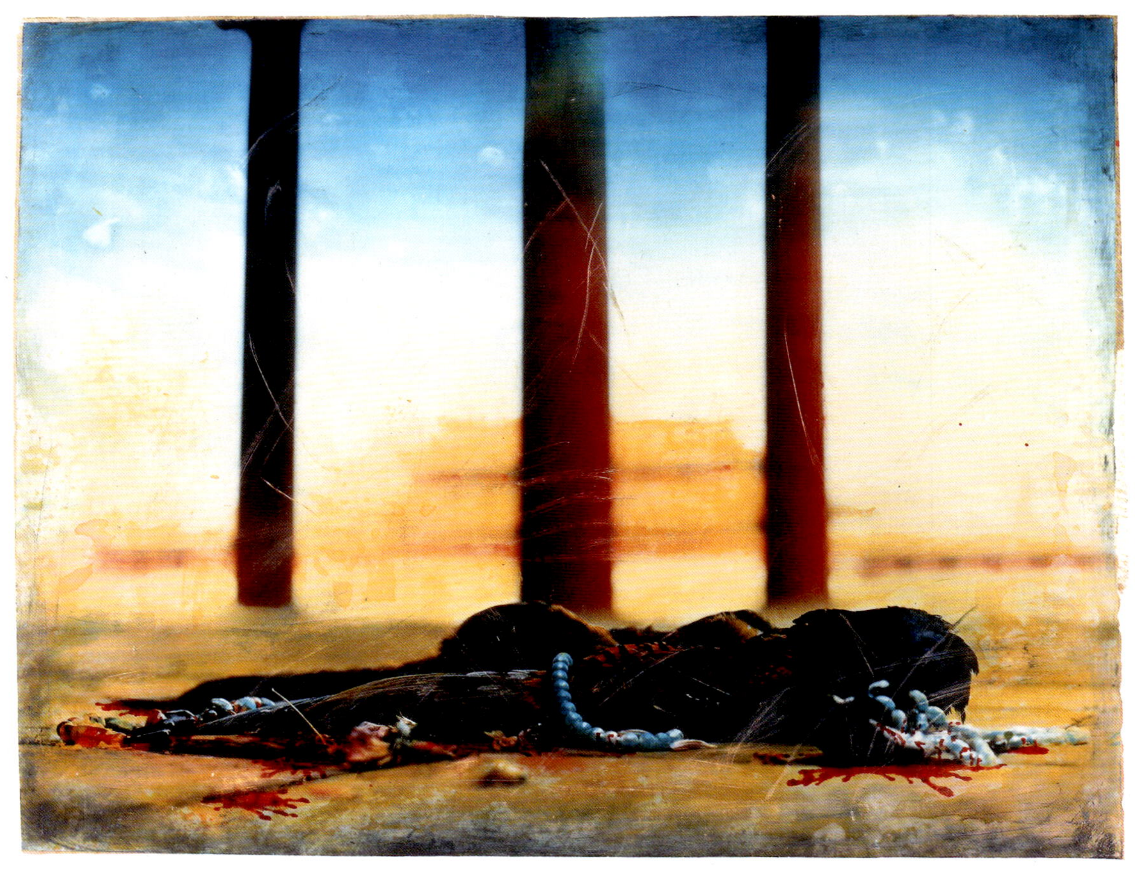

Hong Lei, *Autumn in the Forbidden City (West Veranda)*, 1997

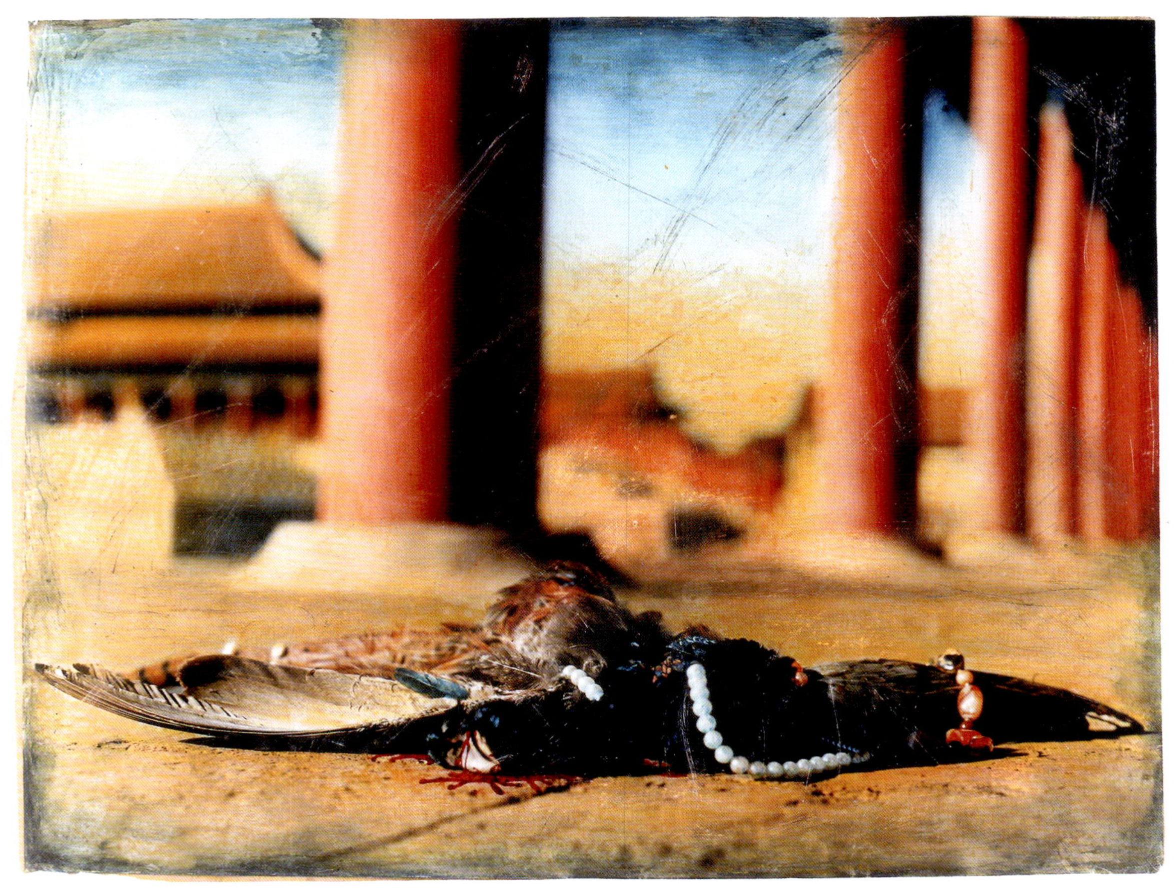

10/10 紫禁城的秋天（太和殿東迴廊） 1997 洪磊

Hong Lei, *Autumn in the Forbidden City (East Veranda)*, 1997

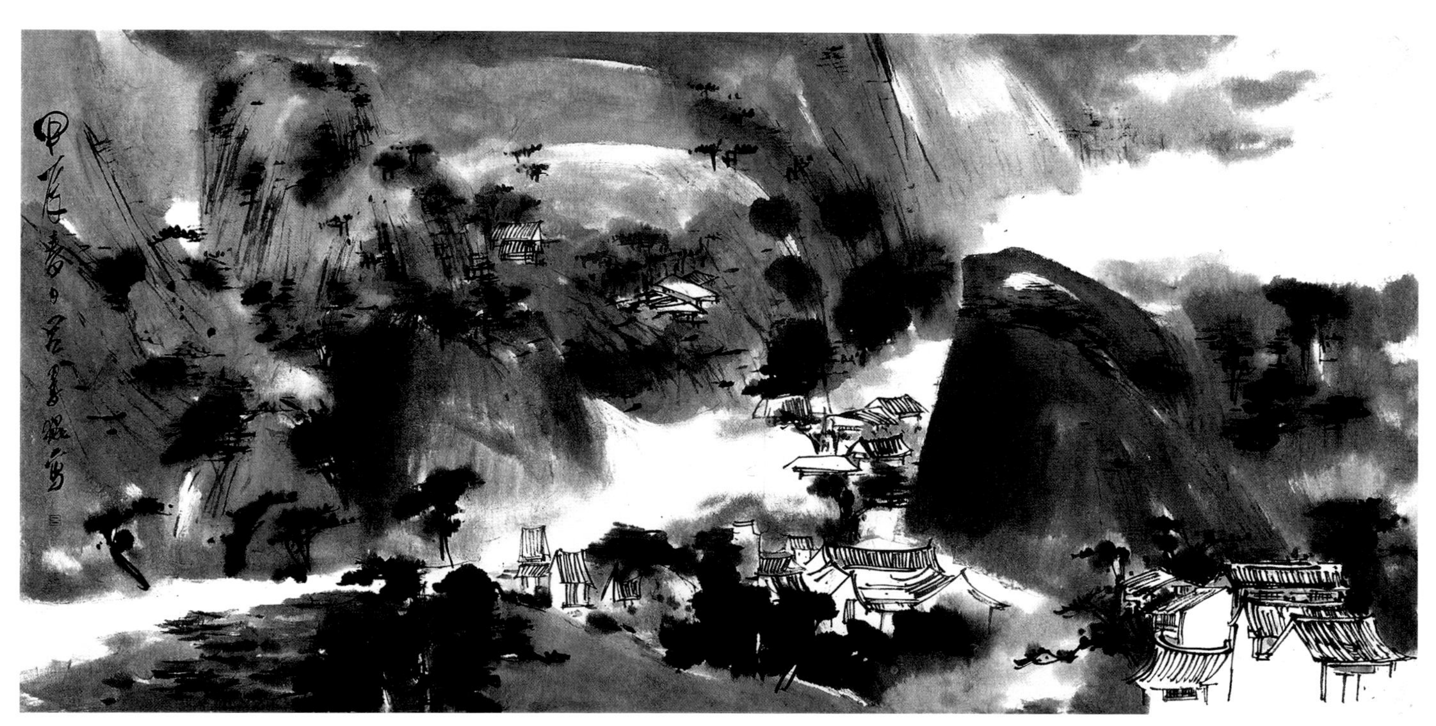

Lui Shou-kwan, *Wood Houses in the Mountains*, 1964

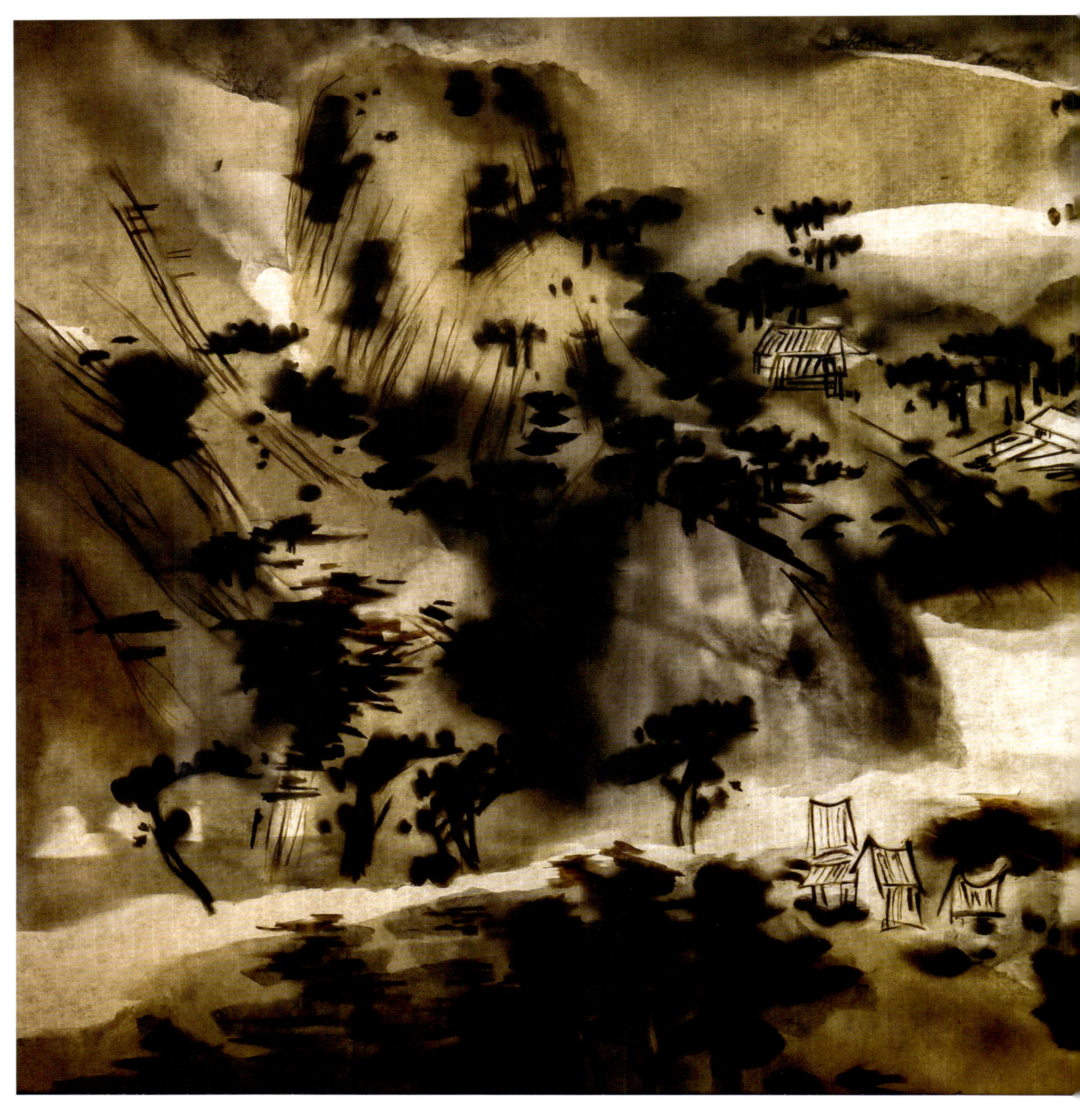

Xu Bing, *Background Story: Ink Variation (from Lui Shou-kwan)*, 2016

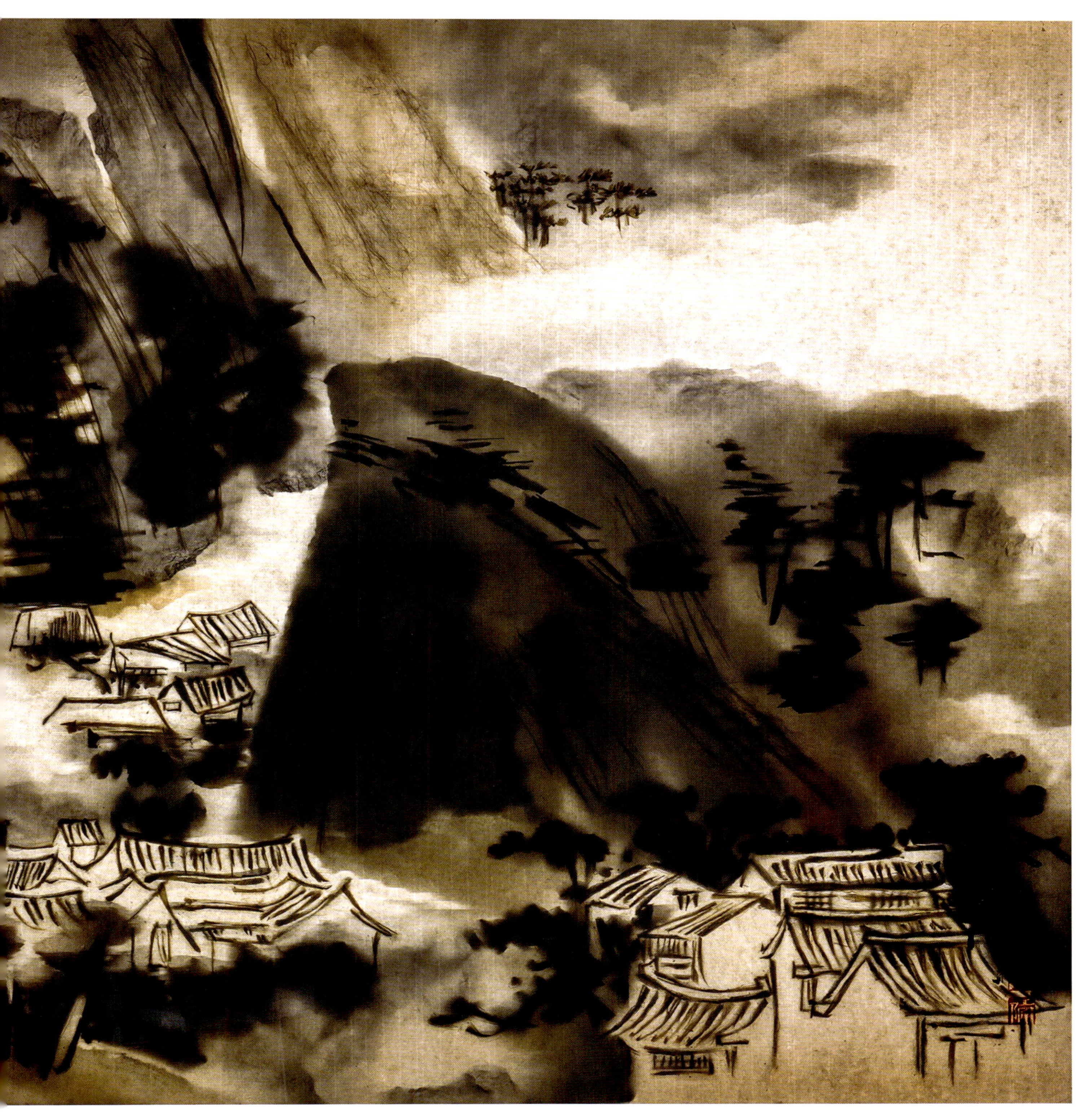

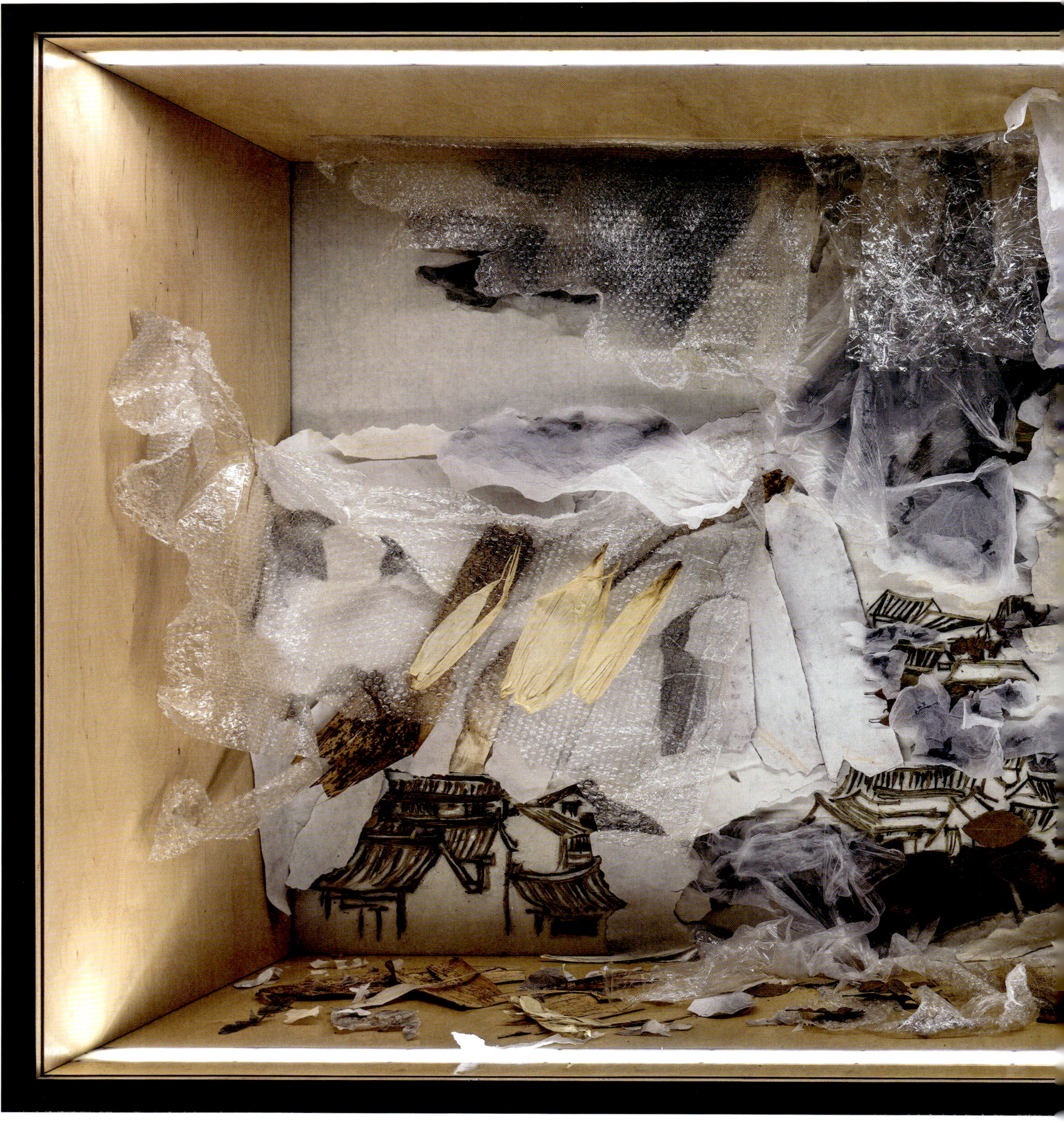

Xu Bing, *Background Story: Ink Variation (from Lui Shou-kwan)*, 2016

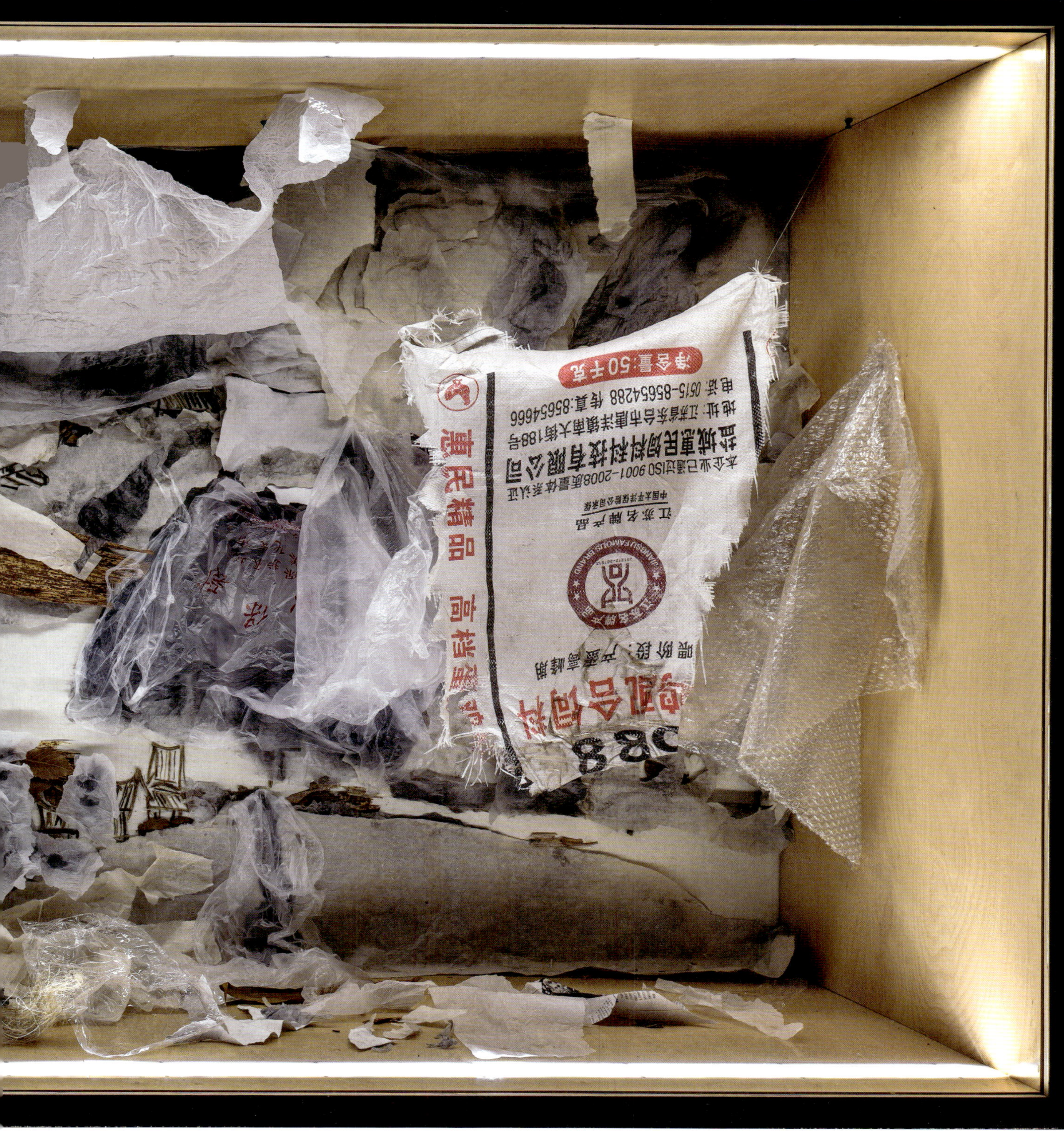
净含量:50千克
电话:0515-85654288 传真:85654666
地址:江苏省东台市唐洋镇南大街188号
盐城惠民饲料科技有限公司
本企业已通过ISO 9001-2008质量体系认证
江苏名牌产品
JIANGSU FAMOUS BRAND
惠民精品

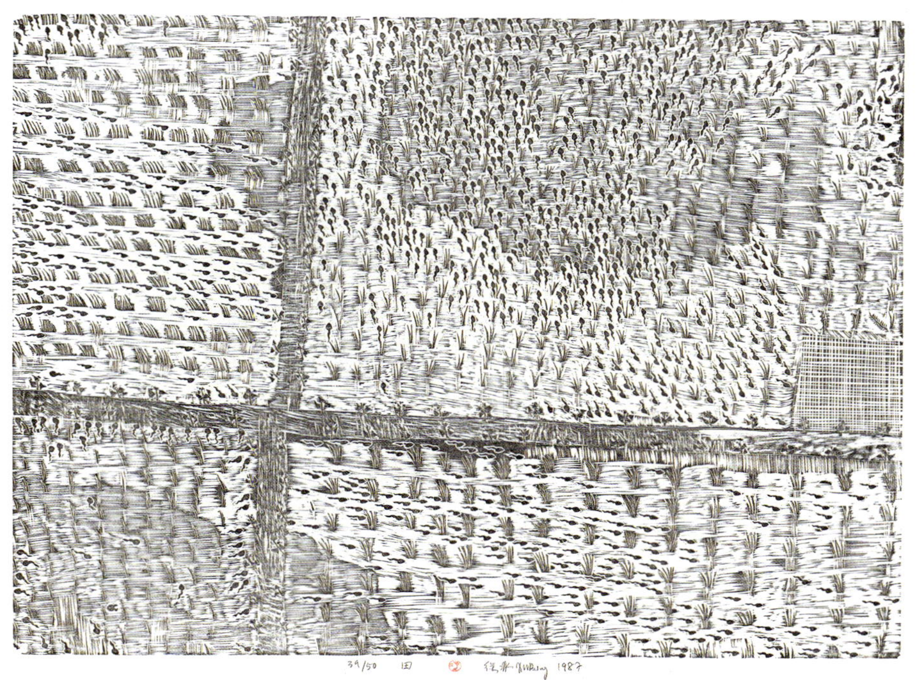

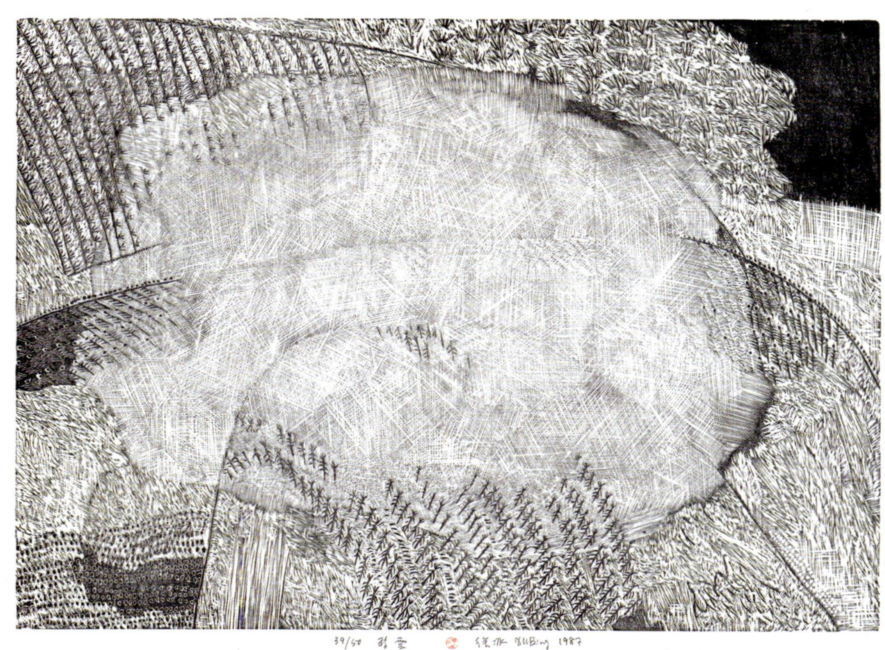

Xu Bing, *Field (from the Fives Series of Repetition)*, 1987
Xu Bing, *Moving Cloud (from the Fives Series of Repetition)*, 1987

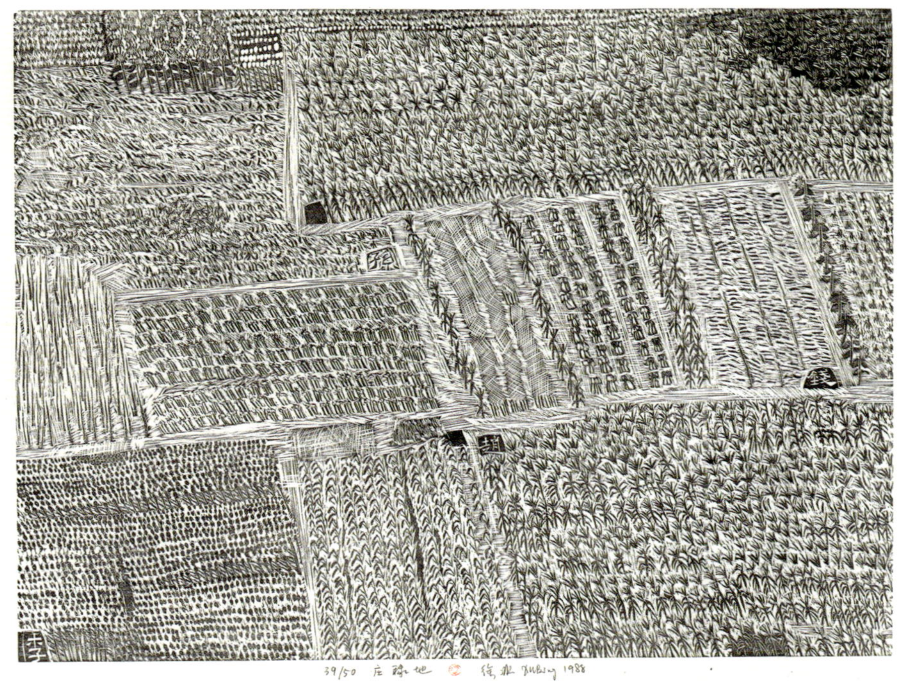

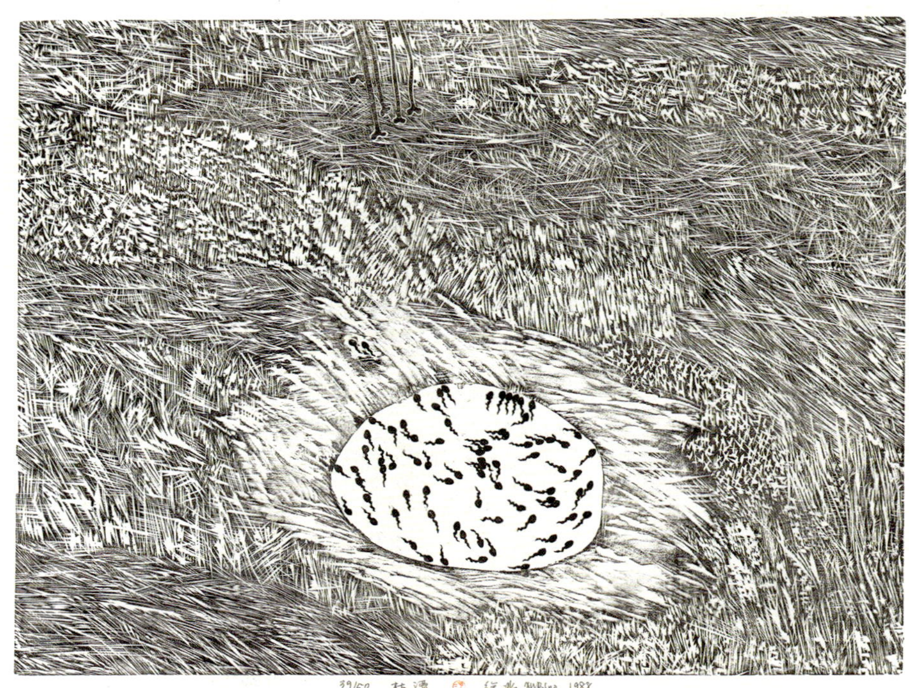

Xu Bing, *Farmland (from the Fives Series of Repetition)*, 1987
Xu Bing, *Withered Pool (from the Fives Series of Repetition)*, 1987

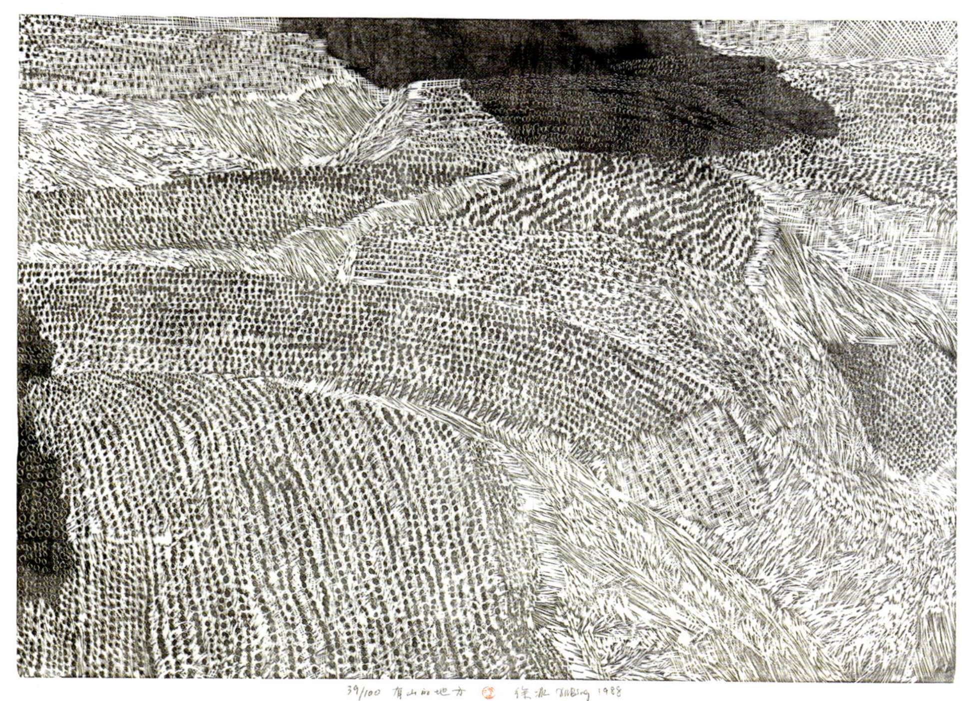

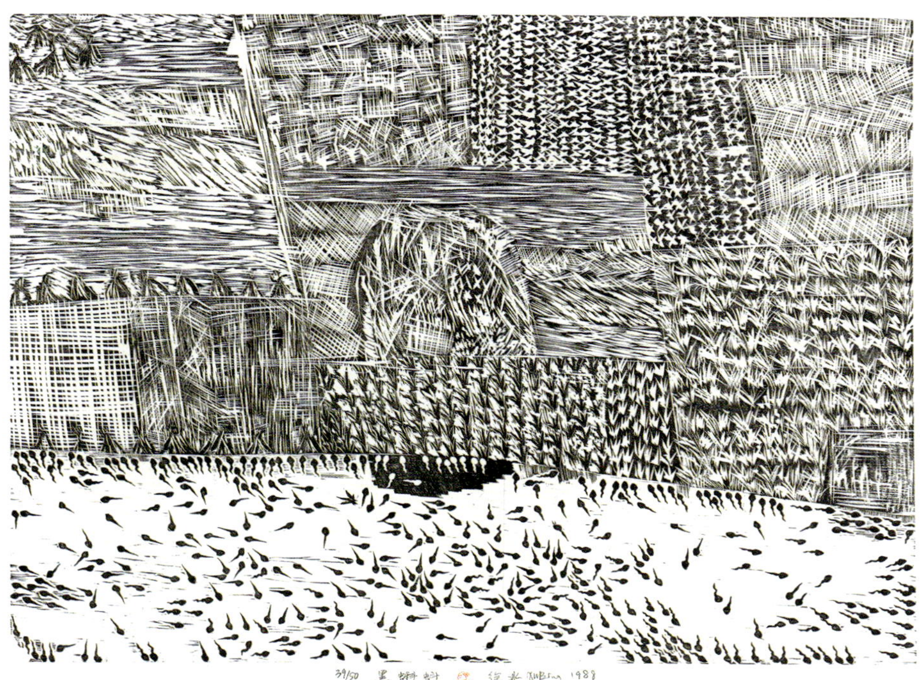

Xu Bing, *Mountain Place (from the Fives Series of Repetition)*, 1987
Xu Bing, *Black Tadpoles (from the Fives Series of Repetition)*, 1987

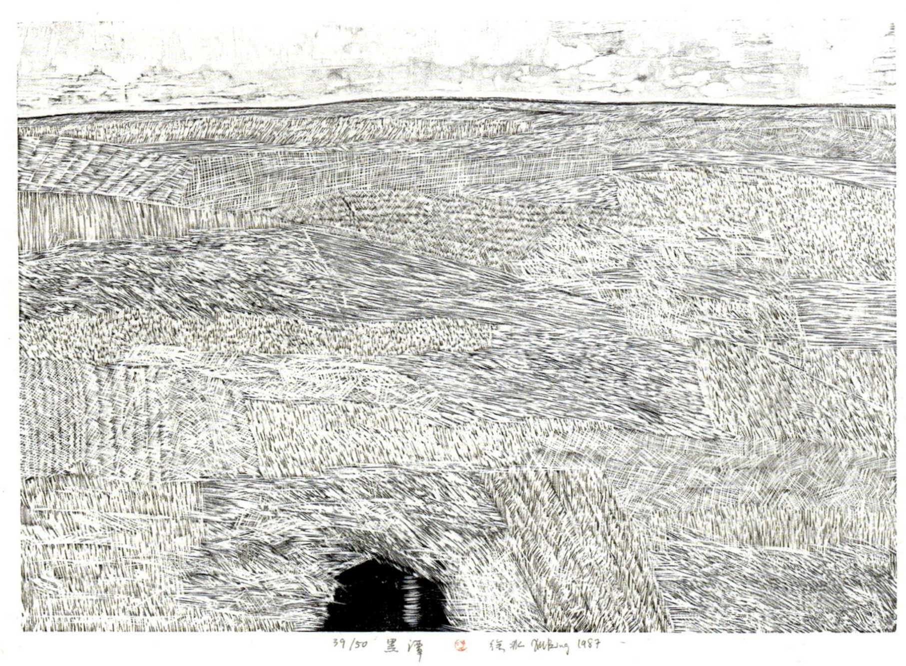

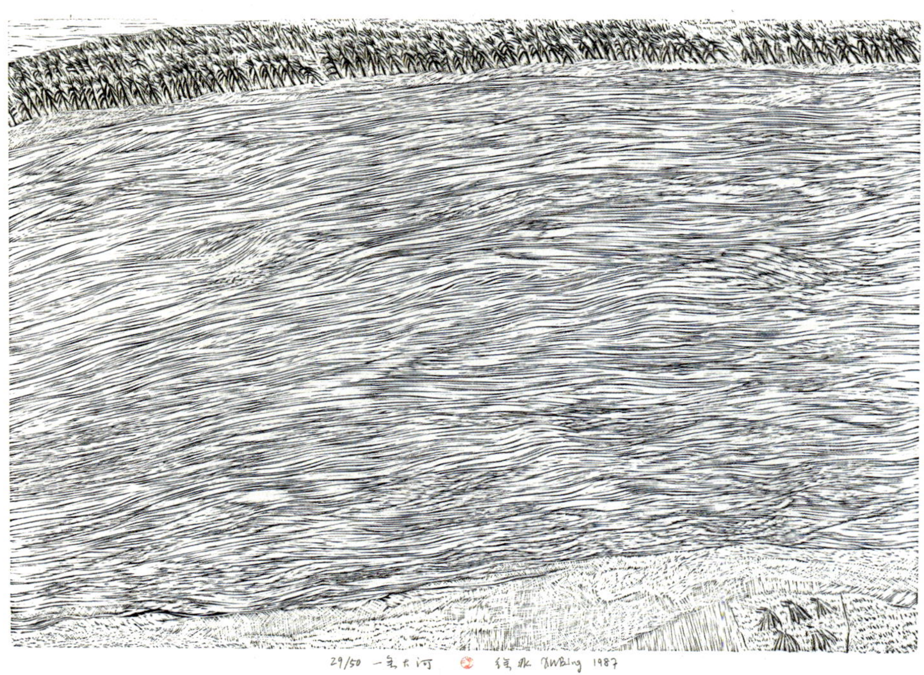

Xu Bing, *Black Pool (from the Fives Series of Repetition)*, 1987
Xu Bing, *Big River (from the Fives Series of Repetition)*, 1987

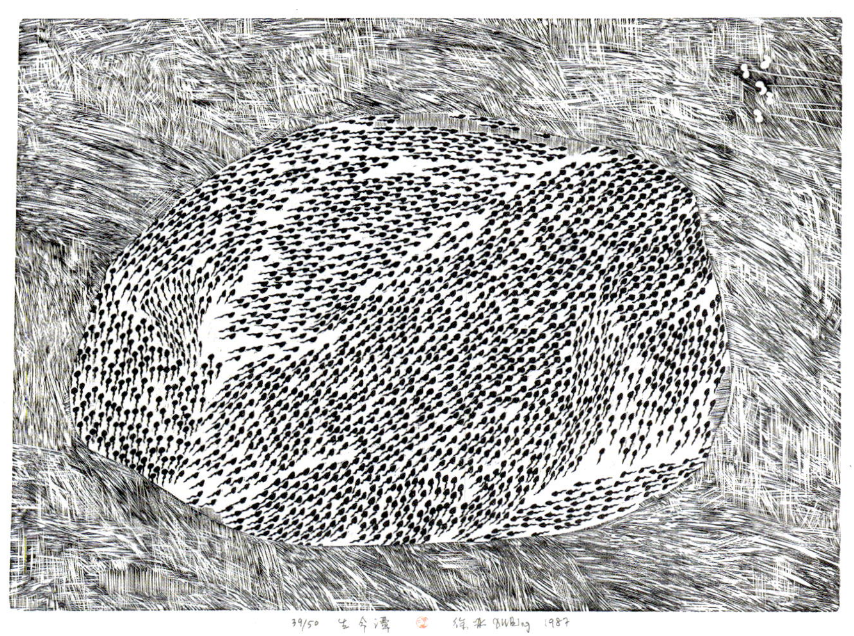

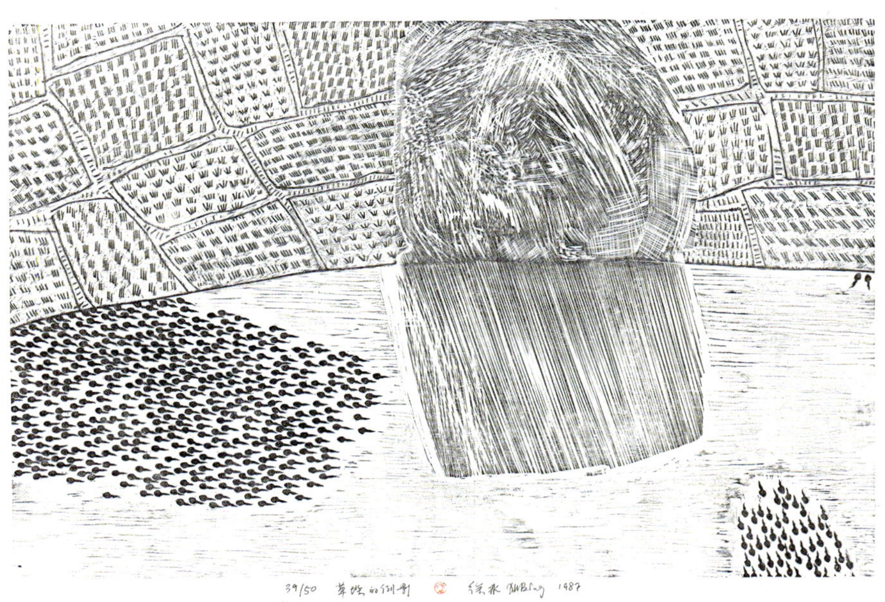

Xu Bing, *Pool of Life (from the Fives Series of Repetition)*, 1987
Xu Bing, *Haystack Reflection (from the Fives Series of Repetition)*, 1987

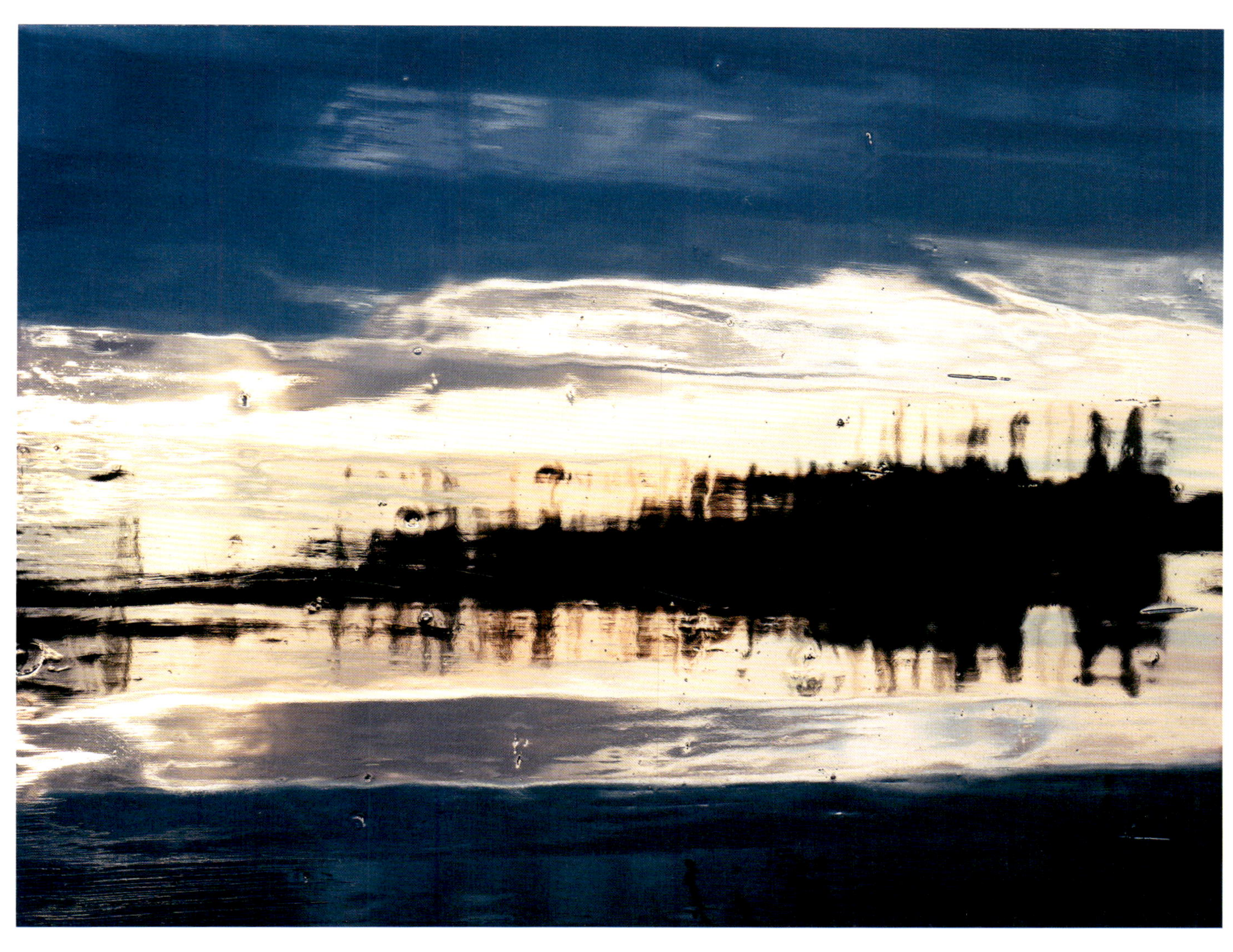

Jorma Puranen, *Icy Prospects # 20*, 2009

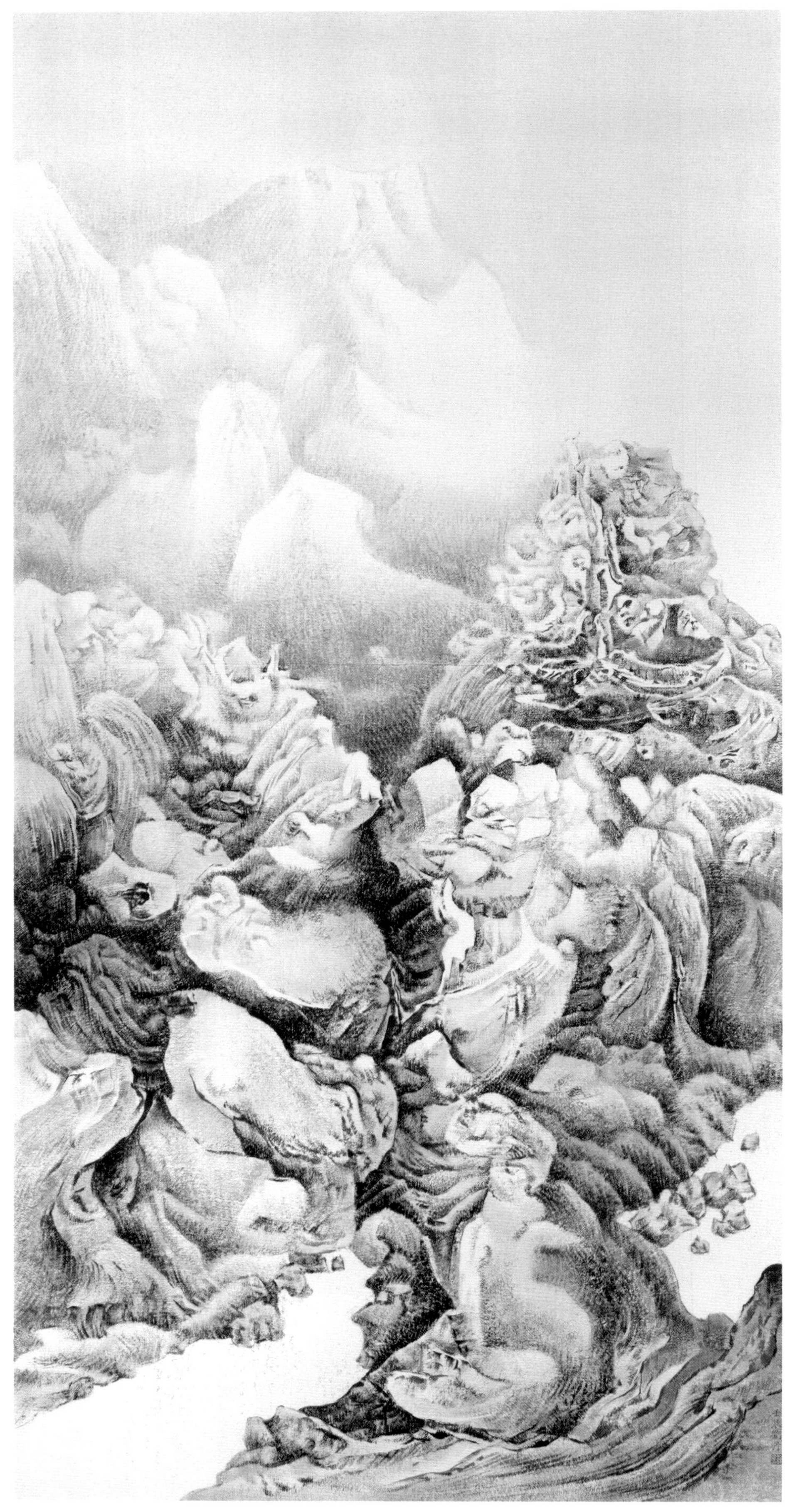

Liu Dan, *Untitled*, 2012

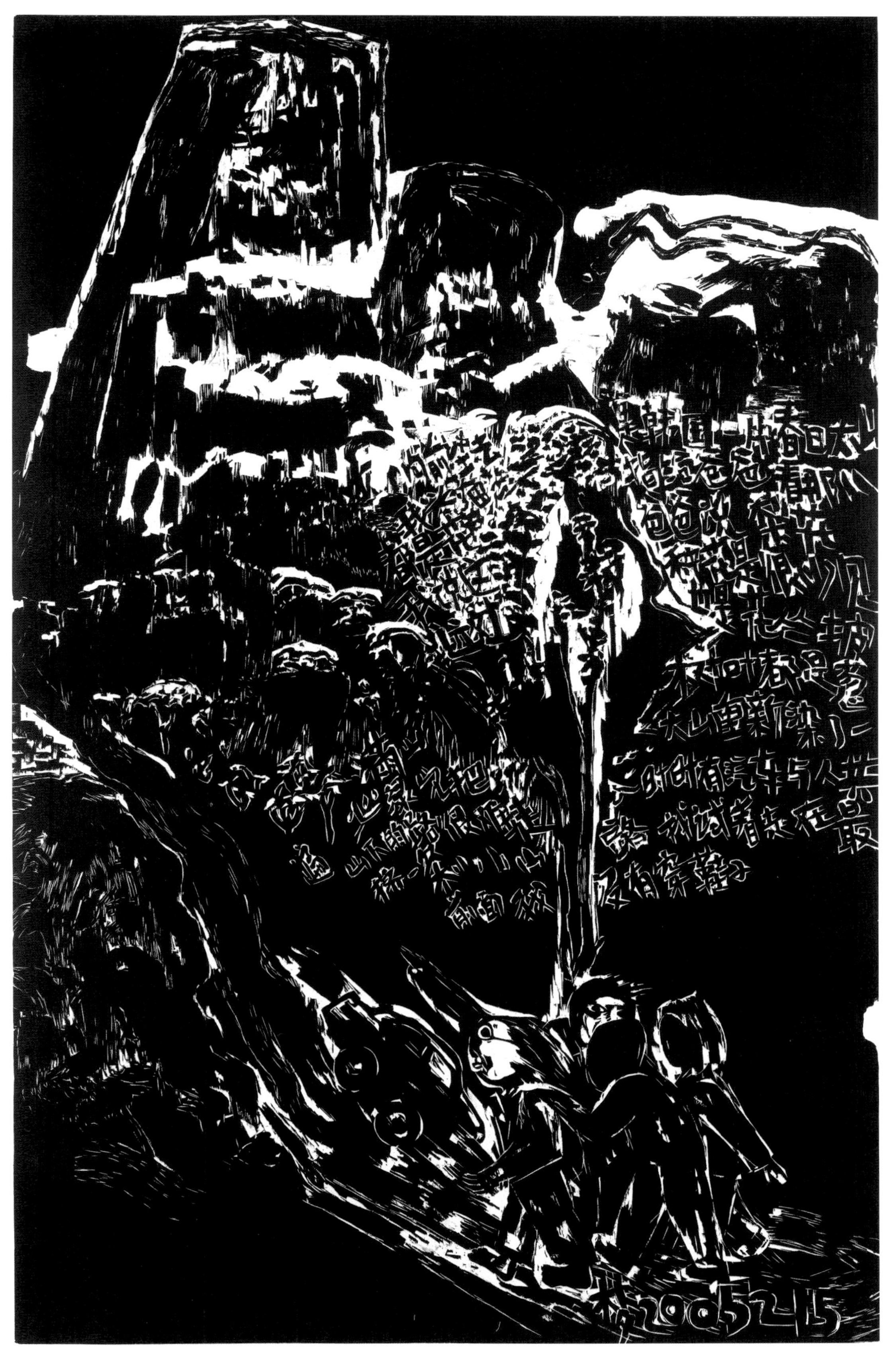

Chen Haiyan, *Dream 2005.2.15, Mountains, Flowers, Crowded People and Cars*, 2009

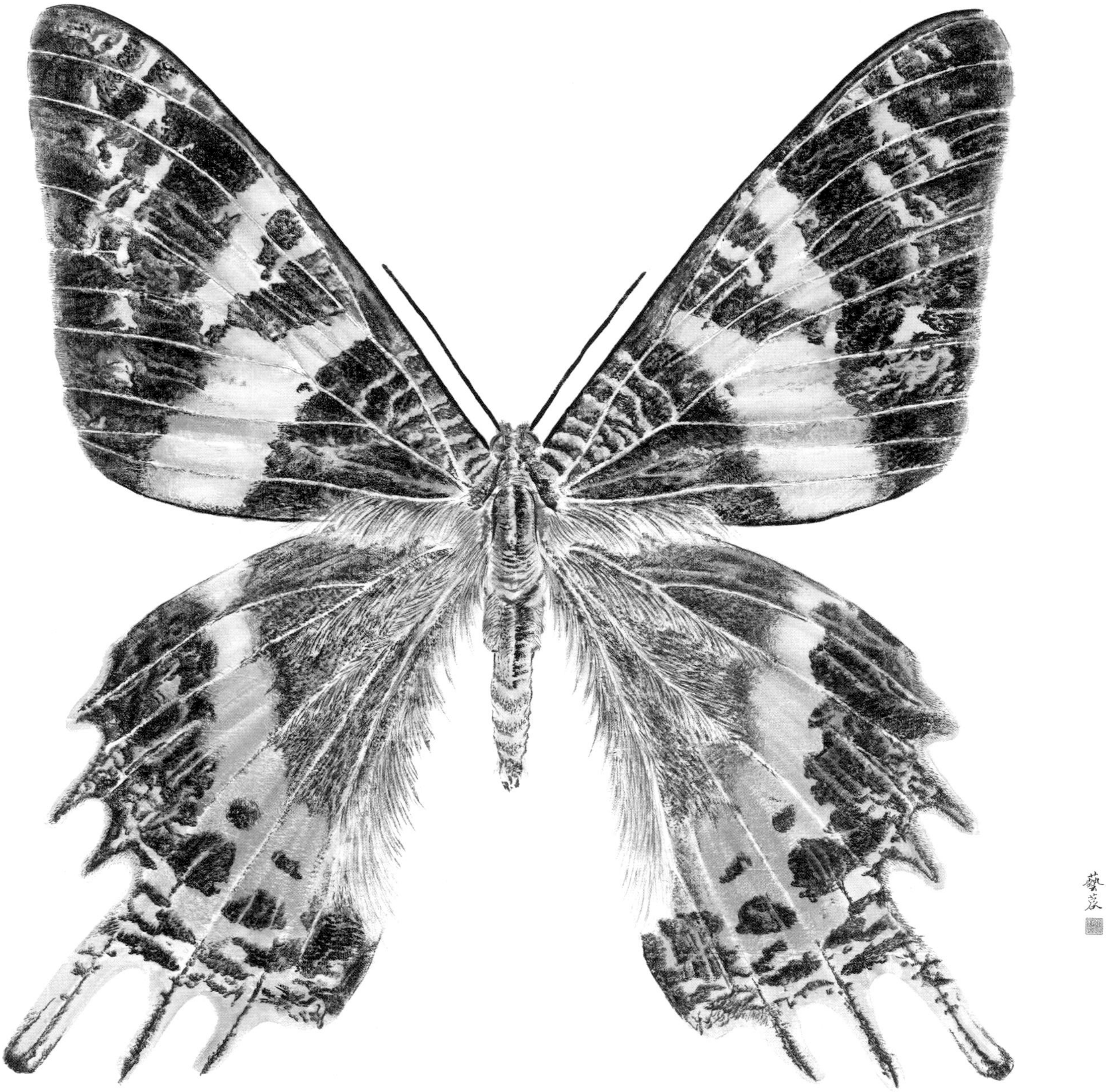

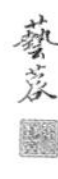

Zhang Yirong, *Butterfly Adrift Lakes and Hills*, 2017

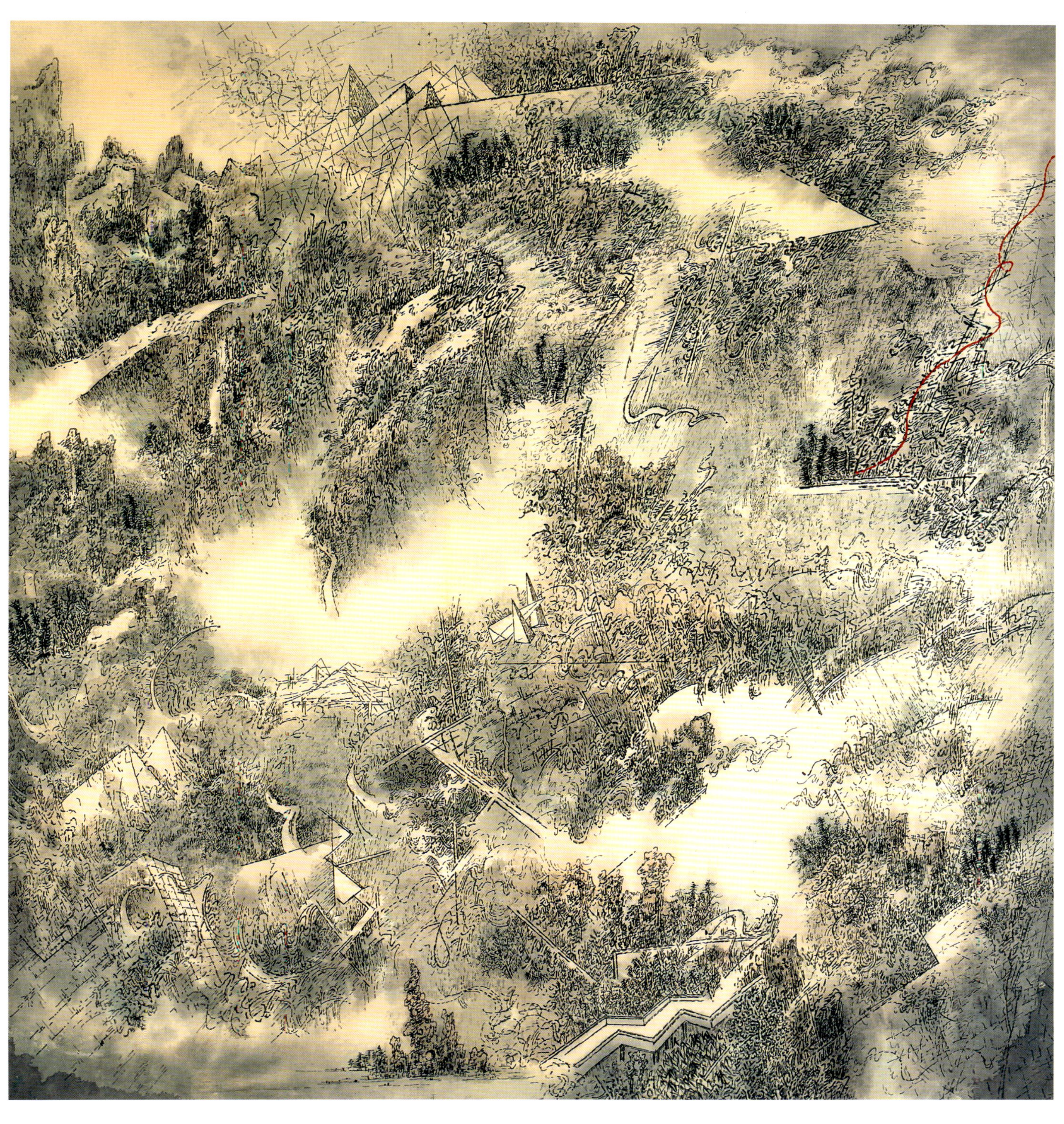

Leung Kui-ting, *Vision 08*, 2008

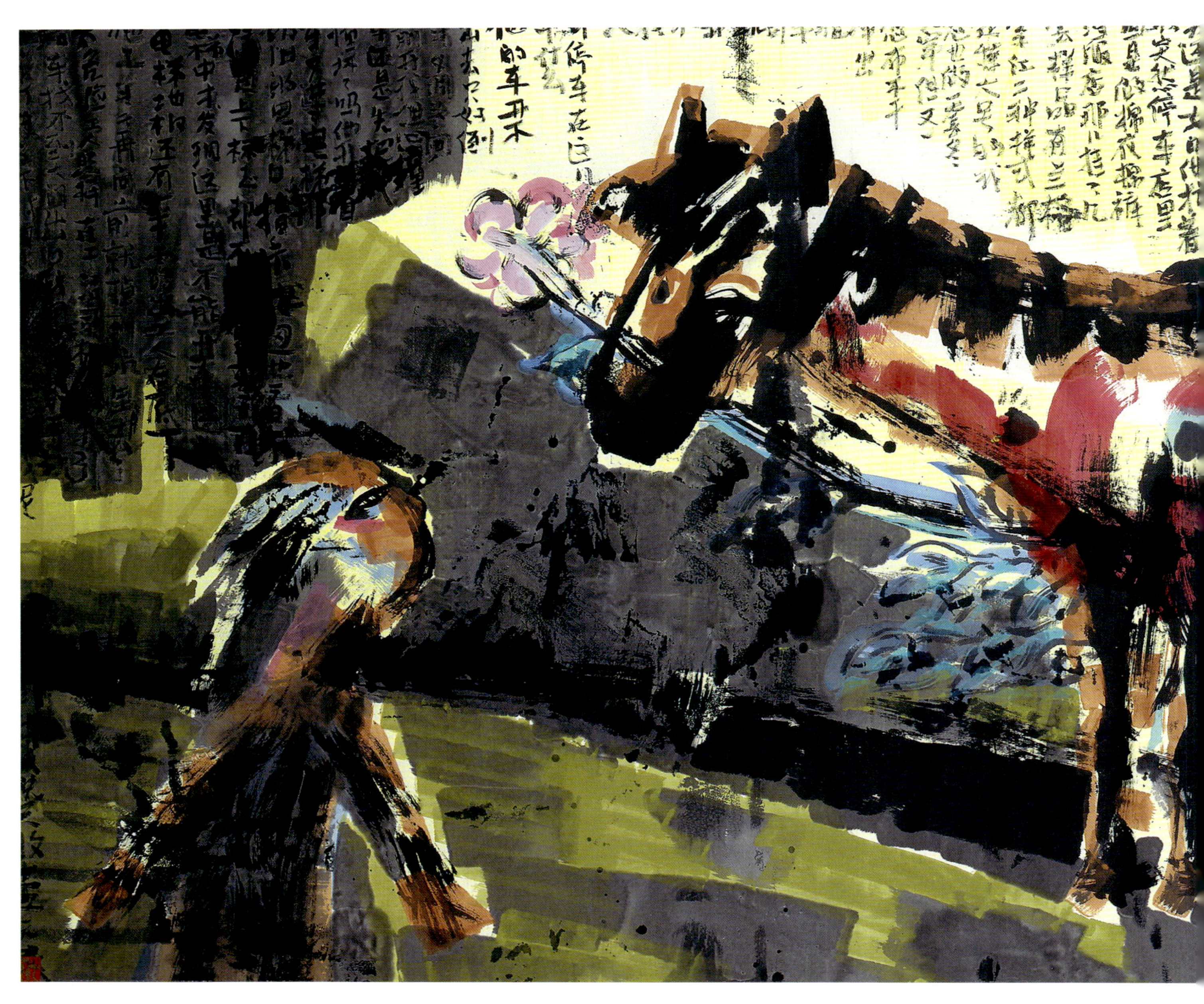

Chen Haiyan, *Horse and Rose*, 2005

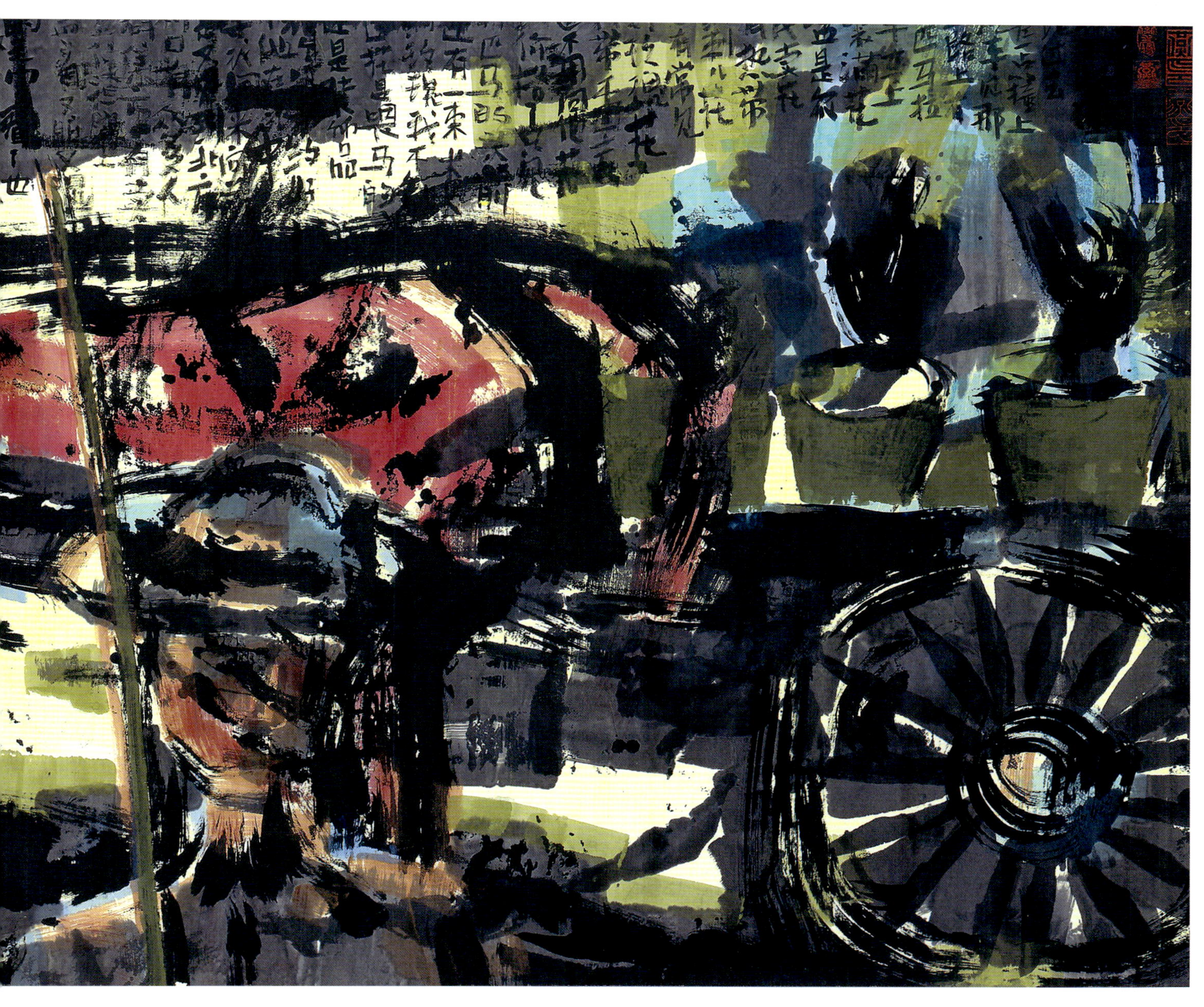

Chu Ko, *The Dreaming Clouds of Wu Mountains*, 2005

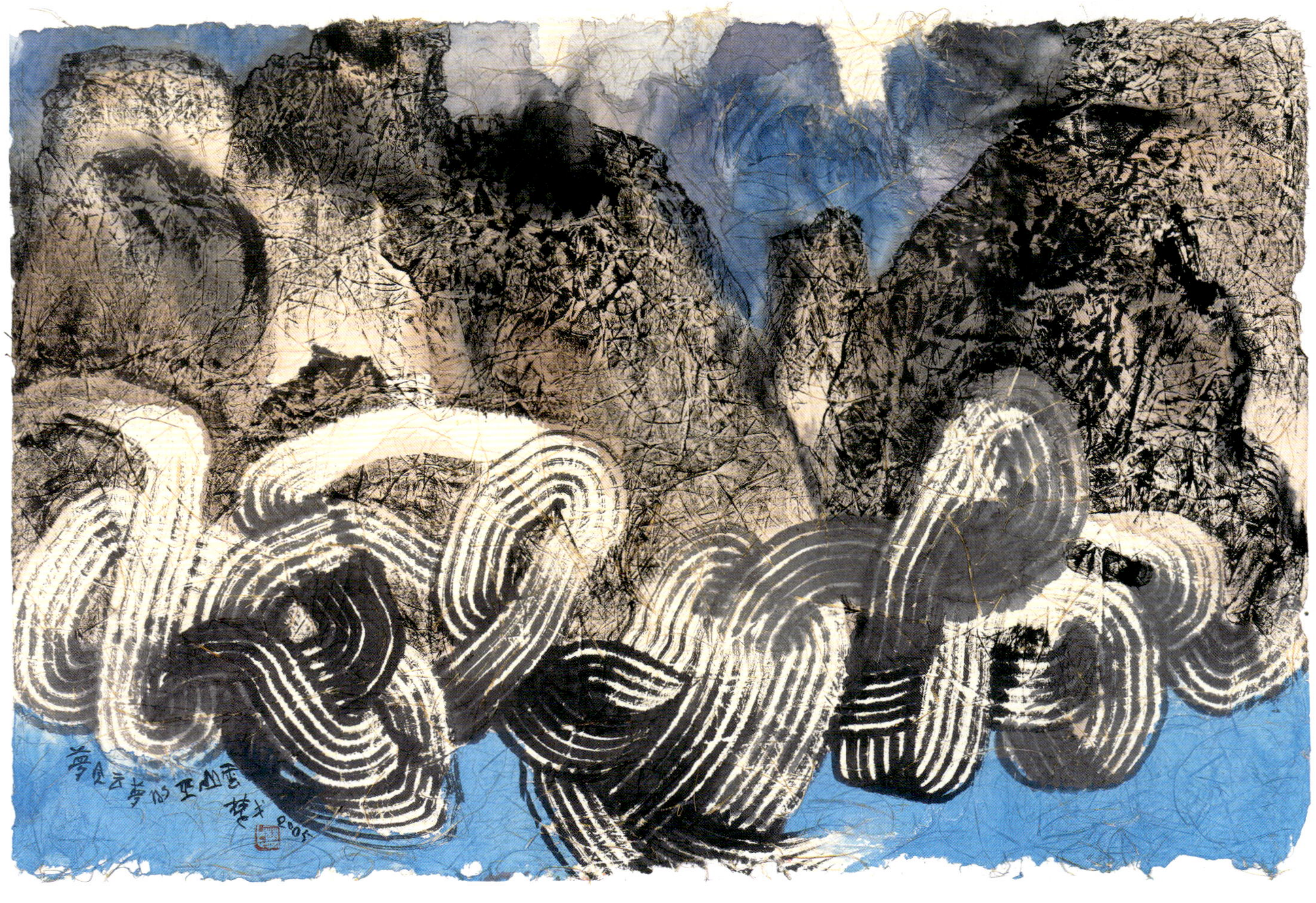

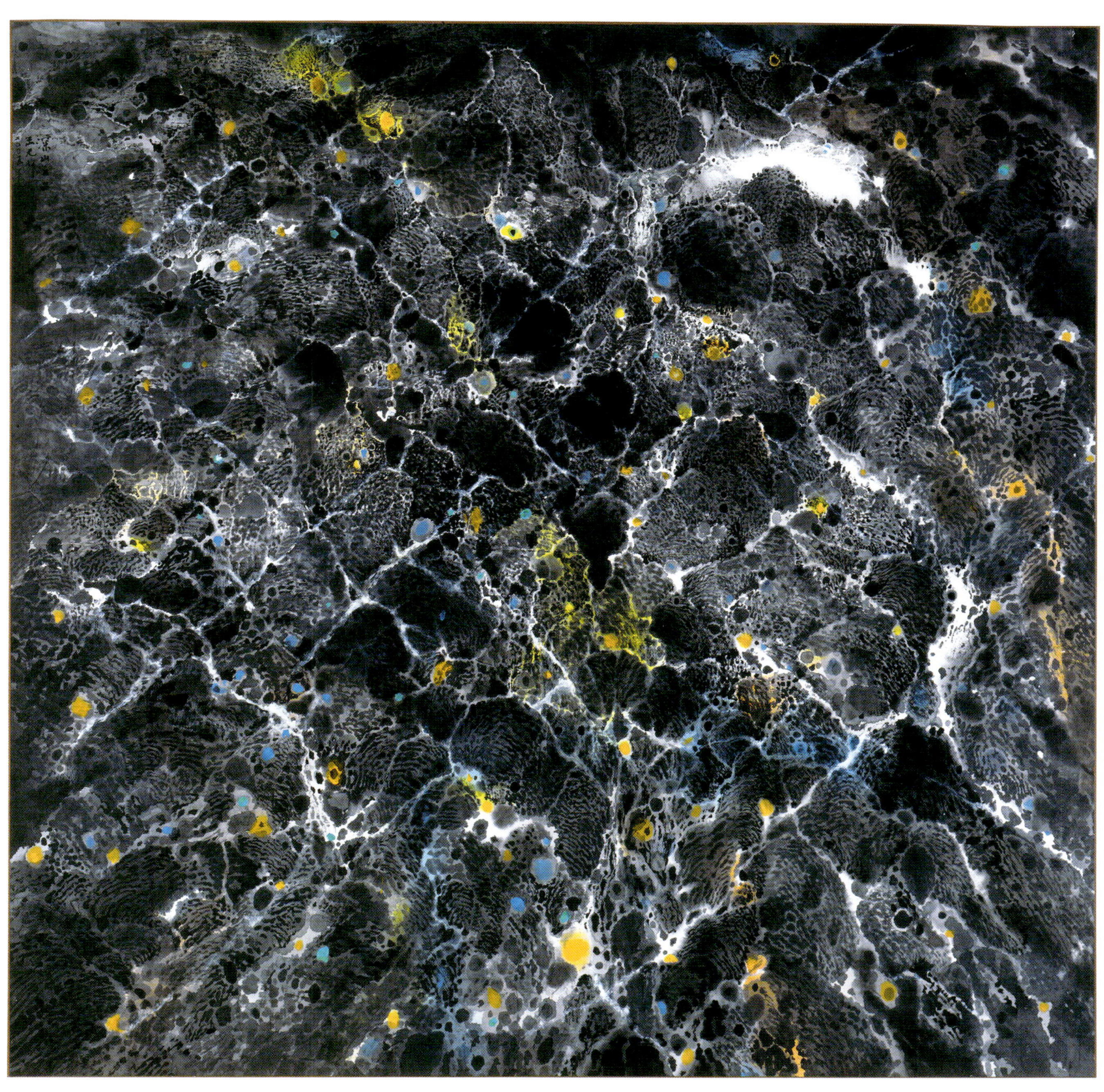

Wucius Wong, *Deep in the Mountains #2*, 2005

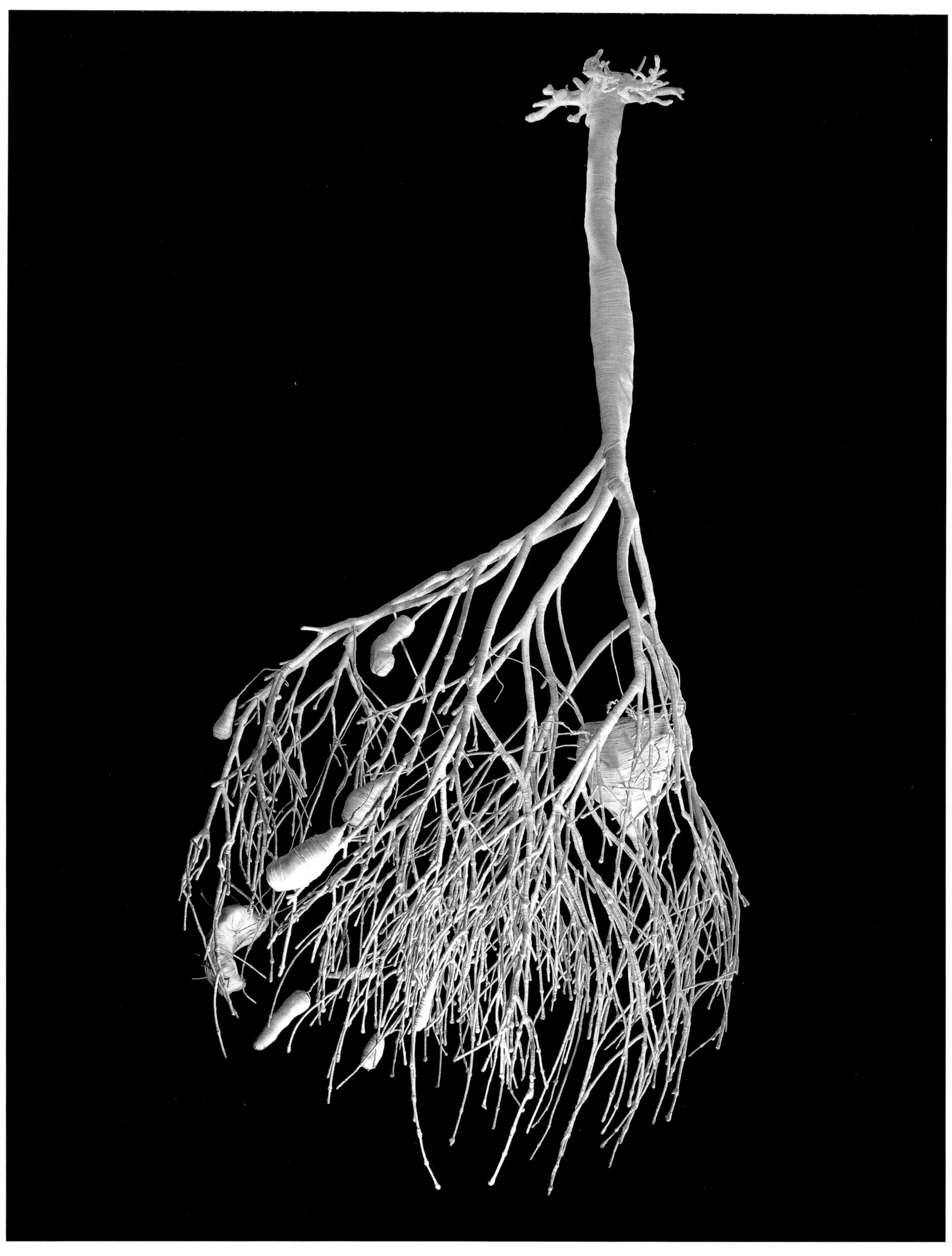

Lin Tianmiao, *The Tree*, 2010

Conclusion In 1985, art critic Li Xiaoshan declared in a highly controversial article, first published in *Jiangsu Pictorial* and later circulated further in *China Fine Arts Weekly*, that Chinese ink painting had reached a dead end—that it did not have a presence in the world of contemporary art, eclipsed in the zeitgeist of the '85 New Wave movement[12] and its penchant for Western mediums. But 1985 marked neither the end nor the reinvention of ink art, for the foundation of contemporary ink art practice is centuries in the making. Just as oil painting had an already centuries-old history in Western art—and was persevering—its foil of ink painting proved persistent. It is not the similarities between ink and Western modernism or global contemporary art practice that sustain the genre's liveliness, but the continuous growth and development of its indelible qualities.

Through these three paradigms of historical ink art, *Ink Dreams* explores the implications of what it means to be "ink" in the contemporary art world. It is neither the material makeup of the genre—ink, brush, and paper—nor the place of origin that defines a contemporary ink artwork, but an engagement with established subjects and aesthetics, three exemplary precedents being meditations, apparitions, and dreamscapes as described above.

To transition the field of ink art into contemporary times requires a revision of the way the genre is defined, as its current context is strikingly different from that of its historical origins. One must consider what has happened since the introduction of Chan painting, *wangliang-hua*, and the literati landscape: the expansion of Buddhism across not only Asia but the entire world, the development of new mediums, the revolutionary impact of the internet and its exponential expansion of cross-cultural communication, the urbanizing physical landscape, among, of course, an overwhelming amount of cultural and artistic development that has occurred over the past two millennia.

This definition of what exemplifies contemporary ink art is neither finite nor complete, nor should it be—new discoveries, considerations, and exceptions can and will be made. For it is the spirit of ink, and not a prescribed set of rules, that has enabled the genre to endure.

12 A general term for the fervent artistic experimentation that occurred in China following the end of the Cultural Revolution, the subsequent loosening of artistic restrictions, and a massive influx of Western artistic influences and materials following the opening of China in the 1980s.

Bibliography

Baas, Jacquelynn. *Smile of the Buddha: Eastern Philosophy and Western Art from Monet to Today*. Berkeley: University of California Press, 2005.

Baas, Jacquelynn, and Mary Jane Jacob, eds. *Buddha Mind in Contemporary Art*. Berkeley: University of California Press, 2004.

Brinker, Helmut, and Hiroshi Kanezawa. *Zen Masters of Meditation in Images and Writings*. Zurich: Artibus Asiae and Museum Rietberg Zurich, 1996.

Bush, Susan. *The Chinese Literati on Painting: Su Shih (1037–1101) to Tung Ch'i-ch'ang (1555–1636)*. Cambridge, Mass.: Harvard University Press, 1971.

Bush, Susan, and Hsio-yen Shih, eds. *Early Chinese Texts on Painting*. Cambridge, Mass.: Harvard University Press, 1985.

Fong, Wen C. *Beyond Representation: Chinese Painting and Calligraphy, 8th–14th Century*. New York and New Haven: The Metropolitan Museum of Art and Yale University Press, 1992.

Köppel-Yang, Martina. *Semiotic Warfare: A Semiotic Analysis, the Chinese Avant-Garde, 1979–1989*. Hong Kong: Timezone 8, 2003.

Lai, Mei Lin. "Lui Shou Kwan & Modern Ink Painting." PhD diss., University of Sydney, 2011.

Li Xiaoshan. "My Views on Contemporary Chinese Painting" (Dangdai zhongguohua zhi wo jian). *China Fine Arts Weekly* (*Zhongguo Meishubao*) (1986).

Lippit, Yukio. "Apparition Painting." *RES: Anthropology and Aesthetics*, no. 55/56 (Spring–Autumn 2009), 61–86, at https://eaa.fas.harvard.edu/files/eaah/files/apparition_painting.pdf.

Morita, Miki. "The Kizil Paintings in the Metropolitan Museum." *Metropolitan Museum Journal* 50 (2015), 115–35, at https://www.journals.uchicago.edu/doi/pdfplus/10.1086/685676.

Paul, Paramita. "Wandering Saints: Chan Eccentrics in the Art and Culture of Song and Yuan China." PhD diss., Universiteit Leiden, 2009, at https://terebess.hu/zen/PPAULThesis.pdf.

Wang, Eugene Y. "Chinese Art: The Story of Haze (Part One)." *Orientations* 49, no. 3 (May–June 2018), 73–85.

Wang, Eugene Y. "Chinese Art: The Story of Haze (Part Two)." *Orientations* 49, no. 4 (July–August 2018), 50–59.

Wu, Hung. "Buddhist Elements in Early Chinese Art (2nd and 3rd Centuries A.D.)." *Artibus Asiae* 47, nos. 3–4 (1986), 263–303, 305–52.

Wynne, Alexander. *The Origin of Buddhist Meditation*. New York: Routledge, 2007.

Artists in the Exhibition

All artworks are promised gifts of the Fondation INK.

OPHÉLIE ASCH

b. Warsaw, 1973

***Battle at the Craters* (*Bataille aux cratères*), 2014**
Acrylic on paper
67⅜ × 37¼ in. (171 × 95 cm)

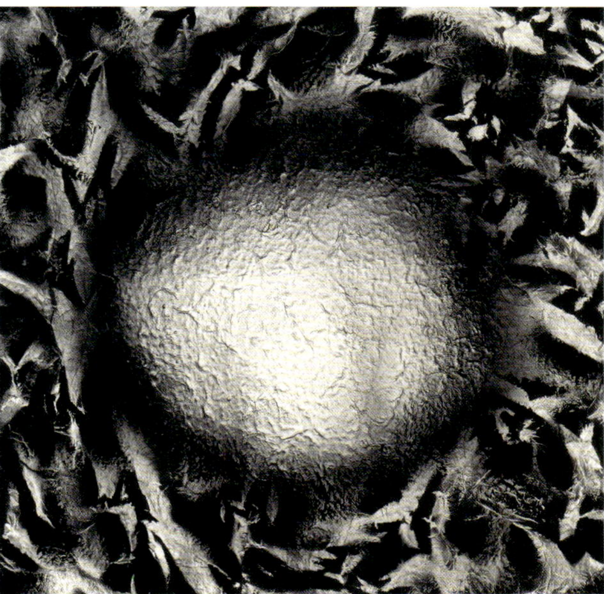

Battle at the Craters (*Bataille aux cratères*), 2014 (detail)

Ophélie Asch was born in Warsaw and now resides and works in Paris. She grew up in a cultured family, as the daughter of two ballet dancers and the granddaughter of Léopold Zborowski, a Polish poet and writer, and an art dealer who represented such painters as Amedeo Modigliani, Marc Chagall, André Derain, Moïse Kisling, and Chaïm Soutine. Asch studied philosophy at the University of Paris Sorbonne and began her career as a photographer and painter in the early 2000s. While many of her photographic series, notably *Rain People* (*Gens de pluie*), focus on human figures situated within nebulous landscapes inundated by water, her paintings have tended toward abstraction. In recent years, Asch has experimented with acrylic paints, producing a series of abstract compositions using both colors and monochromatic tonalities.

Battle at the Craters is one of a series of paintings with similar titles created by Asch between 2010 and 2015. These have been poetically compared to scenes of ruins as well as primordial images of the birth of the universe. This large abstraction, painted with acrylic on paper, presents a vision of a violent, dreamlike world, infused with elements rendered in black, gray, and white pigments that bring to mind such organic structures as interwoven branches and twigs, subterranean mycorrhizal networks, or images of warring birds or frantic swarms of insects. The very title of the painting, *Battle at the Craters*, evokes not only scenes of combat beyond the edge of human perception, but also images of craters made by bombs and meteors. Such works are not so much pictures of the visible world as images of the constantly shifting energies within and underlying the visible, rendering what is invisible to the naked eye but no less real in terms of the forces of nature at work. *Battle at the Craters* is very much about what is seen and unseen—a vision of the world, of the cycle of birth, life, and death, and one that captures a deeper and more complex image of reality. **SL**

Selected Exhibition
Ophélie Asch, Galerie Hopkins, Paris, 2015.

Further Source
Olivier Beer and Sarah Moon, *Gens de pluie: Photographies d'Ophélie Asch* (Paris: Delpire, 2005).

BINGYI

b. Beijing, 1975

Let Me Become the Universe's Plaything, 2018
Ink on paper
$53\frac{15}{16} \times 27\frac{3}{16}$ in. (137 × 69 cm)

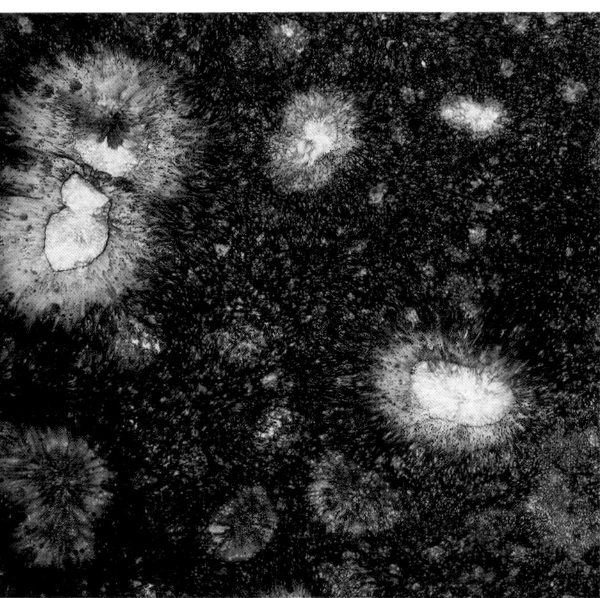

Let Me Become the Universe's Plaything, 2018 (detail)

In *Let Me Become the Universe's Plaything*, part of a series of works related to the notion of *Wanwu* (roughly translated as "the myriad things"), Bingyi experiments with depicting the universe as the ultimate landscape. One naturally first perceives the contents of this painting at a human scale: ripples on a dark body of water, or flowers in a field, viewed from above. In fact, the scene can be read as nearly infinite or, equally, infinitesimal: each puddle a black hole and each light patch the glimmer of a distant star, or microbial cells crawling around a petri dish under a microscope.

The artist leaves the scale and subject of her painting intentionally ambiguous, mutating into any number of scenes that the viewer could imagine. This is accomplished in part through a technique that embodies this combination of macro and micro. She begins with boundless washes of ink, generating the atmosphere of the scene, followed by detailed linework to define her shapes. Bingyi herself considers *Universe's Plaything* an object of meditation, connecting its different viewers through a shared experience and creating a space for deep contemplation, begging the question: Can one perceive the entire universe in a single flower?

Bingyi has a holistic understanding of Chinese art. She has curated exhibitions of Chinese painting since her student days at Mount Holyoke College and completed a PhD in art history at Yale University in 2005, with a dissertation on Han-dynasty painting. Although ink painting is at the core of her oeuvre, Bingyi's practice knows no bounds: she has produced works of performance, installation, sculpture, architecture, and even feature-length film, often synthesizing these manifold practices with ink to create mixed-media works. **SF**

Selected Exhibitions
On the Road/Position Papers/Insertions, 7th Gwangju Biennale, 2008; *Bingyi: Cascade*, Smart Museum of Art, University of Chicago, 2011; *Bingyi: Impossible Landscapes*, INK Studio, Beijing, 2018.

Further Sources
Bingyi: Six Accounts of a Floating Life (New York: Max Protetch Gallery, 2008); Britta Erickson et al., *Bingyi: Impossible Landscapes* (Beijing: INK Studio, 2018); "Words," Bingyi, at bingyi.info/words.

IRMA BLANK

b. Celle, Germany, 1934

Radical Writings, Dal Libro Totale, ca. 1984
Watercolor on paper
12¾ × 9⅞ in. (32.5 × 25 cm)

Radical Writings, Abecedarium 7-1-91, 1991
Oil on canvas
81¼ × 27 9/16 in. (206.5 × 70 cm)

Radical Writings, Dal Libro Totale, ca. 1984 (detail)

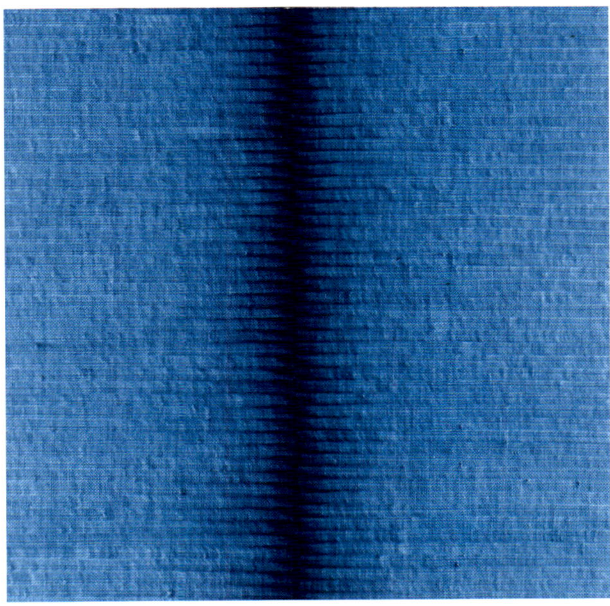

Radical Writings, Abecedarium 7-1-91, 1991 (detail)

"I purify writing. I leave its original, primordial sign, before it becomes writing. Before it is encoded in language." In an interview for the 57th Venice Biennale, the conceptual artist Irma Blank articulates the impetus undergirding her lifelong work: an unrelenting exploration of the ineffable written word. The visual language that Blank has crafted over the five-odd decades of her mature work is, simply put, breathtaking.

Applied to an aging paper, the soft lavender watercolor of *Dal Libro Totale* beckons us. Bound like a book and splayed open, the work smiles deliciously, "Read me." As we approach, though, rather than passages and phrases, words and letters, we are confronted with a gestural nod to writing—repetitive drawn-out strokes, executed slowly and deliberately. These plots of nonscript are punctuated only by blank spaces, which rhythmically break the uniform brushstrokes. This seeming illegibility defines *Abecedarium* as well. Methodically brushed bands, this time in blue oil colors on canvas, recall lines of text. They grow deeper and darker at the center of the canvas, mimicking the spine of a book. The ultramarine blue, favored by Blank, perhaps recalls the ink of the familiar ballpoint pen, which she uses in another series, *Avant-testo*.

The two works nearly bookend the twelve-year-long series *Radical Writings*. While using different materials and formats, these artworks respond to a single underlying notion: the relationship between breath and script. Reading the two works in the context of Blank's oeuvre provides a Rosetta Stone of sorts. The artist's exploration of writing through gestural art began in the 1960s with her series *Eigenschriften* (1968–73), where she used fragments of alphabetical signs to convey the mystification of foreign language. In subsequent series like *Trascrizioni* (1973–79), *Avant-testo* (1990s–early 2000s), and her most recent, ongoing series *Gehen* (2017–), Blank continues to utilize new approaches, such as transcribed texts rendered illegible, meditative application of ballpoint pens in circular motions, and mark-making, capturing time and motion. In *Radical Writings* (1983–95), Blank rejects meaning-bearing script altogether.

So how does one read *Dal Libro Totale* and *Abecedarium*? Simple. Breathe in... **EC**

Selected Exhibitions
Venice Biennales, 2001 and 2017; *Irma Blank: To Be*, Alison Jacques Gallery, London, 2014; *Irma Blank: Paper Works from the Museion Collection*, Museion, Bolzano, Italy, 2018; *Blank*, ICA, Milan, Museo Villa Dei Cedri, Bellinzona, Switzerland, and Bombas Gens Centre d'Art, Valencia, 2020.

Further Sources
Luca Cerizza, *Irma Blank, senza parole* (Bologna: Galleria P420, 2013); Alfredo Cramerotti, *Irma Blank: Paentiadau'r Anadl / Breath Paintings* (Llandudno, Wales: Mostyn Art Gallery, 2015); *Irma Blank* (London: Koenig Books, 2019).

MATTI BRAUN

b. Berlin, 1968

Untitled, 2009
Batik
23⅛ × 77⅛ × 1⅜ in. (58.8 × 196 × 3.5 cm)

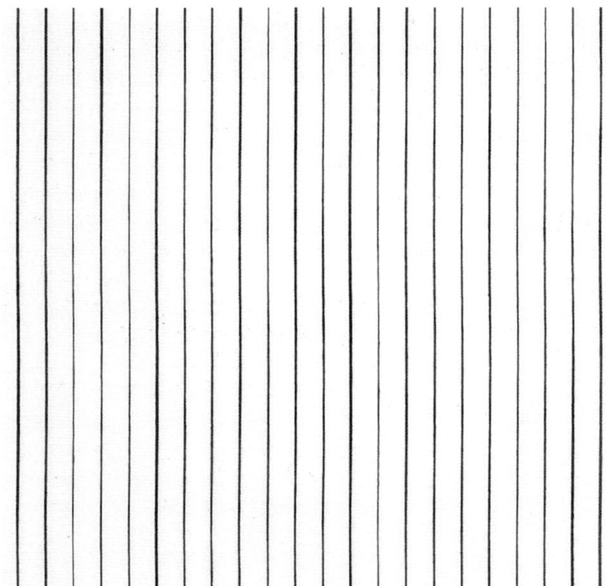

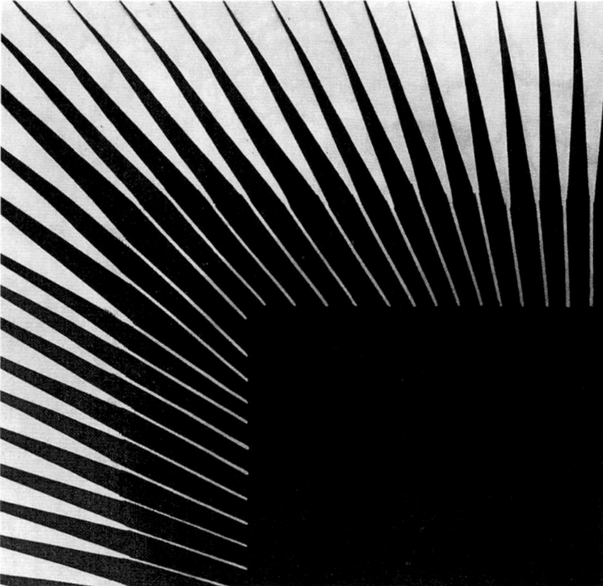

Untitled, 2009 (details)

Born in Berlin, Matti Braun studied at the Städelschule, Frankfurt am Main, and at the Braunschweig University of Art. He is well known for his exploration of cross-cultural themes and especially for his colorfully crafted glass pieces and silk dye batik. Through thorough research of materials, history, and biographical context, Braun often finds intersections between dissimilar cultures, forming subtle interpretations and fictional allusions to stories woven from both physical and conceptual migration and trade.

For *Untitled*, Braun used the traditional, ceremonial method of silk dyeing popular in Indonesia called batik. Batik utilizes a wax or paste resistant dyeing method where the artisan applies wax in selective patterns, then soaks the textiles in dyes that are wax resistant. After the wax has been removed with boiling water, the process can be repeated with multiple colors. Although batik is widely attributed to the Southeast Asian region, similar methods are recorded in ancient Egypt, Nara-period Japan, and Tang-dynasty China. In the 19th century, Dutch and English traders also brought the method to Sub-Saharan Africa, and today the batik process is used in several regions of the continent, especially in Senegal and Nigeria. Braun discovered the batik process through Rudolf Smend of Galerie Smend in Cologne, which specialized in textile art. The artist says, "Through him I became aware of many techniques, a rich heterogenous heritage, the great diversity of approaches in the field, and the work of several artists working in it today."

As seen in *Untitled*, Braun reappropriates the batik technique to create a series of monochromatic works, ranging from light to dark. Thin, black patterned lines radiate from a black center on the white silk; the compositions are reminiscent of both Asian ink wash and Western abstraction. The four canvases are abuzz, each its own unique illustration of energy emerging from empty space. Blending cultural implications and traditions of numerous histories, Braun's works in the *Untitled* series simplify these intricate connections and associations to depict a universally understood, meditative study of the void.

In 1994, Braun won the Peter Mertes Award, Bonner Kunstverein, Germany. He currently resides in Cologne. CY

Selected Exhibitions
Bunta Garbo, Stedelijk Museum Bureau Amsterdam, 2002; *The Alien by Matti Braun*, Project Arts Centre, Dublin, 2005; *Özurfa*, Museum Ludwig, Cologne, 2008.

Further Sources
Christiane Meyer-Stoll et al., *Matti Braun: Kola* (Cologne: W. König, 2009); Sarah Frost et al., *Matti Braun: Salo* (Cologne: W. König, 2011).

CHEN BOLAN

b. Shanghai, 1955

A Street View of Shanghai, 2007

Oil on canvas
35 × $51\frac{7}{16}$ in. (90 × 130 cm)

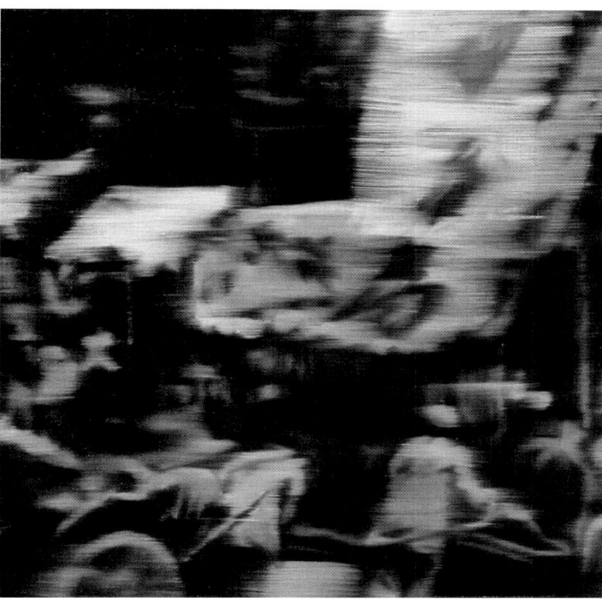

A Street View of Shanghai, 2007 (detail)

Born and raised in Shanghai, Chen Bolan received his art training at Shanghai Normal University in 1980–84. He moved to Japan in 1986, then to England in 1991, and eventually returned to Japan and settled there. Influenced by art in the East and West, Chen's oeuvre shows diverse styles utilizing a variety of materials, mainly ink, beeswax, enamel, and pastel.

A Street View of Shanghai is one of Chen's works in the *Black & White* series that he started in 1994. The painting was based on a photograph he found in a library in London—a street view of Shanghai taken in the 1920s or '30s (fig. 1). The picture resonated with his personal background, so Chen transformed the photographic image into an oil painting. Capturing a mundane moment, the scene shows the rickshaws from behind as they move up the street. Shop banners blow in the wind, the characters on them barely legible. Mimicking the out-of-focus effect of an old black-and-white photograph, the painting evokes a sense of nostalgia. The blurriness contributes to the sensation of an ephemeral moment eluding the viewer like a faded memory.

Chen's canvas is reminiscent of European photorealistic painting of the 1960s and '70s, as exemplified in the works of German artist Gerhard Richter. Richter's realist figurative "photopaintings" make extensive use of the fuzzy appearance of photographs that lack focus or show the movement of the camera or its subject. "I blur things," Richter explained, "to make everything equally important and equally unimportant." *A Street View of Shanghai* reproduces a similar visual appearance. "The vagueness," according to Chen, "seems to enhance the warmth of ambiguous emotions. Meanwhile, it expands the imagination by removing colors, which is the charm of monochromatic paintings." WK

Selected Exhibitions
Galerie Leda Fletcher, Geneva, 2003; Millennium Art Museum, Beijing, 2005; solo exhibitions at Silkland Gallery, Tokyo, 2014.

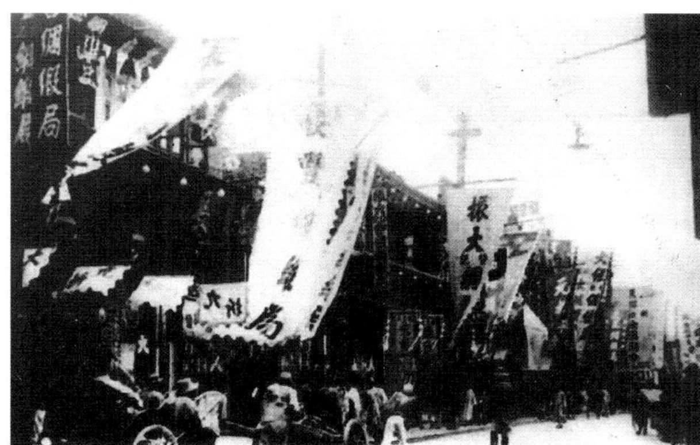

Fig. 1 Source photo for Chen Bolan's *A Street View of Shanghai*, 1920s–30s. Courtesy of the artist

CHEN HAIYAN

b. Fushun, Liaoning Province, China, 1955

Dream 2005.2.15, Mountains, Flowers, Crowded People and Cars, 2009
Woodcut print on paper
63⅞ × 40¼ in. (162.3 × 102.3 cm)

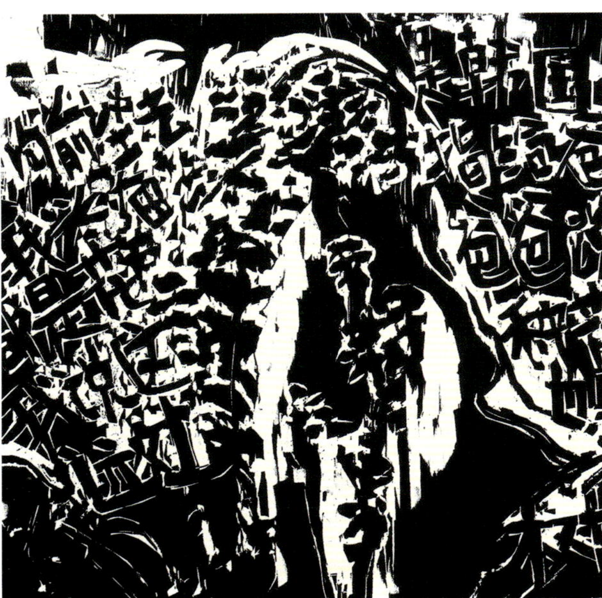

Dream 2005.2.15, Mountains, Flowers, Crowded People and Cars, 2009 (detail)

Chen Haiyan brings her dreams to life in bold, expressionistic prints and paintings, rich with saturated colors and deeply black ink. Her signature process began with small etchings on wood based on entries from her dream diary, which, as her artistic practice developed, became monumental in size. The resulting works evoke both Chinese woodblock carving and German Expressionism, but her style is unique; her strong black forms often conjure feelings of anger, anxiety, or confusion, but equally can convey whimsy and radical softness. By engaging with the fantasy of her sleeping world while grounded in the temporal environment of her Hangzhou studio, the artist creates an outlet for her in-between self: an unbounded dream Chen looking to exist in the earthly world. The events of her dreams often mimic her daily life: dream Chen sees painters and figures from the art academy where she works, passes friends from her waking life on the street, wonders where her son is. She creates a loop of art(life)-inspired-by-dream-inspired-by-life. Dream Chen is likely to encounter unnerving situations, obstacles in her path, and, on occasion, groups of friendly cats.

The works by Chen included in the Fondation INK Collection represent a microcosm of her artistic career. *Dream 1986/6/19 Maqpi* (fig. 1) exemplifies her early work—small, with lots of text on a white ground. *Dream 2005.2.15* reflects the darker, less cluttered aesthetic typical of her later work. Over the past fifteen years, Chen has turned to large-scale painting, showing a clear and developed understanding of color, contrasting the bold, black linework that has marked so much of her career.

The blocky brushwork of *Horse and Rose* is typical of her painting practice; although her woodblock prints always began with a painting on wood, and thus we see similarity in her bold lines and rough, blocky forms, the carving process leaves no space for broken ink (*pomo*) lines or variance in the ink's wetness. While Chen's woodblock carving is far warmer in nature than that of mechanical counterparts, there remains a rigidity to the medium of carving and printing that the artist has escaped in her paintings. **SF**

Selected Exhibitions
China/Avant-Garde, National Art Museum of China, Beijing, 1989; *"I Don't Want to Play Cards with Cézanne" and Other Works: Selections from the Chinese "New Wave" and "Avant-Garde" Art of the Eighties*, Pacific Asia Museum, Pasadena, 1991; *Chen Haiyan: Carving the Unconscious*, INK Studio, Beijing, 2013.

Further Sources
Richard E. Strassberg, ed., *"I Don't Want to Play Cards with Cézanne" and Other Works: Selections from Chinese "New Wave" and "Avant-Garde" Art of the Eighties* (Pasadena: Pacific Asia Museum, 1991); Jaeheung Lee, *Chagall & Chagall: The Artworks of Chen Haiyan* (Daejeon, South Korea: Asia Museum, 2003); *The Enduring Passion for Ink*: "Chen Haiyan's Dreams," directed by Britta Erickson, video, 2013.

Horse and Rose, 2005

Ink and color on xuan paper
57½ × 143¼ in. (146 × 364 cm)

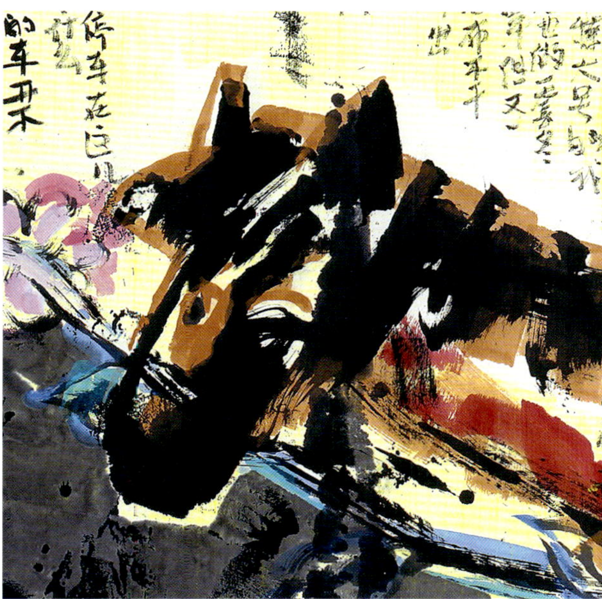

Horse and Rose, 2005 (detail)

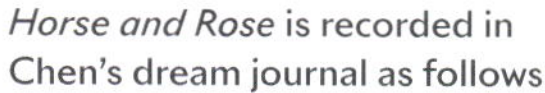

Horse and Rose is recorded in Chen's dream journal as follows:

Dream: July 17, 2005
I am alone and running as fast as I can. I almost crash into a car. On the dirt road ahead I see a horse-drawn cart. The cart is loaded up with flower pots. There are tropical plants with thorns and there are the usual roses. I can't bring them back, so I don't need to ask the price. I see that on the horse's head is a big bouquet of roses. I don't know if the flowers are to feed the horse or for decoration.

I have to meet my son; he is waiting for me at home. As I walk onward, I reach the entrance of a northern village where there is a great multitude of people gathered for market. People are selling things like tofu dregs, bottle caps, and dirty, wet towels. I don't dare buy a flat-bread to eat there.

I get into a taxi and haven't seen whether the driver is male or female. He drives and suddenly stops inside a room. There is a little pathway by a storefront. The people in the store are making cotton-padded pajama pants and tops. I take several pairs but they are all massive. Some are patterned with blue stripes, others with purple. I think to myself that I should make a pair to wear in the winter, but I am also afraid that the cloth is not clean.

The taxi driver parked here isn't looking for fares, so why is it sitting here? His car can't get out from here. He needs to back up, turn around and drive straight ahead. Am I worried that the car will hit me or that I will run into it first? He starts up the car and drives into the elevator. The buttons on that rickety old elevator are worn down and unclear, you can't make out which is up and down. In the middle of driving in the driver discovers that this isn't an elevator that cars can drive into. From the floor of the elevator there's a part where you can see the laborers below at work. The car drives forward and falls into the pit below. So dangerous! As usual, the workers are breaking a sweat. The taxi driver has me show the way. The car can't find the main gate from which to exit. I use my son's mobile phone to call him. But the numbers are wrong. My son is at home waiting for me. This female taxi driver tells me she will only charge me 15 RMB. I tell her it's OK.

Translated by Maya Kóvskaya

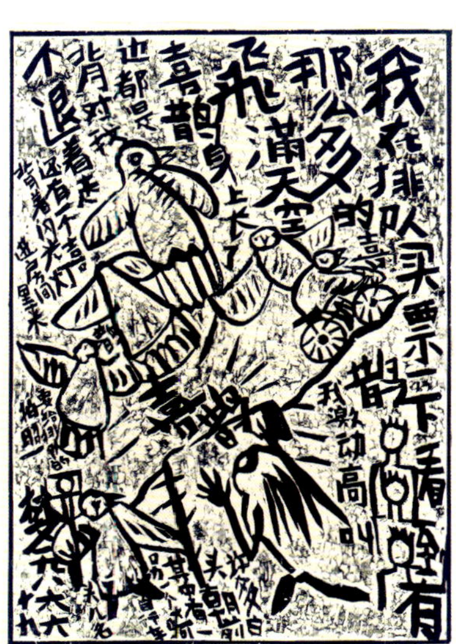

Fig. 1 Chen Haiyan, *Dream 1986/6/19 Maqpi*, 1986. Woodcut print on paper, 39⅜ × 26¾ in. (100 x 68 cm). Fondation INK Collection

MICHAEL CHERNEY

b. New York, 1969

Five Peaks: Eastern, Western, Southern, Central, Northern, 2008
Inkjet print on mitsumata paper
84 × 128 in. (213.4 × 325 cm)

Michael Cherney, also known by his Chinese name Qiu Mai, meaning "autumn wheat," is what one might call an honorary Chinese artist. Drawn to the language and culture of China, Cherney began studying in Taiwan in 1989 and moved to Beijing in 1991. In 1993, after recovering from a serious illness, he was compelled to capture life through his art, and started creating works that fuse contemporary photography techniques and traditional Chinese painting aesthetics.

Cherney's black-and-white photographs fully embrace the philosophical and scholarly foundations of historical *shanshui* ink paintings and often depict historically important sites or mountain vistas seen in the canonical works of Chinese masters. In *Five Peaks: Eastern, Western, Southern, Central, Northern*, his subject is the famous Wulao (Five Masters) peaks of Lushan (Mount Lu) in Jiujiang. Comprised of five cloudy ink washes of mountains dotted at their edges with faint trees, the work has the appearance of a series of hanging scrolls. Winding fog leads the viewer into the scene, recalling compositional techniques used by historical ink masters.

The use of traditional paper as a ground and the scroll mounting reinforce the work's painterly quality. The grain of the photograph takes the place of evident brushwork, both signs of an artist's hand, pulling *Five Peaks* away from the realistic photographic representation of life and further into the realm of Chinese ink painting. SF

Selected Exhibitions
from 2 arises 3: Collaborative Works of Arnold Chang and Michael Cherney, Asian Art Museum, San Francisco, 2014; *Stone and Mist: Chinese Landscape Photography by Michael Cherney*, Nelson Atkins Museum, Kansas City, 2014; *The Heart-Mind Learns from the Eyes*, Three Shadows Photography Art Centre/ +3 Gallery, Beijing, 2018.

Further Sources
Britta Erickson et al., *Reframing: Writings on the Art of Michael Cherney* (Beijing: Peoples Fine Art Publishing House, 2006); Jay Xu et al., *from 2 arises 3: The Collaborative Works of Arnold Chang and Michael Cherney 2009–2014* (New York: Early Spring Press, 2014); Tiffany Wai-Ying Beres and Pi Daojian, *from 2 arises 3: The Collaborative Works of Arnold Chang and Michael Cherney 2014–2017* (Hong Kong: University of Hong Kong Museum and Art Gallery, 2018).

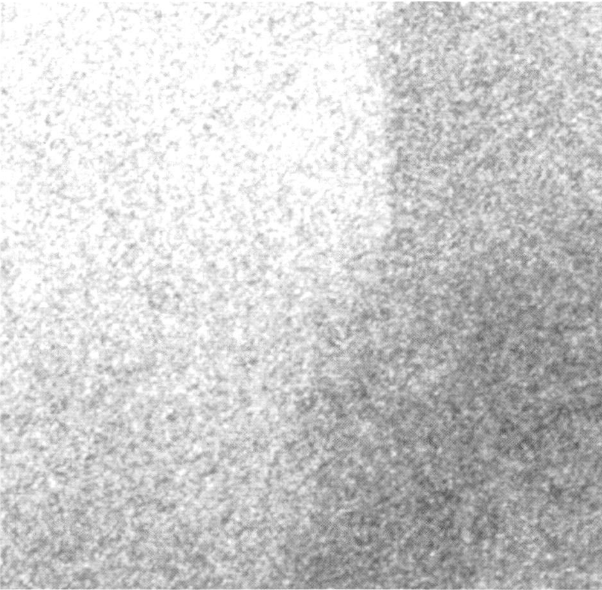

Five Peaks: Eastern, Western, Southern, Central, Northern, 2008 (details)

CHU KO

b. Hunan Province, China, 1931–2011

***The Dreaming Clouds of Wu Mountains*, 2005**
Ink and colors on paper
26 × 37¼ in. (66 × 95 cm)

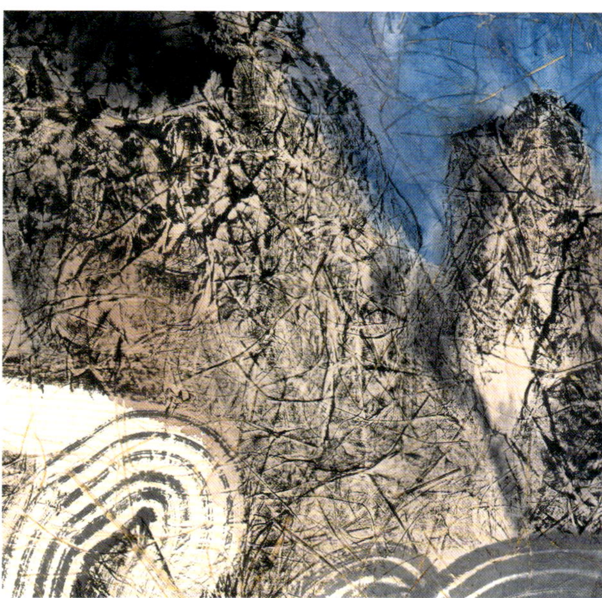

The Dreaming Clouds of Wu Mountains, 2005 (detail)

Born in Hunan Province in mainland China, Chu Ko enlisted in the Nationalist army in 1948 and moved to Taiwan with the government-in-exile in 1949. Originally named Yuan Dexing, he adopted the sobriquet Chu Ko, meaning "the Chu State's dagger-axe," in homage to his home province. The Chu State, which encompassed present-day Hunan, was a powerful state during the Spring and Autumn and Warring States periods (770–221 BCE). Bronze dagger-axes, important military weapons, were fully developed in the Chu State, hence the artist's moniker.

Chu Ko excelled as a poet, painter, sculptor, ceramist, art critic, and art historian. He was also a specialist in ancient Chinese bronzes and worked at the National Palace Museum in Taiwan for over thirty years. Deeply informed by his knowledge of ancient tradition, he frequently incorporated the symbols, motifs, and forms referencing premodern traditions in his works. However, he was not bound by the classical conventions of brush and ink (*bimo*). Rather, he creatively substituted everyday objects such as newspaper, sponges, and rags for a brush, breaking the traditional rules and freely painting his inner landscapes. His fondness for poetry and mastery of calligraphy also permeate his oeuvre. As a prominent art critic, Chu Ko was closely associated with avant-garde movements in Taiwan such as the Fifth Moon Painting Society and the Eastern Painting Society.

The Dreaming Clouds of Wu Mountains, representative of Chu Ko's painting practice, incorporates a symbol of traditional folk art—that of rope braiding—into the landscape. The twisting parallel lines were executed with a special brush invented by the artist: he divided the hair of a wide brush into several subgroups, thus generating several thin lines of paint (six in this work). By manipulating the darkness and density of ink tones and the dynamics of his brush, he played with line, form, and space in an abstracted landscape. In addition, the upper mountains were painted on crumpled paper. A fantastic and majestic dreamscape emerged from Chu Ko's unique style and technique. WK

Selected Exhibitions

Chu Ko: The Unwinding Knot, Pao Galleries, Hong Kong Arts Center, and Alisan Fine Arts, Hong Kong, 1999; *Braid It in Art: The Rope Twisting Art by Chu Ko*, National Museum of History, Taipei, 2004; *Noir d'encre, regards croisés: Hartung et les peintres chinois*, Musée des Arts d'Extrême Orient de la Fondation Baur, Geneva, 2013; *My Way in One Continuous Strand: A Retrospective Exhibition of Chu Ko*, Liang Gallery, Taipei, 2019.

Further Sources

Michael Sullivan, *Art and Artists of Twentieth-Century China* (Berkeley: University of California Press, 1996); Tao Youchun et al., *Braid It in Art: The Rope Twisting Art by Chu Ko* (Taipei: Guoli lishi bowuguan, 2004); Hsiao Chong-Ray, *The Phoenix in Art: Chu Ko* (Kaohsiung: Qingliang yin wenhua shiye youxian gongsi, 2013).

CHUA EK KAY

b. Guangdong Province, China, 1947–2008

***Reflection-Breeze Passes by the Lotus Pond*, 2007**
Ink on paper
35¼ × 37⅞ in. (90 × 96 cm)

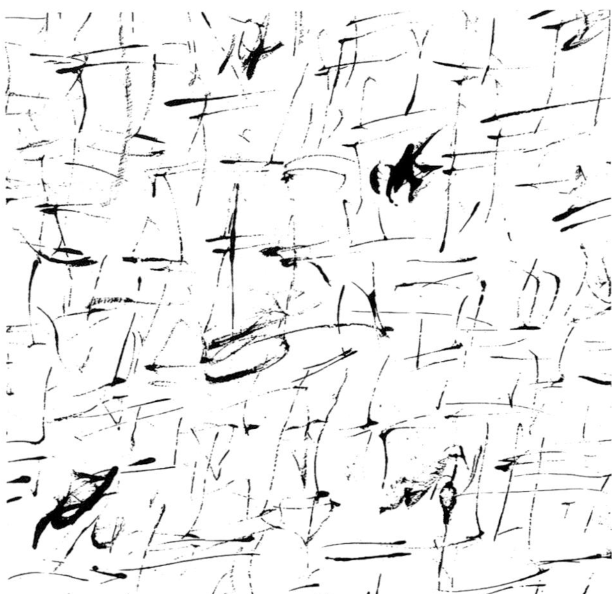

Reflection-Breeze Passes by the Lotus Pond, 2007 (detail)

One of the most successful ink painters in Singapore, Chua Ek Kay was born in Guangdong Province in China and emigrated to Singapore with his family in the 1950s. Before earning an MA from Western Sydney University in Australia, he studied painting and calligraphy with the prominent Chinese Singapore ink painter Fan Chang Tien, who was in the lineage of the Shanghai School of painting that prevailed in the late 19th and early 20th centuries. The cultural environment of the Chinese diaspora community of Chua's youth was more conservative than that in China, and breaking through the confinement of ink painting conventions was especially difficult. Although Chua rooted his practice in the Chinese tradition of ink painting and calligraphy, he continually challenged himself, mining Western modernism and Australian Aboriginal cave painting for innovative techniques and ideas.

A major series of Chua's ink paintings drew inspiration from his memories of Liang Seah Street in Singapore's Chinatown, treating old dwellings, shops, and street scenes as leitmotifs. In his late years, the artist experimented with contemporary mediums and materials, such as prints and paper pulp. *Reflection-Breeze Passes by the Lotus Pond* is a representative work in his well-known series of lotus ponds. Early works in the series showcase the *xieyi* (expressing the spirit) style of Chinese ink painting, exploring spiritual essence through loose brushwork and exaggerated forms. But flowers and leaves are still clearly discernible as such. Later, the lotuses are reduced to the broken branches and dried leaves of late autumn. From there, Chua developed a minimal style with flattened compositions, purely abstract forms, and expressive lines, as shown in this painting. As if some gibberish recorded in illegible calligraphy, it is executed with agitated and forceful brushwork. With only essence remaining, this painting conceptually illuminates the vitality of the lotuses. WK

Selected Exhibitions
Yixi: Recent Paintings of Chua Ek Kay, Shanghai Art Museum, 2005; *Lotus Pond & Water Village*, Cape of Good Hope Art Gallery, Singapore, 2007; *Chua Ek Kay: After the Rain*, National Gallery Singapore, 2015.

Further Sources
Lindy Poh et al., *Chua Ek Kay: Being and Becoming: The Lotus Pond Series* (Singapore: Singapore Tyler Print Institute, 2003); Kian Chow Kwok et al., *Re-visiting Chua Ek Kay: Tribute to the Ink Master* (Singapore: Singapore Tyler Print Institute, 2010); *Being and Becoming Chua Ek Kay*, directed by Jacqueline Smith and Yin Phua, video, 2017; Sara Siew et al., *Chua Ek Kay* (Singapore: National Gallery Singapore, 2019).

MAX COLE

b. Hodgeman County, Kansas, USA, 1937

***Untitled*, 1999**
Ink and wash on Arches paper
22½ × 30 in. (57.2 × 76.2 cm)

Untitled, 1999 (detail)

Max Cole was born and raised in the Midwest of the United States. In 1961, she received a BA at Fort Hays State University and in 1964 completed an MFA at the University of Arizona, Tucson. Cole then worked in both Los Angeles and New York before settling in the Sierra foothills region of Northern California. Inspired by the work of Russian avant-garde artist Kazimir Malevich, Cole's artworks are characterized by simple bands and fields of black, grays, and white, carefully rendered in thin vertical lines. Her practice is underscored by a sense of harmony and serenity produced through diligent, repetitive, freehand mark-making. She spends focused hours in a day, allowing her compositions time to unfold through her motions. Many describe Cole's work as allusions to her childhood, recalling her time spent in the flat, expansive plains of Kansas.

Striations of gray marks vibrate off the surface of *Untitled*. Set against the natural fibers of the paper, the fine lines of ink dance in neat, straight rows, calling to mind a music sheet or the EKG graph of a steady heartbeat. Created by the tension of thousands of hand-drawn lines laid meticulously next to each other, an organic hum emanates from the work. The softness of the piece invites the viewer in for a closer look, where each mark on the paper, although seemingly repetitive, is unique. The size of the piece is immersive and all-encompassing, transporting the viewer into the tranquility of a hypnotic chant.

A fiercely private illustration of the artist's mental landscape, her works are gentle yet passionate, engulfing the viewer in the infinite possibilities of the mind. Cole states of her approach, "I've focused on the border of possibilities and perception, and I believe that the most restrictive limitation is when you abandon focus and admit all possibilities. The result is chaos, which cannot possibly express clarity. The important thing is focus. The limits I work within are not restrictive, because it's like going through a wall into a void that expands infinitely." **CY**

Selected Exhibitions
Museum of Modern Art, Otterndorf, Germany, 1998; *Time and Measure*, Museum Chasa Jaura, Valchava, Switzerland, 2005; *Meditations*, Kunst-Station, Sankt Peter Köln, Germany, 2013.

Further Sources
Reinhard Ermen et al., *Max Cole* (Milan: Charta, 2000); Douglas Dreishpoon and Stephen Zaima, *Max Cole: Works 1970–2018* (Santa Fe: Radius Books, 2018).

DAI GUANGYU

b. Chengdu, Sichuan Province, China, 1955

***Landscape, Ink, Ice*, 2004**
Giclée print on fiber-based paper
47¼ × 63 in. (120 × 160 cm)

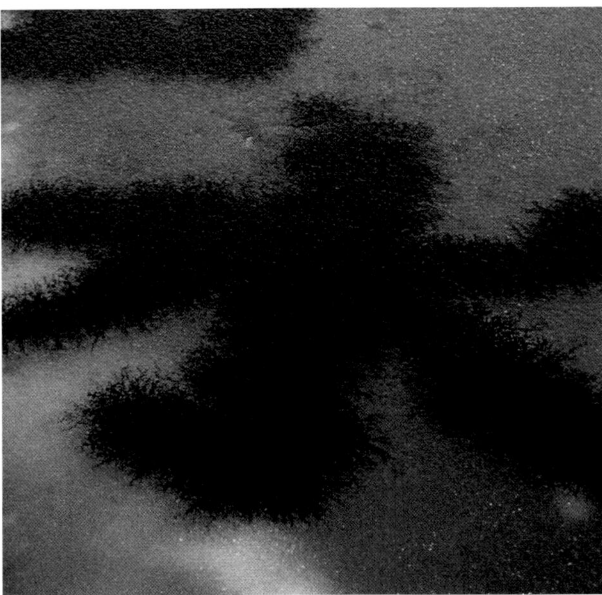

Landscape, Ink, Ice 2004 (detail)

Thick, opaque ink cuts into an icy pond, reading "mountains and waters," or simply "landscape" (*shanshui*). Indeed, distant mountains subtly fringe the composition from above. Water, too, is represented by the slab of ice, which simultaneously figures as the canvas. Reflections of clouds, evident particularly in the second panel of the diptych, add another dimension to the lyrical playfulness between concrete and figurative landscape.

The tension between the first and second panels—left and right respectively—is telling of how natural forces and the dimension of time become active participants in the creative process. In the left panel, the characters can be clearly discerned, though their fractal-like edges foreshadow the passage of time and its effects. The characters in the right panel, now dissipated to the point of abstraction, are almost entirely erased by the natural forces at work. The mountains in the background, in turn, suddenly loom clearer, usurping their textual representation.

Dai Guangyu marries time-based performance art with his long-acquired knowledge of traditional Chinese painting and calligraphy. Yet we are left with neither an ephemeral performance nor a physical output, but rather with their photographic memento—a ghostly apparition. Photography mediates and reframes the moment, translating it into a two-dimensional object. Unlike many of Dai's other ink-based performance works, the artist remains obscured from view. Still, his hand is evident in every aspect of production—from the application of ink to the arrangement of the composition.

Born in Chengdu, Dai quickly became one of the pivotal figures of avant-garde art in Sichuan as well as a leading member of the New Wave art movement of 1985. His experimentation with ink-inspired performance art and his long-standing exploration of the material culminates with *Landscape, Ink, Ice*. Dai's literalization of landscape painting in water and ink takes form as three manifestations of water: landscape (lit. "mountains, water," *shanshui*), ink (lit. "ink water," *moshui*), and ice (lit. "ice water," *bingshui*)—namely, the piece's title. **EC**

Selected Exhibitions
China/Avant-Garde, National Art Museum of China, Beijing, 1989; *When the Waters Recede, the Rocks Appear*, Red Star Gallery, Beijing, 2007; *Endowed with Speech from Birth*, YaFeng Contemporary Art Gallery, Chengdu, 2015.

Further Sources
Bérénice Angremy, *Ink Games: Dai Guangyu* (Shanghai: IFA Gallery, 2008); Silvia Fok, *Life and Death: Art and the Body in Contemporary China* (Bristol: Intellect Books, 2013); Alan Yeung, Dong Xiaokun, and Yang Fan, *Dai Guangyu: Making Traces: The Arts of Participation and Refusal* (Beijing: INK Studio, 2017).

FUNG MING CHIP

b. Guangdong Province, China, 1951

Accidentally Passing, Needle Script, 2015
Chinese ink on xuan paper
71¼ × 95¹¹⁄₁₆ in. (181 × 96 cm)

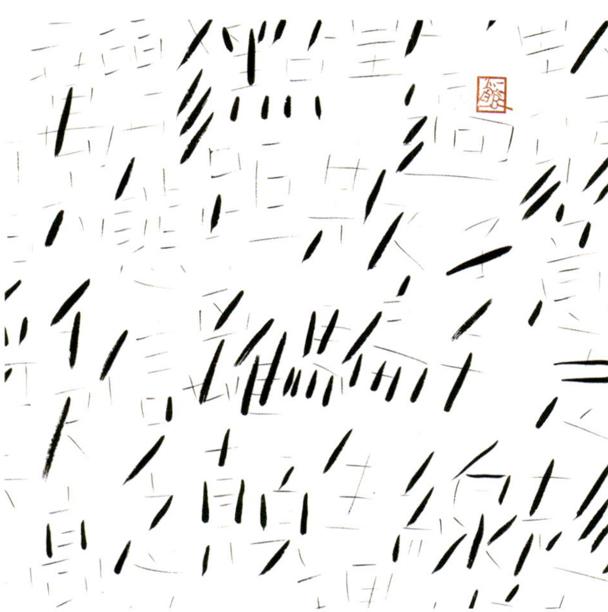

Accidentally Passing, Needle Script, 2015 (detail)

Fung Ming Chip is a self-taught renaissance man, immersing himself in artistic fields ranging from writing and directing to calligraphy and seal carving. His youth was spent in Hong Kong, and in 1977 he moved with his family to New Jersey, near New York City. In 1986, he moved to Taipei, and wrote and directed five plays throughout Taiwan. Since 1986, he has divided his time between Taipei, Hong Kong, and New York, three hubs of contemporary Asian and global art.

In his painting practice, Fung is a reformer of calligraphy, morphing a millennia-old tradition into a practice reflecting contemporary life. His invented scripts, of which he says he has over 100, include sand script, created by blowing dried ink powder—ink sand—over characters written in only water; swirl script, characterized by looping lines; and post-marijuana scripts, which are variable in aesthetic but often include thick, overlapping brushwork. In his needle script, as seen here, Fung considers the spatial relationships of both characters and individual strokes, blurring the divide between the interior and exterior spaces of the characters. On a flight between New York and Asia, he scrawled the poem that inspired the work:

Accidentally Passing
Strong or weak spirit
Follow the whirling engine
Steadily crossing the equator
Quantity quality and pattern are overpowered
Fooling the physical structure
Confusing time and focusing distance
Inverting moon and star
Freezing ideology
Existing will
Exceeding body's limit
36,000 feet up
Looking down at living earth
Searching for unknown future
Looking over to sky
Shrinking eternity
Thinking ahead
Why is there no darkness
(English translation of original Chinese)

Two seals are visible in *Accidentally Passing*, one in the lower left corner and the other on the upper right. Fung began seal carving in 1975, and as is true in much of his artistic practice, has bent and broken the rules of the tradition, often using unconventional shapes, adding images (likening the seal print to a miniature block print), and allowing his characters to trespass over the confines of the seals' carved borders. **SF**

Selected Exhibitions
Noir d'encre—regards croisés: Hans Hartung et les peintres chinois contemporains, Fondation Baur Musée des Arts d'Extrême Orient, Geneva, 2013; *The Magic of Characters: 3000 Years of Chinese Calligraphy*, Museum Rietberg, Zurich, 2015; *Echoes of One Hand Clapping: Picturing Sound in Asian Art*, Princeton University Art Museum, 2016.

Further Sources
Maxwell Hearn, "Interview with Fung Mingchip," The Metropolitan Museum of Art, January 2013, at https://www.metmuseum.org/metmedia/video/collections/asian/interview-with-fung-mingchip; *Fung Ming Chip's Shu-fa Sutra* (Guangzhou: China Art Press, 2015); *Fung Ming Chip: Meme* (Hong Kong: Galerie du Monde, 2017).

GU WENDA

b. Shanghai, 1955

surrealist landscape #3, 1982
Ink on paper
29 9/16 × 189 in. (75 × 480 cm)

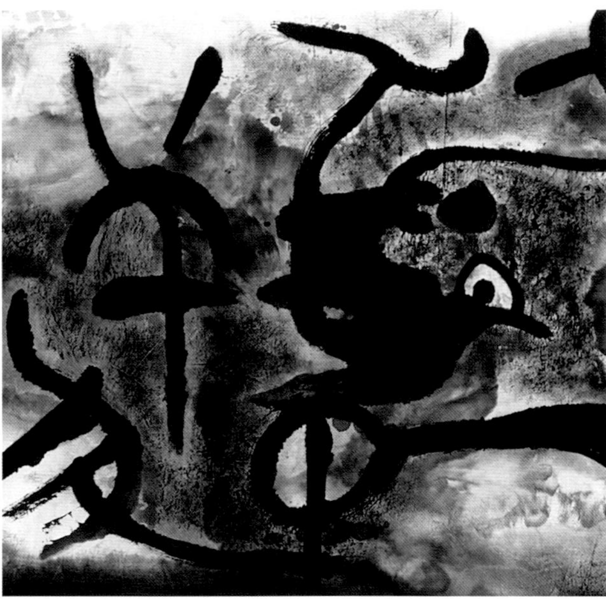

surrealist landscape #3, 1982 (detail)

Born into an intellectual family in Shanghai, gu wenda entered the Shanghai School of Arts and Crafts in 1976, the year the Cultural Revolution ended and higher education was reinstated. He then pursued an MFA at the China Academy of Art in Hangzhou, studying with Lu Yanshao, a master of traditional ink painting. Upon graduation in 1981, gu was retained by the Academy as an assistant professor. Such an educational background would normally prepare one for a successful career as a sophisticated technician in academic art; gu wenda, however, rebelliously chose an unorthodox path and became one of the most influential contemporary avant-garde Chinese artists. In a radical departure from traditional practices, he was the first Chinese artist to fully engage in pseudo-calligraphy, in which the form of characters is intentionally divorced from their content. He also became well known in the 1980s for making installations with language as their critical focus. Moving to the United States in 1987, gu began to incorporate bodily substances and organic matter into his audacious large-scale installations. He garnered international fame with his *United Nations* series created with human hair.

This abstract painting, *surrealist landscape #3*, was done one year after gu wenda graduated from the China Academy of Art. Although employing ink and paper, gu clearly charted a different course from traditional Chinese art of any genre. Well-read in Western culture and philosophy, he drew inspiration from Western abstract art. The indiscernible forms and disordered lines are reminiscent of works by Vasily Kandinsky, while certain combinations of lines resemble characters in seal script, an ancient form of Chinese calligraphy. The notion of "unreadability" in this painting paved the way for the artist's fully developed creation of pseudo-characters in his *mythos of lost dynasties series*, starting in 1983 (fig. 1). Here, the characters are variously detached, synthesized, misplaced, overlapped, miswritten, negated, and inverted. They are, in fact, character-like forms that challenge and inhibit the viewer's attempt to ascribe meaning. **WK**

Selected Exhibitions
Transience: Chinese Experimental Art at the End of the Twentieth Century, Smart Museum of Art, University of Chicago, University of Oregon Museum of Art, and Hood Museum of Art, Dartmouth College, 1999; *United Nations: Babel of the Millennium*, San Francisco Museum of Modern Art, 1999; *Art and China after 1989: Theater of the World*, Guggenheim Museum, New York and Bilbao, and San Francisco Museum of Modern Art, 2017; *The Allure of Matter: Material Art from China*, Los Angeles County Museum of Art and Smart Museum of Art, University of Chicago, 2019.

Further Sources
Chang Tsong-zung et al., *The Mythos of Lost Dynasties: An Ink Painting: Chinese Hair Temple Installation since 1984* (Hong Kong: Hanart TZ Gallery, 1997); Mark H. C. Bessire, ed., *Wenda Gu: Art from Middle Kingdom to Biological Millennium* (Cambridge, Mass.: MIT Press, 2003); Juliette Bianco et al., *Wenda Gu at Dartmouth: The Art of Installation* (Hanover, N.H.: Hood Museum of Art, 2008).

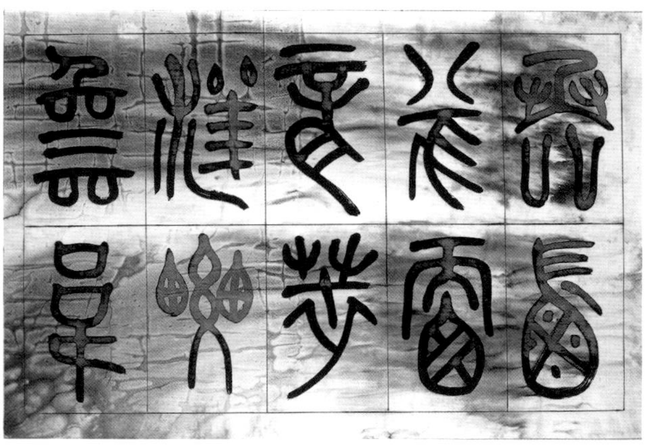

Fig. 1 gu wenda, *mythos of lost dynasties series–pseudo-seal scripture in calligraphic copybook #2*, 1983–86. Ink on paper, 26 × 38 in. (66 × 96.5 cm). Fondation INK Collection

HAI BO

b. Changchun, Jilin Province, China, 1962

Blue Bridge, 2004
Digital print
51 3/16 × 51 3/16 in. (130 × 130 cm)

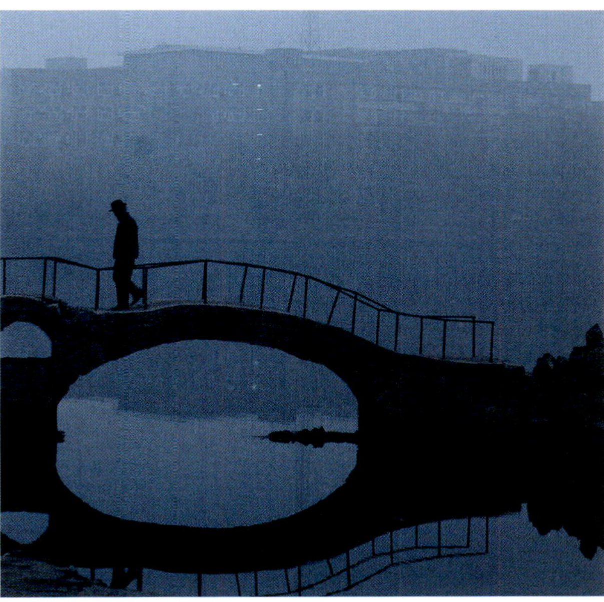

Blue Bridge, 2004 (detail)

Hai Bo received a BA from the Fine Art Institute of Jilin in 1984, and then studied at the Central Academy of Fine Arts in Beijing. While originally trained in printmaking, he turned to photography in the 1980s, and the camera has since become his primary vehicle of expression. Capturing mundane moments and conveying a sense of loss are defining characteristics of Hai's aesthetic. Many of his works focus on the passage of time, as seen in his best-known series titled *Them*. Each work in the series consists of two images—an old photograph and a restaged rendition that the artist created decades later with the same individuals in the same pose. Most of the subjects are family, childhood friends, or acquaintances. The juxtaposition of the two images records the lapse of time, seen in the visible signs of aging, and also documents absence and death, seen in the empty space left by those who are no longer alive.

The series *Them* was inspired by a pair of photographs titled *Bridge*, taken by Hai Bo in 1983 and 2000 respectively. The first photo is a product of Hai's student days and his initial encounters with photography. It captures an unadorned scene of the artist's mother, brother, and sister on a bridge during a spring outing in a park near his hometown. Seventeen years later, Hai revisited the bridge and took another picture with the original angle, although the new version is a color image in which the artist stands alone. *Blue Bridge* notably features the same bridge, although viewed from a different angle. Deeply attached to his family and home in northern China, Hai Bo has stated that the serenity of rural village life is his utopia. Despite its apparent formal simplicity, *Blue Bridge* summons up profound feelings of transience and nostalgia, as well as inescapable melancholy evoked by the photograph's blue tone. **WK**

Selected Exhibitions

Journeys: Mapping the Earth and Mind in Chinese Art, The Metropolitan Museum of Art, New York, 2007; *Perspectives: Hai Bo*, Arthur M. Sackler Gallery, Smithsonian Institution, Washington D.C., 2010; *Photography from the New China*, J. Paul Getty Museum, Los Angeles, 2010; *Hai Bo: The Southern Series*, Pace Gallery, Palo Alto, 2018.

Further Sources

Wu Hung et al., *Between Past and Future: New Photography and Video from China* (Chicago: Smart Museum of Art, 2004); *Hai Bo* (New York: Max Protetch Gallery, 2006); Wang Rui et al., *Hai Bo* (Hangzhou: Zhejiang sheying chubanshe, 2015).

HONG LEI

b. Changzhou, Jiangsu Province, China, 1960

Autumn in the Forbidden City (West Veranda), 1997
Chromogenic print
24 × 30¼ in. (61 × 77 cm)

Autumn in the Forbidden City (East Veranda), 1997
Chromogenic print
24 × 30¼ in. (61 × 77 cm)

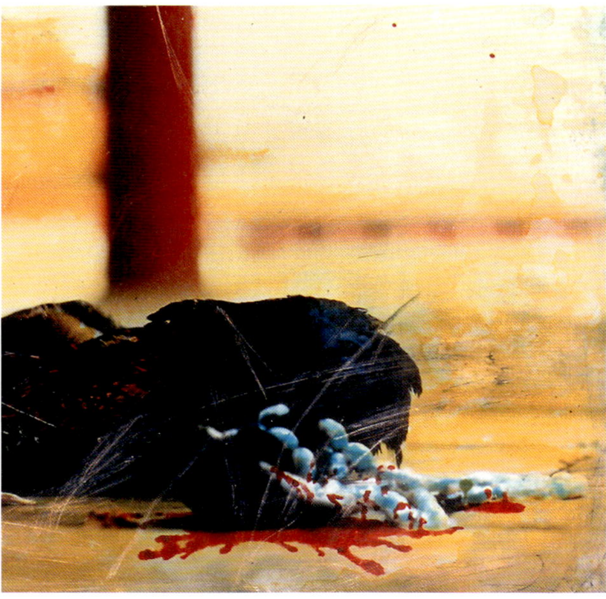

Autumn in the Forbidden City (West Veranda), 1997

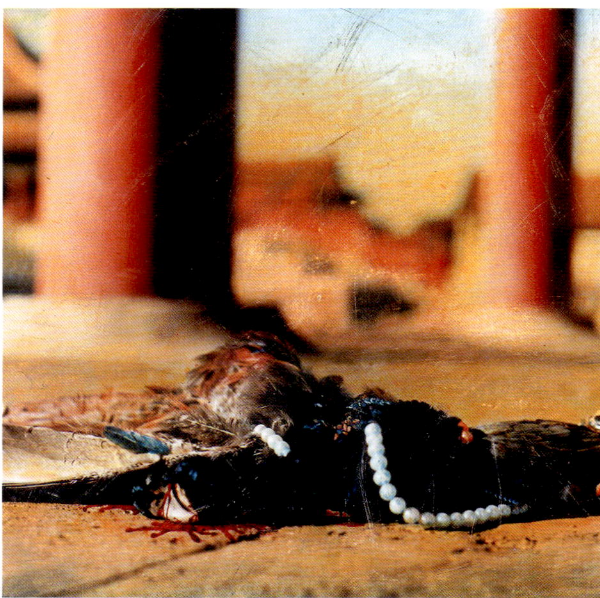

Autumn in the Forbidden City (East Veranda), 1997

Hong Lei studied oil painting (Nanjing Academy of Arts, 1987) and printmaking (Central Academy of Fine Art, 1993), but now works primarily in photography, incorporating digital manipulations into his works. Ink was never his medium of choice, but Hong greatly admires the work of the Song-dynasty imperial court painters, and considers himself a new-age literatus, working in photography with the same spirit that these artists brought to their ink painting practices. In some works, he uses photography to re-create specific ink paintings from Chinese art history, often adding his own dark or eerie edge.

In multiple series, including *Autumn in the Forbidden City*, Hong depicts dead animals enveloped in splashes of decadence, playing with the historical ink art genre of bird-and-flower painting. In *Autumn*, he frames a dead bird—which he has stated may represent himself—in between the columns of a walkway in the Forbidden City, the Ming-dynasty palace complex (built 1406–20) at the center of Beijing. In each photograph, the bird's body is mangled, its blood spilled on the ground in an almost cartoonish splatter; each is wrapped in strands of semiprecious gemstones. The visceral quality of this violence is heightened through the use of what look like scratches to the surfaces of the photographs. An unnatural and conflicting scene in itself, the saturated colors of these photos bring the work further into the realm of the uncanny. SF

Selected Exhibitions
Alors, La Chine?, Centre Pompidou, Paris, 2003; *Seven Worthies*, Today Art Museum, Beijing, 2007; *Perfume This Is Not: Hong Lei New Works*, Shanghai Art Museum, 2012.

Further Sources
Wu Hung and Christopher Phillips, *Between Past and Future: New Photography and Video from China* (Chicago: Smart Museum of Art, 2004); Wu Hung, *Hong Lei: Conversing with the Ancients* (Lincoln: University of Nebraska, 2009).

SHIRAZEH HOUSHIARY

b. Shiraz, Iran, 1955

Torn, 2009
Pencil and white acrylic on canvas
39⅜ × 39⅜ in. (100 × 100 cm)

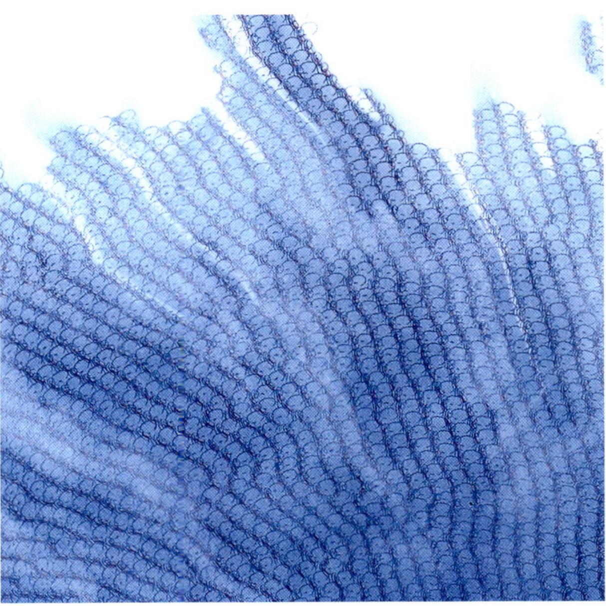

Torn, 2009 (detail)

Shirazeh Houshiary's artworks are characterized by their ethereal quality, their soft yet powerful biomorphic forms radiating energy into space. Her paintings are often produced by the diligent layering of pencil lines paired with acrylic or Aquacryl pigment on canvas, and more recently on aluminum and canvas panels. In *Torn*, serrated fine lines emanate in a gentle spiral, forming a tactile, translucent blue veil across the white canvas. This veil or membrane, a recurring motif in her paintings, can be seen as a metaphor for the barrier that shields us from awareness of our own existence. The meditative undulation of the intricate and meticulously executed blue lines in *Torn* exude an unmistakable spiritual quality, drawing the viewer inward. Transcending the influence of any one religion, Houshiary continually explores the limits of human perception and reality.

Although her works are not tied to any particular culture and her influences are vast, ranging from Kazimir Malevich to the Renaissance masters, Houshiary's veil paintings are often attributed to her study of Sufi poetry and calligraphy. *Torn* stems from the abstraction of two Persian words, forming a geometric web of marks. However, the composition can also be seen through a more universal, metaphysical lens and as an abstracted illustration of the hypnotic energy of the cosmos.

Born in Shiraz, Iran, Houshiary moved to London in 1974 where she received a BA from the Chelsea School of Art in 1979. She was first known for her sculptural work in the 1980s and grouped with contemporaries Richard Deacon and Anish Kapoor. In 1994, she was nominated for the Turner Prize, and she continues to show her work in exhibitions across the globe. CY

Selected Exhibitions
40th Venice Biennale, 1982; *Les Magiciens de la Terre*, Centre Georges Pompidou, Paris, 1989; *Dancing Around My Ghost*, Camden Arts Centre, London, 1993; *Breath*, Battery Park, New York, 2004; *Altar*, St. Martin-in-the-Fields, London, 2011.

Further Sources
Simon Morley, *The Sublime* (London: Whitechapel, 2010); Diana d'Arenberg, "Shirazeh Houshiary," *Ocula Magazine*, May 17, 2018, at https://ocula.com/magazine/conversations/shirazeh-houshiary/; "A Conversation with Shirazeh Houshiary," *Sculpture Magazine*, July 14, 2020, at https://sculpturemagazine.art/a-conversation-with-shirazeh-houshiary/.

HUANG YAN

b. Jilin Province, China, 1966

***Chinese Shanshui Tattoo Series No. 7*, 1999**
Chromogenic print
31½ × 39⅜ in. (80 × 100 cm)

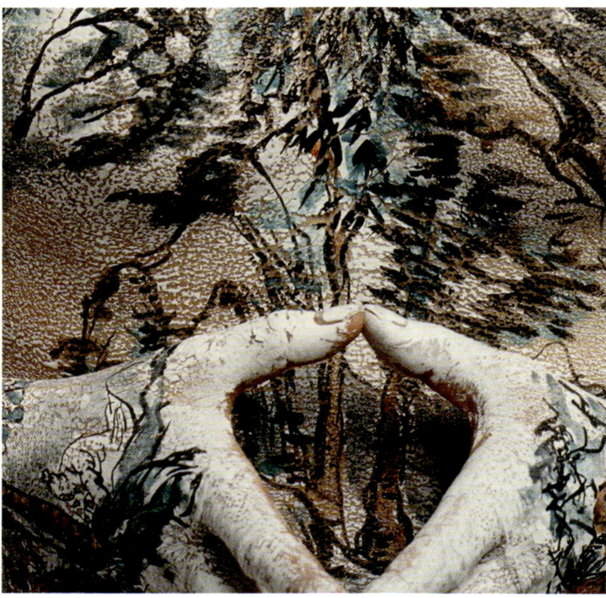

Chinese Shanshui Tattoo Series No. 7, 1999 (detail)

Classically trained artist Zhang Tiemei traces with a brush the whitened torso of her husband, Huang Yan, transforming it into vibrant vistas of landscape painting (*shanshui*). Creeks and ravines, mountains and trees creep up Huang's abdomen and ribcage, covering him up to his neck, then cascading down over shoulders and arms, reaching the tips of his fingers. A hut can be discerned on the back of one hand; on the other, a literatus is lost in thought. There is great intimacy in the very act of producing this work. It speaks to the role of collaboration, raising important issues of artistic agency and creative capital. While Zhang wields the brush, the work is ultimately that of the conceptual artist Huang Yan.

Huang began experimenting with his six-year-long *Chinese Shanshui Tattoo Series* in 1994, later enlisting Zhang's help. He painted classical themes like bird-and-flower motifs and blue-and-green landscapes, first on his face, then later on a variety of unconventional—at times outrageous—surfaces, including bones with flesh still clinging to them, porcelain, and busts of Chairman Mao. The series was propelled by Huang's quest to define the place of traditional painting in contemporary Chinese art. Although some have deemed it facetious, it is evident from Huang's thesis, "The History of Landscape," that his engagement with traditional ink painting is sincere and unironic. "To paint a landscape" he writes, "is to paint man, to paint oneself."

In literati ink painting, the human figure is often ancillary to the landscape. Dwarfed by the scenery, figures at times punctuate it like an afterthought. In Huang's work, the human figure looms large, encompassing the landscape as its very ground. As body becomes canvas, the title of the work, *Chinese Shanshui Tattoo*, suddenly rings truer. While the paint has already begun to fleck off when the photograph is taken, it is more than skin deep. The tradition of ink painting is eternally and indelibly impressed upon the artist's heart. Indeed, as Huang muses: "Under a Chinese intellectual's brush, the 'mountains and rivers' are not a landscape, but a place to open one's heart and confide." **EC**

Selected Exhibitions
Huang Yan, Chinese Contemporary, London, 2005; *Huang Yan Solo Exhibition*, Zhuqizhuan Art Museum, Shanghai, 2007; *Effacement: Huang Yan's China in the 21st Century*, Krannert Art Museum, Champaign, Illinois, 2009; *Longing for Nature*, Museum Rietberg, Zurich, 2020.

Further Sources
The Story of Shan-Shui (Beijing: Red Gate Gallery, 2002); Xindong Cheng, *Huang Yan 1990–2006* (China: Cheng Xindong chuban gongsi, 2006); Eleonora Battiston, *Huang Yan* (Milan: G. Prearo, 2007).

HUANG ZHIYANG

b. Taipei, 1965

***Possessing Numerous Peaks No. S-1226*, 2012**
Marble
9$^{15}/_{16}$ × 13¼ × 6¼ in. (24 × 35 × 16 cm)

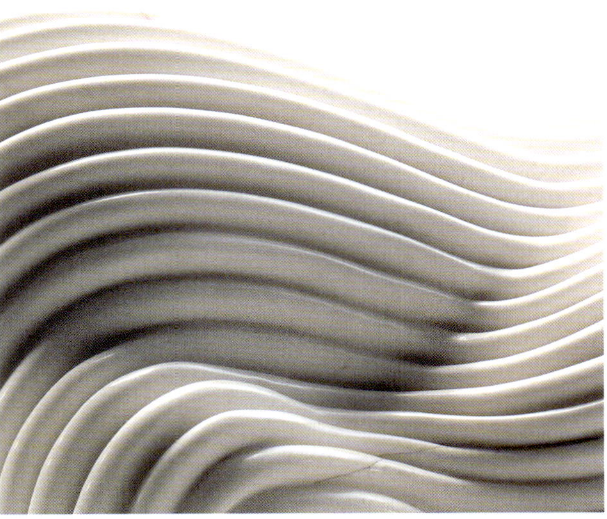

Possessing Numerous Peaks No. S-1226, 2012 (detail)

In his youth, Huang Zhiyang studied ink painting at the Taipei Chinese Cultural University. Principles like the flow of *qi*, essential to ink art, became a foundational part of his practice, and he turned toward imaging a dipolar flow of energy in his painting. Combining this with an interest in biology, Huang relates the flow of *qi* to the physical flow of energy throughout the human body, working on a microscopic scale. What might first appear abstract in his works is actually staunchly physical, though the visual associated with physical energy flow is nonetheless foreign to the average viewer. These works also track the artist's own energy, each piece a phenomenological manifestation of the effort exerted in the creation of the work itself.

After moving to Beijing in 2006, Huang began his *Possessing Numerous Peaks* series, inspired by the towering mountains that surround the city. He has described these mountains as dragons, and in his sculptures we see a shrunken version of these great beasts. The works show a flow of energy through undulating waves, both swirling around the bodies of the dragons and forming their numerous peaks. Emerging out of the tradition of ink landscape painting, the series embodies the same principles of flow and line that are fundamental in ink painting, while utilizing completely contrary materials.

Instead of translucent ink painted in light or forceful strokes, this landscape is formed of solid, opaque, dimensional stone. Instead of the traditional black ink—be it light or dark—the artist chose a stone the color of the standard white painting ground, as if the entire sculpture were negative space. Huang has fully transgressed the rules of ink art, forgoing its definitive materials and subverting standards of color and opacity, but his embodiment of *qi* within a landscape firmly grounds the resulting work within a history of ink painting.

Given Huang's own interests in Buddhism and meditation, it is particularly appropriate that *Possessing Numerous Peaks* evokes a sense of calm, and creates a space for contemplating the very definition of ink art. SF

Selected Exhibitions
City Scenery, Museum of Contemporary Art, Taipei, 2006; *Future Pass: From Asia to the World*, 54th Venice Biennale, 2011; *Huang Zhiyang | The Phenomenology of Life: Chapters in a Course of Study*, National Museum of China and INK Studio, Beijing, 2014.

Further Sources
Chen Yening and Huang Zhiyang, eds., *Huang Zhi Yang 1998–2008* (Taipei: Art & Collection Group, 2008); *Huang Zhiyang | The Phenomenology of Life: Chapters in a Course of Study* (New York: INK Studio, 2014).

JEONG GWANG-HEE

b. Goheung, Jeollanam Province, South Korea, 1967

***The Way of Reflection*, 2017**
Ink on Korean traditional paper (hanji)
63 × 49⅝ in. (160 × 126 cm)

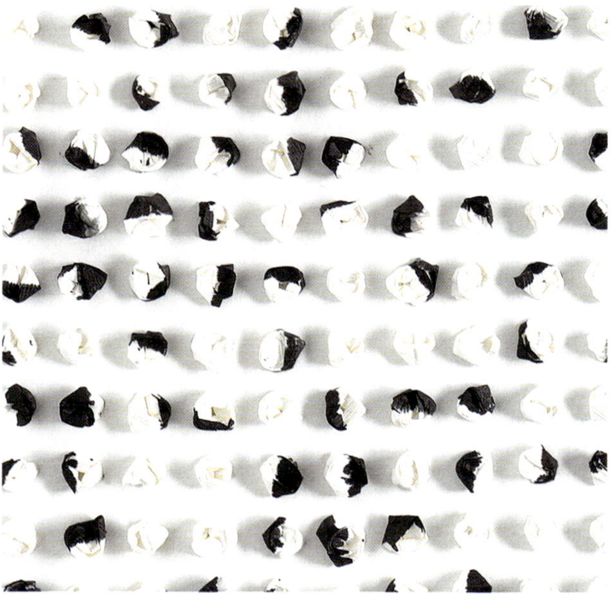

The Way of Reflection, 2017 (detail)

Although ink is a part of Jeong Gwang-Hee's practice, his works are far more than just paintings. In *The Way of Reflection*, he began with sheets of Korean hanji paper, on which are painted his preliminary ink strokes. He then folded and crumpled these pages and assembled a textured ground for the work, which straddles the line between 2D wall art and 3D sculpture. Finally, Jeong added a second layer of ink on top of this base, for a tritonal effect: the pure white paper; the initial marks of ink, muted by the folded paper; and the final ink marks, a deep black.

This piece is part of a larger series of the same name, the crumpling process repeated in each work to create a grid of paper balls. In some of these works, the artist begins with a process of accumulation prior to laying brush to paper, sometimes replacing the hanji with pages from old books, thus adding a third layer of ink in the form of the original printed text. Although his series vary, Jeong frequently employs similar processes of folding or crumpling paper to create a base, then dabs touches of ink on top.

From afar, *The Way of Reflection* looks like a calligraphic or textual grid, each crumpled ball a single cell repeated with countless variations. Closer inspection reveals the labor that went into producing the work: the folded paper, the glimpses of ink, the tidy grid. This technique is one of Jeong's signatures, and conveys the spirit of the artist much like calligraphy might convey self-expression. Trained in both calligraphy and painting, Jeong finds no need to distinguish the two art forms, instead embracing and subverting both to create his distinctive works. He accomplishes a personal goal in this series, of forgoing the material world for abstraction and concept, offering viewers an empty, meditative space. **SF**

Selected Exhibitions
Accumulating Ink, Gwangju Museum of Art, 2014; *Escaping from the Object in Thought*, DaeDam Museum, Damyang, Korea, 2015.

Further Sources
Oh Sewon and Kim Byuldabi, *2009 Artist-Centered Network: Decentered–The First Arko Network Project* (Seoul: Arko Art Center, Arts Council Korea, 2009).

IDRIS KHAN

b. Birmingham, UK, 1978

***Untitled*, 2013**
C-print mounted on aluminum
63 × 118 in. (160 × 300 cm)

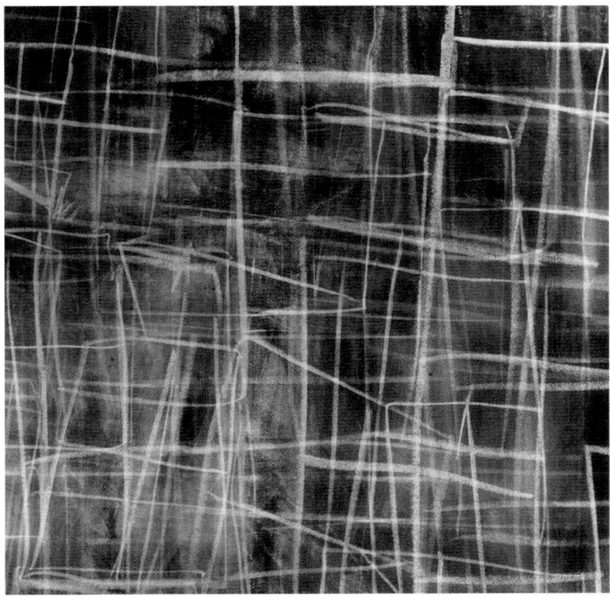

Untitled, 2013 (detail)

Idris Khan was born in Birmingham, England, to a Pakistani father and a Welsh mother; his father is a surgeon and his mother a nurse and pianist. The artist has spoken of the great influence music had on his early life, and this is evident in his work, which includes painting, photography, video, and sculpture. Khan moved to London to attend the Royal College of Art, and London is now his base. He is known for works that are visually complex and deeply layered, which demand and reward excavation. Khan speaks of utilizing photography as a means to explore memory, and just as memories shift over time, his works convey a sense of a world in a state of continuous flux, and of the visible traces of things that once existed but are now transformed into shadows and echoes. In this way, his images embody the sense of an archaeological dig, the excavated results of which remain mysterious even when revealed. Khan manipulates our perceptions of not only space but also time—by collapsing, for example, extended periods into single moments. He has accomplished this in many ways, in one case by combining 2,000 photographs into a single image. Early in his career, Khan produced photographs that looked like drawings, and in many of his more recent works the boundary between the two mediums is ambiguous.

In *Untitled*, Khan creates a mysterious space through a deft combination of painting and photography. The space engendered is simultaneously ordered and elusive, with an unresolved tension that is palpably musical—just as many of his works reflect an interest in and deep knowledge of music. The white lines of *Untitled* dance elegantly across the surface, generating a complex skein against an amorphous field of paler scumbled brushstrokes, all set against a black void. Through abstract means, the artist conjures the illusion of a space full, like the universe itself, of both order and chaos.
SL

Selected Exhibitions
Blue Rhythms, Sean Kelly Gallery, New York, 2019; *The Seasons Turn*, Victoria Miro Gallery, London, 2021.

Further Source
Idris Khan in Conversation with Sarah Thornton, Hirshhorn Museum, Smithsonian Institution, May 30, 2018, at https://hirshhorn.si.edu/event/artist-talk-idris-khan/.

KIM HO-DEUK

b. Seoul, 1950

***San, San* (*Mountain, Mountain*)**, 2018
Ink on cotton (Korean *gwangmok* cloth)
129⅛ × 100 in. (328 × 254 cm)

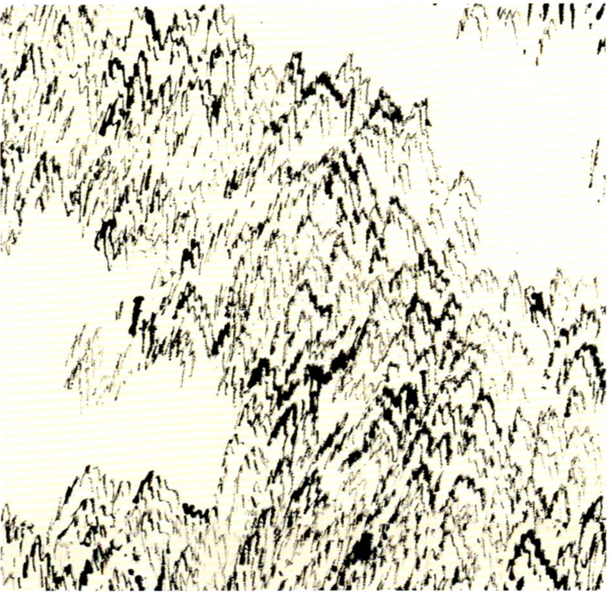

San, San (Mountain, Mountain), 2018 (detail)

Kim Ho-deuk's landscapes are an exploration of *yin* and *yang*, positive and negative space, tradition and modernity, and between-ness, inspired in part by his studies of both Korean and Western art history and painting at Seoul National University. These oppositions are encapsulated in the balance of deep black ink and blank white paper that forms the essence of Kim's painting practice. His approach can be seen as a continuation of *muninhwa*, a Joseon-dynasty scholarly practice of portraying complex concepts through simple brushstrokes.

In his paintings, Kim seldom uses anything but completely opaque black ink, forgoing watery tonal washes; as his brush runs dry, his ink naturally appears lighter, but it is never diluted. Color is always both present and absent from his paintings—as he recognizes that the black ink itself contains every color.

The result is a landscape practice unique to the artist. In his *San, San* series, Kim depicts not a single range or mountain, but hundreds of mountains through the repetition of a basic linear form: a squiggled mountain peak emerging from an immense sea of fog in seemingly empty space. The size of each peak seems at odds with the mist, adding an uncanny, disorienting quality to what might have been a singular view of a landscape. Kim's repeated strokes read variably as contour lines, lines following the flow of *qi* (Korean: *gi*), or, formally, the effect of double-vision.

Although this work appears in the Dreamscapes section of *Ink Dreams*, it could easily have been placed in Meditations. Both formally and conceptually, *San, San* shares the calm emptiness and repetition found there, and even though perceived initially as a landscape, when read as abstract, it shares the minimalist quality of repeating a simple form. **SF**

Selected Exhibitions
Korean Avant-Garde Drawing 1970–2000, Soma Museum of Art, Seoul, 2010; *Abstract It!*, National Museum of Modern and Contemporary Art, Seoul, 2011; *KIM Ho-deuk*, Hakgojae Gallery, Seoul, 2019.

Further Sources
"KIM Ho Deuk," Korean Artist Project with Korean Art Museums, at http://www.koreanartistproject.com/eng_artist.art?method=artistView&flag=artist&auth_reg_no=10; Park Soyoung, *Kim Ho-Deuk* (Yeongcheon, South Korea: Cyan Museum of Art, 2009); Yoon Kew Hong, *Kim Ho Deuk: Layered Space–Between* (Daegu, South Korea: Gallery Bundo, 2014).

KITAMURA JUNKO

b. Kyoto, 1956

Vessel 08-C, 2008
Stoneware
21½ × 6⅛ × 6⅛ in. (54.5 × 15.5 × 15.5 cm)

Vessel 08-G, 2008
Stoneware
4⅜ × 13⅜ × 13⅜ in. (11 × 34 × 34 cm)

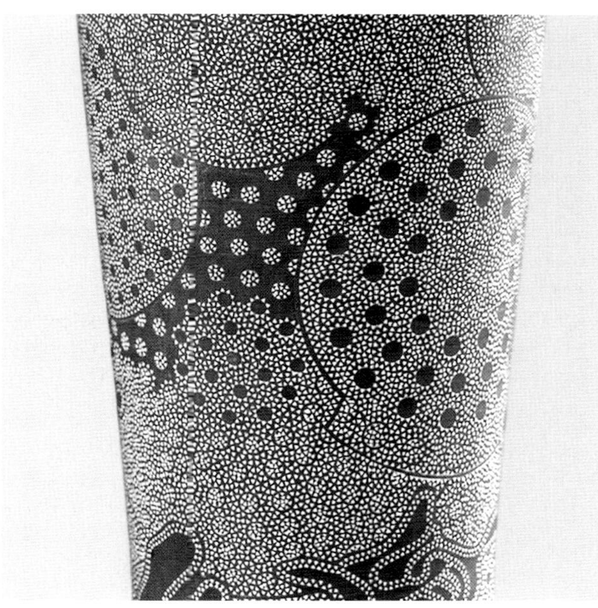

Vessel 08-C, 2008 (detail)

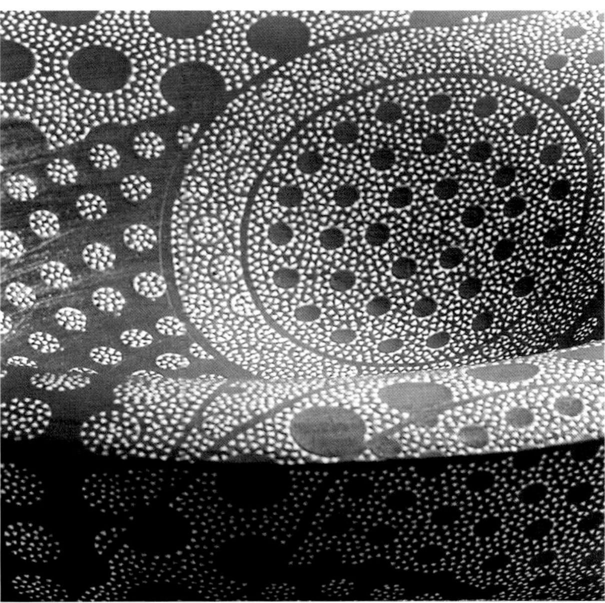

Vessel 08-G, 2008 (detail)

Born in Kyoto, Kitamura Junko is a pioneering Japanese ceramist who creates conceptually daring works that extend the medium far beyond traditional rules of functionality. Originally intending to pursue a career in kimono dyeing, she changed course to the art of ceramic, but an abiding passion for textiles is still evident in her ceramic works decorated with painstakingly intricate lacelike patterns. Two teachers influenced her career choice: Suzuki Osamu, renowned avant-garde ceramic artist and cofounder of the Japanese ceramics group Sōdeisha, and noted ceramist Kondō Yutaka, professor at Kyoto City University of Arts, where Kitamura received an MFA. Her works are also inspired by the organic forms of ancient Japanese pottery from the Jōmon period, as well as the Korean tradition of Buncheong (or Punch'ong) ware in the early Joseon dynasty, featuring slip (liquid clay) inlay and a natural, unassuming style.

These two simple yet dynamic stonewares, signature works by Kitamura, exemplify her production methods. She first shapes a vessel on the potter's wheel, then coats it with dark gray or black slip. When the clay is leather hard, she carves small dots on the surface to create exquisite and dizzying patterns using a sharpened piece of bamboo. After a bisque firing, she coats the vessel with white slip. When dry, she scrapes away the excess slip before firing the piece a final time. Kitamura instills her patterning with what she describes as "both quiet and powerful movement, some [designs] slow and delicate and others fast and bold." Refusing to draw patterns in advance, she prefers to let them emerge organically through the creation process. Taken together, these minuscule concentric dots and geometric indentations suggest snowflakes, celestial constellations, or Japanese textile patterns. Kitamura's imaginative designs and laborious technique have garnered considerable praise and admiration.
WK

Selected Exhibitions
Shifting Paradigms in Contemporary Ceramics, Museum of Fine Arts, Houston, 2012; *Fired Earth, Woven Bamboo: Contemporary Japanese Ceramics and Bamboo Art*, Museum of Fine Arts, Boston, 2013; *Yō Akiyama + Junko Kitamura*, Kakiden Gallery, Tokyo, 2013; *Japanese Ceramics for the Twenty-first Century: The Betsy and Robert Feinberg Collection*, The Walters Art Museum, Baltimore, 2014; *A Moment in Time: Akiyama Yō and Kitamura Junko*, Joan B Mirviss LTD, New York, 2015.

Further Sources
Monochrome: Akiyama Yo + Kitamura Junko (Tokyo: Gyararikochukyo, 2008); Linda Muehlig, ed., *Touch Fire: Contemporary Japanese Ceramics by Women Artists* (Northampton: Smith College Museum of Art, 2009), pp. 49–53; *Fired Earth, Woven Bamboo: Contemporary Japanese Ceramics and Bamboo Art* (Boston: MFA Publications/ Museum of Fine Arts, 2013); Robert Mintz and Joan Mirviss with Betsy Feinberg, *Japanese Ceramics for the Twenty-first Century: The Betsy and Robert Feinberg Collection* (Baltimore: Walters Art Museum, 2014).

MATTI KUJASALO

b. Helsinki, 1946

Painting, 2011
Acrylic on canvas
$68\frac{15}{16} \times 68\frac{15}{16}$ in. (175 × 175 cm)

Painting, 2011 (detail)

Art was a part of Matti Kujasalo's life from an early age. His grandmother, herself an established artist, encouraged him to draw and paint in his youth. After finishing his basic education, he took courses at the Free Art School in Helsinki. From 1964 to 1968, he attended the Academy of Fine Arts of Finland, where he later became instructor and director. Kujasalo visited the United States in 1967 and again in 1970, readily absorbing the influence of American artists Ad Reinhardt and Josef Albers, both known for their geometric, color-blocked approaches to pure abstraction. In 1976, Kujasalo joined the International Workgroup for Constructive Art, a Constructivist group particularly interested in color fields and seriality.

Kujasalo's systematic Constructivist works, like *Painting*, rely on a formal practice of abstract patterning. On an initial colored ground, he lays down strips of tape with widths as small as one-tenth of a millimeter, to create a series of square grids that overlap to form intricate patterns. After each layer of tape is applied to the canvas, he adds a new color of paint, later pulling up the tape to reveal the earlier hues. By repeating this process, Kujasalo creates precise and detailed abstract works.

Beginning in the 1990s, the artist turned to a monochrome black, white, and gray palette with the occasional touch of color. In *Painting*, vibrant colors peek through the final layer of paint—which is always black, here overwhelming almost all of the canvas. The spaces between lines of black paint create windows into the colorful, vibrant world below, with the darker areas receding and the lighter areas coming forward, an energetic optical illusion. **SF**

Selected Exhibitions
Momentum 2011, 6th Nordic Biennial of Contemporary Art, Momentum Kunsthall, Moss; *Matti Kujasalo: A Retrospective 1971–2017*, GASK, Kutná Hora, Czech Republic, 2017; *Cutting Edges: Nordic Concrete Art from the Erling Neby Collection*, Scandinavia House, New York, 2019.

Further Sources
Jorma Hautala, *Matti Kujasalo* (Bergamo: Grafico, 1980); Leonhard Lapin et al., *Matti Kujasalo* (Helsinki: Galerie Anhava, 2010).

LEE UFAN

b. Kyongnam, Korea, 1936

From Point, 1978
Graphite on paper
22¼ × 30⅛ in. (56.6 × 76.5 cm)

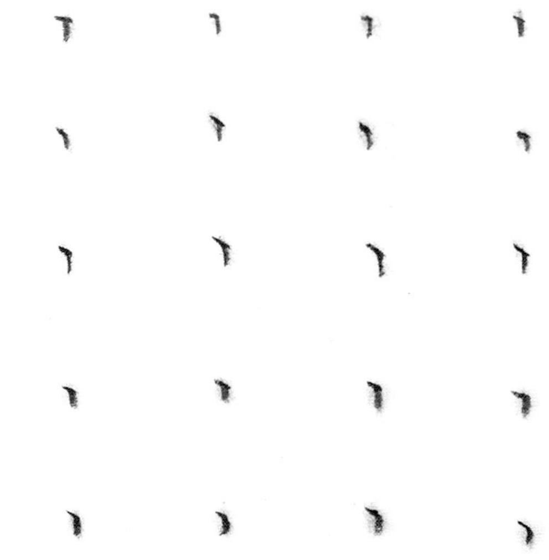

From Point, 1978 (detail)

"The meeting and parting of points are aspects of all things, and this repetitive mechanism demonstrates the infinity of the universe. My *From Point* and *From Line* series are based on this concept of infinity. The cyclic repetition of appearance and disappearance, disappearance and appearance, seen in these series is a theory, a mode of logic, and a method of expression."

As he articulates in *The Art of Encounter*, artist-philosopher Lee Ufan seeks to represent in his *From Point* the concept of infinity as a vector of repetition with endless variation. The slow and deliberate mark-making process constitutes a record and a journal of the artist's bodily movements. Short, hooked marks with blurred edges are applied methodically to plain paper. Spaced evenly, no two are alike; their slight variation within the grid forms a rhythmic, almost musical cadence. They gradually spread across the paper, claiming their presence in the most economical terms. By using minimal gestures to occupy and transform space, Lee applies the concept of blank-leaving (*liu bai*), a Chinese aesthetic principle where areas are intentionally left untouched, counterpoising other elements in the composition. While he acknowledges the concept's influence on his artistic practice, Lee adapts blank-leaving and incorporates it into his own visual language of minimalism, which is decidedly individual and contemporary.

Born in Kyongnam, Korea, and educated in Seoul, Lee moved to Japan in 1956 where he studied philosophy and spearheaded the avant-garde group Mono-ha (School of Things). The movement's fascination with simple materials and the perception of the artist as facilitator is reflected here in the choice of humble materials—graphite and paper—and the notion of the artwork not as the goal of the painting process, but rather as its record. The piece's monochromaticity also speaks to another art movement revolving around Lee, Dansaekhwa (Monochrome Painting), which was based in Japan, Korea, and France and experimented with the manipulation of painting materials. *From Point* may draw on the artist's cultural context and aesthetic proclivities, but it ultimately transcends geographic boundaries and temporal demarcations; it is global, and timeless. **EC**

Selected Exhibitions
Lee Ufan: The Art of Margins, Yokohama Museum of Art, 2005; Lee Ufan Museum, Naoshima, Japan, opened 2010; *Lee Ufan: Marking Infinity*, Solomon R. Guggenheim Museum, New York, 2011; *Lee Ufan: Inhabiting Time*, Centre Pompidou-Metz, 2019.

Further Sources
U-hwan Yi, Alexandra Munroe, Akira Tatehata, and Mika Yoshitake, *Lee Ufan: Marking Infinity* (New York: Guggenheim Museum, 2011); U-hwan Yi, Hans Ulrich Obrist, and Stanley N. Anderson, *The Art of Encounter* (London: Lisson Gallery/Serpentine Gallery, 2018); *Lee Ufan: Open Dimension* (Washington, D.C.: Smithsonian Institution, 2020).

JOEY LEUNG KA-YIN

b. Hong Kong, 1976

Late Rabbit, 2010
Ink, color, biro, and pencil on paper
37⅝ × 39 in. (95.5 × 96.5 cm)

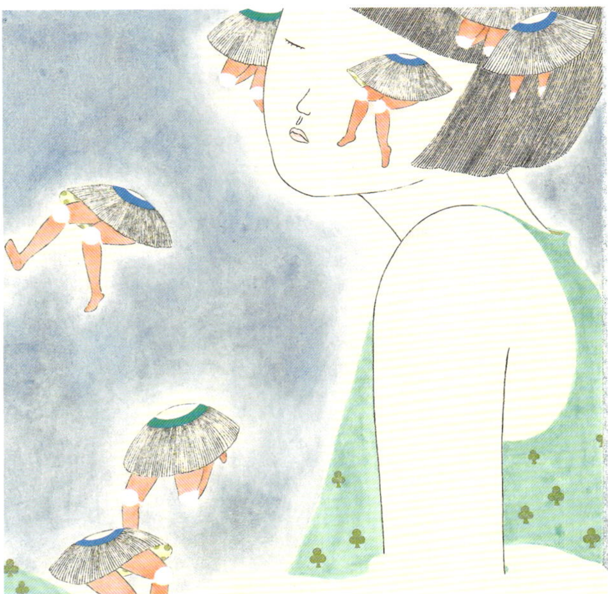

Late Rabbit, 2010 (detail)

Joey Leung Ka-yin combines whimsical themes with the traditional Chinese motifs of birds-and-flowers and mountain landscapes. Her pieces are characterized by fine *gongbi* linework and muted colors, and often feature young, short-haired girls with elfin facial features, communing in the nude with nature. The artist describes the girls as "lazy, bored, not satisfied, and sometimes hav[ing] weird, naughty or destructive thoughts"—we see this in *Late Rabbit* in the small figure at the center-right of the image, wielding a pair of scissors and surrounded by destroyed topiaries.

In her MFA studies at the Chinese University of Hong Kong, Leung synthesized traditional *gongbi* techniques with comic illustration. She utilizes a number of trompe l'oeil techniques throughout her works: emulating brushwork with pen, often drawing over a line multiple times in order to mimic the look of a thick brushstroke; silk brocade, used in traditional mounting methods, drawn with ink and color; and hand-drawn imitations of computer-generated fonts. In *Late Rabbit*, the type reads:

Please forgive me your majesty
You know I am never late
I mistakenly took the wrong path
And was distracted by the flirtatious glances
like a group of jumping fleas
They threw me the sweetest "hello" I have ever heard
I fell headlong into their embrace
Then I lost my way and I didn't know how to find it
That's the reason why I am late

Leung's figures are presented in a pastel fantasy-scape, in which proportions and physical features are often distorted: the young girls as large as the mountain or as small as the lotus pod on which they lounge; their knees popping out of lakes to create grassy islands. In *Late Rabbit*, clouds weave around the elbow and knee of the central figure, her dress a verdant hillside patterned with paved, winding roads and telephone poles. **SF**

Selected Exhibitions
The Pivotal Decade: Hong Kong Art 1997–2007, Chinese Arts Centre [now Centre for Chinese Contemporary Art], Manchester, 2007; *Legacy and Creations: Ink Art vs Ink Art*, Hong Kong Museum of Art, 2010; *A Sense of Place: From Turner to Hockney*, Hong Kong Museum of Art and Tate, London, 2019.

Further Sources
Henry Au-yeung, *The Pivotal Decade: Hong Kong Art 1997–2007* (Hong Kong: Grotto Fine Art, 2007); Tina Liem, *Joey Ka-yin Leung: Cloudy Fairy-Tales* (Hong Kong: Grotto Fine Art, 2010); Henry Au-yeung, *Mollywood* (Hong Kong: Grotto Fine Art, 2018).

LEUNG KUI-TING

b. Guangzhou, Guangdong Province, China, 1945

Vision 08, 2008
Ink on silk
57 7/16 × 53 9/16 in. (146 × 136 cm)

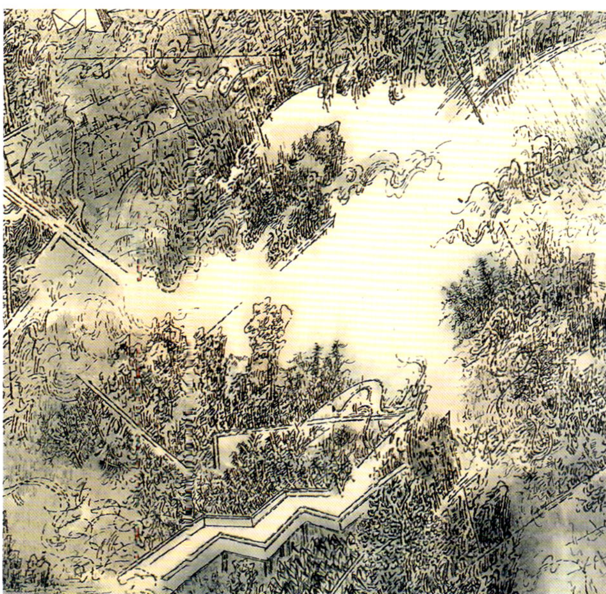

Vision 08, 2008 (detail)

Born in Guangzhou in mainland China, Leung Kui-ting moved to Hong Kong with his family in 1948. A carpenter at a young age, he studied painting in 1964 under Lui Shou-kwan (pp. 79, 157) and Wucius Wong (p. 179), two prominent artists of the New Ink Movement in Hong Kong. Throughout the 1960s, Leung experimented with various mediums, including ink, oil, printmaking, and sculpture, but since the 1980s he has concentrated on ink painting as his primary mode of expression. Most of his works synthesize classical ink painting and modern art, combining subjects such as scholar's rocks, trees, and mountains favored by China's premodern literati with new styles, techniques, and symbols unique to the modern environment.

A representative work of Leung Kui-ting's oeuvre, *Vision 08* depicts a landscape among misty clouds, where the flow of *qi*, or energy, is carefully rendered. For the overall composition, he abandoned the level standpoint used by traditional artists, instead adopting a panoramic aerial view as if seen from an airplane, a perspective that, of course, was not experienced by people in the past. Superimposed on natural scenery are fragmented forms, geometric doodles, and discursive lines that evoke urban architecture, digital signals, or the formation of heaven and earth. Years of experience as a sculptor have enhanced Leung's sensitivity to and appreciation of three-dimensionality, and enabled him to create such spatially complicated and almost incongruous landscapes. Through the medium of traditional ink, brush (sometimes also a pen), and silk, he paints dots, lines, and forms, with lightly colored ink washes. The broken lines are similar to the ox-hair brush texture strokes (*niumao cun*) originated by the Yuan-dynasty master Wang Meng, yet the reference is overwhelmed by Leung's modern twist, where he interweaves and harmonizes Chinese traditional landscape paintings with modern spatial aesthetics. WK

Selected Exhibitions
Contemporary Works from Hong Kong Museum of Art, Vancouver Museum of Art, 1992; *Leung Kui Ting: Roaming Vision + Digital*, Hanart TZ Gallery, Hong Kong, 2011; *The Origin of Tao: New Dimensions in Chinese Contemporary Art*, Hong Kong Museum of Art, 2012; *Noir d'encre, regards croisés: Hartung et les peintres chinois*, Musée des Arts d'Extrême Orient de la Fondation Baur, Geneva, 2013; *Alisan Fine Arts: Celebrating 35 Years of Promoting Chinese Contemporary Art*, Hong Kong Central Library, 2016.

Further Sources
Chang Tsong-zung, ed., *Hong Kong Eye: Hong Kong Contemporary Art* (Milan: Skira, 2012); Chang Tsong-zung, ed., *Geometry of the Spirit: 50 Years of Leung Kui Ting* (Hong Kong: Hanart TZ Gallery, 2014); Tang Hoichiu et al., *A Legacy of Ink: Lui Shou-Kwan 40 Years On* (Hong Kong: Alisan Fine Arts, 2015).

LI HUASHENG

b. Yibin, Sichuan Province, China, 1944–2018

Album 2, 1990s
Ink and color on paper
12 leaves, each 13⅜ × 13⅜ in. (34 × 34 cm)

Li Huasheng began cultivating his control of the brush as a youth, practicing both calligraphy and traditional landscape painting. As a student at the Yangzi River Secondary School, he was surrounded by beautiful natural scenery and spent much of his time sketching. After graduating, he began working in the propaganda unit of the Yangzi River Shipping Corporation traveling through the gorges and painting his dramatic surroundings. At the start of the Cultural Revolution (1966–76), he faced criticism from his peers, who perceived elements of his work as symbolic of a longing for the West. In response, he turned to oil painting in an accepted Socialist Realist style but continued his ink landscape practice in secret. The artist endured criticism and slander from the Chinese government for years but finally began to receive recognition for his ink paintings during the 1980s.

Album 2 is a group of twelve small, originally stand-alone works that were assembled into an album format by Gérard and Dora Cognié with Li, one of two such sets in the Fondation INK Collection representative of his mid-career landscapes. They are painted in his style of loose, watery brushstrokes and brilliantly colored pigments. The varied thin black linework and vast washes in black and gray are typical of his landscapes in the 1980s and '90s. The fluid, rapidly executed marks hint at an interest in abstraction that predates his phenomenological explorations begun in the late 1990s. Notably, his landscape paintings rarely include a straight line—even the small buildings that he sometimes inserts in a composition have impossibly curved walls.

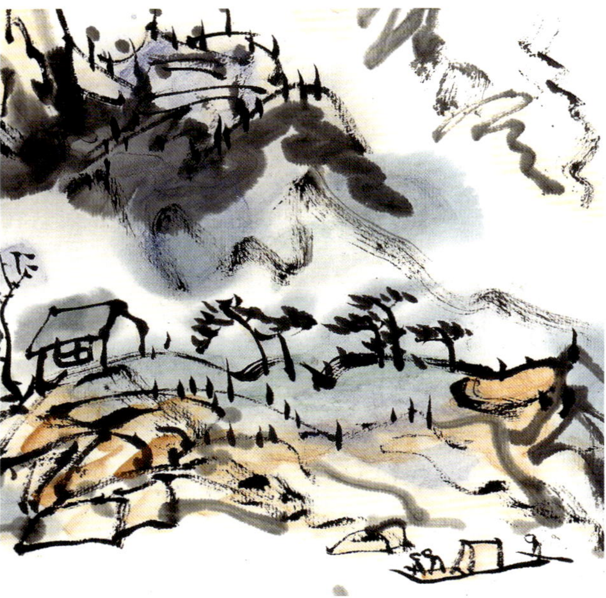

Album 2, 1990s (details)

Untitled, 1998–2000
Ink on paper
56¾ × 72¹⁄₂₆ in. (144 × 183 cm)

104, 2001
Ink on xuan paper
48⅝ × 97⅝ in. (123.5 × 248 cm)

Li's later practice of grid painting was born of an age-old tradition. The act of secluding oneself deep within the mountains and valleys of rural China has a rich history in the world of the Chinese literati. Though the practice has become less common over time, Li dedicated himself to the cultivation of a unique artistic vision through the shielding of the self from outside influences. In 1987, after spending five months in the United States, he grew restless with the traditional techniques he previously employed. Embarking on a ten-year period of retreat, he made multiple trips to the Himalayas, staying in various Tibetan Buddhist monasteries, where, inspired by lines of chanting monks, he began his grid painting.

These works constitute a phenomenological record of Li's life. Like the chanting of monks, the construction of a grid involved a deeply meditative process—each line required patience and emptiness, repeated until the whole ground was filled. The vivacious Li was often able to point to a section of a particular grid and recall the events occurring as he reached that part of the painting. The experiences and thoughts that came to him during the creation of a work—which sometimes extended over months—are forever embodied and embedded in each grid. SF

Selected Exhibitions
Li Huasheng: An Individualistic Artist, Chinese Culture Center, San Francisco, and Alisan Fine Arts, Hong Kong, 1998; *Chinese Maximalism*, Millennium Art Museum, Beijing, UB Anderson Gallery, Buffalo, and Ethan Cohen Fine Arts, New York, 2003; *Li Huasheng: Process, Mind, and Landscape*, INK Studio, Beijing, 2014.

Further Sources
Jerome Silbergeld and Jisui Gong, *Contradictions: Artistic Life, the Socialist State, and the Chinese Painter Li Huasheng* (Seattle: University of Washington Press, 1993); *The Enduring Passion for Ink*: "Li Huasheng's Ambivalence," directed by Britta Erickson and Richard Widmer, video, 2017.

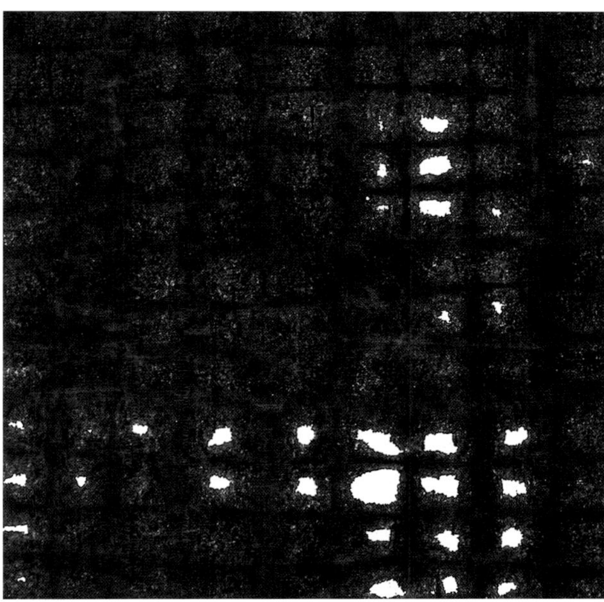

Untitled, 1998–2000 (detail)

104, 2001 (detail)

LI HUAYI

b. Shanghai, 1948

Landscape, 2009
Ink and color on paper
27 × 51 in. (68.6 × 129.5 cm)

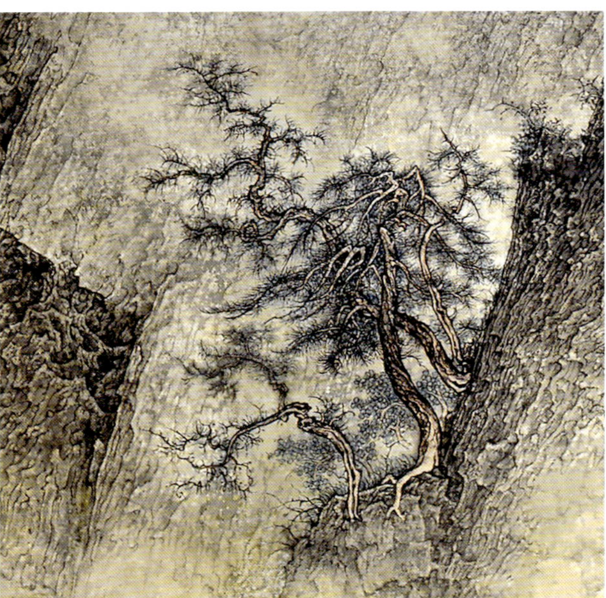

Landscape, 2009 (detail)

Born into a prestigious Shanghai family, Li Huayi studied painting from the age of six under Wang Chuantao, son of the Shanghai School artist Wang Zhen. At sixteen, he was trained by Western-style artist Zhang Chongren. During the Cultural Revolution (1966–76), Li was employed making Socialist Realist propaganda posters. In 1982, he emigrated to the United States and earned an MFA at San Francisco's Academy of Art University.

Li Huayi's training was diverse, but it was the monumental landscapes of the Northern Song dynasty that provided the spark to forge a unique personal style. Here, he renders the trees as crab claws, a typical *cun* texturing stroke used, for instance, in Northern Song artist Guo Xi's *Early Spring* (1072; National Palace Museum, Taipei). And consonant with traditional literati painting, which is more an expression of self through the play of brush and ink, Li's work reflects his inner spirit, not an actual landscape. But unlike those Northern Song precedents which were produced in vertical scroll format, many of Li's large-scale paintings are horizontal. Forgoing the panoramic depiction of mountains characteristic of the Northern Song, he deconstructs the elements of a landscape and recombines them into an abstract scene in which details are amplified. In *Landscape*, the magnificence and dynamics of the geometric mountainlike forms are unmistakably contemporary. The crystalline details of the boulders suggest a microcosm, while the dark, deep creases in the upper center draw the viewer into a mysterious macro-realm. This confusion of micro and macro, placing seemingly contradictory elements within a single field, complicates the viewer's perception.

The artist's working method involves multiple steps. He first lays paper on the floor and pours ink on it. He manipulates the ink with broad flat brushes or by lifting the edges of the paper. Then he mounts the paper on a stiff surface and paints vertically. Finally, he adds details and layers of texture. Particular about materials, Li uses paper custom-made to his specifications of absorbency and strength. His brushes are also specially made or designed by himself. **WK**

Selected Exhibitions
The Monumental Landscapes of Li Huayi, Asian Art Museum of San Francisco, 2004; *Fresh Ink: Ten Takes on Chinese Tradition*, Museum of Fine Arts, Boston, 2010; *Images of the Mind: The Ink Painting of Li Huayi*, National Art Museum of China, Beijing, 2011; *Fantasies on Paper and Enchantments in Gold: Solo Exhibition of Li Huayi*, Suzhou Museum, 2017; *Contemporary Landscapes: Li Huayi*, Honolulu Museum of Art, 2019.

Further Sources
Michael Knight and Kazuhiro Tsuruta, *The Monumental Landscapes of Li Huayi* (San Francisco: Asian Art Museum Chong-Moon Lee Center for Asian Art and Culture, 2004); Michael Knight et al., *Mountain Landscapes by Li Huayi* (London: Eskenazi Gallery, 2007); Kuiyi Shen, *Li Huayi* (New York: Rizzoli, 2018).

LIN TIANMIAO

b. Taiyuan, Shanxi Province, China, 1961

Seeing Shadows No. 35, 2007
Thread and mixed media on canvas
56¾ × 111¾ × 3³⁄₁₆ in. (144 × 284 × 8 cm)

The Tree, 2010
Synthetic bone and thread
137¾ × 63 × 63 in. (350 × 160 × 160 cm)

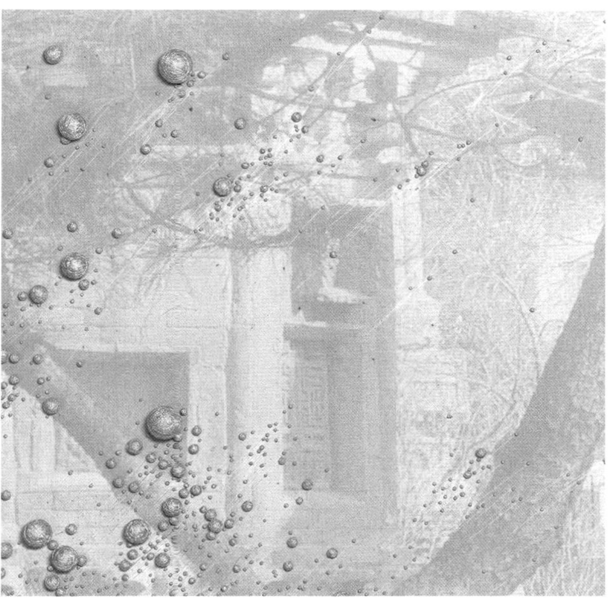

Seeing Shadows No. 35, 2007 (detail)

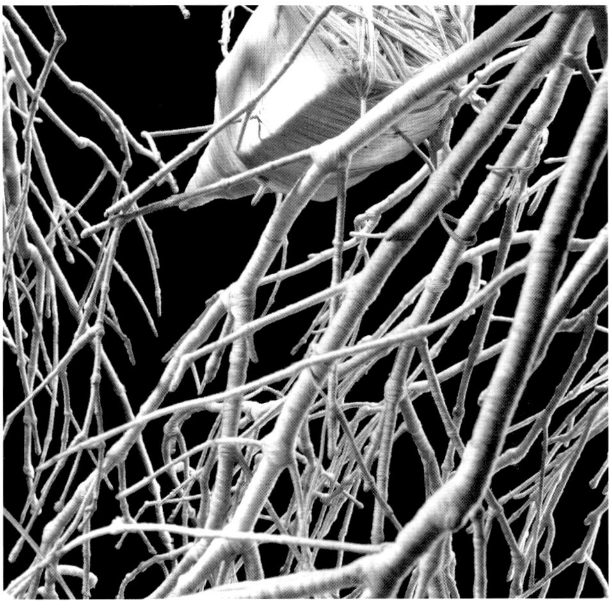

The Tree, 2010 (detail)

One of the most established artists in China today, Lin Tianmiao explores themes of memory, womanhood, and decay through an innovative use of her signature material, white cotton thread. Lin has recalled her introduction to this material: from the age of four, she would help her mother to unwind old pairs of white cotton work gloves that she received periodically as a worker at a state-owned factory. During the Cultural Revolution (1966–76), it was common to collect and conserve such items that might be useful in mending, sewing, or completing other domestic tasks.

After graduating from Capital Normal University in Beijing in 1984, Lin moved with artist-husband Wang Gongxin (p. 111) to New York, where she worked in textile design. A bustling center of contemporary art, the city served as a hub of international influences for Lin. After returning to Beijing in 1995, she began utilizing thread to bind and cover everyday household objects, such as dishes, small appliances, and bicycles, erasing their surfaces by obscuring their original form. This technique has remained a part of her practice, and she often assembles these uncanny objects in large-scale installations.

In 2006, Lin began to experiment with printmaking during an artist's residency at the Singapore Tyler Print Institute. In the series *Seeing Shadows* (2005–12), she combines large-scale photographic prints with white thread. The subjects and imagery of the grayscale photos become blurred, distorted, and at times are completely concealed by threads and woven three-dimensional growths that bubble over the edge of the canvas. They are at once soft and unsettling, both inviting touch and evoking diseased flesh—a dangerous combination.

The Tree, a mature example of Lin's thread-wrapping technique, exemplifies her process in recent works. She begins by creating a sculptural amalgam, often combining synthetic bones with weapons, tools, or instruments. These elements are then covered using white or colored monochrome silk or cotton thread, leaving the viewer to guess at the sculpture's original component parts. A closer look at the unearthly branches of *The Tree* reveals that this is one such chimera—Lin's threads are not wrapping natural wood here, but a combination of synthetic bones and other amorphous materials. Embedded within the web of branches, these mysterious elements evoke the nests of a bird or wasp, or a collection of equally alien internal organs. SF

Selected Exhibitions
Bound Unbound: Lin Tianmiao, Asia Society, New York. 2012; *Seeing Shadow*, Art & Public Gallery, Geneva, 2007; *1.62M: Lin Tianmiao Solo Exhibition*, HOW Art Museum, Wenzhou, China, 2015.

Further Sources
Karen Smith and Pi Li, *Lin Tianmiao: Non Zero* (Beijing: Beijing Tokyo Art Projects, 2004); Lin Tianmiao, *Seeing Shadows* (Beijing: Timezone 8, 2007); Victoria Lu, *Focus on Paper: Lin Tianmiao* (Singapore: Singapore Tyler Print Institute, 2007); Melissa Chiu and Guo Xiaoyan, eds., *Bound Unbound: Lin Tianmiao* (New York: Asia Society, 2012).

LIU DAN

b. Nanjing, Jiangsu Province, China, 1953

Untitled, 2012
Ink on paper
86⅝ × 47¼ in. (220 × 120 cm)

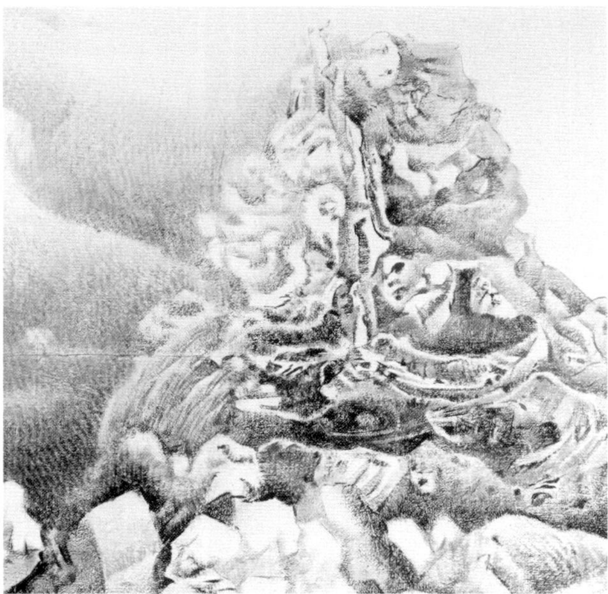

Untitled, 2012 (detail)

Liu Dan embodies the platonic ideal of the contemporary literatus, invoking the spirit of China's historical scholar-officials who expressed themselves freely through painting, calligraphy, and poetry. His works represent the continuation of the literati painting tradition and the recollection of history's greatest ink masters, for one would be hard-pressed to find an artist with more of an engagement with the arts and philosophies of the past. Himself a collector of past master works, Liu's practice is split between the imaging of objects from life—scholar's stones being a favorite subject—and imaginary landscapes, like *Untitled*, that yield a glimpse into his inner world.

Liu Dan's childhood was largely shaped by the programs of the Chinese Communist Party. In 1957, during the Anti-Rightist Campaign, Liu's parents—his father a chemistry professor, his mother a high school English teacher—were targeted as rightist intellectuals. In spite of the antireligious and antihistorical stances of the time, however, and with his grandfather's encouragement, Liu studied the classics from a very young age, in the form of Confucius's sayings, poetry, painting, and calligraphy. He also discovered an interest in Chinese and Western master painters alike, and was particularly drawn to Renaissance artists. From 1981, he lived in the United States for 25 years. Upon his return to China, Liu continued to cultivate his mature artistic practice: black ink on white paper, punctuated with the occasional hint of cinnabar red. While he eschews the use of pigments, his meticulous attention to detail and fine linework recall the traditional technique of *gongbi* brush painting.

In *Untitled*, we see in the foreground the base of a mountain, with water or snow on either side conveyed through Liu's use of negative space. Rising from the snow is a form familiar from classical Chinese mountain landscape paintings. However, a closer look reveals that the rocks that create this mountain are swirling, dreamy, and without the grounding weight of true stone. Hidden caverns in the mountain wall are rendered in Liu's deepest tones of black ink; his lightest tones signal the mountain peaks fading back into a thick mist. **SF**

Selected Exhibitions
Fresh Ink: Ten Takes on Chinese Tradition, Museum of Fine Arts, Boston, 2011; *Ink Unbound: Paintings by Liu Dan*, Minneapolis Institute of Art, 2016; *Liu Dan: New Landscapes and Old Masters*, Ashmolean Museum, Oxford, 2016.

Further Sources
Ackbar Abbas, *Transfigured Echoes: Recent Paintings by Liu Dan* (London: Eskenazi, 2015); Yang Liu and Stephen Little, *Ink Unbound: Paintings by Liu Dan* (Minneapolis: Minneapolis Institute of Art, 2016); Elizabeth Kindall and Liu Yang, "Stories from Liu Dan," Minneapolis Institute of Art, September 22, 2016, at https://vimeo.com/184080907; *The Enduring Passion for Ink:* "Liu Dan's Perfection," directed by Britta Erickson and Richard Widmer, video, 2017.

LIU GUOSONG (LIU KUO-SUNG)

b. Benbu, Anhui Province, China, 1932

Moon Series: It'll Soon Be White All Over, 1970
Ink and colors on paper
36⅛ × 23⅝ in. (91.8 × 60.2 cm)

Moon Series: Daybreak, 2005
Ink and colors on paper, mixed media, and collage
43½ × 22⅝ in. (110.5 × 57.5 cm)

Widely acclaimed as the "Father of Modern Ink Painting," Liu Guosong was born in 1932 in Anhui Province in mainland China and moved to Taiwan in 1949. He was educated in both Chinese and Western painting styles at the National Taiwan Normal University. Constantly challenging the limits of traditional Chinese ink painting, and deeply attuned to the modern art movements of the Western world, Liu cofounded the influential Fifth Moon Painting Society, the most prominent group of Chinese abstract painters of its time in Taiwan. He overturned the traditional mode of Chinese ink painting by experimenting with colors, textures, and techniques, evident in his innovative *shita* (water rubbing), *zimo* (steeped ink), and *penmo* (sprayed ink) practices. He thoughtfully adapted elements from various sources to achieve avant-garde ends, seen in his *Calligraphic Abstraction Series*, *Water Rubbing Series*, *Steeped Series*, and *Tibet Series*, among others.

Liu began the *Moon Series* in 1969, inspired by images of Earth taken by astronauts on Apollo 8, as well as the luminous spheres of light emanating from traditional Chinese lanterns. Watching films of the Apollo team, he connected the idea of space exploration with the panoramic landscapes of the Song dynasty and later, when Chinese artists would paint from an elevated or transcendent perspective, similar to that of an astronaut. These two works from the series were created with one of Liu's signature techniques. First, he collected the thick, long plant fibers that are thrown away as waste in the paper-making process and attached them to the surface to make the so-called "Guosong paper." He then painted on both sides of the sheet. After completing the painting, Liu peeled off the long fibers, revealing the white parts underneath that now function as white lines. The crazy cursive brush style seen here references the Five Dynasties artist Shi Ke as well as Abstract Expressionism. *Daybreak* incorporates a photograph as a collage, inspired by Western art as well as the traditional Chinese folk art of paper cutting (*jianzhi*).

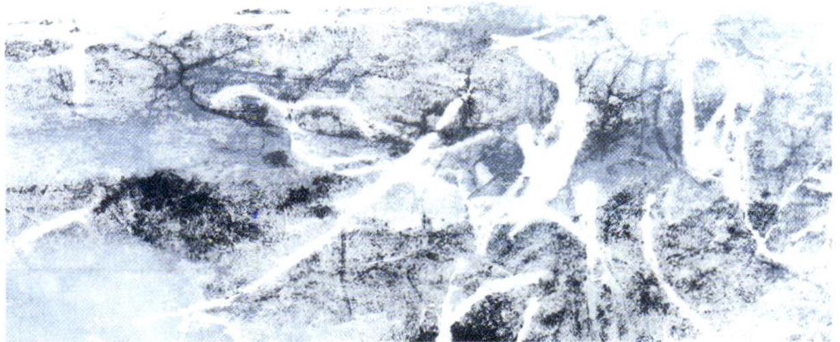

Moon Series: It'll Soon Be White All Over, 1970 (detail)

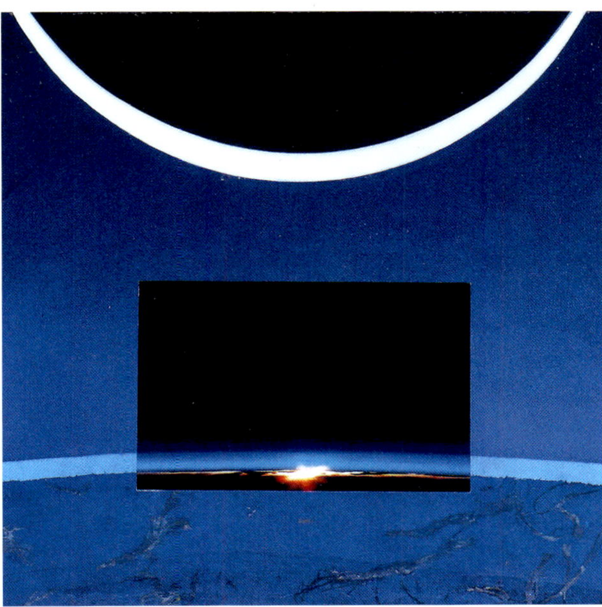

Moon Series: Daybreak, 2005 (detail)

Jiuzhaigou Series #48: Sea of Floating Ice, 2004

Ink, colors, and tracing paper
27¼ × 40 in. (69.3 × 101.5 cm)

Jiuzhaigou Series #48: Sea of Floating Ice, 2004 (detail)

Jiuzhaigou Series #48: Sea of Floating Ice provides another example of Liu's flexible approach to materials. The artist traveled to Jiuzhaigou (literally, "Nine-Stockade Valley") in Sichuan Province for the first time in the winter of 2001. Impressed by the colorful water there, he tried many different ways to re-create the beautiful scenery. Accidentally, he discovered that architect's nonabsorbent tracing paper would be an ideal vehicle for depicting the water of Jiuzhaigou. After many experiments with this new material, Liu invented the *zimo* method used in *Sea of Floating Ice*. He first laid a large sheet of tracing paper on the floor. With the composition already in mind, he carefully sprayed water on the paper, then dripped and sprayed ink and colors to let them mix with the water spontaneously to form an effect of glistening water. Once the "painting" was completed, he laid another sheet of tracing paper on top. When the two sheets adhered, the water, ink, and colors in between seemed to transform into rippling water. Liu then separated the two sheets, cropping and editing to make this fantastical and ethereal image. WK

Selected Exhibitions
Liu Guosong: A Universe of His Own, Hong Kong Museum of Art, 2004; *Sixty Years a Painter: Retrospective Exhibition of Liu Guosong*, Palace Museum, Beijing, 2007; *Revolution/Renaissance: The Art of Liu Kuo-sung*, National Museum of History, Taipei, Museum of Contemporary Art, Singapore, National Museum of Jakarta, and National Art Gallery Kuala Lumpur, 2014; *Echo of the Universe: Ink Art of Liu Kuo-sung*, Chinese Art Museum, Shanghai, 2016; *De la Chine à Taiwan: Les Pionniers de l'abstraction*, Museum of Ixelles, Brussels, 2017; *To the Moon: Liu Kuo-sung*, Kaohsiung Museum of Fine Arts, 2019.

Further Sources
Michael Sullivan, *Liu Guosong* (Taipei: Leland Art House, 1970); P'i Tao-chien et al, *The Universe in Mind: A Retrospective of Liu Kuo-sung* (Taipei: Caituan faren zhonghua wenhua jijinhui, 2002); Li Chu-tsing et al., *Liu Guosong: A Universe of His Own* (Hong Kong: Leisure and Cultural Services Department, 2004); Qiongrui Xiao, *Modern Ink and Wash: Liu Guosong* (Taizhong shi: Guoli Taiwan meishu guan, 2017).

LUI SHOU-KWAN

b. Guangzhou, Guangdong Province, China, 1919–1975

Wood Houses in the Mountains, 1964
Chinese ink and color on paper
24¼ × 47½ in. (61.5 × 120.5 cm)
IP-LSK-04

Zen Painting A69-14, 1969
Ink and color on paper
59$\frac{1}{16}$ × 31⅞ in. (150 × 81 cm)

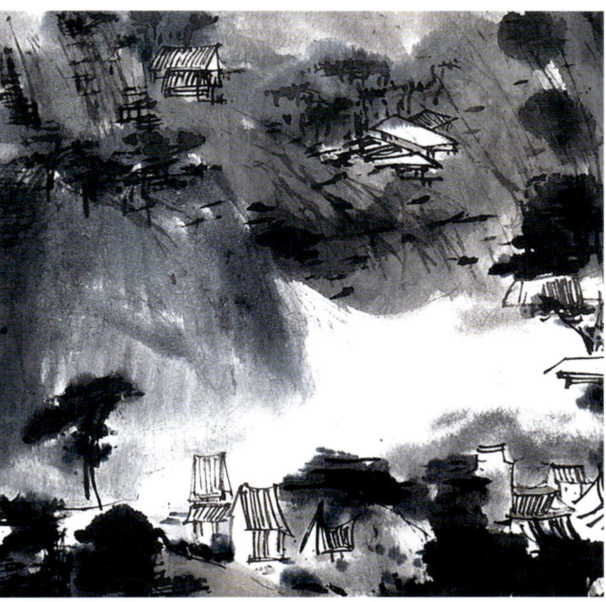

Wood Houses in the Mountains, 1964 (detail)

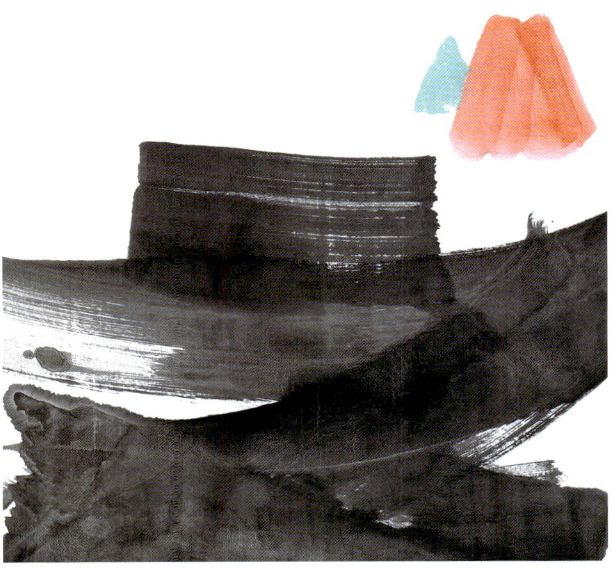

Zen Painting A69-14, 1969 (detail)

Sketchy, expressive dabs sweep across the paper and gather into two masses, broken by a diagonal void. From them emerge mist-enshrouded hills, trees, and houses. At first glance, *Wood Houses in the Mountains* appears to conform to traditional conventions. The panoramic landscape is comprised of the proverbial rolling hills, lush vegetation, and rivers that merge seamlessly into the sky by virtue of plain paper. These landmasses are punctuated by clusters of houses with sloping rooftops and upturned finials recognizable as quintessentially Chinese architecture. The painting also bears an inscription in cursive script, "Composed by Lui Shou-kwan on a spring eve in the *jiachen* year (1964)" (*jiachen chunxi Lü Shoukun xie*), followed by the artist's seals. The work appears monochromatic, in the manner of traditional painting in which Lui Shou-kwan was steeped from early childhood, being the son of the prominent painter, Lui Canming. Yet, careening from the aphorism of the five hues of plain ink, Lui Shou-kwan sneaks in a subtle tonality.

Indeed, the work appears to occupy an inflection point between Lui's search for traditional ink and his flavor of abstraction. Though distinctly figurative, the stocky, almost heavy-handed strokes are reminiscent of his groundbreaking *Zen Paintings* series, exemplified by the eponymous 1969 work illustrated here. As its broad strokes erupt into splattered ink, *Zen Painting* conjures the Buddhist notion of sudden enlightenment, reinforced by the inscription, "Dharma without hindrance, hindrance without dharma" (*fa wu zhang, zhang wu fa*), citing Qing artist Shitao's treatise on painting. All this underscores Lui's instrumental role in the New Ink Movement in Hong Kong as a leading figure and mentor for a generation of ink abstract painters, including Wucius Wong (p. 179) and Leung Kui-ting (p. 175).

Lui's work establishes a thoughtful dialogue between traditional painting and the search for new iterations of Chinese ink art. This dialogue is extended in Xu Bing's interpretation of *Wood Houses in the Mountains* (pp. 158–61). Again, reflecting a new path to a familiar composition, new methods to a well-established visual language. **EC**

Selected Exhibitions
In Search of Zen: The Art of Lui Shou-kwan, National Art Museum of China, Beijing, 2013; *A Legacy of Ink: Lui Shou-kwan 40 Years On*, Alisan Fine Arts, Hong Kong, 2015; *Lui Shou-kwan Centenary Exhibition: Abstraction, Ink and Enlightenment*, Ashmolean Museum, Oxford, 2018; *Longing for Nature*, Museum Rietberg, Zurich, 2020.

Further Sources
Lui Mui Sin-ping, *Lui Shou-kwan, 1919–1975* (Hong Kong: Lui Mui Sin-ping, 1979); *The Manuscripts of Lui Shou-kwan* (Hong Kong: Hong Kong Chinese University Press, 2005); *Lui Shou-kwan: Zen Ink Art* (Hong Kong: Alisan Fine Arts, 2013).

MIN BYUNG HUN

b. Seoul, 1955

***Snow Land Sky Fog Gloom*, 2005**
Gelatin silver print
41 × 48 1/16 in. (104 × 122 cm)

Snow Land Sky Fog Gloom, 2005 (detail)

Min Byung Hun is a native of Seoul. Prior to becoming a photographer, he pursued careers as a musician, vocalist, and electronics engineer. In the 1980s, he studied in the studio of Korean photographer Soon Tae Hong. Min's work has ranged from images of sky, water, and snow to nudes. In speaking of his photographs, he has stated, "I aim to focus on the small things, the trivial things, the things that change naturally, and I really personally empathize with those elements."

Snow Land Sky Fog Gloom is part of a series of photographs created in 2005, the individual works of which share the same title. These black-and-white photographs present images of Korea's landscape enveloped in snow and fog. In many of these scenes, the boundaries between earth and sky merge or mirror each other. Min's skill in capturing subtle monochromatic images brings to mind traditions of East Asian painting, as seen, for example, in early Korean ink landscapes of the Goryeo and early Joseon dynasties. In Min's photographs, the actions of mist and snow create images in which formal distinctions between solid and void become blurred and even irrelevant. Even his photographs of cities are so often obscured by mist and fog that they are barely recognizable as urban environments. Underlying the visual ambiguity are Daoist concepts widely disseminated in Korea for many centuries, pointing to the fluid boundary between existence and nonexistence. As the *Daode jing*, the classic Daoist text attributed to the ancient sage Laozi, paradoxically states, "Being and nonbeing have the same origin." This idea underlies such fundamental Daoist concepts as these: that all knowledge is fleeting and all facts relative. Min echoes these sentiments when he describes his work as "akin to the aftertaste of the night's dream lingering on in the early morning." SL

Further Source
Emmanuelle de L'Écotais, "Byung Hung MIN," Korean Artist Project with Korean Art Museums, at http://www.koreanartistproject.com/eng_artist.art?method=artistView&flag=artist&auth_reg_no=22.

PARK SEO-BO

b. Yecheon, North Gyeongsang Province, South Korea, 1931

Ecriture No. 080222, 2008
M xed media with Korean hanji paper on canvas
57⅛ × 48¹⁄₁₆ in. (145 × 122 cm)

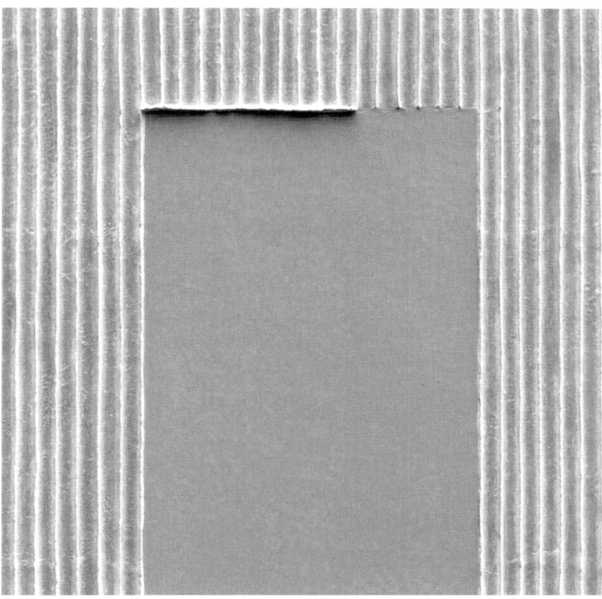

Ecriture No. 080222, 2008 (detail)

Park Seo-Bo is one of the most eminent artists in Korea today. He is the "father" of the Dansaekwa movement of abstract, minimalist, monochromatic art that emerged in South Korea in the 1970s, embedding spirituality and self-emptying into his work through repeated action. Over the past half-century, Park's oeuvre has been anchored by his ongoing *Ecriture* series, which evolved with the artist as his practice matured.

Ecriture was born out of frustration. In the late 1960s, Park watched his three-year-old son as he toiled over his handwriting, trying to fit his characters into the squares of his older brother's gridded practice paper. After writing and erasing again and again, he finally scribbled over the crumpled paper in defeat. This inspired the first iterations of *Ecriture*, which consisted of Park scrawling pencil over wet white paint on canvas, constituting a quiet record of the artist's hand and his arduous process. The second stage of the series, begun in the 1990s, involved experimentation with furrows of neutral colors on wet hanji paper, forgoing the act of scrawling but preserving the systematic, repeated linear patterning of the first phase.

Finally, the third stage, which encompasses *Ecriture No. 080222*, began at the turn of the century. The series had grown with Park for more than four decades, and as the 20th century ended, the artist confronted a new and unfamiliar digital era. It was then that *Ecriture*, ever a vehicle for Park's own spiritual development and self-emptying, became a therapeutic space for the viewer as well. Both muted and saturated colors, subtly shifting between the furrows of the paper, are employed as tools of healing. Here, a soft blue-gray changes when viewed from differing angles or under different lighting. In the center of Park's signature furrows, one finds peace in a "breathing hole," a flat zone that offers the eye—and the spirit—a place of rest and emptiness. **SF**

Selected Exhibitions
Dansaekhwa, 56th Venice Biennale, Palazzo Contarini-Polignac, 2015; *From Lee Ungno to Lee Ufan: Korean Artists in France*, Musée Cernuschi, Paris, 2015; *Park Seo-Bo: The Untiring Endeavorer*, National Museum of Modern and Contemporary Art, Seoul, 2019.

Further Sources
Kate Lim, *Park Seo-Bo: From Avant-Garde to Ecriture* (Singapore: Booksactually, 2014); *Park Seo-Bo: The Untiring Endeavorer* (Seoul: National Museum of Modern and Contemporary Art, 2019).

ANTOINE PENTSCH

b. Budapest, 1925–2012

Untitled, 1989
Etching print on paper
22¼ × 29¹⁵⁄₁₆ in. (57 × 76 cm)

Untitled XII, 2000
Mixed media: etching print on BFK Rives paper and aquarelle
22¼ × 29¹⁵⁄₁₆ in. (57 × 76 cm)

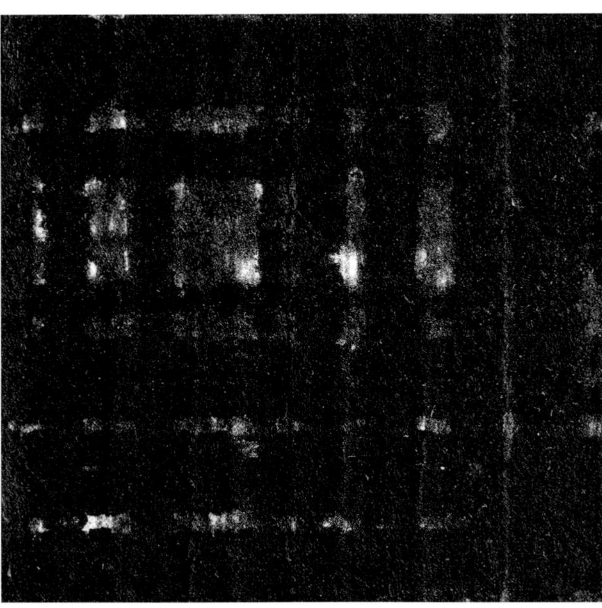

Untitled, 1989 (detail)

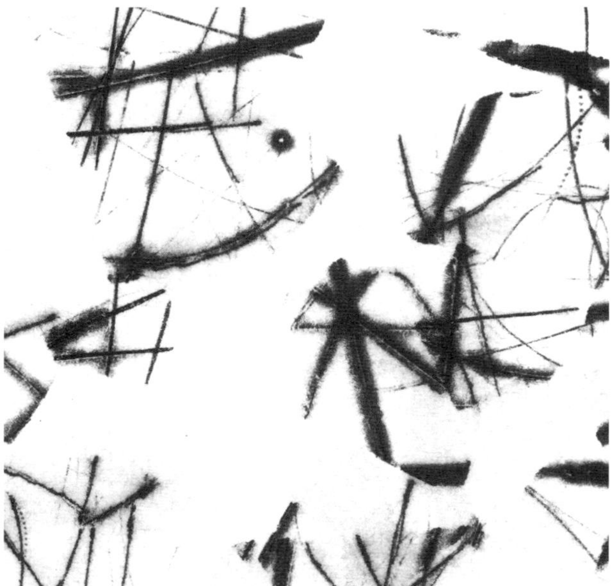

Untitled XII, 2000 (detail)

Antoine Pentsch was born in Budapest and emigrated with his family to Paris when he was five. From 1970 until his death in 2012, he lived and worked in Montreal. He was enormously creative as a painter and printmaker, and was also known as a poet. Pentsch taught art at the University of Quebec in Montreal and a guest course on printmaking at Mary Baldwin University in Virginia. His prints from the 1970s include ethereal works created solely by embossing into the paper.

Untitled (1989) presents an imaginary alphabet suggesting cuneiform or an esoteric musical score. In the writing of the artist's "text," there is considerable variation in the symbols' size and the force with which they were etched in the metal printing plate. Even the characters' individual structures vary enormously. Somehow the work combines the elegant format of a proclamation with the informality of a handwritten letter.

A significantly different work is *Untitled XII* (2000), presenting an abstract black-and-white matrix evoking images of dystopian subterranean architecture, or of looking into the heart of an impossibly complex mathematical equation. As remote as the artist's world appears, its otherworldly presence becomes part of our reality. Pentsch's universe is simultaneously alien and strangely familiar. **SL**

Selected Exhibitions
Noir et blanc, La Galerie d'Art Lionel Groulx, Montreal, 1995; *Antoine Pentsch: Masques*, Galerie Bernard, Montreal, 2012.

Further Source
La Poétique d'Artiste, Édition du Silence, Montreal, 1995.

JORMA PURANEN

b. Helsinki, 1951

Icy Prospects # 20, 2009
Chromogenic print
64 3/16 × 79 1/8 in. (163 × 201 cm)

Icy Prospects # 20, 2009 (detail)

Born in Helsinki, Jorma Puranen is one of the most influential contemporary photographers in Finland. He began his career in the early 1970s and is considered the "founding father" of the Helsinki School of photography, based at the School of Arts, Design and Architecture at Aalto University. He has twice been awarded the National Prize for Finnish Photography, in 1992 and 2010. Puranen is best known for his series that explore the themes of time, memory, loss, and the legacy of colonialism. Among these are his manipulated photographs based on antique Finnish glass-plate negatives found in museum archives, and his series that re-present Old Master portrait paintings in the dim, pre-electric indoor lighting of the 17th and 18th centuries.

Beginning with a trip to the far north of Finland in 1970, and over the course of subsequent visits, Puranen has devoted much of his work to documenting the human history and natural beauty of the Sámi region, most of which lies north of the Arctic Circle. This is the ancient land known as Lapland, home to such indigenous minorities as the Utsjoki, Enontekiö, Inari, and Sodankylä. Puranen's series celebrating these native peoples and their history was inspired by a set of portrait photographs taken by French photographer G. Roche in Lapland in 1884, during Prince Roland Bonaparte's expedition to the Sámi region. After studying and copying many of the original 19th-century photographs housed in the Musée de l'Homme in Paris, Puranen had his large-scale photographic copies transferred to acrylic plates, with which he created a series of installations in the snow of the arctic wilderness, themselves subsequently documented by the artist in large-scale photographs.

Icy Prospects # 20 is one of a series of haunting images of the Sámi region's arctic wilderness. These consist of time exposures taken of the landscapes as reflected on wood boards painted with highly reflective black acrylic paint. In the resulting images, the wood grain of the boards plays a key role as the ground against which the artist created dreamlike images that hinge on the fluid border between painting and photography. **SL**

Selected Exhibitions
Arctische Archiv, Villa Oppenheim, Berlin, 2007; *Icy Prospects, Photology Gallery*, Milan, 2008.

Further Source
Liz Wells, *Jorma Puranen: Icy Prospects* (Ostfildern: Hatje Cantz, 2009).

QIU SHIHUA

b. Zizhong, Sichuan Province, China, 1940

Untitled, 1994
Oil on canvas
71¼ × 141¾ in. (181 × 360 cm)

Untitled, 1994 (detail)

To fully grasp the images of Qiu Shihua's works takes time. A quick glance yields merely white paint on canvas, akin to Ad Reinhardt or Robert Rauschenberg. For those willing to take the time, however, Qiu's works slowly reveal themselves as complex landscapes, painted in atmospheric, loose washes of not white or gray, but blues, reds, and yellows.

The artist never trained in ink painting, due in part to his belief that traditional *shanshuihua* (landscape painting) had reached its apex and could not be improved upon. He instead studied Socialist Realist oil painting at the Xi'an Academy of Fine Arts, graduating in 1962, just a few years before the beginning of the Cultural Revolution (1966–76). Qiu then worked in the coal-mining town of Tongchuan, north of Xi'an, producing billboards and posters for a movie theater. In 1981, he visited Europe, where he studied French Impressionism and lighting.

In the late 1980s, Qiu changed course: he ceased painting from life and began to focus on the concept behind his art, in particular, the traditional Chinese principle of *qiyun*, or spirit resonance—the idea of capturing the spirit of a subject as opposed to formally depicting its likeness so that this spirit may resonate with future generations. Obliging his viewers to engage with his paintings at length to allow the subject to emerge from a seemingly blank canvas, Qiu also communicates his own spirit, sharing with us the time he himself has dedicated to the piece. **SF**

Selected Exhibitions
The Yi School: Thirty Years of Chinese Abstract Art, CaixaForum, Madrid, 2008; *Qiu Shihua: Landschaft, Licht und Stille*, Museum Pfalzgalerie Kaiserslautern, Germany, 2012; *Empty/Not Empty*, Galerie Urs Meile, Beijing and Lucerne, 2020.

Further Sources
Christopher W. Mao, ed., *Insight: Paintings by Qiu Shihua* (New York: Chambers Fine Art, 2005); Huang Zhuan, ed., *Qi Yun: The International Traveling Exhibition of Chinese Abstract Art* (Shenzhen: OCT Contemporary Art Terminal of He Xiangning Art Museum, 2007); Britta Buhlmann and Udo Kittelmann, *Qiu Shihua* (Düsseldorf: Richter & Fey, 2012).

RHEE KIBONG

b. Seoul, 1957

***Wet Psyche—No Wind*, 2010**
Acrylic, Plexiglas, and mixed media on canvas
94½ × 70⅞ in. (240 × 180 cm)

Wet Psyche—No Wind, 2010 (detail)

Rhee Kibong's process begins with a charcoal sketch in tones of gray and black, the carbon blended to varying degrees by the artist's fingertips. He then translates the sketch to canvas, painting the first layer of the scene using dark and muted colors to make dotted brushstrokes, softened by mists of water. After this layer is completed, he adds a swath of white fabric, muffling the image below. Next he paints a second layer atop the fabric, as if certain branches and leaves are peeking through the thick haze. A Plexiglas pane, slightly raised off of the canvas, bears the final painted layer.

The effect is a spectral landscape shrouded in a mixed-media fog. Here, Rhee subverts the traditions of both sculpture and painting, creating a shallow depth that allows for infinite shifting variations. Rather than simply presenting a flattened, two-dimensional image, the artist invites the viewer into the misty scene through the small space between Plexiglas and canvas.

Rhee earned both his BFA (1981) and MFA (1985) from Seoul National University. His artistic promise was recognized early on—just a year after graduating with a bachelor's degree, his work was already being shown internationally. In 1986, he was awarded the Grand Prize for his entry in the Grand Art Exhibition of Korea, held at the National Museum of Modern and Contemporary Art in Gwacheon, and in 1994 he received the Total Art Prize. **SF**

Selected Exhibitions
6th Asia Pacific Triennial of Contemporary Art, Queensland, Australia, 2009; *Korean Painting Now*, National Taiwan Museum of Fine Arts, Taichung, 2012; *Neo-Naturalism*, Ilwoo Space, Seoul, 2017.

Further Sources
Sabine Lee, *Rhee, Ki Bong* (Seoul: Kukje Gallery, 2007); Yu Jinsang et al., *Kibong Rhee: The Wet Psyche* (Seoul: Kukje Gallery, 2008); Koh Wonseok et al., *Kibong Rhee: The Cloudium* (Seoul: Arko Art Center and Arts Council Korea, 2012).

SHI GUORUI

b. Shanxi Province, China, 1964

***New Beijing CCTV*, 2007**
Gelatin silver print, unique camera obscura
55⅛ × 89 in. (140 × 226 cm)

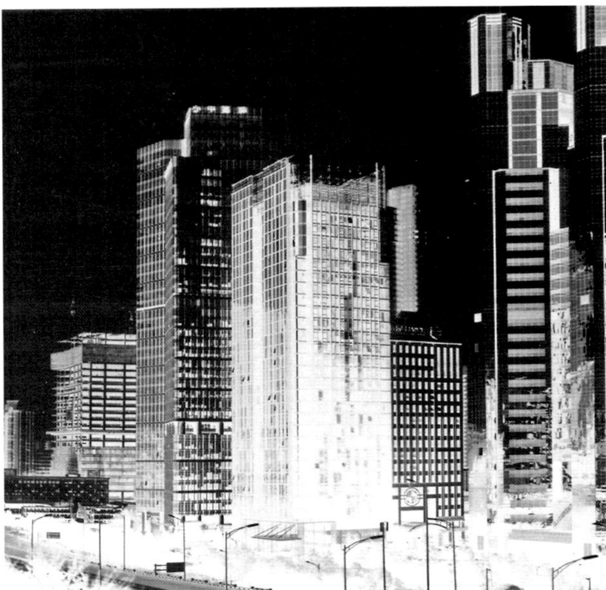

New Beijing CCTV, 2007 (detail)

The tiniest glimmer of light brings to life entire cities through Shi Guorui's oversized pinhole cameras. Well-versed in the philosophies of Mozi (ca. 470–ca. 391 BCE), who discovered the properties of light passing through a pinhole camera that cause an image to flip, Shi began making his own pinhole cameras in 1996. Three years later, he started experimenting with the camera obscura, and in 2002 created his first room-sized camera obscura work.

Over the course of Shi's career, he has cultivated a bodily intimacy with the camera obscura, combining the scientific with the emotional: while he positions the lens based on mathematical calculations, the exposure time of each photo is based on the artist's intuition. In a way, these works are performances, an exercise in Shi's corporeal understanding of the photographic process. He spends the entirety of each lengthy exposure—sometimes as long as seven hours—sitting inside the camera in total darkness. This meditative experience is concluded when he feels the artwork is finished, a determination that has less to do with the precise moment to end an exposure in order to produce a "perfect" image and more to do with the artist's sense that the meditation has been completed.

Most of Shi's photographs depict black-and-white land- or cityscapes, surreal in their reversed lighting and sense of calm. *New Beijing CCTV* is no exception. On the left side of the image, Shi has captured the construction of the CMG Guanghua Road Office Area, designed by renowned architects Rem Koolhaas and Ole Scheeren as the headquarters for China Central Television (CCTV). Because of the long exposure necessary in Shi's technique, no one car or person can be pinpointed within the scene; rather, the highway in the lower right quadrant appears ghostly, barren, with only faint tracks indicating the far-off, flowing traffic. **SF**

Selected Exhibitions
Shi Guorui: Reproduction and Refashioning, de Young Museum, San Francisco, 2007; *Uncanny Perceptions: Camera Obscura by Shi Guorui*, Chinese Contemporary Gallery, New York and Beijing, 2007; *Shi Guorui: Ab/Sense-Pre/Sense*, Thomas Cole National Historic Site, Catskill, New York, 2019.

Further Sources
Carol Yinghua Lu and Sue-an van der Zijpp, *New World Order: Contemporary Installation Art and Photography from China* (Groningen, Netherlands: Groninger Museum, 2008); Katherine Don and Britta Erickson, *Shi Guorui: Rebirth. Camera Obscura Works by Shi Guorui 2001–2011* (Los Angeles: L&M Arts, 2011); Maxwell K. Hearn, *Ink Art: Past as Present in Contemporary China* (New York: The Metropolitan Museum of Art, 2013).

HIROSHI SUGIMOTO

b. Tokyo, 1948

Lightning Fields 119, 138, 143, 2009
Three gelatin silver prints
Each 23 × 18½ in. (58.4 × 47 cm)

Hiroshi Sugimoto is one of the most gifted photographers active in the world today. Born in Tokyo in 1948, he graduated from Rikkyo University in 1970, followed by travels through Russia, Poland, and Western Europe. He visited Los Angeles in 1971, then studied fine art there at the ArtCenter College of Design from 1972 to 1974, focusing on photography. In 1974, Sugimoto moved to New York and now divides his time between there and Tokyo. Perhaps best known for his transcendental photographs of the sea and of early 20th-century movie theater prosceniums, Sugimoto has also created beautiful photographic series comprising images of museum dioramas, modernist architecture, waxwork-museum figures, drive-in theaters, and Buddhist sculptures, among other subjects. Significantly, he is also a serious and well-informed collector of fossils, Asian and European antiquities, and traditional Japanese art, particularly Buddhist art. Throughout his career, Sugimoto has focused on black-and-white photography and has continued to use an early 20th-century box camera as his primary photographic instrument.

In discussing his series *Lightning Fields*, Sugimoto has referenced early experiments with electricity by such pioneers as Benjamin Franklin, Michael Faraday, and William Henry Fox Talbot (the discoverer of the photosensitive properties of silver alloys and the inventor of positive-negative photographic imaging). To pursue and document his own experiments with the effects of electricity, Sugimoto set up in his darkroom a 400,000-volt Van de Graaff generator that sent bolts of electrostatic energy through film onto a metal table, at times manipulating the sparking bolts of electricity with an armory of metal kitchen utensils. Of the images that resulted, often resembling branching trees, vascular systems, and high-energy cosmic events, Sugimoto has stated, "I see the spark of life itself, the lightning that struck the primordial ooze." **SL**

Selected Exhibitions
Conceptual Forms and Mathematical Models, The Phillips Collection, Washington, D.C., 2015; *Lost Human Genetic Archive*, Tokyo Photographic Art Museum, 2016; *Gates of Paradise*, Japan Society, New York, 2017; *Quatro Ragazzi*, MOA Museum of Art, Atami, 2018; *Past Vitam*, Kyoto City KYOCERA Museum of Art, 2019.

Further Sources
Hiroshi Sugimoto: Dioramas (New York: Matsumoto Editions, 2014); Philip Larratt-Smith, ed., *Hiroshi Sugimoto: Black Box* (New York: Aperture, 2016); *Hiroshi Sugimoto: Theaters* (New York: Matsumoto Editions, 2016).

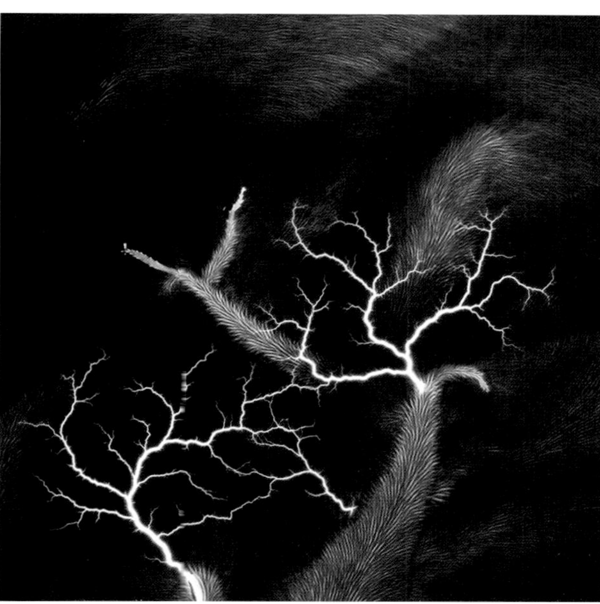

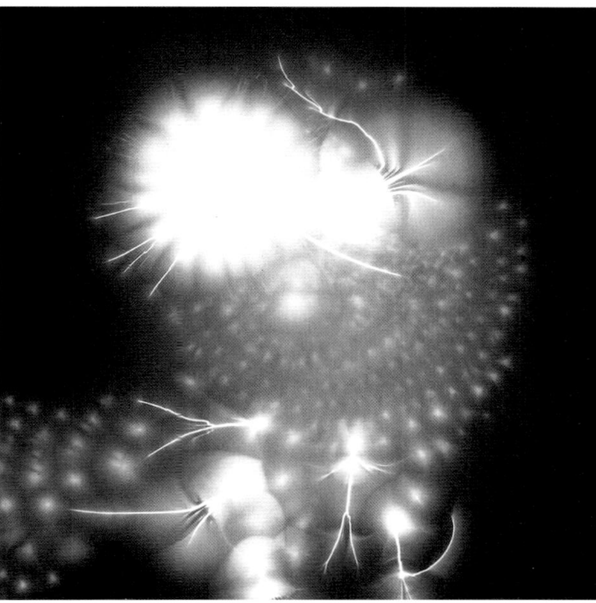

Lightning Fields 119, 138, 2009 (details)

SUNAGAWA HARUHIKO

b. Fukuoka, Japan, 1946

Convergence, 2005–7
Wood, glass, and concrete molding
39⅜ × 59¹⁄₁₆ × 59¹⁄₁₆ in. (100 × 150 × 150 cm)

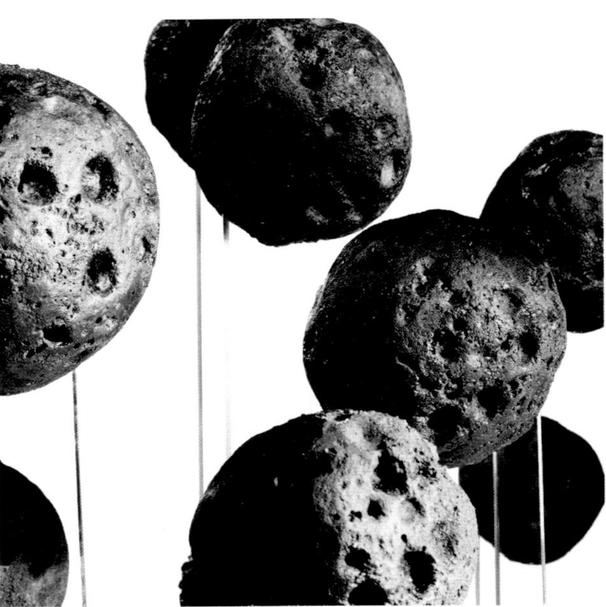

Convergence, 2005–7 (detail)

Upon entering the artist's studio, one is struck by the near absence of the typical mess of splattered paint and scattered tools that usually goes hand-in-hand with the profession. One is met, instead, with neatly laid out compasses and rulers, glass slabs, and graph papers, spaced evenly atop an elongated table. Thoughtfully sketched diagrams and small calculations jotted here and there reflect the importance of precision in the artist's practice. The workspace is as polished and minimal as the works themselves.

Sunagawa Haruhiko was born in Fukuoka, Japan, in 1946. He studied physics at Tokyo University of Science before leaving for London to pursue an education in painting and drawing at Hammersmith College of Art. He relocated to France in 1975 where he currently resides. Sunagawa's academic background in the sciences unmistakably inform his exploration of a visual language that captures movement, time, and natural phenomena. Gravitating toward Geometric, Kinetic, and Optical art, Sunagawa cites Victor Vasarely, Jesús Rafael Soto, and Carlos Cruz-Diez as well as Russian Constructivists like Kazimir Malevich and El Lissitzky as influential figures for the development of his personal style. Above all, Sunagawa is inspired by nature.

Convergence is composed of a multitude of cast cement spheres of varying size bearing irregular indentations. The rough, solid orbs are suspended atop narrow slabs of fragile glass, affixed to a wood podium. A tinge of black is mixed into the paint of the raised platform to soften the harsh white, adding calmness and tranquility, the artist explains. Through the interplay of light and shadow; the arrangement of spheres from small to large along a semicircular track that stretches from back right to front and left; and harnessing our shifting gaze as we approach it, the work is anything but still. Like beads rebounding when dropped on the floor, or atoms shooting away from a single file, *Convergence* ultimately captures movement in space. EC

Selected Exhibitions
Exposition retrospective, Musée Bourdelle, Paris, 1993; *Transpositions*, Galerie Denise René, Paris, 2006; *Sunagawa*, Galerie Akié Arichi, Paris, 2016.

Further Sources
Sunagawa: Prix Bourdelle 1991 (Paris: Musée Bourdelle, 1993); *Sunagawa*, a Hibou Production SARL documentary, directed by Pierre François Prouteau, produced by Jean-Philippe Raymond, 2015.

WANG GONGXIN

b. Beijing, 1960

Sun Set 5, 2004
Chromogenic print
38³⁄₁₆ × 47⁵⁄₈ in. (97 × 121 cm)

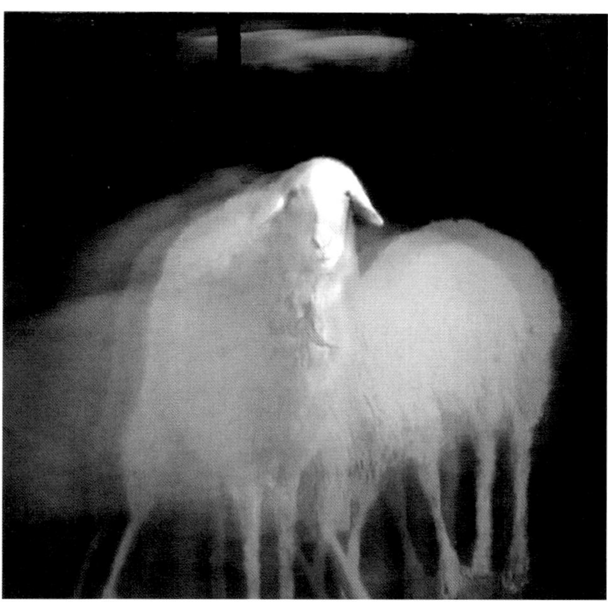

Sun Set 5, 2004 (detail)

The sun has already set on the glum view. Vestiges of iridescence linger in the sky like a distant memory. As our eyes adjust to the darkness, a construction site comes into view. A herd of sheep meanders among bare pillars of poured concrete. Their soft ovine figures, dimly hallowed, vest the scene with an uncanny atmosphere. Wandering aimlessly within this unfinished skeleton of brutalist architecture, they appear out of place, and lost.

The print is one of a set of five, all featuring Beijing, where Wang Gongxin was born and raised. In the late 1980s and early '90s, when Wang was living in Brooklyn with his wife, artist Lin Tianmiao (pp. 98, 181), his native city was undergoing rapid transformation following Deng Xiaoping's reforms. Entire neighborhoods were razed to the ground, making room for an unprecedented burst of construction, as China juggernauted toward urbanization and modernization. When the couple returned to Beijing in 1994, the city was unrecognizable; Wang found himself lost in his own hometown. And so, harnessing new developments in editing software such as Photoshop, he set out to bear witness to this new reality in his series *Sun Set*. He photographed the altered cityscape, desaturating the vignettes to appear as if viewed through night-vision goggles. Onto pictures of ruin and rebuild, Wang overlapped digitally manipulated images—like apparitions, haunting their old stomping grounds.

Both *Sun Set 2* (fig. 1) and *Sun Set 5* were photographed in the Beijing metropolitan area. While the latter depicts new construction in what used to be farmland, the former captures the ruins of a traditional *siheyuan* courtyard, an architectural artifact of old Beijing, much like the one in which Wang himself grew up. Set against a dilapidated facade of an old house, three eerily illuminated chairs hover over the rubble like specters of a long-forgotten conversation. The tension between the superimposed images and their now-altered locales comes to define the series, blurring the boundaries between old and new, urban and rural, reality and memory, as the sun sets on an era. EC

Selected Exhibitions
Wang Gongxin: My Sun, Asia Society, New York, 2012; *Wang Gongxin: Video Artist*, National Gallery of Victoria, Melbourne, 2014; *Art and China after 1989: Theater of the World*, Solomon R. Guggenheim Museum, New York, 2017.

Further Sources
Wang Gongxin and Lin Tianmiao, *Here? or There?* (Beijing: Timezone 8, 2006); Hao He, *Wang Gong Xin: Works 1993–2008* (Beijing: Timezone 8, 2008); Claire Roberts, *Wang Gongxin: Video Artist* (Melbourne: National Gallery of Victoria, 2014).

Fig. 1 Wang Gongxin, *Sun Set 2*, 2004. Chromogenic print, 38³⁄₁₆ × 47⁵⁄₈ in. (97 × 121 cm). Fondation INK Collection

WANG TIANDE

b. Shanghai, 1960

Untitled, 2013
Ink and incense burns on paper
$78\frac{15}{16} \times 168\frac{1}{8}$ cm (200.5 × 427 cm)

To fully appreciate Wang Tiande's technique, one must first understand its lore. The burning and layering for which Wang is now known came out of a chance happening, when, in 2002, ash from the artist's cigarette fell onto his paper, searing a hole into the surface. In his practice today, he intentionally burns his ground, using a lit stick of incense in place of a brush to "paint" his landscapes and calligraphy.

The resulting work encapsulates two types of negative space: the white, unburnt part of the paper, and the hole left by the burning incense stick. Wang fills the latter space by placing an ink-and-paper painting under the burnt paper, half-hiding the layer beneath, half-allowing it to peek through. In *Untitled*, the burnt and painted layers each depict a different landscape with different calligraphy, some of the black ink showing through the white paper, giving us not two but three different image planes: the negative-space incense drawing; the calligraphy visible through this drawing as incomplete, cut-off wisps; and the muted but complete calligraphy discernible through the thin white paper.

Wang is highly knowledgeable in his field, first attending the College of Art in Shanghai in 1981, then graduating from the Chinese Painting Department of the Zhejiang Academy of Fine Arts (now China Academy of Art) in Hangzhou in 1988. He went on to receive a PhD from the China Academy of Art calligraphy department in 2014, and now teaches as a professor of art at Fudan University in Shanghai. **SF**

Selected Exhibitions
Inside Out: New Chinese Art, San Francisco Museum of Modern Art and Asia Society, New York, 1998; *Ink Art*, The Metropolitan Museum of Art, New York, 2014; *Over Mountains and Across Valleys: Wang Tiande Solo Exhibition*, Guangdong Museum of Art, Guangzhou, China, 2017.

Further Sources
Christopher W. Mao, ed., *Made by Tiande* (New York: Chambers Fine Art, 2004); Yeewan Tina Pang and Fan Dian, *Wang Tiande: Landscape Transformations* (Hong Kong: Alisan Fine Arts, 2007); Allison Gorsuch et al., eds., *One Meter Seventy-Three* (Shanghai: Contrasts Gallery, 2008).

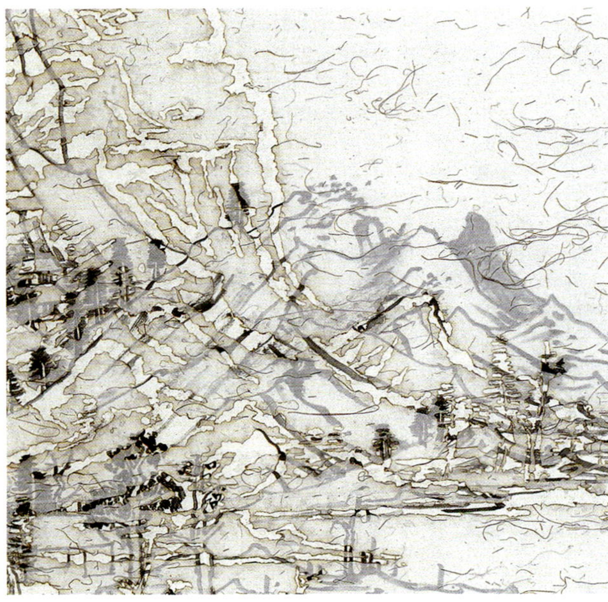

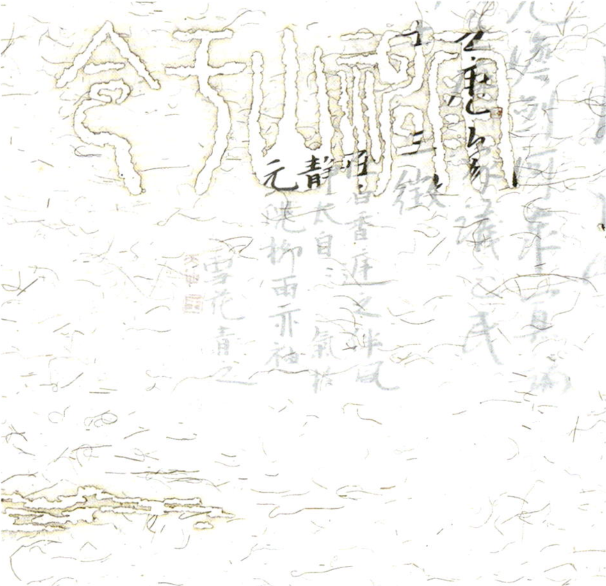

Untitled, 2013 (details)

WUCIUS WONG

b. Guangzhou, Guangdong Province, China, 1936

Deep in the Mountains #2, 2005
Ink and color on paper
37 × 37 in. (94 × 94 cm)

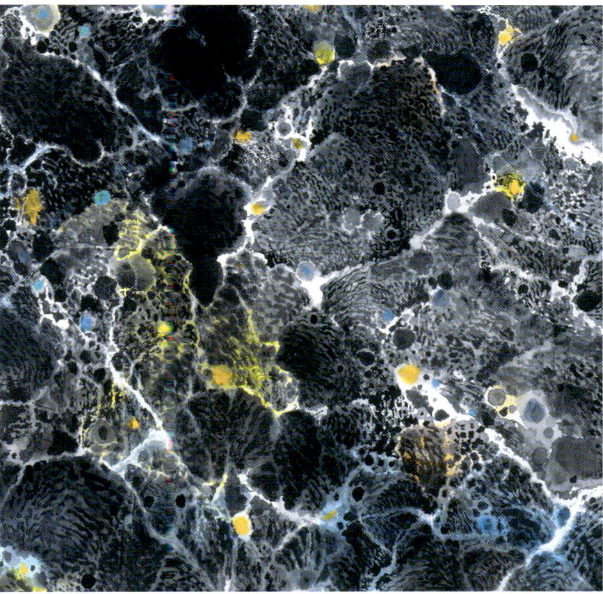

Deep in the Mountains #2, 2005 (detail)

White fissures creep like cracks in an old wall. They splinter and penetrate throbbing planes of splattered ink. Zap! A yellow flash suddenly bursts onto the surface, illuminating the textured ground with a phosphorous glow. The electrified plane pulsates and shimmers as the eye moves fitfully from one blue flash to another, and another. Quickening and spreading across the paper, they gradually connect and form into an organic tapestry, a grid of neural synapses in a microscopic rendering of brain activity.

But wait, is it a microscopic view or a macroscopic one? With this thought, we are catapulted into outer space, suddenly gazing at otherworldly topographies as if from an unfathomable distance, like an orbiting satellite in a silent void. Cerebral capillaries rearrange themselves before us into mountainous ridges; white veins become valleys and ravines in a sprawling landscape. We're suspended in midair between this irreconcilable micro/macro ambiguity. "Conflicting space provides an absurd spatial situation which seems impossible for us to interpret," Wucius Wong writes in his *Principles of Two-dimensional Design*. "Two visual experiences are in serious conflict with each other and cannot be reconciled. The situation is absurd because it does not exist in reality. Somehow it evokes a strange visual tension which offers many interesting possibilities . . ."

Wong, one of the leading figures of the Hong Kong New Ink Movement, was born in Guangdong and moved to Hong Kong at a young age, studying under the influential ink artist Lui Shou-kwan (pp. 79, 157). After pursuing higher education in North America, he returned to Hong Kong, venturing into a multifaceted career as a painter, scholar, poet, and design artist. Of his implementation of graphic design theory in ink painting, Wong writes in *A Legacy of Ink*: "I did not cease to pursue painting in my spare time [while teaching design at the Chinese University of Hong Kong], creating compositions with design concepts." *Deep in the Mountains #2* exemplifies Wong's characteristic style, which plays with angle and perspective, synthesizing graphic design and painting. **EC**

Selected Exhibitions
Mountain Thoughts, Minneapolis Institute of Art, 1987; *At the East-West Crossroads: The Art of Wucius Wong*, Hong Kong Museum of Art, 2006; *Myriad Visions of Wucius Wong*, Art Institute of Chicago, 2009; *Longing for Nature*, Museum Rietberg, Zurich, 2020.

Further Sources
Jay Xu, "Searching for Mountains No. 2," *Art Institute of Chicago Museum Studies* 34, no. 1 (2006), 38–39; *Wucius Wong* (Singapore: iPreciation, 2008); Wucius Wong, *Wang Wuxie wenji* [An Anthology of Wang Wuxie] (Guangzhou: Huacheng chubanshe, 2014).

WU CHI-TSUNG

b. Taipei, 1981

Still Life 012-Buttercup Tree, 2019
Single-channel video, 6 min., 58 sec.

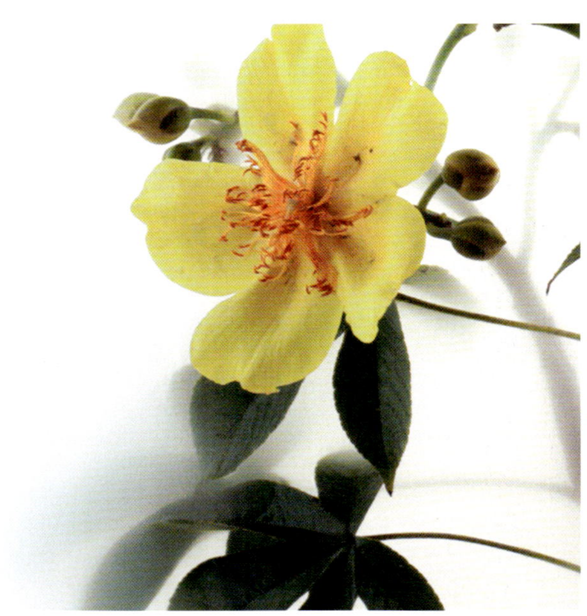

Still Life 012-Buttercup Tree, 2019 (detail)

Born in Taiwan and now living in Berlin, Wu Chi-Tsung does not see himself as a "Chinese contemporary artist," but instead as a combination of new and old, Eastern and Western traditions. He considers his works to be in the *spirit* of painting—himself trained as an oil painter—although painting is notably absent from his current practice. Wu's *Still Life* series was inspired by traditional Chinese ink art and the desire to translate this tradition into video. For his *Landscape in the Mist Series*, which employs a similar technique, Wu found inspiration in the paintings of 19th-century French realist Jean-Baptiste-Camille Corot. One finds a similarity in Corot's layers of blurry trees and the landscapes of Wu's video works, the latter shrouded in what looks like a thick fog.

However, in *Still Life 012-Buttercup Tree*, the mist is not mist, the tree is not a tree, and the still life only *appears* still—it is actually a nearly static video, advancing at a lethargic pace. In *Buttercup Tree*, Wu depicts the gradual progression of water being poured into a glass tank and submerging a cutting of buttercup flowers that has been dislocated from the earth. Wu uses these tricks to simulate a scene from a gardenscape, captured as heavy clouds of mist roll through. In both subject matter and composition, the artist presents viewers with a work in the same mode as a traditional bird-and-flower ink painting, showing a spray of branches against a blank white backdrop. Traditionally, this backdrop would be the pure white of blank paper. Here, brush and paper are absent but not missed. **SF**

Selected Exhibitions
Wu Chi-Tsung: Recalibrate, Centre for Chinese Contemporary Art, Manchester, 2013; *Far from East*, Künstlerhaus Bethanien, Berlin, 2017; *Wu Chi-Tsung Solo Exhibition*, MoT+++, Ho Chi Minh City, 2018.

Further Sources
Yunyi Lau, "An Interview with Wu Chi-Tsung," *The Artling*, April 25, 2018, at https://theartling.com/en/artzine/an-interview-with-wu-chi-tsung/; *Far from East* (Berlin: Künstlerhaus Bethanien, 2017); "IN FOCUS: Wu Chi-Tsung | Applying Traditional Practices to Contemporary Photography," PHOTOFAIRS, 2019, at https://www.photofairs.org/news/focus-wu-chi-tsung-applying-traditional-practices-contemporary-photography?fbclid=IwARomAFaPF3edruKP8byA8Wxk YHZp99uBf5yrBOd7vQbnEoPVJx1QCU_dJT8.

XU BING

b. Chongqing, China, 1955

Background Story: Ink Variation (from Lui Shou-kwan), 2016
Multimedia installation
47¼ × 94½ in. (120 × 240 cm)

Field (from the Fives Series of Repetition), 1987
Woodblock print on paper
21⅝ × 27 in. (55 × 68.7 cm)

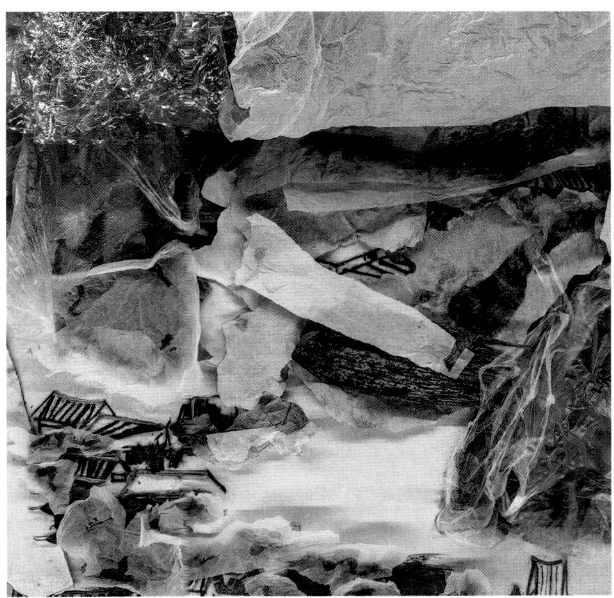

Background Story: Ink Variation (from Lui Shou-kwan), 2016 (detail)

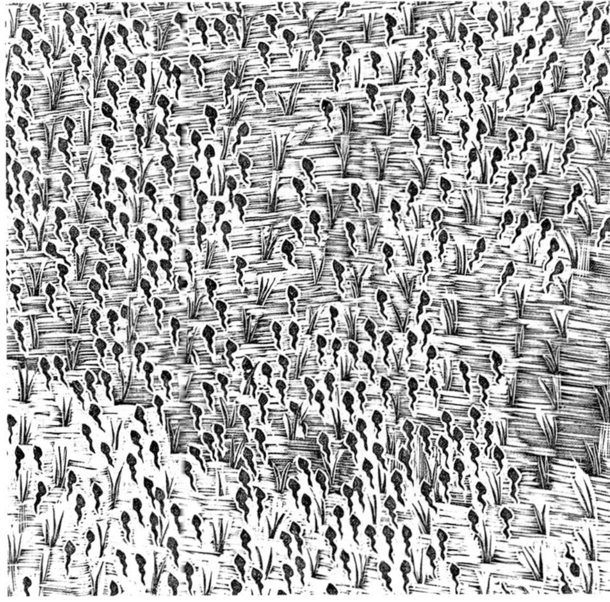

Field (from the Fives Series of Repetition), 1987 (detail)

Moving Cloud (from the Fives Series of Repetition), 1987
Woodblock print on paper
20¼ × 28⅜ in. (51.5 × 72 cm)

Farmland (from the Fives Series of Repetition), 1987
Woodblock print on paper
21⅝ × 28⅜ in. (55 × 72 cm)

Withered Pool (from the Fives Series of Repetition), 1987
Woodblock print on paper
21½ × 28½ in. (54.5 × 72.5 cm)

Mountain Place (from the Fives Series of Repetition), 1987
Woodblock print on paper
20⅞ × 28½ in. (53 × 72.5 cm)

Black Tadpoles (from the Fives Series of Repetition), 1987
Woodblock print on paper
21⅝ × 29½ in. (54.8 × 74.8 cm)

Black Pool (from the Fives Series of Repetition), 1987
Woodblock print on paper
19⅞ × 28 in. (50.5 × 71 cm)

Big River (from the Fives Series of Repetition), 1987
Woodblock print on paper
20⅞ × 28¹⁵⁄₁₆ in. (53 × 73.5 cm)

Pool of Life (from the Fives Series of Repetition), 1987
Woodblock print on paper
19⅞ × 26⅞ in. (50.4 × 68.2 cm)

Haystack Reflection (from the Fives Series of Repetition), 1987
Woodblock print on paper
18⅝ × 28¼ in. (47.4 × 71.7 cm)

One of the most established figures in contemporary Chinese art, Xu Bing combines historical modes and subject matter with an interest in semiotics and globalization. Throughout his career, he has explored themes of environmentalism, urban life, and the international mixing of languages, mainly through his primary medium of printmaking, but branching out into installation, sculpture, and performance as well. In 1999, Xu received the MacArthur "Genius" Award for his artistic innovation.

After high school, in 1974, Xu left his home of Beijing as a part of the Down to the Countryside Movement, in which educated urban youths were sent to work on farms. He then trained as a printmaker at the Central Academy of Fine Arts, earning an MFA in 1987. The *Five Series of Repetition*, presented as his thesis project, indicates a deep interest in the very process of printing. Xu made impressions of his woodblocks throughout their different stages: the first round an uncut block, yielding an allover inky black composition, the last almost entirely white negative space after he carved away most of the block's surface. The works illustrated here show the midway point of the artist's process: the scenes of farmland were fully etched into the woodblocks before he began chipping away at these forms, erasing them from the print.

Background Story: Ink Variation (from Lui Shou-kwan) is one in an ongoing series of multimedia installations by Xu that draws inspiration from historical Chinese painters. Each work in the series rethinks a canonical ink precedent. Here, from the front we see the fine brushwork and subtle tonal variations of an ink master, but from behind it is revealed that Xu's landscape was not made from brush and ink, nor grounded on paper or silk. Instead, we find an open-back light box cluttered with layers of debris: thin plastic bags mimic loose ink washes; linework is emulated using the stems and blades of dried plants. It is, nonetheless, an ink artwork, sharing the spirit and appearance of an ink painting, as well as engaging with the history of copying as both a sign of respect and a method of learning that has been part of Chinese ink art practice for centuries.

Dora and Gérard Cognié selected Lui Shou-kwan's *Wood Houses in the Mountains* (1964; p. 157) as the basis for Xu Bing's variation, and the two pieces have been paired for the installation of *Ink Dreams*. **SF**

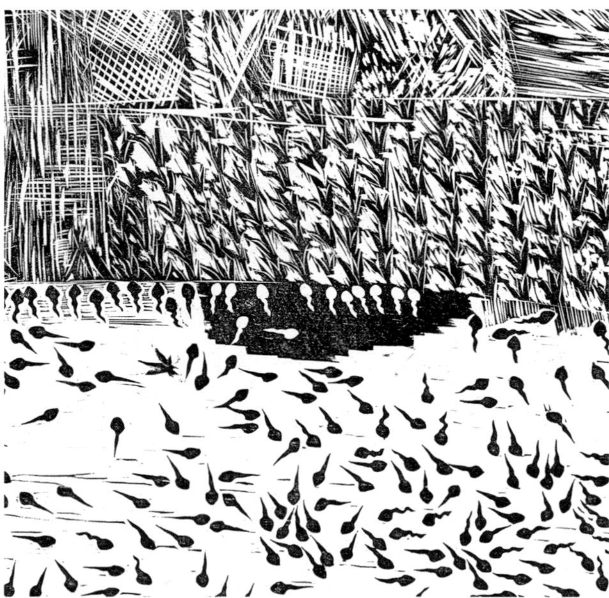

Black Tadpoles (from the Fives Series of Repetition), 1987 (detail)

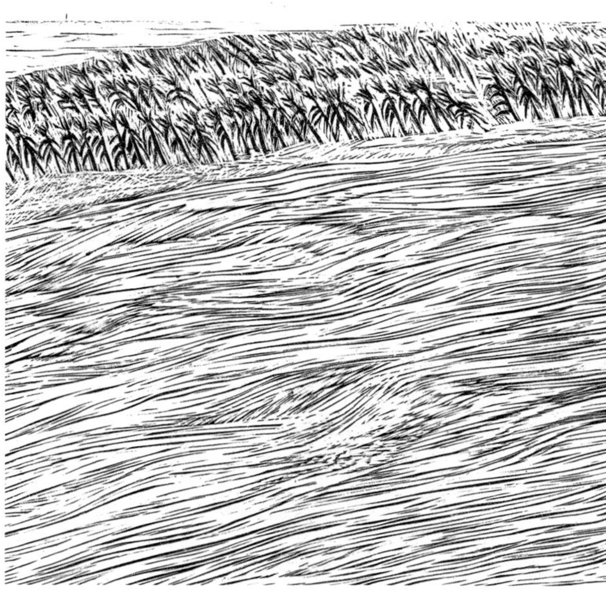

Big River (from the Fives Series of Repetition), 1987 (detail)

Selected Exhibitions

Word Play: Contemporary Art by Xu Bing, Smithsonian Institution, Washington, D.C., 2001; *Xu Bing: A Retrospective*, Taipei Fine Arts Museum, 2014; *Background Story: A New Approach to Landscape Painting*, Chazen Museum of Art, Madison, Wisconsin, 2015; *Xu Bing*, United Art Museum, Wuhan, 2017; *Xu Bing: Thought and Method*, Ullens Center for Contemporary Art, Beijing, 2018.

Further Sources

Britta Erickson, *Words without Meaning, Meaning without Words: The Art of Xu Bing* (Washington, D.C., and Seattle: Smithsonian Institution and University of Washington Press, 2001); Carolyn C. Guile, ed., *Reading Space: The Art of Xu Bing* (Hamilton, N.Y.: Colgate University, 2009); *Xu Bing: A Retrospective* (Taipei: Taipei Fine Arts Museum, 2014).

YAN BINGHUI

b. Tianjin, China, 1956

Monument, 1993
Ink on paper
70⅛ × 38⅝ in. (178 × 98 cm)

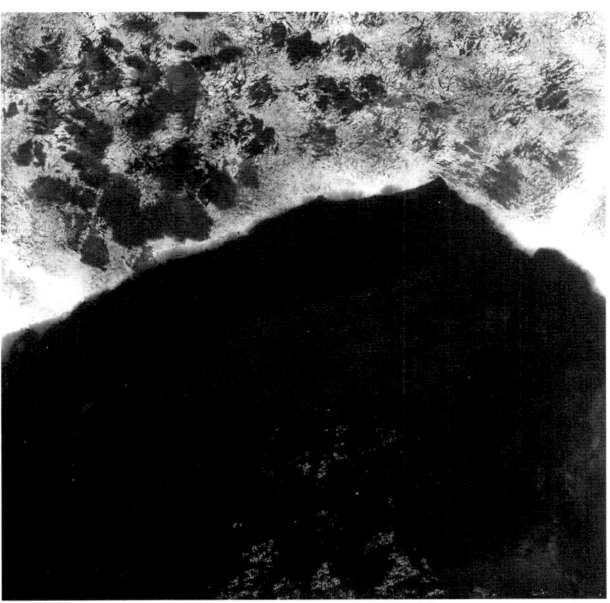

Monument, 1993 (detail)

Two large masses occupy the picture space, one a shadow of the other. The solid form in the foreground is rendered in repeated dabs of ink in varying qualities and values, layered again and again. Its contours are achieved by an irregular application of saturated brush, resulting in whirlpools and blurred edges. At the center, the brush grows drier. Hints of exposed paper yield a textured effect, suggesting a rugged surface. This technique of applying thick ink using a relatively dry brush, known as "burnt ink" (*jiaomo*), is characterized by spontaneous, splintered strokes. Behind it, a faint nimbus repeats the silhouette in a similar manner, though in reverse. This time, wet dabs are applied to the center, as if overcast by the adjacent form, while dry brush is used on the fringe. Unmistakable marks of brush bristles in this imperfect sphere show no attempt to hide the artist's hand. As the title's literal translation, *Empty Form* (*Kongxiang*), suggests, the work bears Daoist overtones, evoking the concept of *yin* and *yang*, and perhaps the universe, which is conceived of in traditional thought as a square (earth) and a circle (heavens).

Yan Binghui is one of the prominent figures of the '85 New Wave movement, whose work was featured in the groundbreaking exhibition *China/Avant-Garde* in 1989. While many artists of his generation broke with the medium of traditional ink altogether, for Yan it was a source of inspiration. His art defies classification. As Fan Di'an observes, "It is neither abstraction nor expressionism…Neither is it abstract expressionism." And Zheng Yan notes, "Neither New Ink nor Experimental Ink quite captures his style." Indeed, "defying many categories and aspects," Yan muses, "ink art is ultimately the art of the mind and soul." **EC**

Selected Exhibitions
Inside Out: New Chinese Art, MoMA PS1, New York (traveling exhibition), 1998; *Yan Binghui: Ink Painting Exhibition*, Academy of Fine Arts, Tianjin, 2005; *The Yi School: Thirty Years of Chinese Abstract Art*, CAIXA Forum, Madrid, 2008; *Ren: Yan Binghui*, Wanying Art Museum, Shijiazhuang, 2015.

Further Sources
Shuangxi Yin, Yu Zhang, and Daojian Pi, *Heibai shi: Zhongguo dangdai shiyan shuimo, 1992–1999* [Black and White: Contemporary Chinese Experimental Ink] (Wuhan: Hubei meishu chubanshe, 1999); *Binghui bimo (1986–2000)* (Wuhan: Hubei meishu chuban she, 2001); Zheng Yan et al., *Ren: Yan Binghui* (Shijiazhuang: Wanying Art Museum, 2015).

YANG JIECHANG

b. Foshan, Guangdong Province, China, 1956

Fingerprint: Right Ring Finger, 1992–94
Ink and glue on xuan paper and gauze
96½ × 91⅜ in. (245 × 232 cm)

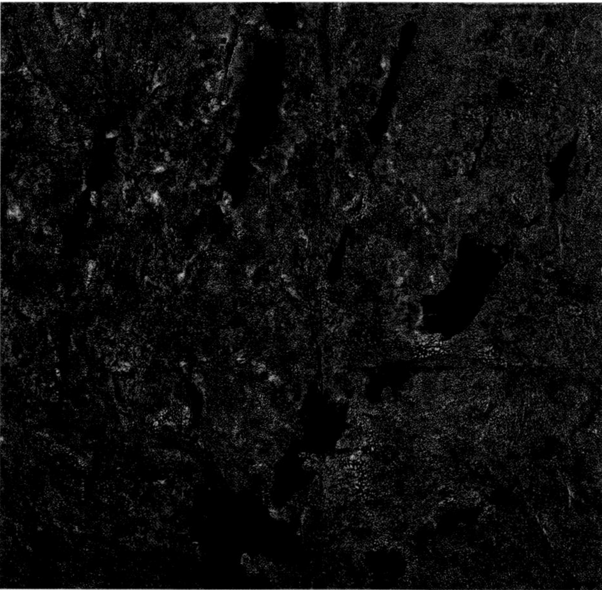

Fingerprint: Right Ring Finger, 1992–94 (detail)

Yang Jiechang has approached his artistic education holistically, pulling from not only a formal academic curriculum at the Zhejiang Academy (graduating 1982), but also Daoist and Chan Buddhist studies at Mount Luofu and Guangxiao Temple, both in Guangdong Province. These philosophies lend his work a meditative, repetitive quality, expressed as a dialogue between control and chaos.

In 1988, Yang moved to Germany, where he lived in a small apartment and worked in a studio space two floors underground. Though this was a miserable period in his life, he was on the brink of international recognition: the next year, he created a series of works *in situ* for the exhibition *Magiciens de la Terre* at the Centre Pompidou in Paris. These were the first pieces in his *100 Layers of Ink* series, in which he painted layer upon layer of ink onto gauze and xuan paper, no longer worried about conserving materials, as they were provided by the museum. *Fingerprint: Right Ring Finger*, an early example from the series, is part of a small subset of *100 Layers* based on fingerprints.

In addition to his primary materials of ink, gauze, and xuan paper, Yang incorporates alum, glue, and earth, creating a signature contrast of matte black and luminous reflective surfaces. While from some viewpoints, the works in the *100 Layers* series appear infinitely black, at other angles they appear almost white where light bounces off the top layers of glue. In the *Fingerprint* series, the glue mixture is applied in whorls to create and highlight the ridges of a fingerprint—a symbol of identity, a signature itself.

At first glance, one might compare these works to those of Ad Reinhardt, Mark Tobey, or Kazimir Malevich. However, Yang has aptly pointed out that many Western artists, like Tobey, were inspired by East Asian art. He asks, "Why not say those artists imitated me?" **SF**

Selected Exhibitions
Yang Jiechang—I Often Do Bad Things, Deichtorhallen/Phoenixhalle, Hamburg, 2014; *Earth Roots: Yang Jiechang Paintings, 1985–1999*, INK Studio, Beijing, 2017; *No-Snadow Kick*, Shanghai Duolun Museum of Modern Art, 2018; *Yang Jiechang: 3 Souls 7 Spirits*, Minsheng Art Museum, Shanghai, 2019.

Further Sources
The Enduring Passion for Ink: "Yang Jiechang's Gu and Qi," directed by Britta Erickson and Richard Widmer, video, 2017; Martina Köppel-Yang, ed., *I Often Do Bad Things: Yang Jiechang: Texts and Works, 1982–2016* (Dortmund: Verlag Kettler, 2017); Britta Erickson and Alan Yeung, *Yang Jiechang: Earth Roots: Paintings, 1985–1999* (Beijing: INK Studio, 2017).

YANG SHIH-CHIH (EMILY S. C. YU)

b. Qingdao, Shandong Province, China, 1949

Modern Landscape, 2008
Ink, paper, and collage
78¾ × 177¼ in. (200 × 450 cm)

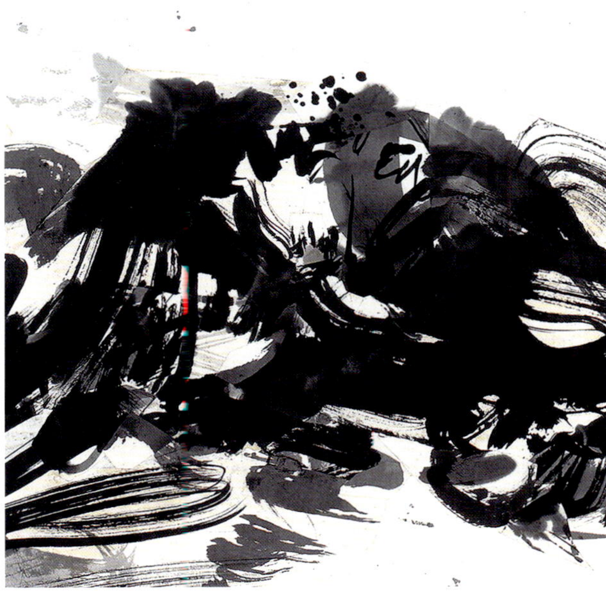

Modern Landscape, 2008 (detail)

Yang Shih-Chih was born in Qingdao in mainland China and then moved to Taiwan. She finished business school to fulfill her parents' expectations. With her passion for art, however, she made a bold transition and came to the United States to study art at San Francisco State University in the late 1970s and early '80s. Yang's early works are abstract paintings with oil or acrylic on linen. In the early 2000s, she started a creative experiment with ink and xuan paper, which later became her signature practice, as shown in *Modern Landscape*. Although it looks like an ink painting, it is actually a collage. Yang spontaneously painted on a large sheet of paper without any set plan in mind, like a child drawing according to pure instinct. Then she flipped the sheet over and cut it into pieces; the painting on the other side did not interfere with her judgment on what to keep or to remove. The fragments became Yang's new "brushstrokes," which she pasted together to form a unique work of art.

Random, adventurous, challenging, and surprising—by unveiling the hidden relationship between the seemingly unrelated strokes, Yang endows the image with a sense of time and fluidity. While the clusters of fragments are assembled, the space within the image is in a constant state of flux. The image gradually takes shape and eventually reaches its equilibrium, resulting in a complete yet mutable space. This process enables Yang to enter a new realm where traditional ink painting retains its unique character but its conventions are subverted. In Yang Shih-Chih's long search for a "holistic perspective," she constantly explores dialogues between traditional and modern, Chinese art and Western art. WK

Selected Exhibitions
Unconventional Strokes, IT Park Gallery, Taipei. 2007; *Where to Where*, 107 Gallery, Taichung, Taiwan, 2013; *Let Strokes Take Their Course*, Show Gallery, Kaohsiung, Taiwan, 2016.

Further Sources
Emily S. C. Yang 1981–1995: 15 Years—A Survey (Xinzhu, Taiwan: Qinghua daxue yishu zhong xin, 1997); Yang Shih-Chih, *The Co-existentiality in Visual Experience* (Taipei: self-published, 2002); Yang Shih-Chih, *Yang Shih-Chih's Art: 2013* (self-published, 2013); Yang Shih-Chih, *Let Strokes Take Their Course* (self-published, 2016).

YAO JUI-CHUNG

b. Taipei, 1969

Wonderful: Secret Lover in Golden House, 2007
Pen, ink, and gold leaf on handmade paper
55⅛ × 18⅛ in. (140 × 46 cm)

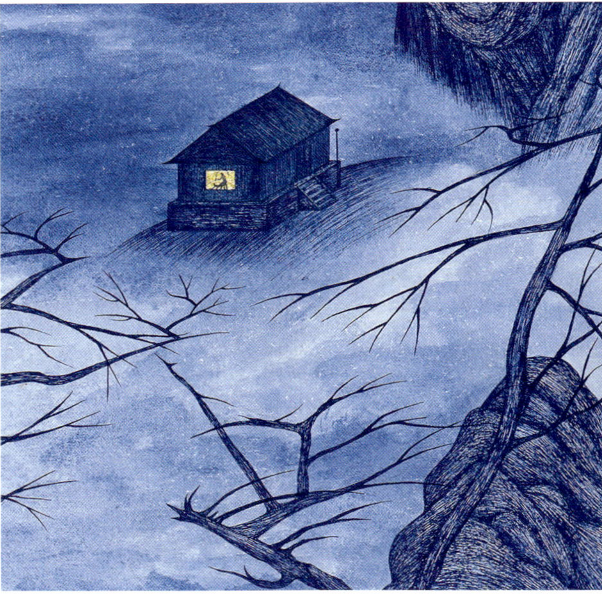

Wonderful: Secret Lover in Golden House, 2007 (detail)

Born in 1969, Yao Jui-Chung is recognized as one of the most innovative Taiwanese artists of his generation. He received his training at Taipei National University of the Arts in 1994 and represented Taiwan at the Venice Biennale in 1997. His father, originally from mainland China, was a traditional ink painter in the literati circle of the great calligrapher Yu Youren. But Yao is a rebel. His artworks run against both tradition and the mainstream with seemingly beautiful images but unabashedly provocative intent. A versatile artist, he is well known for his works on paper, but he has also experimented with photography, installation, performance, video, and sculpture. In addition, he is a curator, art critic, and art historian dedicated to evaluating and promoting Taiwanese contemporary art.

Yao Jui-Chung is famous for his series of "fake landscapes"—landscape paintings in bright colors and decorated with gold leaf. The compositions are reminiscent of traditional Chinese paintings, but their themes intentionally usurp the so-called orthodoxy. *Wonderful: Secret Lover in Golden House* is a typical work in the series. In a traditional painting, an isolated hut normally suggests a lofty scholar's reclusion among mountains and rivers. Yao, however, depicts a secret lover in a house with flamboyant gold color. Although influenced by the eccentric landscapes of late Ming painters like Wu Bin and Chen Hongshou, Yao abandons traditional materials and techniques, as well as the literati aesthetic of *ya* (elegance). The ostentatious gold and almost superficially bright colors in his fake landscapes are decorative features that might be considered *su* (vulgar) in the orthodox sense. The themes expressed are even more blatantly opposed to Confucian norms. Yao turns literati pursuits into the trivial matters of contemporary life, such as surfing the internet (instead of writing calligraphy), playing *majiang* (instead of chess), etc. A way to converse with his father, Yao's fake landscapes address, in an eclectic way, the contradiction between the unavoidable influences of China's traditions and the striving for his own identity in the present. **WK**

Selected Exhibitions
Good Times, Tina Keng Gallery, Taipei, 2014; *Golden Land*, Goedhuis Contemporary, London, 2015; *Golden Landscape*, Dong Gallery, Taipei, 2018; *Longing for Nature*, Museum Rietberg, Zurich, 2020.

Further Sources
Brian A. Kennedy et al., *Everything Will Fall into Ruin: Yao Jui-Chung* (Taipei: Taipei shili meishu guan, 2006); Yao Jui-Chung, *The Ruined Islands* (Taipei: Tianyuan chengshi wenhua, 2014); Yao Jui-Chung, *Incarnation* (Taipei: Diancang yishu jiating gufen youxian gongsi, 2017).

ZHANG YIRONG

b. Shaanxi Province, China, 1979

Butterfly Adrift Lake and Hills, 2017
Chinese ink on paper
49¼ × 49¼ in. (125 × 125 cm)

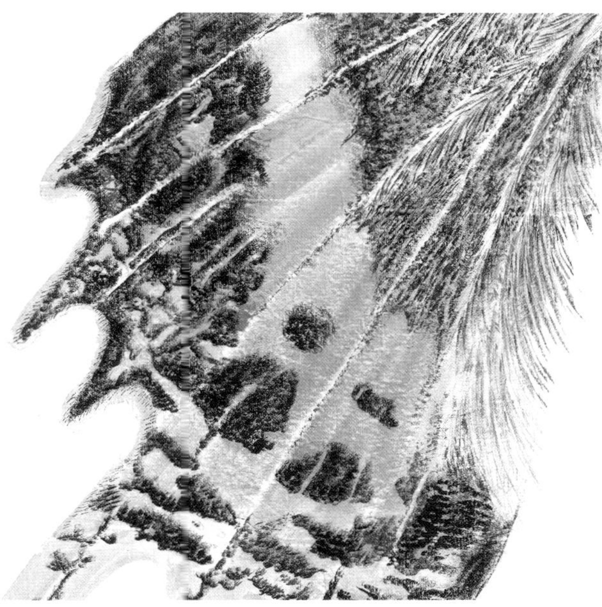

Butterfly Adrift Lake and Hills, 2017 (detail)

In a small town in northern Shaanxi, Zhang Yirong grew up watching her father paint murals for local temples and monasteries. She quickly turned from passive observer to active artist and became a painting prodigy herself, winning the National Children's Painting Competition golden prize at the age of five.

After pursuing an unfulfilling career in media, Zhang met ink painter Tai Xiangzhou, who encouraged her to return to art. She then began cultivating her *gongbi* linework, which would become an integral element of her signature style, by painting large copies of historical works. In 2005, Zhang began to apprentice under ink artist and *gongbi* master Liu Dan (p. 170), observing his otherwise private practice on a daily basis. His influence is clear: they share compositional elements, like a strong use of negative space, as well as techniques, with fine linework indicating a thorough understanding of the medium of ink.

A butterfly, one of Zhang's favorite subjects, forms the bounds of this work. The panes of its wings contain an entire world: rocks, trees, and pools of water. "Adrift lake and hills," the butterfly itself mirrors the nature below in its shimmering wings, showing us the landscape that it perceives in the captured moment. But the butterfly also has a symbolic meaning in Chinese ink and literati culture, recalling a story by the fourth-century BCE sage Zhuangzi, who dreamed of himself as a butterfly and awoke to question whether he was a butterfly dreaming of himself as a human. The work thus encompasses two dreamscapes: the scene reflected in the wings of the butterfly, and the possibility that the painting itself is a dream.
SF

Selected Exhibitions
Beyond the Jade Terrace, Alisan Fine Arts, Hong Kong, 2014; *Ink Painting of Zhang Yirong*, Catherine Palace, Moscow, 2017; *Women Ink | China Hong Kong*, Alisan Fine Arts Aberdeen and Central, Hong Kong, 2019.

Further Sources
Tiffany Beres, *Beyond the Jade Terrace* (Hong Kong: Alisan Fine Arts, 2014); Daphne King Yao, *Tai Xiangzhou and Zhang Yirong: One with the Universe* (Hong Kong: Alisan Fine Arts, 2017).

ZHANG YU

b. Tianjin, China, 1959

Divine Light Series No. 7: Floating Incomplete Circle, 1994
Ink on paper
96½ × 91⅜ in. (245 × 232 cm)

Fingerprint 2007, 2007
Water on xuan paper
75⅝ × 39⅜ in. (192 × 100 cm)

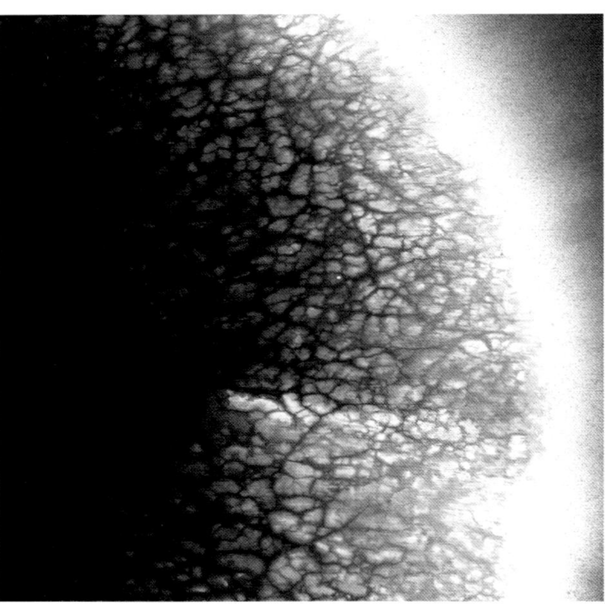

Divine Light Series No. 7: Floating Incomplete Circle, 1994 (detail)

Fingerprint 2007, 2007 (detail)

Although repetitive action is an important aspect in the work of many Chinese artists, few have committed to a single technique with as much consistency as Zhang Yu. He first worked with the motif of repeated fingerprints as early as 1991, then paused for a decade-long break, returning to the practice in 2001 when he felt he had established himself on the international art scene.

The *Divine Light Series* was produced during this interim and represents a rare exception to his fingerprint practice. Zhang created the work as an exploration of the bounds of ink, an experiment in combining Chinese ink and Western techniques, with the subject of a mysterious primeval light. In the series, he worked to erase his own voice, consciously painting in a way that left no trace of brushstrokes, and choosing a subject disconnected from his own lived experience. The resulting piece bears no trace of the artist's hand, as if the divine light itself materialized the work.

Zhang's fingerprint works, on the other hand, are at once self-portraits, rubbings, and meditations: repeated stamps of his fingerprint in water, red ink, or black ink. Though the fingerprint is understood as a marker of one's unique identity, its ubiquitousness in Zhang's oeuvre erases its singularity, presenting it instead as both a tool and a material. These pieces can be read as performance works, and his printed papers as documents of those performances—records of his life and act of artistic creation. From a spiritual mindset, he is enacting a process of self-cultivation that requires great patience and willpower, repeating the same small mark until his paper is completely covered.

In *Fingerprint 2007*, Zhang used only water to impress his fingerprint upon the paper. His series of water-only fingerprints deemphasizes the two-dimensional patterning of the mark, and instead shows us an impression in the round, each motion creating a small indent in the surface of the paper. **SF**

Selected Exhibitions
Cultivation Practice: Exhibition of Zhang Yu's Fingerprint Works 1991–2013, Gwangju Museum of Art, 2013; *Zhang Yu: The Form of Notion/Thought*, Guangdong Museum of Art, Guangzhou, 2014; *Mountain Plan: Water. Ink. Mountain*, Guangdong Museum of Art, Guangzhou, and Feng Chia University, Taichung, 2018.

Further Sources
Fingerprints: Traces of Zhang Yu's Self-Cultivation (Taichung: Da Xiang Art Space, 2009); Feng Boyi, ed., *Self-Cultivation—Zhang Yu's Fingerprint Works 1991–2011* (Beijing: China Today Art Museum Publishing House, 2011).

ZHENG CHONGBIN

b. Shanghai, 1961

***Dissolved Geometry B*, 2012**
Ink and acrylic on xuan paper
113⅜ × 33½ in. (288 × 85 cm)

***Dissolved Geometry C*, 2012**
Ink and acrylic on xuan paper
113⅜ × 33½ in. (288 × 85 cm)

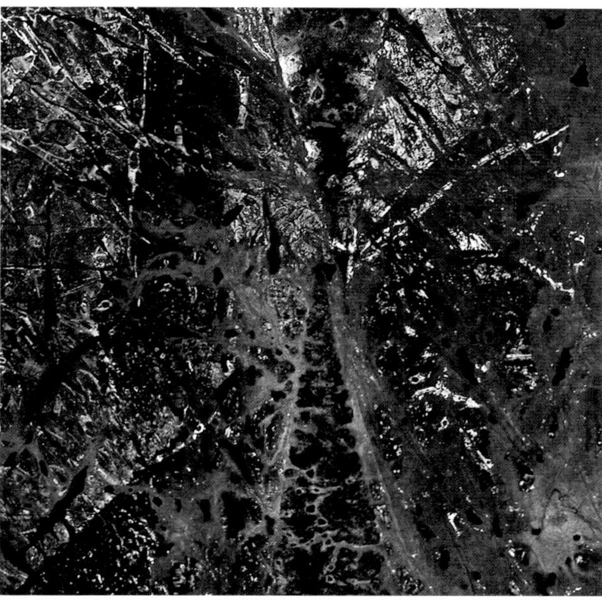

Dissolved Geometry B, 2012 (detail)

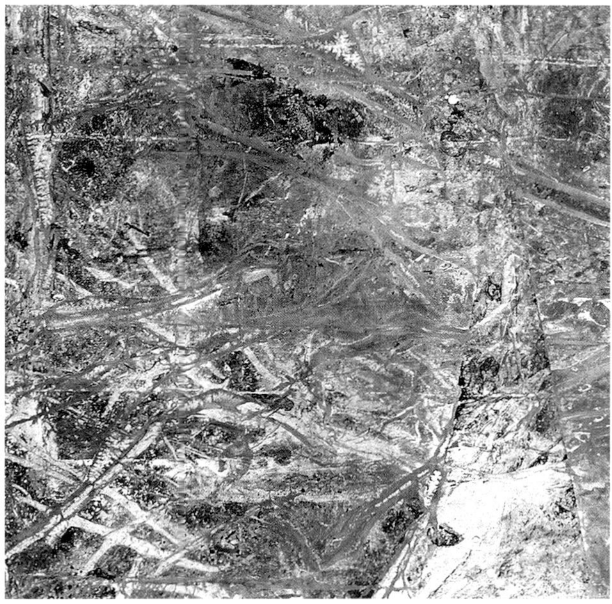

Dissolved Geometry C, 2012 (detail)

Zheng Chongbin was inspired by the modest artists of his childhood neighborhood. He recalls watching his retired neighbors—who he later learned had been demoted from their political positions during the Cultural Revolution (1966–76)—as they painted their daily pieces, and was drawn to the ritual of this practice. He studied traditional Chinese ink painting under Mu Yilin and Chen Jialing before attending the Zhejiang Academy of Fine Arts in Hangzhou. After graduating in 1984, he stayed on as a teacher until 1988. Desiring to incorporate more gesture into his artwork, he later broke from the guidelines of his masters to create larger-scale abstractions using a wide *paibi* brush, and combining Chinese ink with Western acrylic. Zheng's unique method, in which he paints on both the front and the back of xuan paper with different mediums, generates a distinctive contrast of light and dark, blending and resistance, Chinese and Western materials; it is through this technique that he produced the singular aesthetic seen in *Dissolved Geometry B* and *Dissolved Geometry C*.

Unique to ink is the quality of flowing in the same way as water, and the capturing of water's movement in time through evaporation. After a work-in-progress dries, what remains is the impression of this movement—the ghost of the water's flow and energy. The energy of Zheng's ink is allowed to run in certain places and forced to stop in others, where it meets the resistance of the acrylic paint. The artist makes room for the unpredictable as he folds, unfolds, and flips the paper, letting the ink and acrylic create their own effects on each sheet of xuan. His works at once appear minimal, abstract, and expressionistic, summoning up images of Abstract Expressionist and modern Chinese painting alike.

Zheng moved to the United States in 1989, as the first person to receive the international fellowship at the San Francisco Art Institute. After earning an MFA there in 1991, the artist remained in California, incorporating elements of American installation and light-based artwork into his oeuvre.
SF

Selected Exhibitions
Impulse, Matter, Form, INK Studio, Beijing, 2013; 56th Venice Biennale, 2015; *Liquid Space*, Ryōsokuin Temple Kenninji, Kyoto, 2019; *I Look for the Sky*, Asian Art Museum, San Francisco, 2020.

Further Sources
Britta Erickson, *Zheng Chongbin: Impulse, Matter, Form* (Beijing: INK Studio, 2014); Lisa Claypool and Masahiro Terada, *Liquid Space: Zheng Chongbin Light, Space, Installation* (Kyoto: Shibunkaku Works, 2019).

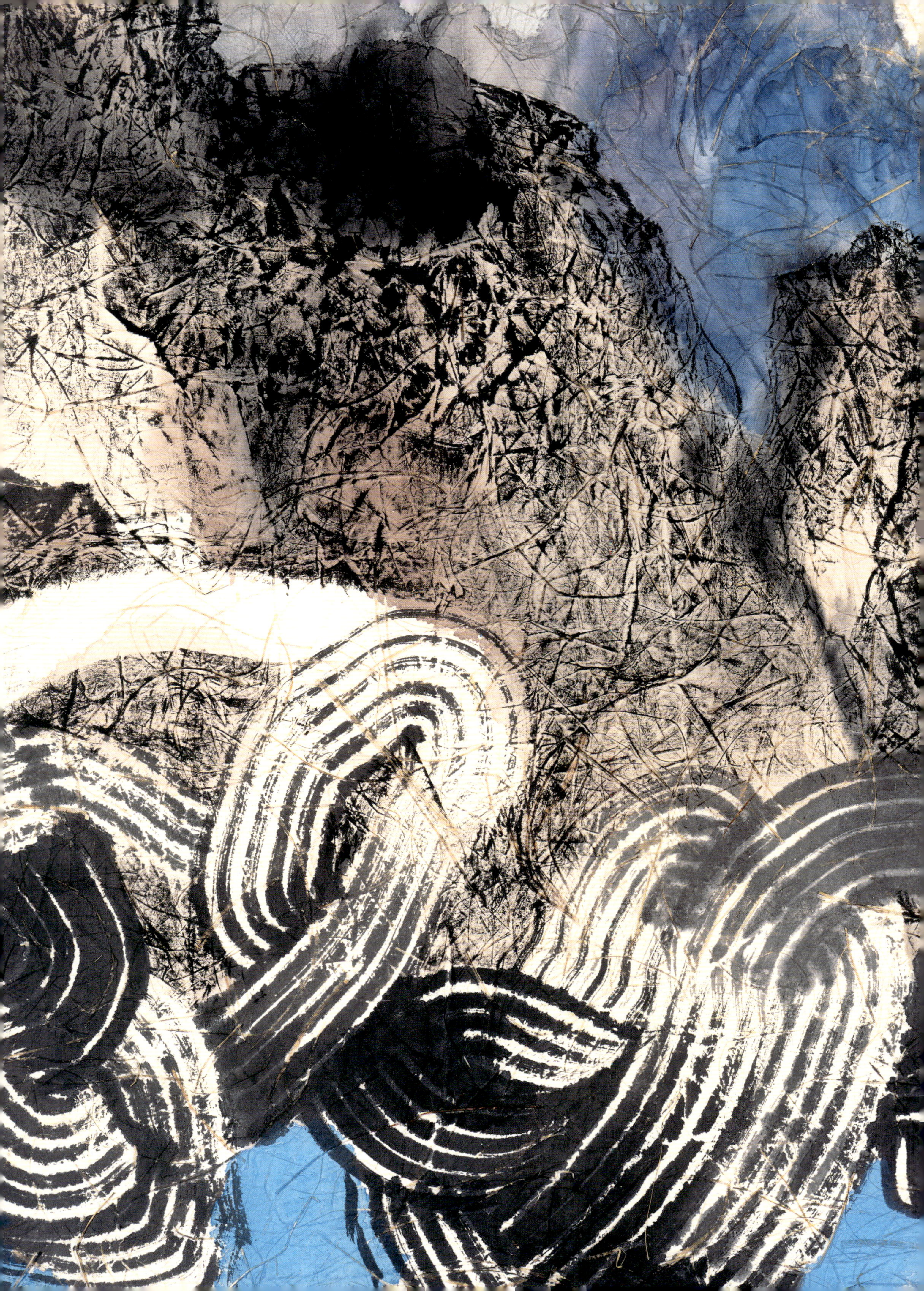

Index

Page numbers in *italics* denote illustrations.

A

absence, 37, 88, 90, 91, 93, 199, 209

negative space, 43, 203, 206, 216, 230, 234, 239

Abstract Expressionist, 44, 217, 241

Academy of Art University, San Francisco, 214

Accidentally Passing, Needle Script (Fung), *59*, 197, *197* (detail)

acrylic on canvas

Painting (Kujasalo), *72*, 208, *208* (detail)

Torn (Houshiary), *85*, 201, *201* (detail)

Wet Psyche–No Wind (Rhee), 93, *110*, 225, *225* (detail)

acrylic on paper

Battle at the Craters (Bataille aux cratères) (Asch), *45* (detail), *77*, 185, *185* (detail)

Dissolved Geometry B (Zheng), *95*, 241, *241* (detail)

Dissolved Geometry C (Zheng), *95*, 241, *241* (detail)

Ajanta Caves, Aurangabad, Maharashtra, India, 40, *40*, 41

Albers, Josef, 208

Album 2 (Li Huasheng), *127* (detail), *131–34*, 212, *212* (details)

alum, 93, 236

aluminum, 205

Amitabha Buddha, 40, 41

Siddhartha Gautama, 40, 42

An Shigao, 40

Anti-Rightist Campaign, 216

apparitions, 34, 37, 87–93, *94–121*, 182

ArtCenter College of Design, Los Angeles, 227

Asch, Ophélie, 185

Battle at the Craters (Bataille aux cratères), *45* (detail), *77*, 185, *185* (detail)

Australian Aboriginal cave painting, 194

Autumn in the Forbidden City (East Veranda) (Hong), *155*, 200, *200*

Autumn in the Forbidden City (West Veranda) (Hong), *154*, 200, *200*

B

Background Story: Ink Variation (from Lui Shou-kwan) (Xu), *125* (detail), 126, *158–61*, 233, *233* (detail), 234

batik

Untitled (Braun), *66–69*, 188, *188* (details)

Battle at the Craters (Bataille aux cratères) (Asch), *45* (detail), *77*, 185, *185* (detail)

Beat poets, 44

Beijing, 200, 203, 229, 234

Autumn in the Forbidden City (East Veranda) (Hong), *155*, 200, *200*

Autumn in the Forbidden City (West Veranda) (Hong), *154*, 200, *200*

Capital Normal University, 215

Central Academy of Fine Arts, 199, 200, 234

New Beijing CCTV (Shi), *112–13*, 226, *226* (detail)

Big River (from the Fives Series of Repetition) (Xu), *166*, 233, *234* (detail)

bimo, 193

Bingyi, 19, 46, 186

Let Me Become the Universe's Plaything, *78*, 186, *186* (detail)

bird-and-flower paintings, 35, 200, 202, 210, 232

Black Pool (from the Fives Series of Repetition) (Xu), *166*, 233

Black Tadpoles (from the Fives Series of Repetition) (Xu), *165*, 233, *234* (detail)

Blank, Irma, 19, 26, 46, 187

Radical Writings, Abecedarium 7-1-91, *83*, 187, *187* (detail)

Radical Writings, Dal Libro Totale, *82*, 187, *187* (detail)

blank-leaving concept, 209

Blue Bridge (Hai), *147*, 199, *199* (detail)

Bonaparte, Roland, 223

Braun, Matti, 188

Untitled, *66–69*, 188, *188* (details)

broken-ink lines, 190

Bronze Age, 13

brush-and-ink technique, 193

Buddha, 40, 41, 42, 46

Buddhism, 37, 40–44, 182, 203

chaitya worship hall, *40*

See also Chan Buddhism; Zen Buddhism

Buncheong (or Punch'ong) ware, 207

Burnouf, Eugène, 43

burnt-ink technique, 235

Butterfly Adrift Lakes and Hills (Zhang Yirong), *173*, 239, *239* (detail)

C

Cage, John, 44

calligraphy, 23, 25, 37, 193, 196, 204, 212, 216, 230, 238

history, 13–15

illegible, 194

reformer, 197

seal script, 198

mythos of lost dynasties series–pseudo-seal scripture in calligraphic copybook #2 (gu), 198, *198*

Sufi, 201

cameras, 189, 199

box, 227

obscura, 199

pinhole, 199

Capital Normal University, Beijing, 215

Castiglione, Giuseppe, 34–35

Qianlong Emperor in Ceremonial Armor on Horseback, The, *34*

Central Academy of Fine Arts, Beijing, 199, 200, 234

Centre Pompidou, Paris, 236

ceramics, 18, 30, 46

Vessel 08-C (Kitamura), *74*, 207, *207* (detail)

Vessel 08-G (Kitamura), *75*, 207, *207* (detail)

Chu Ko, *The Dreaming Clouds of Wu Mountains*, 2005 (detail)

chaitya worship hall, 40
Chan Buddhism, 37, 41, 42, 43, 44, 46, 88, 182, 236
Chang, Johnson, 21
Changchun, Jilin Province
 Fine Art Institute of Jilin, 199
chants, 44, 195, 213
characters, Chinese, 13, 93, 189, 197, 198, 221, 222, 237
 Chinese Shanshui Tattoo Series No. 7 (Huang Yan), *128* (detail), *152*, 202, *202* (detail)
 mythos of lost dynasties series—pseudo-seal scripture in calligraphic copybook #2 (gu), 198, *198*
Chelsea School of Art, London, 201
Chen Bolan, 189
 Street View of Shanghai, A, *103*, 189, *189* (detail)
Chen Haiyan, 129, 190–91
 Dream 1986/6/19 Maqpi, 190, *191*
 Dream 2005.2.15, Mountains, Flowers, Crowded People and Cars, *2* (detail), *171*, 190, *190* (detail)
 Horse and Rose, *176–77*, 191, *191* (detail)
Chen Hongshou, 238
Chen Jialing, 241
Cherney, Michael, 35, 192
 Five Peaks: Eastern, Western, Southern, Central, Northern, *36* (detail), *140–41*, 192, *192* (details)
China Academy of Art (formerly Zhejiang Academy of Fine Arts), Hangzhou, Zhejiang Province, 198, 230, 236, 241
China/Avant-Garde (1989), 235
China Fine Arts Weekly, 182
Chinese Shanshui Tattoo Series No. 7 (Huang Yan), *128* (detail), *152*, 202, *202* (detail)
Chinese University of Hong Kong, 210, 231
Chu Ko, 22, 193
 Dreaming Clouds of Wu Mountains, The, *178*, 193, *193* (detail), *242* (detail)
Chu Teh-Chun, 21, 26
Chua Ek Kay, 194
 Reflection-Breeze: Passes by the Lotus Pond, *56*, 194, *194* (detail)
Cognié, Dora, 12, 17, 21, 23, *27*, 28, *31*, 34
 collecting, 24–25, 212, 234
 Fondation Dora, 11
 profession, 11
 travels, 24, 28, 29
 See also Fondation INK
Cognié, Gérard, 20, 25, 27
 collecting, 17–18, 21–30, 212, 234
 profession, 11
 travels, 17, 21, 28, 29, 30
 See also Fondation INK
Cole, Max, 19, 46, 195
 Untitled, *80*, 195, *195* (detail)
collages
 Modern Landscape (Yang Shih-Chih), *138–39*, 237, *237* (detail)
 Moon Series: Daybreak (Liu Guosong), *149*, 217, *217* (detail)
College of Art, Shanghai, 230
comic illustration, 210
Communist China, 44, 216
conceptual artists, 187, 202
Confucianism, 40, 238
Confucius, 216
Constructivists, 208, 228
contemplation, 40, 41, 42, 46, 186
Convergence (Sunagawa), *62–63*, 228, *228* (detail)
Corot, Jean-Baptiste-Camille, 232
court painting, 34, 200
Cruz-Diez, Carlos, 228
Cultural Revolution, 26, 182n12, 198, 212, 214, 215, 224, 241
cun texturing stroke, 214
cursive script, 13, 219

D
Dahlberg, Jonas, 26
Dai Guangyu, 196
 Landscape, Ink, Ice, 93, *106–7*, 196, *196* (detail), *254* (detail)
Dansaekhwa movement, 209
Daode jing, 220
Daoism, 40, 220, 235
Deep in the Mountains #2 (Wong), *9* (detail), *179*, 231, *231* (detail)
Deng Xiaoping, 229
dharma, 219
Dissolved Geometry B (Zheng), *95*, 241, *241* (detail)
Dissolved Geometry C (Zheng), *95*, 241, *241* (detail)
Divine Light Series No. 7: Floating Incomplete Circle (Zhang Yu), 91, *92* (detail), *119*, 240, *240* (detail)
Dong Qichang
 Wanluan Thatched Hall, *124*, 126
Down to the Countryside Movement, 234
Dream 1986/6/19 Maqpi (Chen Haiyan), 190, *191*
Dream 2005.2.15, Mountains, Flowers, Crowded People and Cars (Chen Haiyan), *2* (detail), *171*, 190, *190* (detail)
Dreaming Clouds of Wu Mountains, The (Chu), *178*, 193, *193* (detail), *242* (detail)
dreamscapes, 34, 37, 126, 129, *130–81*, 193, 206, 239

Early Spring (Guo Xi), 90, 214
Eastern Painting Society, 193
eccentric landscapes, 238
Ecriture No. 080222 (Park), *65*, 221, *221* (detail)
emptiness, 206, 213, 221
 self-emptying, 41, 221
empty space, 19, 188, 199, 204, 206
energy, 19, 22, 26, 188, 201, 203, 241
 electrostatic, 227
 qi, 13, 211
 qiyun, 124
enlightenment, Buddhist, 40, 42, 219
enlightenment era, European, 43
ensō, 43
etchings
 Untitled (Pentsch), *71*, 222, *222* (detail)
 Untitled XII (Pentsch), *57*, 222, *222* (detail)

F
fabrics, 93, 225
 batik, 187
 cotton, 215
 gwangmok cloth, 206
 silk, 90, 124, 188, 210, 211, 215, 234
 See also thread-wrapping technique
Fan Chang Tien, 194
Fan Kuan, 90
fantasy-scape, 210
Faraday, Michael, 227
Farmland (from the Fives Series of Repetition) (Xu), *164*, 233, 234
Field (from the Fives Series of Repetition) (Xu), *163*, 233, *233* (detail)
Fifth Moon Painting Society, 193, 217
Fine Art Institute of Jilin, Changchun, 199
Fingerprint 2007 (Zhang Yu), *49*, 240, *240* (detail)
Fingerprint: Right Ring Finger (Yang Jiechang), *6* (detail), 93, *97*, 236, *236* (detail)
Five Dynasties period, 217
Five Peaks: Eastern, Western, Southern, Central, Northern (Cherney), *36* (detail), *140–41*, 192, *192* (details)
Fletcher, Leda, 22
Fluxus, 44
folk art, 193, 217
Fondation Dora, Geneva, 11
Fondation INK, 11–12, 15, 17–30
Franklin, Benjamin, 227
From Point (Lee), *55*, 209, *209* (detail)
Fudan University, Shanghai, 230
Fung Ming Chip, 14, 29, 197
 Accidentally Passing, Needle Script, *59*, 197, *197* (detail)

G
German Expressionism, 190
globalization, 234
glue, 93, 235
Gogh, Vincent van, 44
gold leaf, 238
Gong Kai, 88
gongbi technique, 93, 210, 216, 239
Goryeo dynasty, 220
grids, 44, 204, 208, 209, 213
gu wenda, 198
 mythos of lost dynasties series—pseudo-seal scripture in calligraphic copybook #2, 198, *198*
 surrealist landscape #3, *100–101*, 198, *198* (detail)
Guanxiu, 41, 42, 44
Guo Xi, 90
 Early Spring, 90, 214
gwangmok cloth, 206

H
Hai Bo, 129, 199
  Blue Bridge, *147*, 199, *199* (detail)
Hammersmith College of Art, London, 228
Han dynasty, 13, 40, 186
Han Lei, 21
Hanart TZ Gallery, Hong Kong, 21
Hangzhou, Zhejiang Province
  China Academy of Art, 198, 230, 236, 241
hanji, 204, 221
Haystack Reflection (from the Fives Series of Repetition) (Xu), *167*, 233
Heart Sutra, The (Wang Dongling), 12
Helsinki
  Academy of Fine Arts of Finland, 208
  Free Art School, 208
  School of Photography, 223
Hinduism, 40, 43
Hong Kong, 11, 29, 197
  Chinese University of Hong Kong, 210, 231
  New Ink Movement, 211, 219, 231
Hong Lei, 21, 129, 200
  Autumn in the Forbidden City (East Veranda), *155*, 200, *200*
  Autumn in the Forbidden City (West Veranda), *154*, 200, *200*
Horse and Rose (Chen Haiyan), *176–77*, 191, *191* (detail)
Houshiary, Shirazeh, 19, 201
  Torn, *85*, 201, *201* (detail)
hua, 14
  shanshuihua, 224
  shuimohua, 35
  wanglianghua, 88, 90, 91, 93, 182
Huang Yan, 129, 202
  Chinese Shanshui Tattoo Series No. 7, *128* (detail), *152*, 202, *202* (detail)
Huang Zhiyang, 203
  Possessing Numerous Peaks No. S-1226, *32–33* (detail), *81*, 203, *203* (detail)
Hu Chongxian, 35
  Jade Green Straws (Zhang Daqian and Hu Chongxian), *37*
Hu Zhifu, 88

I
Impressionism, 224
Impressionists, 44
India, 40, 43
ink and wash, 35, 42
  Untitled (Cole), *80*, 195, *195* (detail)
ink art, 12, 15, 23, 34, 93, 129, 182
  aesthetics, 12, 17, 18, 19, 34, 35, 88, 192, 209
  definition, 18, 23, 26, 37, 182, 203
  history, 12–15, 26–27, 34–35, 37, 90–91, 93, 126, 203
  traditional, 23, 198, 202, 211, 219, 235, 237, 238
Ink Art: Past as Present in Contemporary China (2013), 29
inscriptions, 13, 37, 219
installation, 18, 28, 37, 186, 198, 215, 223, 232, 238, 241
  Background Story: Ink Variation (from Lui Shou-kwan) (Xu), *125* (detail), 126, *158–61*, 233, *233* (detail), 234
International Workgroup for Constructive Art, 208

J
Jade Green Straws (Zhang Daqian and Hu Chongxian), *37*
Jan, Elvira, 21, 26
Japan, 40, 43, 188, 207
Jataka texts, 40
Jeong Gwang-Hee, 204
  Way of Reflection, The, *4* (detail), *61*, 204, *204* (detail)
Jiangsu Pictorial, 182
jiaomo technique, 235
Jing Hao, 14, 90
Jiuzhaigou, Sichuan Province, 218
Jiuzhaigou Series #48: Sea of Floating Ice (Liu Guosong), 12, 91, *109*, 217–18, *218* (detail)
Jōmon period, 207
Joseon dynasty, 206, 207, 220
Juran, 90

K
Kandinsky, Vasily, 198
Kangxi, Emperor, 34
Khan, Idris, 26, 83, 205
  Numbers, 12
  Untitled, *104–5*, 205, *205* (detail), *252* (detail)
Kim Ho-deuk, 129, 206
  San, San (Mountain, Mountain), *153*, 206, *206* (detail)
  studio, *22*
Kitamura Junko, 46, 207
  Vessel 08-C, *74*, 207, *207* (detail)
  Vessel 08-G, *75*, 207, *207* (detail)
Kizil Caves, Xinjiang Uyghur Autonomous Region, China, 41, *41*
Kondō Yutaka, 207
Koolhaas, Rem, and Ole Scheeren, 226
Korea, 40, 209, 220, 221, 225
  See also South Korea
Kujasalo, Matti, 46, 208
  Painting, *72*, 208, *208* (detail)
Kyoto City University of Arts, 207

L
landscape, 14, 123–29, 186, 203, 206, 223, 230, 232, 234, 239
  blue-and-green, 202
  Buddhist, 41, 43
  eccentric, 238
  inner, 37, 124, 126, 142n11, 193, 214
  "History of Landscape, The," (Huang Yan), 202
  literati, 182, 202, 214
  misty, 90–91, 206, 211, 216, 219, 220, 225, 232
  Modern Landscape (Yang Shih-Chih), *138–39*, 237, *237* (detail)
  mountain, 25, 91, 206, 210, 216
  shanshui, 93, 196, 202
  Chinese Shanshui Tattoo Series No. 7 (Huang Yan), *128* (detail), *152*, 202, *202* (detail)
  shanshuihua, 224
  surrealist landscape #3 (gu), *100–101*, 198, *198* (detail)
  traditional, 211, 212
  urban, 126, 182
  xinjing, 124n11
Landscape (Li Huayi), *142–43*, 214, *214* (detail)
Landscape, Ink, Ice (Dai), 93, *106–7*, 196, *196* (detail), *254* (detail)
Laozi, 220
Late Rabbit (Leung Ka-yin), *151*, 210, *210* (detail), *249* (detail)
layering, 88, 93, 201, 204, 205, 208, 214, 225, 230, 232, 235
  100 Layers of Ink series (Yang Jiechang), 236
  of debris, 234
Lecht, Suzanne, 23
Lee Ufan, 209
  From Point, *55*, 209, *209* (detail)
Let Me Become the Universe's Plaything (Bingyi), *78*, 186, *186* (detail)
Leung Ka-yin, Joey, 210
  Late Rabbit, *151*, 210, *210* (detail), *249* (detail)
Leung Kui-ting, 129, 211, 219
  Vision 08, *175*, 211, *211* (detail)
Li Gongnian, 90
Li Huasheng, 19, 26, 27, *27*, 28, 44
  104, *52*, 213, *213* (detail)
  Album 2, *127* (detail), *131–34*, 212, *212* (details)
  Untitled, *27*, *73*, 213, *213* (detail)
Li Huayi, 129, 214
  Landscape, *142–43*, 214, *214* (detail)
Li Jin, 11
Li Xiaoshan, 182
Liang Kai, 88
Light and Space artists, 44
Lightning Field 119 (Sugimoto), *115*, 227, *227* (detail)
Lightning Field 138 (Sugimoto), *117*, 227, *227* (detail)
Lightning Field 143 (Sugimoto), 12, *116*, 227
likeness, 14, 124, 224
Lin Tianmiao, 215, 229
  Seeing Shadows No. 35, *86–87* (detail), 88, *98–99*, 215, *215* (detail)
  Tree, The, *16* (detail), *181*, 215, *215* (detail)
Lissitzky, El, 228
literati, 124, 126, 129, 182, 211, 213, 238, 239
  painting, 202, 214, 216
liu bai concept, 209
Liu Dan, 126, 216, 239
  Untitled, *10* (detail), 11, *170*, 216, *216* (detail)

Liu Guosong (Liu Kuo-Sung), 22, 17, 217
brushes in studio, *28*
Jiuzhaigou Series #48: Sea of Floating Ice, 12, 91, *109*, 217–18, *218* (detail)
Moon Series: Daybreak, *149*, 217, *217* (detail)
Moon Series: It'll Soon Be White All Over, *122–23*, *148*, 217, *217* (detail)
Lokaksema, 40
London
Chelsea School of Art, 201
Hammersmith College of Art, 228
Royal College of Art, 205
Los Angeles
ArtCenter College of Design, 227
Los Angeles County Museum of Art
gift from Fondation INK, 11–12, 15, 29, 30
Lotus Sutra, 43
Lu Yanshao, 198
Lui Canming, 219
Lui Shou-kwan, 17, 46, 211, 219, 231
Wood Houses in the Mountains, *157*, 219, *219* (detail), 234
Zen Painting A69-14, *47* (detail), *79*, 219, *219* (detail)
luohan, 42, *42*
Lyrical Abstraction, 21, 26

M
Ma Yuan, 43
MacArthur "Genius" Award, 234
majiang, 238
Malevich, Kazimir, 195, 201, 228, 236
marble
Possessing Numerous Peaks No. S-1226 (Huang Zhiyang), *32–33* (detail), *81*, 203, *203* (detail)
Martin, Agnes, 44
meditation, 19, 40, 41, 46, 91, 203
theme in ink art, 25, 27, 34, 37, 39–46, *47–85*, 126, 129, 182, 186, 206, 240
meditative process, 44, 46, 187, 201, 213, 226
melancholy, 199
memory, 189, 205, 215, 223, 229
Mi Fu, 90
"Mi tradition" of painting, 90, 91
Mi Youren, 90
Michaux, Henri, 21, 26
Min Byung Hun, 26, 220
Snow Land Sky Fog Gloom, 88, *89* (detail), *102*, 220, *220* (detail)
mindfulness, 44
Ming dynasty, 200, 238
minimalism, 46, 209
Minimalists, 44
mitsumata paper, works on
Five Peaks: Eastern, Western, Southern, Central, Northern (Cherney), *36* (detail), *140–41*, 192, *192* (details)
modernism, 182, 194
Modern Landscape (Yang Shih-Chih), *138–39*, 237, *237* (detail)
Mogao Caves, Dunhuang, Gansu Province, China, 41n6
monochrome, 13, 42, 44, 126, 185, 188, 189, 208, 215, 219, 220, 221
Dansaekhwa movement, 209
Mono-ha, 209
Monument (Yan), *76*, 235, *235*
Moon Series: Daybreak (Liu Guosong), *149*, 217, *217* (detail)
Moon Series: It'll Soon Be White All Over (Liu Guosong), *122–23*, *148*, 217, *217* (detail)
Mountain Place (from the Fives Series of Repetition) (Xu), *165*, 233
Moving Cloud (from the Fives Series of Repetition) (Xu), *163*, 233
Mu Yilin, 241
Musée de l'Homme, Paris, 223
muninhwa painting, 206
Muñoz, Isabel, 26
Muqi, 43
mythos of lost dynasties series–pseudo-seal scripture in calligraphic copybook #2 (gu), 198, *198*

N
National Palace Museum, Taipei, 193
National Taiwan Normal University, Taipei, 217
negative space, 43, 203, 206, 216, 230, 234, 239
Neolithic period, 13
New Beijing CCTV (Shi), *112–13*, 226, *226* (detail)
New Ink Movement, 211, 219, 231, 235
New Wave movement, 182, 196, 235
nostalgia, 189, 199
Nouvelle École de Paris, 21, 26

O
ox-hair brush texture strokes, 211

P
paibi brush, 241
Painting (Kujasalo), *72*, 208, *208* (detail)
Pali texts, 43
paper, 25
burnt, 230
crumpled, 193, 204, 221
"Guosong," 217
hanji, 204, 221
mitsumata, 192
tracing, 218
xuan, 191, 197, 213, 236, 240, 241
paper-cutting folk art, 217
Paris, 21, 22
Centre Pompidou, 236
Musée de l'Homme, 223
Nouvelle École de Paris, 21, 26
School of Paris, 21
University of Paris Sorbonne, 185
Paris-Pekin (2002), 21
Park Seo-Bo, 91, 221
Ecriture No. 080222, *65*, 221, *221* (detail)
penmo technique, 217
Pentsch, Antoine, 222
Untitled, *71*, 222, *222* (detail)
Untitled XII, *57*, 222, *222* (detail)
performance, 26, 46, 186, 196, 226, 234, 239, 240
photographic work, 21, 26, 35, 93, 129, 189
Autumn in the Forbidden City (East Veranda) (Hong), *155*, 200, *200*
Autumn in the Forbidden City (West Veranda) (Hong), *154*, 200, *200*
Blue Bridge (Hai), *147*, 199, *199* (detail)
Chinese Shanshui Tattoo Series No. 7 (Huang Yan), *128* (detail), *152*, 202, *202* (detail)
Five Peaks: Eastern, Western, Southern, Central, Northern (Cherney), *36* (detail), *140–41*, 192, *192* (details)
Icy Prospects # 20 (Puranen), *169*, 223, *223* (detail)
Jade Green Straws (Zhang Daqian and Hu Chongxian), *37*
Landscape, Ink, Ice (Dai), 93, *106–7*, 196, *196* (detail), *254* (detail)
Lightning Field 119 (Sugimoto), *115*, 227, *227* (detail)
Lightning Field 138 (Sugimoto), *117*, 227, *227* (detail)
Lightning Field 143 (Sugimoto), 12, *116*, 227
Moon Series: Daybreak (Liu Guosong), *149*, 217, *217* (detail)
New Beijing CCTV (Shi), 11, *112–13*, 226, *226* (detail)
Seeing Shadows No. 35 (Lin), *86–87*, 88, *98–99*, 215, *215* (detail)
Snow Land Sky Fog Gloom (Min), 88, *89* (detail), *102*, 220, *220* (detail)
Sun Set 2 (Wang Gongxin), 229, *229*
Sun Set 5 (Wang Gongxin), *111*, 229, *229* (detail)
Untitled (Khan), *104–5*, 205, *205* (detail), *252* (detail)
"photopainting," 189
Plexiglas, 93, 225
pollution, 126
pomo lines, 190
Pool of Life (from the Fives Series of Repetition) (Xu), *167*, 233
Pop, 44
Possessing Numerous Peaks No. S-1226 (Huang Zhiyang), *32–33* (detail), *81*, 203, *203* (detail)
principles of Chinese painting, 124
Puranen, Jorma, 19, 223
Icy Prospects # 20, *169*, 223, *223* (detail)

Q
qi, 13, 203, 206, 211
qiyun, 224
qiyun shendong, 13, 124
Qianlong Emperor in Ceremonial Armor on Horseback, The (Castiglione), *34*
Qing dynasty, 219
Qiu Shihua, 19, 224
Untitled, 46, *50–51*, 224, *224* (detail)
Qiu Zhijie, 11

R

Radical Writings, Abecedarium 7-1-91 (Blank), *83*, 187, *187* (detail)
Radical Writings, Dal Libro Totale (Blank), *82*, 187, *187* (detail)
Rauschenberg, Robert, 224
reality, 14, 42, 44, 129, 185, 201, 229
- *shi*, 14
- *zhen*, 14

Reflection-Breeze Passes by the Lotus Pond (Chua), *56*, 194, *194* (detail)
Reinhardt, Ad, 44, 208, 224, 236
repetition, 19
- theme in ink art, 37, 44–45, 129, 206, 209

resonance, 18, 19
- *qiyun*, 124, 224
- *qiyun shendong*, 13

Rhee Kibong, 225
- *Wet Psyche—No Wind*, 93, *110*, 225, *225* (detail)

Richter, Gerhard, 189
Rikkyo University, Tokyo, 227
ritual bronze vessels, 13
Roche, G., 223
rope braiding, 193
Royal College of Art, London, 205
rubbings, 240
- water, 217

S

Sámi region, Finland, 223
sanfanjiuran coloring technique, 93
San Francisco
- Academy of Art University, 214
- Buddhist temple in, 44
- San Francisco Art Institute, 241
- San Francisco State University, 237

San, San (Mountain, Mountain) (Kim), *153*, 206, *206* (detail)
Sanskrit texts, 43
scholar-officials, 216
scholar's rocks, 25, 211
School of Paris, 2[illegible]
script, 187
- *Accidentally Passing, Needle Script* (Fung), *59*, 197, *197* (detail)
- cursive, 13, 219
- *mythos of lost dynasties series—pseudo-seal scripture in calligraphic copybook #2* (gu), 198, *198*
- post-marijuana, 197
- seal, 198

sculpture, 18, 204, 225
- Buddhist, 40, 41, 227
- *Convergence* (Sunagawa), 46, *62–63*, 228, *228* (detail)
- *Possessing Numerous Peaks No. S-1226* (Huang Zhiyang), *32–33* (detail), *81*, 203, *203* (detail)
- *Tree, The* (Lin), *16* (detail), *181*, 215, *215* (detail)
- *See also* stoneware

seal
- carving, 197
- script, 198

Seeing Shadows No. 35 (Lin), *86–87*, 88, *98–99*, 215, *215* (detail)
self-cultivation, 19, 240
self-emptying, 221
self-expression, 124, 126, 204, 214
self-portraits, 240
self-taught, 197
Seoul National University, 206, 225
Shang dynasty, 13
Shanghai, 17, 19, 21, 28, 29
- College of Art, 230
- Fudan University, 230
- School of Arts and Crafts, 198
- Shanghai Normal University, 189
- Shanghai School, 194, 214
- *Street View of Shanghai, A* (Chen Bolan), *103*, 189, *189* (detail)

shanshui, 93, 192
- *Chinese Shanshui Tattoo Series No. 7* (Huang Yan), *128* (detail), *152*, 202, *202* (detail)

shanshuihua, 224
Shi Guorui, 11, 226
- *New Beijing CCTV*, 11, *112–13*, 226, *226* (detail)

Shi Ke, 41, 42, 217
shita, 217
Shitao, 219
shuimohua, 35
Siddhartha Gautama, 40, 42
siheyuan, 229
"Silk Road," 40
Singapore, 11
- Liang Seah Street, 194
- Singapore Tyler Print Institute, 215

Six Dynasties period, 13
Smend, Rudolf, 188
Snow Land Sky Fog Gloom (Min), 88, *89* (detail), *102*, 220, *220* (detail)
Socialist Realist style, 44, 212, 214, 224
Sōdeisha, 207
Song dynasty, 43, 124, 200, 217
- Northern Song dynasty, 90, 124, 126, 214
- Southern Song dynasty, 88

Soon Tae Hong, 220
Soto, Jesús Rafael, 228
South Korea, 11, 28, 29, 30, 221
- *See also* Korea

Spring and Autumn period, 193
Still Life 012-Buttercup Tree (Wu), 91, *120–21*, 232, *232* (detail)
stoneware
- *Vessel 08-C* (Kitamura), *74*, 207, *207* (detail)
- *Vessel 08-G* (Kitamura), *75*, 207, *207* (detail)

Street View of Shanghai, A (Chen Bolan) *103*, 189, *189* (detail)
studio
- of Chen Haiyan, 190
- of Kim Ho-deuk, *22*
- of Li Huasheng, *27*
- of Liu Guosong, *28*
- of Sunagawa Haruhiko, 228
- of Wang Tiande, 21
- of Yang Jiechang, 236
- of Zhang Yu, *25*

studio visits, 21, 24, 25, *26*, *27*, 28, 29
su (vulgar), 238
Su Shi, 124
Sufi poetry and calligraphy, 201
Sugimoto, Hiroshi, 19, 26, 91, 227
- *Lightning Field 119*, *115*, 227, *227* (detail)
- *Lightning Field 138*, *117*, 227, *227* (detail)
- *Lightning Field 143*, 12, *116*, 227

Sun Set 2 (Wang Gongxin), 229, *229*
Sun Set 5 (Wang Gongxin), *111*, 229, *229* (detail)
Sunagawa Haruhiko, 46, 228
- *Convergence*, *62–63*, 228, *228* (detail)

surrealist landscape #3 (gu), *100–101*, 198, *198* (detail)
sutras, 44, 46
- *Heart Sutra, The* (Wang Dongling), 12
- Lotus Sutra, 43

Suzuki Osamu, 11, 207
symbolism, 43

T

Tai Xiangzhou, 239
Taipei
- National Palace Museum, 193
- National Taiwan Normal University, 217
- Taipei Chinese Cultural University, 203
- Taipei National University of the Arts, 238

Taiwan, 11, 22, 30, 193, 197, 217, 238
Talbot, William Henry Fox, 227
Tang dynasty, 13, 42, 188
Tek, Budi, 15
thread-wrapping technique
- *Seeing Shadows No. 35* (Lin), *86–87*, 88, *98–99*, 215, *215* (detail)
- *Tree, The* (Lin), *16* (detail), *181*, 215, *215* (detail)

Tobey, Mark, 236
Tokyo
- Rikkyo University, 227
- Tokyo University of Science, 228

Torn (Houshiary), *85*, 201, *201* (detail)
Tree, The (Lin), *16* (detail), *181*, 215, *215* (detail)

U

Ullens, Myriam and Guy, 21
University of Paris Sorbonne, 185
Untitled (Braun), *66–69*, 188, *188* (details)
Untitled (Cole), *80*, 195, *195* (detail)
Untitled (Khan), *104–5*, 205, *205* (detail), *252* (detail)
Untitled (Li Huasheng), *27*, *73*, 213, *213* (detail)
Untitled (Liu Dan), *10* (detail), 11, *170*, 216, *216* (detail)

Untitled (Pentsch), *71*, 222, *222* (detail)
Untitled (Qiu), 46, *50–51*, 224, *224* (detail)
Untitled (Wang Tiande), *144–45*, 230, *230* (details)
Untitled XII (Pentsch), *57*, 222, *222* (detail)

V
Vaisravana, *42*
Vasarely, Victor, 228
Venice Biennale, 187, 238
verisimilitude, 91
Vessel 08-C (Kitamura), *74*, 207, *207* (detail)
Vessel 08-G (Kitamura), *75*, 207, *207* (detail)
videos
Still Life 012-Buttercup Tree (Wu), 91, *120–21*, 232, *232* (detail
Vietnam, 11, 23, 24, 28
viharas, 40
Viola, Bill, 44
violence, 200
Vision 08 (Leung Kui-ting), *175*, 211, *211* (detail)

W
Wang Chuantao, 214
Wang Dongling, 11, 14
Heart Sutra, The, 12
Wang Gongxin, 93, 215, 229
Sun Set 2, 229, *229*
Sun Set 5, *111*, 229, *229* (detail)
Wang Hui
Clearing after Rain over Streams and Mountains, 91, *91*
Wang Meng, 211
Wang Tiande, 17, 21, 27, 29, 230
Untitled, *144–45*, 230, *230* (details)
Wang Zhen, 214
wanglianghua, 88, 90, 91, 93, 182
Wanluan Thatched Hall (Dong Qichang), *124*, 126
wanwu, 46, 186
Warring States period, 193
watercolors
Radical Writings, Dal Libro Totale (Blank), *82*, 187, *187* (detail)
Way of Reflection, The (Jeong), *4* (detail), *61*, 204, *204* (detail)
Wei Ligang, 29
Wet Psyche—No Wind (Rhee), 93, *110*, 225, *225* (detail)
Whitman, Walt, 44
Withered Pool (from the Fives Series of Repetition) (Xu), *164*, 233
Wonderful: Secret Lover in Golden House (Yao), *137*, 238, *238* (detail)
Wong, Wucius, 129, 211, 219, 231
Deep in the Mountains #2, *8–9* (detail), *179*, 231, *231* (detail)
Wood Houses in the Mountains (Lui), *157*, 219, *219* (detail), 234
woodblock prints, 190, 234
See also individual titles under Xu Bing
woodcut prints
Dream 1986/6/19 Maqpi (Chen Haiyan), 190, *191*
Dream 2005.2.15, Mountains, Flowers, Crowded People and Cars (Chen Haiyan), *2* (detail), *171*, 190, *190* (detail)
Wu Chi-Tsung, 232
Still Life 012-Buttercup Tree, 91, *120–21*, 232, *232* (detail)
Wuzhun Shifan, 88

X
Xi'an Academy of Fine Arts, Shaanxi Province, 224
Xie He, 124
xieyi, 194
xinjing, 124n11
Xu Bing, 126, 219, 233–34
Background Story: Ink Variation (from Lui Shou-kwan), *125* (detail), 126, *158–61*, 233, *233* (detail), 234
Big River (from the Fives Series of Repetition), *166*, 233, *234* (detail)
Black Pool (from the Fives Series of Repetition), *166*, 233
Black Tadpoles (from the Fives Series of Repetition), *165*, 233, *234* (detail)
Farmland (from the Fives Series of Repetition), *164*, 233, 234
Field (from the Fives Series of Repetition), *163*, 233, *233* (detail)
Haystack Reflection (from the Fives Series of Repetition), *167*, 233
Mountain Place (from the Fives Series of Repetition), *165*, 233
Moving Cloud (from the Fives Series of Repetition), *163*, 233
Pool of Life (from the Fives Series of Repetition), *167*, 233
Withered Pool (from the Fives Series of Repetition), *164*, 233
xuan paper, works on
104 (Li Huasheng), *52*, 213, *213* (detail)
Accidentally Passing, Needle Script (Fung), *59*, 197, *197* (detail)
Dissolved Geometry B (Zheng), *95*, 241, *241* (detail)
Dissolved Geometry C (Zheng), *95*, 241, *241* (detail)
Fingerprint 2007 (Zhang Yu), *49*, 240, *240* (detail)
Fingerprint: Right Ring Finger (Yang Jiechang), *6* (detail), 93, *97*, 236, *236* (detail)
Horse and Rider (Chen Haiyan), *176–77*, 191, *191* (detail)

Y
ya (elegance), 238
Yan Binghui, 235
Monument, *76*, 235, *235*
Yang Jiechang, 236
Fingerprint: Right Ring Finger, *6* (detail), 93, *97*, 236, *236* (detail)
Yang Shih-Chih, 237
Modern Landscape, *138–39*, 237, *237* (detail)
Yao Jui-Chung, 238
Wonderful: Secret Lover in Golden House, *137*, 238, *238* (detail)
yin and *yang*, 206, 235
Yin Zhaoyang, 21
Yongzheng, Emperor, 34
Yu Youren, 238
Yuan dynasty, 211
Yuz Museum, Shanghai, 15

Z
Zao Wou-Ki, 21, 26
Zborowski, Léopold, 185
Zen Buddhism, 37, 43, 44, 46
Zen Painting A69-14 (Lui), *47* (detail), *79*, 219, *219* (detail)
Zhang Chongren, 214
Zhang Daqian, 35, 37
Zhang Daqian and Hu Chongxian
Jade Green Straws, *37*
Zhang Tiemei, 202
Zhang Yanyuan, 13–14
Zhang Yirong, 239
Butterfly Adrift Lakes and Hills, *173*, 239, *239* (detail)
Zhang Yu, 25, 44, 240
Divine Light Series No. 7: Floating Incomplete Circle, 91, *92* (detail), *119*, 240, *240* (detail)
Fingerprint 2007, *49*, 240, *240* (detail)
Zhao Ji, 90
Zhao Yi, 13
Zhejiang Academy of Fine Arts (now China Academy of Art), Hangzhou, 198, 230, 236, 241
Zheng Chongbin, 19, 93, 241
Dissolved Geometry B, *95*, 241, *241* (detail)
Dissolved Geometry C, *95*, 241, *241* (detail)
Zhirong, 88
Zhiweng Ruojiang, 88
Zhuangzi, 239
zimo, 217, 218

Joey Leung Ka-yin, *Late Rabbit*, 2010 (detail)

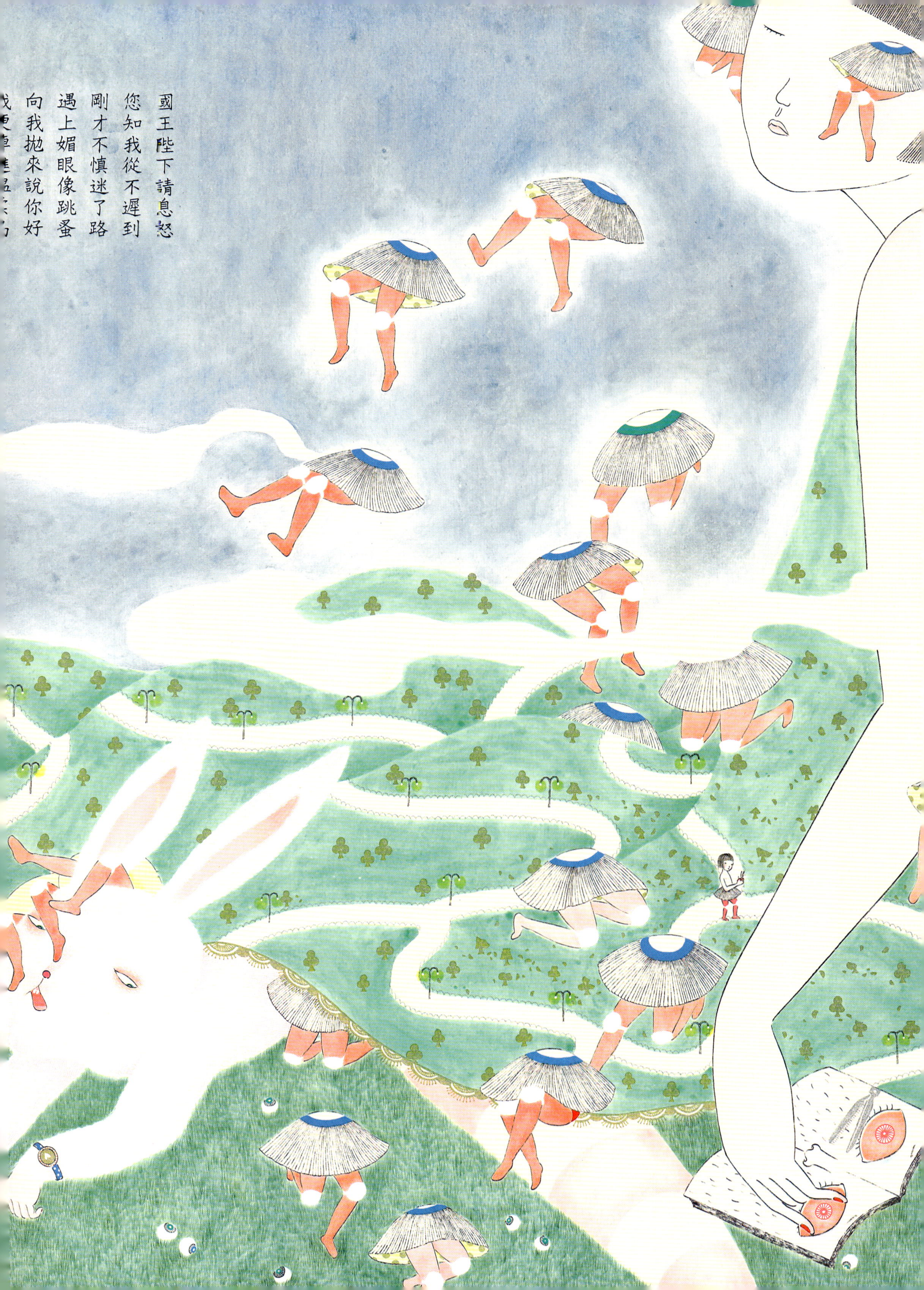
國王陛下請息怒
您知我從不遲到
剛才不慎迷了路
遇上媚眼像跳蚤
向我拋來說你好

Acknowledgments

I begin these acknowledgments by expressing my profound thanks to the visionary collectors Gérard and Dora Cognié, whose Fondation INK has made a generous and significant promised gift of global ink art to LACMA. I first met Gérard Cognié at Art Basel Hong Kong in 2016 and, upon my first visit to the collection, was immediately taken by its quality and depth. In 2018, at Art Basel Hong Kong, Michael Govan, LACMA's CEO and Wallis Annenberg Director, and the Cogniés jointly announced the promised gift to LACMA of 400 contemporary artworks from the Fondation INK Collection.

My sincere thanks to Michael Govan and to Zoë Kahr, Deputy Director for Curatorial and Planning, both of whom supported the genesis of our relationship with the Cogniés and provided valuable advice as our collaboration evolved.

My special thanks to scholars Britta Erickson and Craig Yee for introducing me to the Cogniés, and for their support toward this project's realization.

A special word of thanks to Gérard and Dora Cognié for having generously shared their vast knowledge of contemporary ink art with our curatorial team.

Special recognition and thanks go to Susanna Ferrell, LACMA's Wynn Resorts Assistant Curator of Chinese Art. She has directed every aspect of this project, and her curatorial and scholarly skills are fully evident in the exhibition and its catalogue. We are also deeply grateful to the Fondation INK, LACMA's Asian Art Council, Mark and Jennifer McCormick, Susan R. Stockel, and Stephen O. Lesser for their generous support of this catalogue and its production.

My sincere thanks to Wan Kong, The Mozhai Foundation Assistant Curator of Chinese Art; Einor K. Cervone, The Mozhai Foundation Curatorial Fellow; and Celia Yang, Major Gift Officer and Head of Director's Strategic Initiatives, Asia, all of whom contributed to the catalogue and assisted in the exhibition's planning. In addition, I am deeply grateful to Vikki Cruz, Curatorial Administrator of the Chinese and Korean Departments, who effortlessly oversaw and managed the exhibition's communications and planning.

Many individuals assisted in this project's preparation, and we would like to thank them here: Fiona Amitai and Stephanie Fleet of Alison Jacques Gallery, Bingyi, Chen Bolan, Chen Haiyan, Michael Cherney, Max Cole, Kaeli Deane, Normand Desrosiers, Shadi Mirsepassi and Rute Ventura of Lisson Gallery, Gu Renming, gu wenda, Shirazeh Houshiary, Charlotte Grey Jackson of Charlotte Jackson Fine Art, Yu-yeon Kim, Joey Leung Ka-yin, Hansi Liao and Leng Lin of Pace Gallery, Lin Lee, Liu Guosong, Jesebel Qiu, Sunagawa Haruhiko, Linda Tang, Cassie Tao, Yim Tom and Fung Ming Chip, Yvonne Tsai of Red Gold Fine Art, Yan Binghui, Daphne King Yao of Alisan Fine Arts, Alan Yeung, Wang Gongxin, and Zheng Chongbin.

At LACMA, our thanks go to Fred Goldstein, former Senior Vice President, General Counsel, and Secretary; Victoria Behner, Martin Sztyk, and Carolyn Oakes in Exhibition Programs; Registrar Hannah Gibson; and Julia Latané in Art Preparation and Installation. This catalogue would not have been realized without the critical direction and dedication of Publisher Lisa Gabrielle Mark. Philomena Mariani brought skill and affability to the editing of the text, while Dawson Weber in Rights and Reproductions assisted in obtaining images and keeping the publication on track. The beautiful catalogue design was conceived by Lorraine Wild and Xiaoqing Wang of the Green Dragon Office, Los Angeles. Kathleen Preciado compiled the index. Finally, our thanks go to Elizabeth Gerber and Vivian Lin for their roles in creating the exhibition's educational programming.

Stephen Little
Florence and Harry Sloan Curator of Chinese Art
Head, Chinese, Korean, and South & Southeast Asian Departments

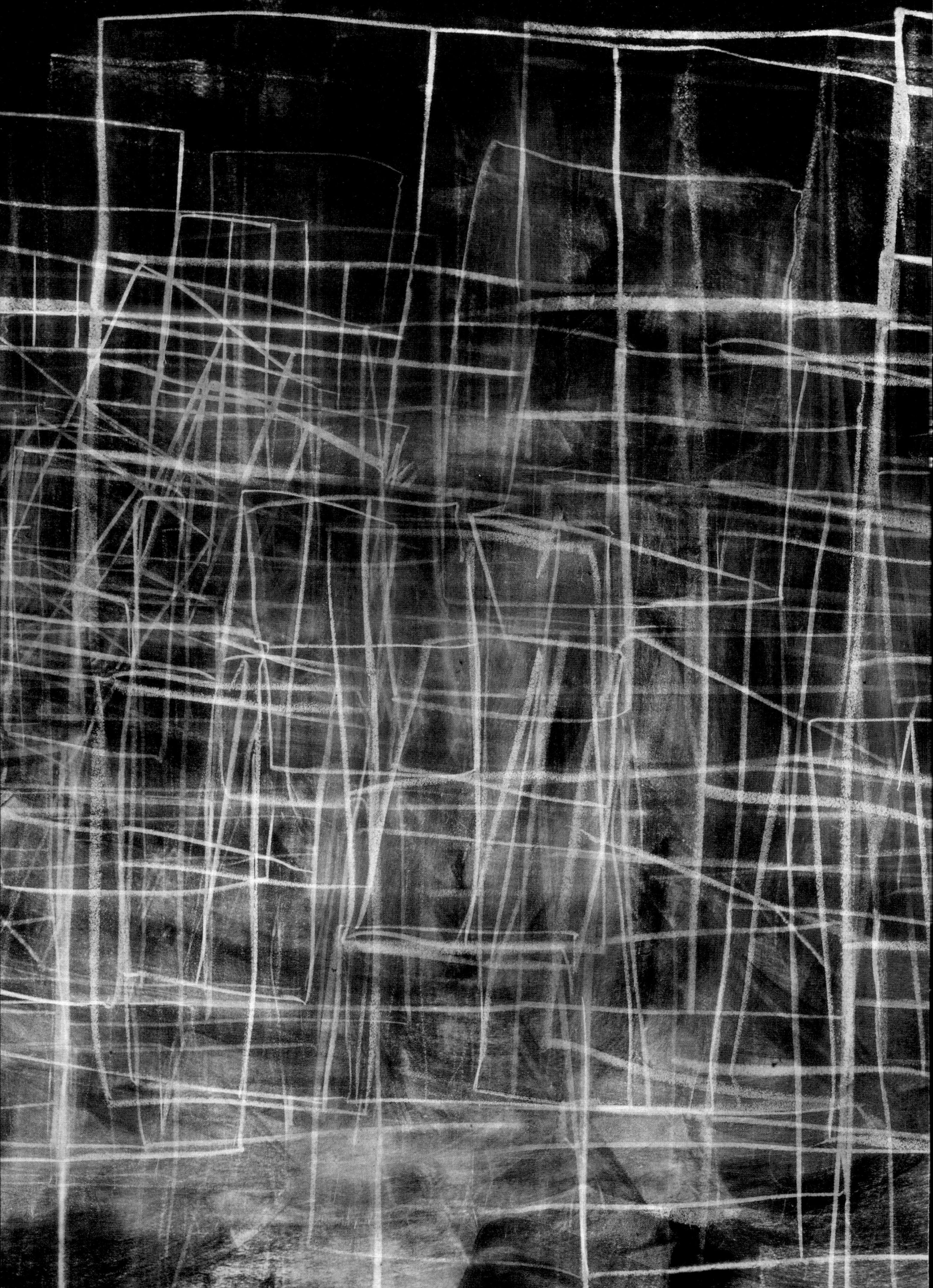

Idris Khan, *Untitled*, 2013 (detail)

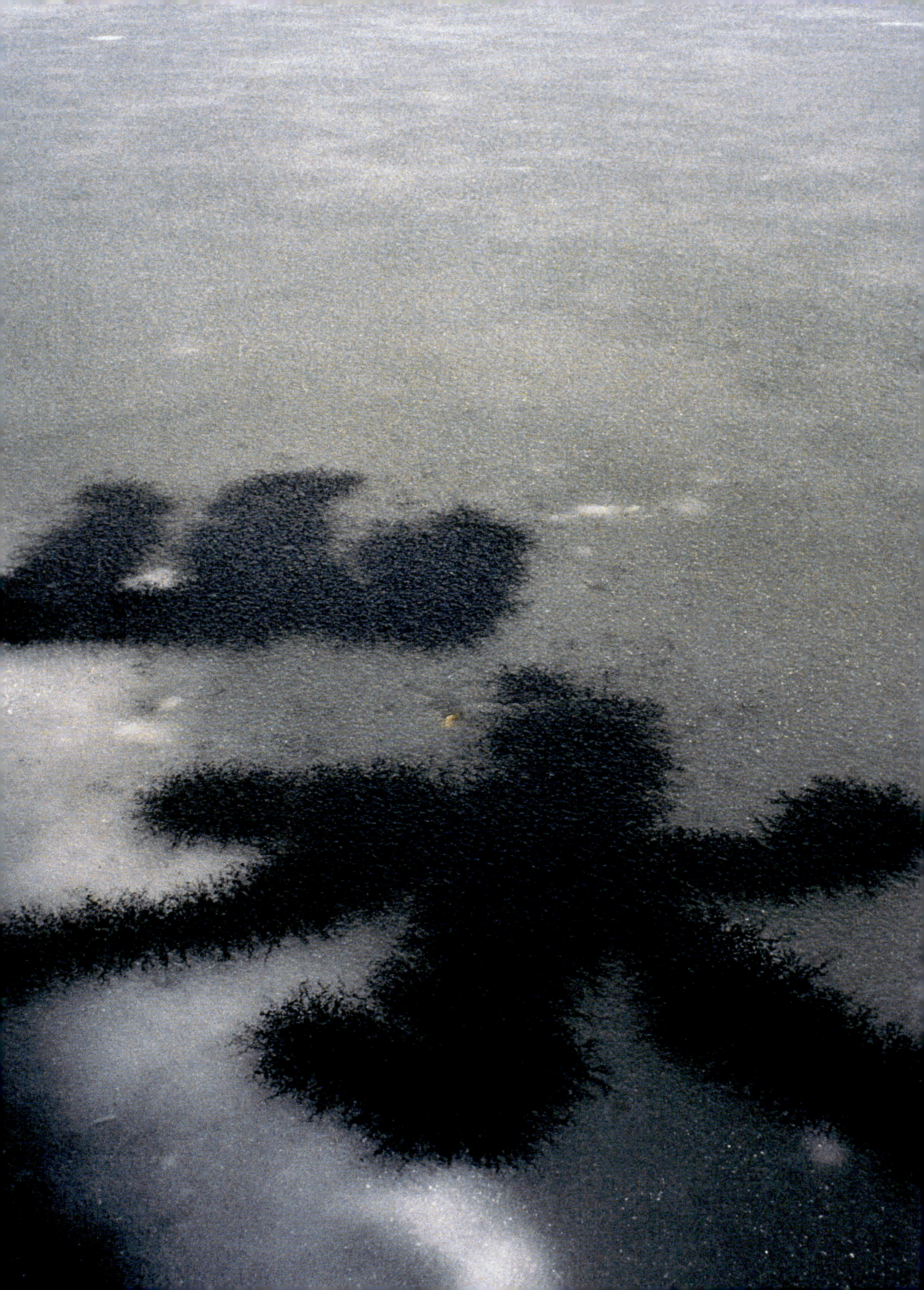

Photo Credits

Works and photographs are reproduced courtesy of the creators and lenders of the materials depicted. The following images, keyed to page number, are those for which additional or separate credits are due. Unless otherwise noted, all photos are by Maurice Aeschimann, Geneva, courtesy of the Fondation INK.

Cover, pp. 78, 186: © 2021 Bingyi
pp. 2, 171, 176–77, 190, 191 top: © 2021 Chen Haiyan, photos courtesy of the artist
pp. 4, 61, 204: © 2021 Jeong Gwang-Hee, photos courtesy of the artist
pp. 6, 97, 236: © 2021 Yang Jiechang
pp. 8–9, 179, 231: © 2021 Wucius Wong
pp. 10, 170, 216: © 2021 Liu Dan
pp. 16, 86–87, 98–99, 181, 215: © 2021 Lin Tianmiao
pp. 20, 22, 28, 31: photos by Susanna Ferrell
p. 25: photo by Dora Cognié
p. 27: photo by Britta Erickson
pp. 32–33, 81, 203: © 2021 Huang Zhiyang
p. 34: image source: The Palace Museum, Beijing/image © 2021 The Palace Museum, Beijing
pp. 36, 140–41, 192: © 2021 Michael Cherney, photos courtesy of the artist
p. 37: © 2021 Hu Chongxian and Zhang Daqian, courtesy of the family members of the artists and the Yuz Foundation
pp. 38–39, 52–53, 73, 131–34, 212–13: © 2021 Li Huasheng Art Foundation
p. 40: Shawshots/Alamy Stock Photo
p. 41: installation view, M WOODS Beijing, 2018, photo: Yang Dongxu, © 2021 M WOODS
pp. 42 left, 91: digital images courtesy of www.metmuseum.org
p. 42 right: photo © 2021 The Trustees of the British Museum. All rights reserved.
pp. 45, 77, 185: © 2021 Ophélie Asch
pp. 47, 79: © 2021 Helen Ting
pp. 49, 92, 119, 240: © 2021 Zhang Yu
pp. 50–51, 224: © 2021 Qiu Shihua
pp. 55, 209: © 2021 Artists Rights Society (ARS), New York/ADAGP, Paris
pp. 56, 194: © 2021 Estate of Chua Ek Kay
pp. 57, 71, 222: © 2021 Estate of Antoine Pentsch
pp. 59, 197: © 2021 Fung Ming Chip
pp. 62–63, 228: © 2021 Sunagawa Haruhiko
pp. 65, 221: © 2021 Park Seo-Bo, photos courtesy of the artist and Kukje Gallery, Seoul
pp. 66, 188 top: © 2021 Matti Braun, photos © Hans Georg Gaul, courtesy of the artist and Esther Schippers, Berlin
pp. 67–69, 188 bottom: © 2021 Matti Braun, photos © Serge Hasenböhler, courtesy of the artist and Esther Schippers, Berlin
pp. 72, 208: © 2021 Matti Kujasalo
pp. 74–75, 207: © 2021 Kitamura Junko
pp. 76, 235: © 2021 Yan Binghui
pp. 80, 195: © 2021 Max Cole
pp. 82, 187 top: © 2021 Irma Blank, photos by Michael Brezinski, courtesy of the artist and Alison Jacques Gallery, London
pp. 83, 187 bottom: © 2021 Irma Blank
pp. 85, 201: © 2021 Shirazeh Houshiary, photos by Ellen Page Wilson, courtesy of the artist
pp. 89, 102, 220: © 2021 Min Byung Hun and Leehwaik Gallery, Seoul, photos courtesy of the artist and Leehwaik Gallery, Seoul
p. 90: photo courtesy of the National Palace Museum, Taipei
pp. 95, 241: © 2021 Zheng Chongbin
pp. 100–101, 198: © 2021 gu wenda
pp. 103, 189 top: © 2021 Chen Bolan
pp. 104–5, 205, 252: © 2021 Idris Khan
pp. 106–7, 196, 254: © 2021 Dai Guangyu
pp. 109, 122–23, 148, 149, 217–18: © 2021 The Liu Kuo-sung Archives
pp. 110, 225: © 2021 Rhee Kibong
pp. 111, 229: © 2021 Wang Gongxin
pp. 112–13, 226: © 2021 Shi Guorui
pp. 115–17, 227: © 2021 Hiroshi Sugimoto, courtesy of Fraenkel Gallery, San Francisco
pp. 120–21, 232, 256: © 2021 Wu Chi-Tsung Studio, digital images courtesy of Wu Chi-Tsung Studio
p. 124: Wikimedia Commons
pp. 125, 158–61, 233 top: © 2021 Xu Bing Studio, photos by Fang Chao
pp. 127, 138–39, 237: © 2021 Yang Shih-Chih (Emily S. C. Yu)
pp. 128, 152, 202: © 2021 Huang Yan
pp. 137, 238: © 2021 Yao Jui-Chung
pp. 142–43, 214: © 2021 Li Huayi
pp. 144–45, 230: © 2021 Wang Tiande
pp. 147, 199: © 2021 Hai Bo, courtesy of Pace Gallery
pp. 151, 210, 249: © 2021 Joey Leung Ka-yin, photos courtesy of the artist
pp. 153, 206: © 2021 Kim Ho-deuk
pp. 154–55, 200: © 2021 Hong Lei
pp. 157, 219: © 2021 Helen Ting
pp. 163–67, 233 bottom, 234: © 2021 Xu Bing Studio
pp. 169, 223: © 2021 Jorma Puranen, photos courtesy of the artist
pp. 173, 239: © 2021 Zhang Yirong, photos courtesy of the artist and Alisan Fine Arts, Hong Kong
pp. 175, 211: © 2021 Leung Kui-ting
pp. 178, 193, 242: © 2021 Estate of Chu Ko
p. 189 bottom: photo courtesy of Chen Bolan
p. 191 bottom: © 2021 Chen Haiyan

Dai Guangyu, *Landscape, Ink, Ice*, 2004 (detail)

Cover Bingyi, *Let Me Become the Universe's Plaything*, 2018 (detail)

p. 2 Chen Haiyan, *Dream 2005.2.15, Mountains, Flowers, Crowded People and Cars*, 2009 (detail)

p. 4 Jeong Gwang-Hee, *The Way of Reflection*, 2017 (detail)

p. 6 Yang Jiechang, *Fingerprint: Right Ring Finger*, 1992–94 (detail)

pp. 8–9 Wucius Wong, *Deep in the Mountains #2*, 2005 (detail)

pp. 32–33 Huang Zhiyang, *Possessing Numerous Peaks No. S-1226*, 2012 (detail)

pp. 38–39 Li Huasheng, *104*, 2001 (detail)

pp. 86–87 Lin Tianmiao, *Seeing Shadows No. 35*, 2007 (detail)

pp. 122–23 Liu Guosong, *Moon Series: It'll Soon Be White All Over*, 1970 (detail)

Published in conjunction with the exhibition
Ink Dreams: Selections from the Fondation INK Collection

This exhibition was organized by the Los Angeles County Museum of Art.

Generous support for the publication was provided by Fondation INK, the Asian Art Council, and Mark and Jennifer McCormick. Additional funding was provided by Susan R. Stockel and Stephen O. Lesser.

Itinerary
Los Angeles County Museum of Art
September 19–December 12, 2021

Copublished in 2021 by
Los Angeles County Museum of Art
5905 Wilshire Boulevard
Los Angeles, CA 90036
(323) 857-6000
www.lacma.org

and

DelMonico Books • D.A.P.

For LACMA
PUBLISHER Lisa Gabrielle Mark
PROJECT MANAGEMENT Dawson Weber
EDITOR Philomena Mariani
INDEXER Kathleen Preciado
RIGHTS AND REPRODUCTIONS Dawson Weber, with Sarah Applegate
ADMINISTRATIVE SUPPORT Tricia Cochée
DESIGNERS Lorraine Wild and Xiaoqing Wang for Green Dragon Office
COLOR SEPARATIONS Echelon Color, Santa Monica

For DelMonico Books
PRODUCTION DIRECTOR Karen Farquhar

This book is typeset in Riviera Nights by Swiss Typefaces.

Library of Congress Cataloging-in-Publication Data
Names: Ferrell, Susanna, editor. | Cervone, Einor K. | Erickson, Britta. | Kong, Wan. | Little, Stephen, 1954- | Yang, Celia. | Los Angeles County Museum of Art organizer, host institution.
Title: Ink dreams: selections from the Fondation INK collection / edited by Susanna Ferrell; with additional contributions by Einor K. Cervone, Britta Erickson, Wan Kong, Stephen Little, Celia Yang.
Description: Los Angeles : Los Angeles County Museum of Art; New York: DelMonico Books·D.A.P., 2021. | Includes bibliographical references and index. | Summary: Published in conjunction with the exhibition Ink Dreams: Selections from the Fondation INK Collection--Provided by publisher.
Identifiers: LCCN 2021010606 | ISBN (hardcover)
Subjects: LCSH: Art, Modern--20th century --Exhibitions. | Art, Modern--21st century--Exhibitions. | Ink painting, Chinese--Exhibitions. | Art--Private collections--Switzerland--Exhibitions. | Fondation INK--Exhibitions.
Classification: LCC N6487.L67 L6755 2021 | DDC 709.04--dc23
LC record available at https://lccn.loc.gov/2021010606

A CIP record for this book is available from the British Library

ISBN 978-1-942884-98-9

Printed and bound in Singapore